PROFESSIONAL
TIZEN™ APPLICATION DEVELOPMENT

PROFESSIONAL

Tizen™ Application Development

PROFESSIONAL

Tizen™ Application Development

Hojun Jaygarl
Cheng Luo
Yoonsoo Kim
Eunyoung Choi
Kevin Bradwick
Jon Lansdell

wrox™
A Wiley Brand

Professional Tizen™ Application Development

This edition first published 2014
© 2014 Samsung Electronics Co. Ltd.
Registered office

John Wiley & Sons Ltd, The Atrium, Southern Gate, Chichester, West Sussex, PO19 8SQ, United Kingdom

For details of our global editorial offices, for customer services and for information about how to apply for permission to reuse the copyright material in this book please see our website at www.wiley.com.

The right of the author to be identified as the author of this work has been asserted in accordance with the Copyright, Designs and Patents Act 1988.

Wiley also publishes its books in a variety of electronic formats. Some content that appears in print may not be available in electronic books.

Designations used by companies to distinguish their products are often claimed as trademarks. All brand names and product names used in this book are trade names, service marks, trademarks or registered trademarks of their respective owners. The publisher is not associated with any product or vendor mentioned in this book. This publication is designed to provide accurate and authoritative information in regard to the subject matter covered. It is sold on the understanding that the publisher is not engaged in rendering professional services. If professional advice or other expert assistance is required, the services of a competent professional should be sought.

Limit of Liability/Disclaimer of Warranty: The publisher and the author make no representations or warranties with respect to the accuracy or completeness of the contents of this work and specifically disclaim all warranties, including without limitation warranties of fitness for a particular purpose. No warranty may be created or extended by sales or promotional materials. The advice and strategies contained herein may not be suitable for every situation. This work is sold with the understanding that the publisher is not engaged in rendering legal, accounting, or other professional services. If professional assistance is required, the services of a competent professional person should be sought. Neither the publisher nor the author shall be liable for damages arising herefrom. The fact that an organization or website is referred to in this work as a citation and/or a potential source of further information does not mean that the author or the publisher endorses the information the organization or website may provide or recommendations it may make. Further, readers should be aware that Internet websites listed in this work may have changed or disappeared between when this work was written and when it is read.

Trademarks: Wiley, Wrox, the Wrox logo, Wrox Programmer to Programmer, and related trade dress are trademarks or registered trademarks of John Wiley & Sons, Inc. and/or its affiliates, in the United States and other countries, and may not be used without written permission. Tizen is a registered trademark of the Linux Foundation. All other trademarks are the property of their respective owners. John Wiley & Sons, Ltd. is not associated with any product or vendor mentioned in this book.

A catalogue record for this book is available from the British Library.

978-1-118-80926-6 (paperback)
978-1-118-80924-2 (ebook)
978-1-118-80925-9 (ebook)

Set in 9.5pt Sabon LT Std-Roman by MPS Limited, Chennai, India.

Printed in the United Kingdom by TJ International

To my wife, Hana. Without you all this wouldn't have been possible.

—HOJUN

To my wife, Tong; my daughter, Mary; my son, Luke; and mom and dad, with love.

—CHENG

To my beloved wife, Yungsuk; my kids, Yunggyun, Yungjun, and Yeeun; and my parents, Inhyung and Boksun. You made writing this book possible.

—YOONSOO

As my workmate and even more my husband, Joonwoo, your devotion and support for me is always the basis for everything.

—ERIN

To Julia and Iliya, for the mountains and the laughter.

—JON

ABOUT THE AUTHORS

HOJUN JAYGARL is a software architect and developer with experience developing software in a number of languages. He started in software development for venture companies at the age of 20, developing Windows and web applications. After working at venture companies for 5 years, Hojun moved to Samsung Electronics to develop embedded software of smart appliances. He then left Samsung to pursue a PhD in Computer Science at Iowa State University. He studied software engineering and developed an automated testing framework. After getting his PhD, Hojun came back to Samsung and developed bada and the Tizen native framework. Currently he is working on new smartphone applications for intelligence and big data.

CHENG LUO is a mobile application developer and technical evangelist with extensive experience developing mobile applications on different platforms, including Maemo, Symbian, bada, Android, and Tizen. He started his application development on early mobile devices, such as Compaq iPaq 3630 and Nokia N770 using C and C++ based on Linux.

Cheng currently works as a developer advocate in the Amazon EU office in Luxembourg. Prior to joining the Amazon Appstore team in Europe, Cheng lead a team of bada and Tizen experts in Samsung Europe. He has developed a number of open source projects in bada and Tizen and has spoken at various international conferences and developer events.

Cheng holds a M.Sc. in Networking Technologies from Aalto University in Finland. He and his family currently reside in Luxembourg

YOONSOO KIM is a Tizen platform architect who is actively participating in the development of Tizen, considering desired platform qualities such as security, reliability, maintainability, and performance.

Yoonsoo reviews all Tizen native C++ API changes to ensure that all APIs are easy to use, hard to misuse, easy to extend, and have good performance. Yoonsoo also actively maintains the coding idiom with clear rationales so that Tizen developers can decide which guide they should follow for their daily development, which is very important in the environment of a large team and complex software.

EUNYOUNG CHOI is a technical documentation leader with software development experience in the telephony, sensor, and content frameworks based on Tizen and bada.

KEVIN BRADWICK is a web developer from South Wales who has spent the majority of his working career building websites and web applications with HTML(5), PHP, and JavaScript. His passion is for developing smart solutions that improve and enable good user experience on the web. Kevin started his career in graphic design but quickly became captivated by the creative possibilities that could be achieved in web development.

Kevin currently works as a Senior Web Developer at the BBC, where he works on products relating to location services. His work is primarily concentrated in front-end development, where he develops and maintains the BBC's JavaScript mapping library in addition to web components that interact with various location APIs. Kevin has also formed his company, KodeFoundry, which provides bespoke web solutions for companies that want cutting-edge digital solutions.

JON LANSDELL is a technical writer, trainer, and developer whose professional path was set in 1985 when he met his first Apple Macintosh. Spending the next 20 years as a Mac developer, running developer training courses and, while at the legendary Steam Radio Limited, providing developer support for Apple, first in the UK and then to developers worldwide, John has spent most of his career creating content to try to make developers' lives easier.

Jon moved into mobile, first at Symbian and Nokia, before joining Samsung, where he spent three years in the Developer Cooperation Group, creating technical content including videos, sample code, and blog posts to support developers using bada, Samsung's Android technologies such as S-Pen, and, of course, Tizen. He is now a freelance technical writer and trainer. Jon is also co-author of *Introduction to bada: A Developer's Guide* (Wiley, 2010) and *Tizen for Dummies* (Wiley, 2013, Custom Edition).

CREDITS

**ASSOCIATE DIRECTOR—
BOOK CONTENT MANAGEMENT**
Martin Tribe

ASSOCIATE PUBLISHER
Chris Webb

ASSOCIATE COMMISSIONING EDITOR
Ellie Scott

MARKETING MANAGER
Lorna Mein

ASSISTANT MARKETING MANAGER
Dave Allen

EDITORIAL MANAGER
Rev Mengle

SENIOR PROJECT EDITOR
Sara Shlaer

PROJECT EDITOR
John Sleeva

EDITORIAL ASSISTANT
Annie Sullivan

TECHNICAL EDITOR
Jon Lansdell

SENIOR PRODUCTION EDITOR
Kathleen Wisor

PROOFREADER
Sarah Kaikini, Word One

INDEXER
Johnna VanHoose Dinse

COVER DESIGNER
Wiley

ACKNOWLEDGMENTS

I would like to thank my co-author and supervisor (ex-supervisor now), YoonSoo Kim; I have learned many things from you. I could not have been involved with this book without Justin Hong, the founder of bada and a Tizen native framework leader; thanks for giving me this opportunity. I was very glad to work with Cheng Luo. We first met at a Tizen conference in San Francisco, and I still have a very fun photo taken with him. My colleagues have been so supportive and patient while I was writing this book and deserve my thanks. Last but not least, the biggest thanks go to my family and Hana. Your love and support actually complete this book.

—Hojun

A big thank you to my former colleagues at Samsung. It's been a unique and inspiring experience to work with you. Your trust and encouragement made all the difference while I was writing this book.

I want to thank my co-author and technical editor, Jon Lansdell, and the project editor, John Sleeva. Without their patience and endless support, this book would not have been possible.

Most of all, I must thank my wife, Tong. Your love and support has been instrumental in completing this book.

—Cheng

Thanks to Okhyun Kim and Justin Hong for giving me the opportunity to write this book. I especially thank my colleague, Alvin Kim, for always sharpening my knowledge through challenging questions. Finally, I'd like to thank my colleagues for their support, encouragement, advice, and valuable time reviewing this book.

—Yoonsoo

First of all, I would like to thank Justin Hong for giving me the opportunity to write this book. Thanks also to Ellie Scott and John Sleeva for their enthusiasm and efforts in achieving the publication schedule with many authors.

—Erin

I'd like to thank my mother and father, Graziella and John, for supporting me during my college and university years. Your support has helped guide me to where I am today. I'd also like to thank my wife, Zoe, for her ongoing support and patience whilst I have been building my career.

—Kevin

My thanks go to John Sleeva for his hard work and dedication to keeping us on track, together with his patience and humour in the face of a project that turned out to be far more of a challenge than any of us anticipated. Thanks also to Ellie Scott for her determination to get the project done and for keeping us going when we didn't believe we could do it. Most of all I'd like to thank the other authors for sticking with it through all the rewrites and for creating a piece of work that you should be proud of.

—JON

CONTENTS

PART IV: ADVANCED TIZEN

CHAPTER 18: MULTITHREADING   433

CHAPTER 19: INTER-APPLICATION COMMUNICATION AND HYBRID APPLICATIONS   457

INTRODUCTION

AS THIS INTRODUCTION IS BEING WRITTEN, a new range of smart devices is attracting a lot of attention. The operating system that powers these devices is not Android, or iOS, or even Windows Phone. In fact the devices aren't smartphones at all: The Samsung Gear 2 and Gear 2 Neo are smartwatches, and they're running the Tizen operating system. Tizen is designed for multiple device categories and soon you're likely to find it powering devices from smartphones to smart TVs, and from wearables to driveables (the Tizen IVI project for in-vehicle infotainment in cars and buses certainly falls into the latter category). With Tizen smartphones set to hit the market this year, now is the perfect time to learn how to create applications for a smart device platform with a lot of potential.

Professional Tizen Application Development shows you how to write Tizen smartphone applications. While Tizen supports multiple device profiles, this book is focused on the Tizen mobile profile, designed for portable, connected devices, including smartphones and tablets. However, as new forms of Tizen devices are announced, you'll find that what you learn in this book will provide a good foundation for creating Tizen applications, no matter what device you're developing for.

Tizen is open source and HTML5 centric. Developers can create applications using HTML, JavaScript, and CSS, taking advantage of Tizen's support for the W3C HTML5 specifications, and a web engine that is tuned to get the best performance out of these technologies. You can use the Tizen Web Device APIs to access device features, such as sensors, contacts, and calendars, which are not included in the W3C APIs.

Tizen also supports a set of C++ APIs for creating native applications. While Tizen web apps are powerful, certain device features are available only from native applications, and in some cases there's no substitute for the power and performance of native code. Tizen gives you the choice, and this book covers both kinds of applications. Whether you're a web developer or a C++ guru, in this book you'll find code examples to help you create full-featured Tizen applications.

WHO THIS BOOK IS FOR

This book is for intermediate level and experienced developers. You're not expected to be an expert JavaScript or C++ programmer, but you do need to have a good working knowledge of either, or both, languages, depending on whether your interest lies in web or native application development. Although it would be helpful for you to be familiar with another mobile platform such as iOS or Android, it is not essential to understand and work through the examples.

If you are the kind of developer who learns by writing code, then this book is for you. Everything is explained using code examples, so if you are just looking for a technical introduction to what Tizen can do, then you'll find what you need; but if you want to dive in and use the examples to help jump-start your application, you're just the reader we had in mind.

WHAT THIS BOOK COVERS

This book explains how to write both web and native applications for Tizen mobile devices. The first few chapters introduce the Tizen IDE and development tools, such as the Simulator, Emulator, and debugger, before web applications and then native applications are covered in detail. After working through the book, you should be able to write applications that take advantage of all the features offered by a Tizen mobile device.

HOW THIS BOOK IS STRUCTURED

This book is comprised of 19 chapters, divided into 4 parts. Each chapter is organised in such a way that you can dip in and out as needed to find information on the subject you're looking for, including code.

- ➤ **Part I, "Getting Started,"** helps you get familiar with the Tizen IDE and developer tools.

  - ➤ Chapter 1, "An Introduction To Tizen," walks you through installing the Tizen SDK and creating a "Hello World" application for both a web app and a native app. The origins of Tizen and what makes the platform different are also explained in this chapter.

  - ➤ Chapter 2, "Tizen Application Packages," examines how applications are packaged in both web and native formats and explains the core concepts of features, privileges, and application signing.

  - ➤ Chapter 3, "Tizen Development Tools," shows you how to use the Emulator and Event Injector to test and debug both web and native applications. The Web Simulator, used for running and testing web applications, is also covered.

- ➤ **Part II, "Tizen Web APIs,"** explains how to use some of the most important W3C APIs and how to use the Tizen Device APIs to access features not included in the W3C specifications.

  - ➤ Chapter 4, "Web Application Fundamentals," explains the architecture of the Tizen Web Runtime, introduces the Tizen Device APIs, and shows you how to build a web app with the UI Builder.

  - ➤ Chapter 5, "Location-Based Services," shows how to use the Google Maps API to draw a map, add markers, and make use of geocoding. Finding the device location with the W3C Geolocation API is also demonstrated, as well as testing location features in the Web Simulator.

  - ➤ Chapter 6, "Multimedia," demonstrates how to use the Content Manager Device API to discover content on the device, and then moves on to HTML5 multimedia features such as playing audio and video and accessing the device's camera with the Media Capture API.

  - ➤ Chapter 7, "Sensors and Other Hardware," walks you through the creation of a golf game that demonstrates how to make use of the W3C Device Orientation API. How to access near field communication (NFC) features on the device, including reading and writing tags and peer-to-peer mode, is then explained.

➤ Chapter 8, "Messaging Services," introduces the Tizen Messaging Device API, which enables sending and receiving SMS, MMS, and e-mail messages and how to search for messages. The chapter includes the source code for an e-mail sender application.

➤ Chapter 9, "Contacts and Calendars," explains how to use two Tizen Device APIs, Contact and Calendar, to manipulate address books, contacts, and calendars.

➤ **Part III, "Tizen Native APIs,"** covers the native UI and application frameworks and the APIs used for creating native applications.

➤ Chapter 10, "Native UI Applications," introduces the building blocks of a Tizen UI application, including frames, forms, and events. The chapter walks you through creating an application with the New Project wizard and updating it to handle UI events.

➤ Chapter 11, "Native Application Fundamentals," explains the idioms and programming style used by the Tizen native APIs, including error handling and core data types such as strings and collections.

➤ Chapter 12, "Native UI Controls," covers the different types of UI controls and key concepts such as containers, the coordinate system, and listeners.

➤ Chapter 13, "Multimedia and Content," provides a practical introduction to the multimedia features of the Tizen native framework, including playing audio and video and capturing video and images from the camera.

➤ Chapter 14, "Telephony and Networking," details the features you need to create connected applications, such as Wi-Fi Direct, NFC, and Bluetooth, as well as sending and receiving SMS and e-mail messages.

➤ Chapter 15, "Location and Social Services," shows you how to track the location of a device and make use of location region tracking. The second part of the chapter deals with social services, including managing the address book and calendar, and adding events and tasks.

➤ Chapter 16, "Advanced UI and Graphics," describes advanced graphics features such as animations, and new ways of interacting with the user such as image and face recognition, speech recognition, and text-to-speech.

➤ Chapter 17, "I/O and Internationalisation," focuses on storing data in a file or database, and using Tizen's internationalisation features to adapt to different languages, text encodings, and number and date formats.

➤ **Part IV, "Advanced Tizen,"** provides practical examples of techniques that help make your applications more powerful.

  ➤ Chapter 18, "Multithreading," demonstrates the native APIs for multi-thread programming, including threads, events, and mutexes, and provides example code showing inter-thread communication.

  ➤ Chapter 19, "Inter-Application Communication and Hybrid Applications," shows you how to combine a native application and a web application into one hybrid package, and use inter-application communication to enable them to work together.

WHAT YOU NEED TO USE THIS BOOK

The version of the Tizen SDK used in this book is 2.2.1, released in November 2013. Visit the Tizen developer website at `developer.tizen.org` to download the latest version of the SDK and check the release notes for any late-breaking changes.

The Tizen SDK can be run on Mac OS X, Windows, and Linux. See Chapter 1 for more details regarding required system configurations.

CONVENTIONS

To help you get the most from the text and keep track of what's happening, we've used a number of conventions throughout the book.

> **WARNING** *Boxes like this one hold important, not-to-be-forgotten information that is directly relevant to the surrounding text.*

> **NOTE** *Notes, tips, hints, tricks, or asides to the current discussion are offset and placed in italics like this.*

As for styles in the text:

➤ We *highlight new* terms and important words when we introduce them.

➤ We show keyboard strokes like this: Ctrl+A.

➤ We show filenames, URLs, and code within the text like so: `persistence.properties`.

➤ We present code in two different ways:

```
We use a monofont type with no highlighting for most code examples.
We use bold to emphasize code that's particularly important in the present context.
```

SOURCE CODE

As you work through the examples in this book, you may choose either to type in all the code manually or to use the source code files that accompany the book. All of the source code used in this book is available for download at http://www.wrox.com. You will find the code snippets from the source code are accompanied by a download icon and note indicating the name of the program so you know it's available for download and can easily locate it in the download file. Once at the site, simply locate the book's title (either by using the Search box or by using one of the title lists) and click the Download Code link on the book's detail page to obtain all the source code for the book.

> **NOTE** *Because many books have similar titles, you may find it easiest to search by ISBN; this book's ISBN is 978-1-118-80926-6.*

Once you download the code, just decompress it with your favorite compression tool. Alternately, you can go to the main Wrox code download page at http://www.wrox.com/dynamic/books/download.aspx to see the code available for this book and all other Wrox books.

ERRATA

We make every effort to ensure that there are no errors in the text or in the code. However, no one is perfect, and mistakes do occur. If you find an error in one of our books, such as a spelling mistake or a faulty piece of code, we would be very grateful for your feedback. By sending in errata you may save another reader hours of frustration and at the same time you will be helping us provide even higher quality information.

To find the errata page for this book, go to http://www.wrox.com and locate the title using the Search box or one of the title lists. Then, on the book details page, click the Book Errata link. On this page you can view all errata that has been submitted for this book and posted by Wrox editors. A complete book list, including links to each book's errata, is also available at www.wrox.com/misc-pages/booklist.shtml.

If you don't spot "your" error on the Book Errata page, go to www.wrox.com/contact/techsupport.shtml and complete the form there to send us the error you have found. We'll check the information and, if appropriate, post a message to the book's errata page and fix the problem in subsequent editions of the book.

P2P.WROX.COM

For author and peer discussion, join the P2P forums at p2p.wrox.com. The forums are a web-based system for you to post messages relating to Wrox books and related technologies and interact with other readers and technology users. The forums offer a subscription feature to e-mail you topics of interest of your choosing when new posts are made to the forums. Wrox authors, editors, other industry experts, and your fellow readers are present on these forums.

At http://p2p.wrox.com you will find a number of different forums that will help you not only as you read this book, but also as you develop your own applications. To join the forums, just follow these steps:

1. Go to p2p.wrox.com and click the Register link.

2. Read the terms of use and click Agree.

3. Complete the required information to join as well as any optional information you wish to provide and click Submit.

4. You will receive an e-mail with information describing how to verify your account and complete the joining process.

> **NOTE** *You can read messages in the forums without joining P2P but in order to post your own messages, you must join.*

Once you join, you can post new messages and respond to messages other users post. You can read messages at any time on the web. If you would like to have new messages from a particular forum e-mailed to you, click the Subscribe to this Forum icon by the forum name in the forum listing.

For more information about how to use the Wrox P2P, be sure to read the P2P FAQs for answers to questions about how the forum software works as well as many common questions specific to P2P and Wrox books. To read the FAQs, click the FAQ link on any P2P page.

PART I
Getting Started

An Introduction to Tizen

WHAT'S IN THIS CHAPTER?

➤ Discovering Tizen

➤ Installing the SDK

➤ Creating your first Tizen web application

➤ Creating your first Tizen native application

WROX.COM CODE DOWNLOADS FOR THIS CHAPTER

The wrox.com code downloads for this chapter are found at www.wrox.com/go/ professionaltizen on the Download Code tab. After decompressing the downloaded Zip file you will have `HelloWorldNative` and `HelloWorldWeb` directories with the finished application.

This chapter provides a brief introduction to Tizen, including the project's history, the way it's organized, and what makes it unique. Although it provides some good reasons to develop for Tizen, it's likely you already know the potential of the platform, so the chapter quickly turns into a practical introduction.

You will learn how to set up the Tizen development environment, and get started with both web and native application development. You'll then create the Hello World Tizen application using both the web and native application frameworks, and see how easy it is to use the UI Builder and get started with writing code.

DISCOVERING TIZEN

The Linux Foundation announced the Tizen project in September 2011 and the Tizen Association was formed in 2012 to drive industry engagement and support for the project. Tizen as a platform hasn't emerged from nowhere. It's an evolution of the previous Linux-based platforms: MeeGo and LiMo. The Tizen platform embraces the latest standards, such as HTML5 and web-centric technologies, to provide a robust unified experience across multiple devices.

At the time of writing, the latest version of Tizen is 2.2.1. Compared to the initial release, it has a lot of new features and APIs, and the IDE and related tools have also been enhanced. In this chapter, you'll discover how the platform has evolved, look at some of Tizen's most important features, and see why you need to learn about Tizen programming.

We'll start with the two governance bodies behind the Tizen Platform: the Tizen Association and the Tizen Project.

The Tizen Association and Tizen Project

Tizen is an open-source, standards-based, cross-architecture software platform designed for multiple device categories such as smartphones, tablets, in-vehicle infotainment systems, and smart TVs. Tizen platform development is led by two bodies: the Tizen Association and the Technical Steering Group (TSG). The Tizen Association and the TSG are complementary to each other in terms of the marketing and technical directions of Tizen.

The Tizen Association is a mobile operator-led, industry consortium chartered with actively developing the ecosystem around Tizen, which includes marketing presence, gathering of requirements, identification and facilitation of service models, and overall industry marketing and brand awareness. You can find out more at www.tizenassociation.org.

The Tizen Project resides within the Linux Foundation and is governed by the TSG, which is the primary decision-making body for the open-source project and whose focus is the development and delivery of the platform itself. Currently the TSG has two members: Intel and Samsung. The Tizen brand is actually owned by the Linux Foundation, not by any single company.

The Tizen Ecosystem

As an open-source software platform, Tizen provides many opportunities to application developers, platform developers, and original equipment manufacturers (OEMs). Together, these groups comprise the key components of the Tizen ecosystem.

The application developers are important to any mobile ecosystem because they are the ones who create the best applications and user experience for the end user. If you think of ecosystems as the battlefields of the platform war, application developers are in the front line. System integrators are those who squeeze every last ounce of performance from mobile chipsets and GPUs, and write the device drivers to work with sensors and other hardware. An open-source platform like Tizen offers huge opportunities to these developers.

The operators and OEMs might be described as the commanders and generals of the platform war. Operators choose to add Tizen-enabled devices to their networks and deploy their own services on those devices, for functions such as billing and promotions. OEMs are those who make the products that use Tizen, and decide what features will appear on these devices.

Another key element of the Tizen ecosystem is the Tizen Store, which was announced and demonstrated in February 2013 at the Tizen 2.0 release event. Currently the Tizen Store is still under development and not open to the public, but Tizen application developers may submit their applications for the certification process via the seller website.

The mobile platform war is actually one of the ecosystems. The platform that can create a bigger and healthier ecosystem is the one more likely to win the leading position in the market, and to gather more application developers around it. That brings us to the main question: Why should you choose to develop for the Tizen platform?

REASONS FOR PROGRAMMING IN TIZEN

Tizen is still a new platform with a lot of potential. Compared to other mobile platforms, it is the only platform that has all these characteristics:

➤ Tizen is based on standards.

➤ Tizen is open.

➤ Tizen is heterogeneous.

➤ Tizen has industry support.

Tizen Is Based on Standards

Tizen's primary focus for application development is HTML5, a set of standards that is well supported by the industry. It is rapidly merging as the preferred development environment for mobile developers. According to the results of HTML5 compatibility test published on the HTML5 Test website (`http://www.html5test.com`), the Tizen browser tops the HTML5 benchmarking test amongst all other mobile platforms.

Not only is the Tizen browser compatible with more HTML5 features, but it also performs better. Tizen web apps achieve a frame rate of more than 60 frames per second (fps) when displaying graphics using WebGL technologies. This makes Tizen a capable environment for developing 3D and animations applications even in HTML5.

Tizen Is Open

Another characteristic of Tizen is its openness. This refers not only to the platform's source code, but also the governance model.

During the Tizen 3.0 announcement at the Tizen Developer Summit in South Korea in 2013, it was stated that beginning with version 3.0, Tizen will embrace a governance model that is even more open than the current model. The Tizen source code is currently uploaded to the tizen.org git repository only at particular milestones, which means that developers can't access the nightly build of Tizen source code for features as they are being developed. Beginning with Tizen 3.0, all source code will be available on the tizen.org git repository as it is being developed. Developers will be able to download the latest source code from tizen.org, build it, and try out the latest features. Any developer will be able to contribute to the project, and recommendations for and contributions of new Tizen features will be publicly available on the JIRA server, the issue-tracking system used by Tizen Project. Developers will also be able to vote and influence the Tizen roadmap.

All this makes Tizen a truly open platform, especially compared to the closed governance model of Android.

Tizen Is Heterogeneous

Tizen was designed with multiple device profiles in mind. Currently two profiles are under active development: for mobile devices and in vehicle infotainment (IVI) systems. In the future you're likely to find Tizen in PCs, printers, TV set top boxes, and even cameras. In fact, the first official Tizen-enabled device is a camera, the Samsung NX300M. At Mobile World Congress in 2014, Samsung also announced Gear 2, a Tizen-powered smart watch.

From Tizen 3.0 onwards, there will be one codebase that can be configured to support multiple profiles and architectures. The potential of the Tizen platform is considerably bigger than other mobile-only platforms. For application developers, this offers the enticing prospect of writing one application not only for many devices of the same type, but also for a whole range of different types of devices.

> **NOTE** *When we use the word "Tizen" in this book, we are referring to the mobile profile of the Tizen platform.*

Tizen Has Industry Support

Tizen is backed by a large group of industry leaders that form the Tizen Association board. The board includes many operators and device manufacturers and at the time of writing consists of Samsung, Intel, Fujitsu, Huawei, KT Corporation, LG, NTT DOCOMO, Orange, SK Telecom, and Vodafone.

The Tizen Association recently launched the Tizen Association Partner Program, which consists of 36 companies in different areas across a diverse set of connected device manufacturers, operators, application developers, and software vendors. In February 2014, the Tizen Association announced that an additional 15 partners had joined the Tizen Association Partner Program, including Baidu, ZTE, and SoftBank Mobile.

INSTALLING THE TIZEN SDK

Now that you've heard the reasons why you should learn Tizen programming, it's time to get practical and start your development by downloading and installing the Tizen SDK.

The examples in this book make use of version 2.2.1 of the Tizen SDK, which was released in November 2013. You can download the latest version of the SDK from the Tizen developer website: `https://developer.tizen.org/downloads/tizen-sdk`.

Prerequisites

The Tizen developer website (`https://developer.tizen.org/downloads/sdk/installing-sdk/prerequisites-tizen-sdk`) lists all the prerequisites for running the Tizen SDK on different operating systems. Here are the system requirements for the most common platforms — Ubuntu 12.04 or 12.10 (32- or 64-bit), Microsoft Windows XP (32-bit) Service Pack 2 or later, Microsoft Windows 7 (32- or 64-bit), Apple Mac OS X 10.7 Lion (64-bit), or Apple Mac OS X 10.8 Mountain Lion (64-bit):

➤ At least a dual-core 2 GHz CPU

➤ At least 2GB of RAM

➤ At least 3GB of free disk space

➤ A local admin account

The Java Runtime Environment (JRE) version 6 or later is required for all operating systems.

> **NOTE** *Please make sure you install the JRE instead of the Java Development Kit (JDK). The links provided from the developer site do not include a direct JRE download link, so you will need to choose the correct version.*

Installing the SDK

The Tizen SDK consists of two parts: the Tizen IDE and the Tizen SDK image. The Tizen IDE is based on the Eclipse IDE but integrates additional Tizen-specific development tools. The Tizen SDK image can be downloaded from the network during the installation or downloaded separately as a Zip package.

The Tizen SDK supports Windows, Ubuntu, and Mac OS X operating systems. The installation process is fairly simple and is well documented on the Tizen developer website (`https://developer.tizen.org`).

> **NOTE** *If you install the SDK on Mac OS X 10.7.5 or later and an error dialog appears (see Figure 1-1), when you launch the Install Manager, you may need to change your security settings temporarily to prevent the OS X Gatekeeper feature from blocking the installation.*
>
> *Choose Apple Menu ⇨ System Preferences, open the Security preference pane and click the General tab. Under the heading "Allow applications downloaded from," choose the Anywhere radio button. You should now be able to launch the Install Manager.*
>
> *Once you've finished installing the Tizen SDK, restore your settings to the previous state.* 
>
>
> **"inst-manager.app" is damaged and can't be opened. You should eject the disk image.**
>
> "inst-manager.app" is on the disk image "tizen-sdk-mac64-v2.2.71.dmg". Safari downloaded this disk image on 21 November 2013 from developer.tizen.org.
>
> Cancel   Eject Disk Image
>
> **FIGURE 1-1**

To install the Tizen SDK, you need to download the latest Install Manager from `https://developer.tizen.org/downloads/tizen-sdk`. Once you have downloaded the Install Manager, you can choose to install the Tizen SDK from the network or local file.

Once the Install Manager is running, you can choose to install the SDK from the network by clicking the Next button, agree to the terms and conditions, and select the components you want to install. This is the default option when installing the SDK.

You can also install the SDK from the local SDK image or select the previous version of the SDK by clicking the Advanced button (see Figure 1-2).

FIGURE 1-2

To install an SDK version other than the latest version from the network, click the Package server radio button, shown in Figure 1-3. This gives you the option to choose which package server you want to use, and which version of the SDK image to install.

To install the SDK from the local SDK image, click the SDK image radio button and choose the image file that you downloaded as a Zip file.

> **NOTE** *If you use Safari on Mac OS X, ensure that the Preferences ➪ General ➪ Open "safe" files after downloading option is unchecked. Otherwise Safari will extract the SDK image file automatically and the Install Manager won't be able to find the Zip file.*

Once you have successfully installed the Tizen SDK, you are ready to launch the Tizen IDE.

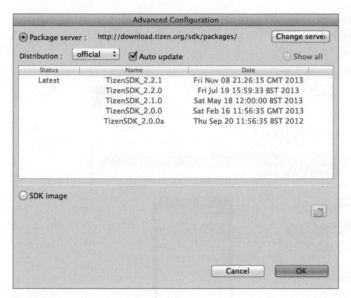

FIGURE 1-3

CREATING THE TIZEN HELLO WORLD WEB APPLICATION

It's traditional for a getting-started tutorial to begin with the Hello World example application, and this chapter is no exception. The Tizen Hello World application demonstrates quite a few features of the SDK and gives you a good start in Tizen programming.

The Hello World example you will create in this section does three simple things:

➤ Presents an OK button on the screen when it is launched

➤ Prints "Hello World" to the screen when the OK button is clicked

➤ Exits when the user clicks the hardware Back key

The simplest way to create a Hello World project is to use the New Project wizard. The New Project wizard provides several templates to use. There are four predefined template types:

➤ **Basic** — A blank application with minimum files and resources to run a Tizen application

➤ **Tizen Web UI Framework** — A set of templates with all the necessary files for creating a web application using the Tizen UI framework

➤ **jQuery Mobile** — A set of templates containing all the necessary files and libraries for creating web applications using the jQuery Mobile framework

➤ **Tizen Web UI Builder** — A set of templates containing all files to create a web application using the integrated Tizen Web UI Builder

To launch the New Project wizard and choose a template, follow these steps:

1. In the IDE, choose File ⇨ New ⇨ Tizen Web Project. The New Tizen Web Project dialog will be displayed as shown in Figure 1-4.

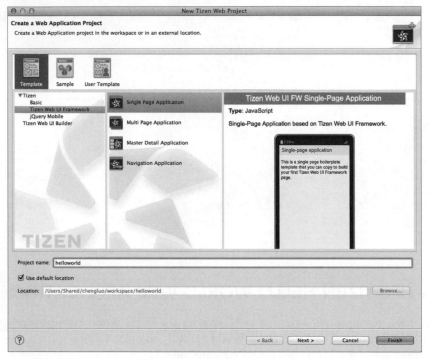

FIGURE 1-4

2. Choose the template that suits your needs. For this helloworld project, select Single Page Application from the Tizen Web UI Framework template options.

3. In the Project name field, give your project a name. The example application uses "helloworld."

4. Click the Finish button.

After you finish the preceding steps, the New Project wizard creates the basic web application structure for you, and this will be the foundation of your Tizen web application project.

The New Project wizard generates folders and files for your Hello World project, as shown in Figure 1-5.

Don't worry too much about the details of each of the files and folders for now; they are explained in more detail in Chapters 2–4.

FIGURE 1-5

To display the "Hello World" text and an OK button, make the following changes to the index .html file as highlighted in the following code listing:

1. Change the auto-generated text between the `<div data-role="content">` tags to `<p id="labelOk"></p>`.

2. Add a new `<div>` with `"data-role=button"`.

INDEX.HTML

```
!DOCTYPE html>
<html>

<head>
    <meta charset="utf-8"/>
    <meta name="description" content="A Tizen Web UI FW single-page template generated
     by Tizen Web IDE"/>
    <meta name="viewport" content="width=device-width,user-scalable=no"/>

    <link rel="stylesheet" href="tizen-web-ui-fw/latest/themes/tizen-white/tizen-web-ui-
     fw-theme.css" name="tizen-theme"/>
    <title>Tizen Web IDE - Template - Tizen - Tizen Web UI Framework - Single-
     Page</title>
    <!--NOTE:
        jquery.js and web-ui-fw.js must be included.
        DO NOT REMOVE below code!
    -->
    <script src="tizen-web-ui-fw/latest/js/jquery.js"></script>
    <script src="tizen-web-ui-fw/latest/js/tizen-web-ui-fw-libs.js"></script>
    <script src="tizen-web-ui-fw/latest/js/tizen-web-ui-fw.js"
        data-framework-theme="tizen-white"></script>

    <!-- NOTE:
        Additional scripts and css files are to be placed here.
        You can use jQuery namespace($) and all functionalities in jQuery
        in your script.  For example:

            <script src="main.js"></script>
            <link rel="stylesheet" href="my.css">
    -->
    <script type="text/javascript" src="./js/main.js"></script>
    <link rel="stylesheet" type="text/css" href="./css/style.css"/>
</head>

<body>
    <div data-role="page">
        <div data-role="header" data-position="fixed">
            <h1>Single-page application </h1>
        </div><!-- /header -->

        <div data-role="content">
            <p id="labelOk"></p>                            //(1)
        <div data-role="button" id="buttonOk">OK</div>      //(2)
        </div><!-- /content -->

        <div data-role="footer" data-position="fixed">
```

```
            <h4>Footer content</h4>
        </div><!-- /footer -->
    </div><!-- /page -->
</body>
</html>
```

The `main.js` JavaScript file in the `/js` folder is generated by the New Project wizard and contains the code for interacting with the user. To implement the button click and hardware Back key event, use the jQuery `bind()` method to add the event callback to the OK button with the ID `buttonOk` that you added in the preceding `index.html` file. The hardware Back key event callback `backEvent()` is implemented automatically by the New Project wizard.

You've now completed your first Hello World Tizen web application. The completed `main.js` JavaScript file is shown below. Run the application by choosing Run ➪ Run As ➪ Tizen Web Simulator Application in the Tizen IDE.

MAIN.JS

```javascript
var backEventListener = null;

var unregister = function() {
    if ( backEventListener !== null ) {
        document.removeEventListener( 'tizenhwkey', backEventListener );
        backEventListener = null;
        window.tizen.application.getCurrentApplication().exit();
    }
}

//Initialise function
var init = function () {
    // register once
    if ( backEventListener !== null ) {
        return;
    }

    // TODO:: Do your initialisation job
    console.log("init() called");

    var backEvent = function(e) {
        if ( e.keyName == "back" ) {
            try {
                if ( $.mobile.urlHistory.activeIndex <= 0 ) {
                    // if first page, terminate app
                    unregister();
                } else {
                    // move previous page
                    $.mobile.urlHistory.activeIndex -= 1;
                    $.mobile.urlHistory.clearForward();
                    window.history.back();
                }
            } catch( ex ) {
                unregister();
```

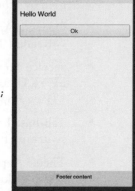

```
            }
        }
    }

    // add eventListener for tizenhwkey (Back Button)
    document.addEventListener( 'tizenhwkey', backEvent );
    backEventListener = backEvent;
    $("#buttonOk").bind( 'click', function (){
      document.getElementById("labelOk").innerHTML="Hello World";
    });
};

$(document).bind( 'pageinit', init );
$(document).unload( unregister );
```

Figure 1-6 shows the result when the Hello World project runs in the Simulator.

FIGURE 1-6

> **NOTE** *You can find much more information about the Web Simulator in Chapter 3, "Tizen Development Tools."*

CREATING THE HELLO WORLD TIZEN NATIVE APPLICATION

Beginning with the Tizen SDK 2.0, it's possible to develop native applications using the Tizen native application framework. In this section, you'll learn how to create the same Hello World example you built in the previous section using the native application framework.

The easiest way is still to use the New Project wizard. This time you'll use the Tizen Native Project wizard, shown in Figure 1-7.

The Tizen Native Project wizard provides different types of templates to choose from to create native applications:

➤ **Empty Application** — An empty project with minimum files.

➤ **Form-based Application** — A set of templates to create a simple project based on a form.

➤ **IME Application** — A template is suitable for creating an IME application project based on a form. This requires a partner-level privilege to run the application.

FIGURE 1-7

➤ **Library Application** — A set of templates to create different types of libraries that can be used by other applications.

➤ **OpenGL Application** — A set of templates to create simple projects based on GlPlayer or GlRender. The view of this project can be based on the Tizen native `Form` or `Frame`.

➤ **Service Application** — A set of templates to create simple service applications that don't have a UI and always run in the background (e.g., DynamicBox provider). See Chapter 2, "Tizen Application Packages," for more details about the DynamicBox.

➤ **Tab-based Application** — A set of templates to create tab-based applications with tab-switching functions.

➤ **Theme Application** — A set of templates to create themes that can be used for the home screen or lock screen.

To create a simple Hello World native application, follow these steps:

1. In the IDE, choose File ⇨ New ⇨ Tizen Native Project. The New Project window will be displayed (refer to Figure 1-7).

2. Choose the template that suits your needs. For this helloworld project example, select Form-based Application template ⇨ Without SceneManager, as shown in Figure 1-8.

3. Add a name for your project. In this example it is named helloworld2.

4. Click the Finish button.

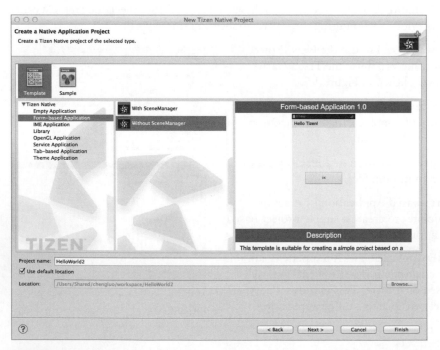

FIGURE 1-8

Once the preceding steps are finished, the New Project wizard will generate necessary folders and files you will need to start your native application.

> **NOTE** *You can find more details about the contents of these files and folders in Chapter 2, while native applications are covered in detail from Chapter 10 onwards.*

You need to pay attention to two files within the Hello World application: the `IDL_FORM.xml` file in the `/res/screen-size-normal` folder and the `HelloWorld2Form.cpp` file in the `/src` folder.

First you need to make the changes to the application UI, which requires editing the `IDL_FORM.xml` file. Double-click the `IDL_FORM.xml` file to open the native UI Builder which is integrated into the Tizen IDE.

To add the "Hello World" text and the OK button as you did in the web application, follow these steps:

1. Select the Text Box from the Toolbox panel, and drag it to the form. Highlight the Text field from the Properties panel of the Text Box, and type **Hello World** as shown as Figure 1-9.

2. The OK button is automatically generated by the template you selected, so you don't need to do anything with the button.

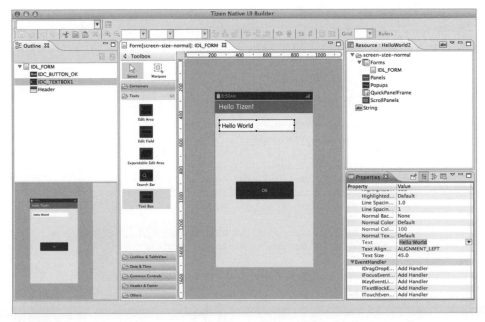

FIGURE 1-9

The next step is to make corresponding changes in the source code of the form, which is the HelloWorld2Form.cpp file. In fact, the New Project wizard does most of the work here. It creates the hardware Back key event handler called OnFormBackRequested(), and it implements the callback for the button click event OnActionPerformed() in the following code listing:

HELLOWORLD2FORM.CPP

```
#include "HelloWorld2Form.h"
#include "AppResourceId.h"

using namespace Tizen::Base;
using namespace Tizen::App;
using namespace Tizen::Ui;
using namespace Tizen::Ui::Controls;

HelloWorld2Form::HelloWorld2Form(void)
{
}

HelloWorld2Form::~HelloWorld2Form(void)
{
}

bool
HelloWorld2Form::Initialize(void)
{
        result r = Construct(IDL_FORM);
        TryReturn(r == E_SUCCESS, false, "Failed to construct form");

        return true;
}
result
HelloWorld2Form::OnInitializing(void)
{
        result r = E_SUCCESS;

        // TODO: Add your initialisation code here

        // Setup back event listener
        SetFormBackEventListener(this);

        // Get a button via resource ID
        Tizen::Ui::Controls::Button* pButtonOk =
                static_cast< Button* >(GetControl(IDC_BUTTON_OK));
        if (pButtonOk != null)
        {
                pButtonOk->SetActionId(IDA_BUTTON_OK);
                pButtonOk->AddActionEventListener(*this);
        }

        return r;
}
```

```
result
HelloWorld2Form::OnTerminating(void)
{
        result r = E_SUCCESS;

        // TODO: Add your termination code here

        return r;
}

void
HelloWorld2Form::OnActionPerformed(const Tizen::Ui::Control& source, int actionId)//(1)
{
        switch(actionId)
        {
        case IDA_BUTTON_OK:
                AppLog("OK Button is clicked!\n");
                break;
        default:
                break;
        }
}

void
HelloWorld2Form::OnFormBackRequested(Tizen::Ui::Controls::Form& source)//(2)
{
        UiApp* pApp = UiApp::GetInstance();
        AppAssert(pApp);
        pApp->Terminate();
}
```

(1) is the callback method for handling actions triggered by Controls, such as the OK button.

(2) is the callback method for handling the hardware Back key.

Again, don't worry too much about how to use the UI Builder, as it's discussed in more detail in Chapter 3.

SIGNING THE HELLO WORLD APPLICATION

There is one more step before you can run your Hello World sample application on the Emulator or device: signing and verifying your application. This step is required for both web and native applications.

Register the certificate in your security profiles by opening the Security Profiles window in the Tizen IDE: Select Windows ⇨ Preferences ⇨ Tizen SDK ⇨ Security Profiles. Figure 1-10 shows the Security Profiles window.

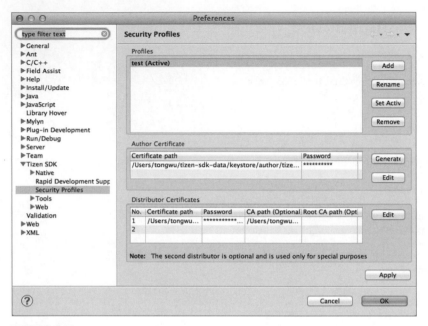

FIGURE 1-10

To add a signed profile, follow these steps:

1. Click the Add button in the Profiles panel, and provide a name for your profile. In the example it's called "test".

2. Click the Generate button in the Author Certificate panel, where you are asked to fill in some information about your author certificate. If you already have an author certificate, you can click the Edit button and choose your certificate from there.

> **NOTE** *You can also use the tools provided by the Tizen SDK to generate your author certificate. To run the certificate generator tool, go to the* `<TIZEN_SDK_HOME>/tools/certificate-generator` *directory and run* `certificate-generator.sh` *in the shell if you are using Ubuntu or Mac OS X, or run the* `certificate-generator.bat` *file from the command line if you are using Windows. Alternatively, use the Generate button from the Security Profiles window.*

3. At least one distributor certificate is required, and by default this is filled in automatically with the distributor certificate provided by the Tizen SDK. The second distributor certificate is optional and is used only for a specific purpose. More information on signing can be can be found in Chapter 2.

Once you have the security profile set up, you are ready to launch your Hello World application on the Emulator or the device. For information about how to launch your application on the Emulator, see Chapter 3.

SUMMARY

This chapter covered a lot of ground — a Tizen history lesson, the details of how a project is organized, what makes Tizen different, and why you should start creating Tizen applications.

After a brief look at the potential of Tizen development, you moved on to creating a Hello World application — both a web version and one using the native APIs. In this chapter, you launched the web application on the Web Simulator, and you may have taken a sneak peek ahead to Chapter 3 to learn how to launch applications in the Emulator.

The foundation provided in this chapter should enable you to now look at Tizen development in more detail. Chapter 2 delves into the contents of Tizen application packages, for both web and native applications, while Chapter 3 looks at the tools provided with the Tizen IDE.

Tizen Application Packages

WHAT'S IN THIS CHAPTER?

➤ Web and native application packages

➤ Inside a hybrid application

➤ Features and privileges

➤ Signing your application

This chapter explains how an application is packaged and installed on a Tizen device. The application package is what you'll upload to the Tizen store or make available from your own web page, application aggregator, or telecom operator's store. Therefore, it's essential to know how Tizen application packaging and installation works before diving into application development. Tizen supports web apps, native apps, and hybrid apps, which combine web and native apps into one application package. You'll learn how each type of application is packaged and discover the contents of an application's configuration and manifest files.

Two fundamental concepts of the Tizen platform, features and privileges, are covered in detail. Features are optional capabilities, such as camera flash or GPS, which may or may not be provided on a particular Tizen device and which an application may require to operate properly. Privileges restrict access to certain APIs to protect the integrity of the device and safeguard the user's data. This chapter explains the different levels of privileges and how you can specify features and privileges in your application.

Finally, application signing is introduced, showing you how to sign your application with author and distributor signatures and how to prepare your application for app store distribution.

PACKAGING A WEB APPLICATION

Tizen supports running web apps based on HTML5, JavaScript, and CSS. A web application is packaged into the .wgt package format. The .wgt package is basically a Zip archive file containing the files and directories shown in Table 2-1.

TABLE 2-1: Contents of a Web Application Package

NAME	DESCRIPTION
`config.xml`	Application configuration data
`icon.{png|gif|ico|svg}`	Application default icon. Various icon file types are supported.
`index.{html|htm|svg|xhtml|xht}`	Application default start file. Various start file types are supported.
`css/`	Directory for CSS source files
`js/`	Directory for JavaScript source files
`locales/`	Directory for localised resources

Figure 2-1 shows the directory structure after a web application is installed.

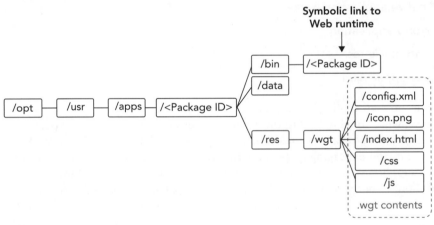

FIGURE 2-1

As you can see, the contents of the .wgt package are installed in the res/wgt directory. The executable in the bin/ directory is a symbolic link to the /usr/bin/wrt-client executable file which is the web runtime. This is shown in the following console output from the sdb shell:

```
sh-4.1$ pwd
/opt/usr/apps/82mdTohKfQ/bin
sh-4.1$ ls -l *
lrwxrwxrwx 1 root root 19 2013-11-30 13:33 82mdTohKfQ.DynamicBox -> \
/usr/bin/wrt-client
sh-4.1$
```

The most important file inside a .wgt package is config.xml, which describes the web application itself. The format of the config.xml file conforms to the W3C standard for packaged web apps and adds some Tizen-specific extensions.

> **NOTE** *The W3C web application packaging standard is described on the W3C website at* `http://www.w3.org/TR/widgets/`.

The main elements of `config.xml` are described in the following list:

- ➤ **Application name** — `<name>` element.

- ➤ **Application version** — `<widget version="x.y.z">` attribute.

- ➤ **Application start file** — `<content src="start_file_name.html"/>` element. This file is shown in the browser when an application is launched.

- ➤ **Application icon file** — `<icon src="icon_file_name.png" />` element. This icon is shown on the home screen or by a launcher application.

- ➤ **Author information** — `<author>` element.

- ➤ **Features required** — `<feature>` element. List any required features here. Each feature has a corresponding URL from which you can obtain more information about the feature. For example, `http://tizen.org/feature/network.push` specifies that the application requires the push service, which may not be supported by all devices. The "Using Optional Features" section in this chapter explains how the feature concept may affect distribution of your application and how to handle optional features.

- ➤ **Tizen-specific extensions:**

  - ➤ **Privileges required** — `<tizen:privilege>` element. List any privileges that your application requires here. Like features, each privilege has a corresponding URL from which you can obtain more information about the privilege. For example, `http://tizen.org/privilege/application.launch` specifies that the application requires access to the APIs used to launch other applications or to register the application for a conditional launch. The "Using Privileged APIs" section in this chapter explains how the privilege concept may affect API usage.

  - ➤ **App id** — `<tizen:application id="...">` attribute. The unique application identifier, which is composed of an alphanumeric package ID and the application name. The package ID is automatically generated by the IDE.

  - ➤ **Required platform version** — `<tizen:application required_version="">` attribute. This specifies the minimum required platform on which the application can run.

  - ➤ **Application controls** — `<tizen:app-control>` element. You can specify multiple application controls. The application control is a Tizen-specific mechanism which allows an application to make use of certain functionality provided by another application, which might include a media player or web browser, for example. You should include the `<tizen:src>`, `<tizen:operation>`, `<tizen:uri>`, and `<tizen:mime>` elements to specify any service your application provides to others.

➤ **Dynamic boxes** — `<tizen:app-widget>` element. You can specify multiple dynamic boxes. The dynamic box is a small area which shows some dynamically updated content from another application directly on the home screen. The label, icon, or content of the dynamic box is specified using the `<tizen:box-label>`, `<tizen:box-icon>`, and `<tizen:box-content>` elements, respectively, within the `<tizen:app-widget>` element. The box content is displayed by a special application called a *dynamic box viewer*, which is an application typically running on the home screen and preinstalled by Tizen device manufacturers.

The DynamicBoxViewer sample application in the Tizen SDK is provided as a Tizen native application, whereas the DynamicBox application, which provides the content, is a web application. Figure 2-2 shows the DynamicBoxViewer (on the left) and DynamicBox (on the right) samples running.

You don't need to know every detail about each element of the `config.xml` file because Tizen IDE provides a configuration editor. Double-clicking the `config.xml` file in the Tizen IDE launches the configuration editor, shown in Figure 2-3.

FIGURE 2-2

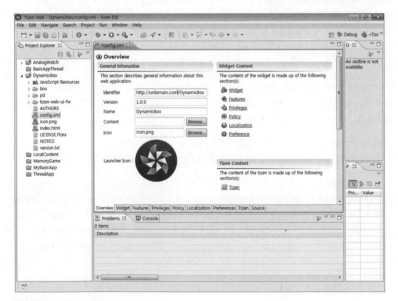

FIGURE 2-3

The configuration editor makes it easy to change application settings without having to edit the XML by hand. In Figure 2-3, the configuration editor is used to change the value of the Identifier in the Dynamic Box app to `http://urdomain.com/DynamicBox`. If this value is saved, then clicking the Source tab will display the updated XML source, including the modified `<id>` value:

```xml
<?xml version="1.0" encoding="UTF-8"?>
<widget
    xmlns="http://www.w3.org/ns/widgets"
    xmlns:tizen="http://tizen.org/ns/widgets"
    id="http://urdomain.com/DynamicBox"
    version="1.0.0" viewmodes="maximized">
    <tizen:app-widget
        id="82mdTohKfQ.DynamicBox.default"
        primary="true">
        <tizen:box-label>Web dynamicbox</tizen:box-label>
        <tizen:box-icon src="icon.png"/>
        <tizen:box-content src="box/index.html">
            <tizen:box-size>1x1</tizen:box-size>
            <tizen:box-size>2x1</tizen:box-size>
            <tizen:box-size>2x2</tizen:box-size>
            <tizen:pd
                src="pd/index.html"
                width="720" height="200"/>
        </tizen:box-content>
    </tizen:app-widget>
    <tizen:application
        id="82mdTohKfQ.DynamicBox"
        package="82mdTohKfQ"
        required_version="1.0"/>
    <icon src="icon.png"/>
    <name>DynamicBox</name>
    <tizen:setting
        screen-orientation="portrait"
        context-menu="enable"
        background-support="disable"
        encryption="disable"
        install-location="auto" hwkey-event="enable"/>
</widget>
```

PACKAGING A NATIVE APPLICATION

Tizen also supports running native apps, written using C++ and the Tizen native APIs. A native application is packaged into the .tpk package format. The .tpk package is a Zip file which contains the predefined directories and files described in Table 2-2.

TABLE 2-2: Contents of a Native Application Package

NAME	DESCRIPTION
bin/	Application executable binaries directory
data/	Application private data directory

continues

TABLE 2-2 *(continued)*

NAME	DESCRIPTION
info/	Application metadata directory. The manifest.xml file resides in this directory.
lib/	Application libraries directory
res/	Application resources directory
setting/	Application preferences directory
shared/	Sharable directory between applications

Figure 2-4 shows the directory structure after a native application is installed.

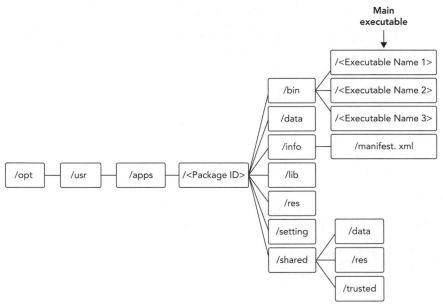

FIGURE 2-4

As you can see, the directories and files in a .tpk package are installed in a hierarchy within the package file itself. You will also notice that there are multiple executables in the bin/ directory in this example, because multiple native applications can be included in one package.

> **NOTE** *Chapter 19, "Inter-Application Communication and Hybrid Applications," contains more details about combining more than one application into an application package.*

The most important file inside a .tpk package is info/manifest.xml, which describes the native application itself. The manifest.xml file should conform to the Tizen native package manifest specification. The XML elements and attributes contained in the `manifest.xml` file are described in the following list. There are many elements in common between the `config.xml` file used for web applications and the native `manifest.xml` file.

➤ **Applications** — `<Apps>` element. Multiple applications can be bundled into one package. Each application inside a native application package is specified with its own XML element: either `<UiApp>` or `<ServiceApp>`. A `UiApp` is an application with a UI, while a `ServiceApp` runs in the background without a UI. A typical multi-application package consists of one `UiApp` and one or more `ServiceApps`.

➤ **Application name** — `<UiApp … Name="...">` or `<ServiceApp … Name="...">` attributes. Used in the same way as the `<name>` element in the `config.xml` file of a web application.

➤ **Application package ID** — `<Id>` element. This is the same as the package ID part of the `<tizen:application id="...">` attribute for web applications. It is an auto-generated alphanumeric package identifier.

➤ **Application version** — `<Version>` element. Specified in the same way as the `<widget version="x.y.z">` attribute in the `config.xml` file of a web application.

➤ **Required API version** — `<ApiVersion>` element. This element specifies the minimum platform version on which the application can run.

➤ **Application icon file** — `<Icon>` element. The icon shown on the home screen by a home (or launcher) application as an icon.

➤ **Features required** — `<Requirements>` element. Features required by your application are listed beneath this element. Web and native applications share the same URLs for required features. See the "Using Optional Features" section later in this chapter for more details.

➤ **Privileges required** — `<Privileges>` element. The privileges an application needs are listed beneath this element. Web and native applications share the same URLs for required privileges. The "Using Privileged APIs" section in this chapter explains how the privilege concept may affect API usage.

➤ **Application controls** — `<AppControls>` element. This is used in the same way as the `<tizen:app-control>` element in the `config.xml` file of a web application. You should specify `OperationId`, `MimeType`, and `UriScheme` attributes through a `<Capability>` element underneath the `<AppControl>` element for each provider of an application control.

➤ **Dynamic boxes** — `<AppWidgets>` element. Used in the same way as the `<tizen:app-widget>` element in the `config.xml` file of a web application. Specify an `<AppWidget>` element for each dynamic box underneath the `<AppWidgets>` element. Describe the dynamic box's display name, preview image, and size using the `<DisplayNames>` and `<Sizes>` elements.

Just like the configuration editor for a web application, the Tizen IDE provides a native application manifest editor, as shown in Figure 2-5.

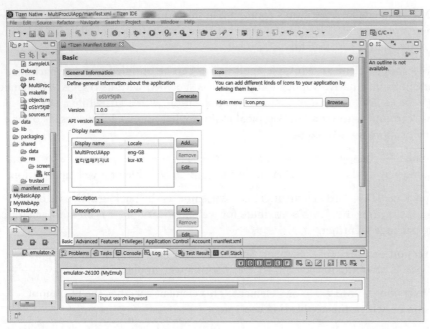

FIGURE 2-5

If you click the `manifest.xml` tab at the bottom of the manifest editor window, you can see the XML source. For example, Figure 2-5 shows the display name field being edited in the MultiProcUiApp sample. Once this change is made and the manifest file saved, here's what the XML source will look like:

```xml
<?xml version="1.0" encoding="UTF-8" standalone="no"?>
<Manifest xmlns="http://schemas.tizen.org/2012/12/manifest">
 <Id>oSbY5tjiIh</Id>
 <Version>1.0.0</Version>
 <Type>C++App</Type>
 <Requirements>
   <Feature Name="http://tizen.org/feature/screen.size.normal">
     true
   </Feature>
 </Requirements>
 <Apps>
   <ApiVersion>2.1</ApiVersion>
   <Privileges>
     <Privilege>
       http://tizen.org/privilege/application.launch
     </Privilege>
   </Privileges>
   <UiApp
     LaunchingHistoryVisible="True" Main="True"
     MenuIconVisible="True" Name="MultiProcUiApp">
     <UiScalability
       BaseScreenSize="Normal" CoordinateSystem="Logical"
       LogicalCoordinate="720"/>
     <UiTheme SystemTheme="White"/>
     <DisplayNames>
```

```
        <DisplayName Locale="eng-GB">
          MultiProcUiApp
        </DisplayName>
        <DisplayName Locale="kor-KR">
          멀티앱패키지UI
        </DisplayName>
      </DisplayNames>
      <Icons>
        <Icon Section="MainMenu" Type="Xhigh">icon.png</Icon>
      </Icons>
      <LaunchConditions/>
      <Notifications>
        <Notification Name="Ticker">On</Notification>
        <Notification Name="Sound">On</Notification>
        <Notification Name="Contents">Off</Notification>
        <Notification Name="Badge">On</Notification>
      </Notifications>
    </UiApp>
  </Apps>
</Manifest>
```

PACKAGING A HYBRID APPLICATION

Tizen supports hybrid application packages, which are typically composed of a web application providing the UI and one or more native apps which take care of background services. The hybrid application package is a Zip file with a .wgt file extension, similar to the web application package. The contents of the package are a combination of a web application package and a native application package, as shown in Table 2-3.

TABLE 2-3: Contents of a Hybrid Application Package

NAME	DESCRIPTION
bin/	Directory for the native application executable(s) and a symbolic link to the web runtime.
data/	Application private data directory.
info/	Directory for native application metadata. The manifest.xml file resides in this directory.
lib/	Directory for native application libraries.
res/	Directory for native application resources and web application contents.
res/wgt/	Root directory for the web application. The web application icon file, web application sta rt file, css/ directory, and js/ directory reside inside this directory.
setting/	Directory for application preferences.
shared/	Native application sharable directory.

Figure 2-6 shows the directory structure after a hybrid application package has been installed.

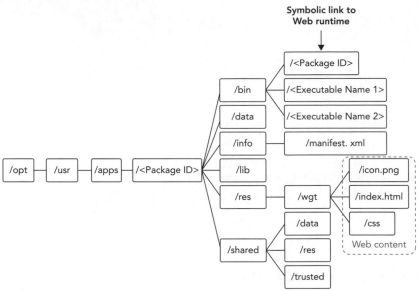

FIGURE 2-6

As you can see, the web and native application files are installed in the same directories as normal web and native applications. The Tizen IDE provides a sample hybrid application consisting of HybridWebApp, which provides the UI, and HybridServiceApp, a native application that has no UI and implements the background tasks. After loading both applications into the IDE, you can combine them into one hybrid application package by making the HybridWebApp refer to the HybridServiceApp.

To set up a project reference between the UI and service application, right-click the web application in the IDE and choose Properties ⇨ Project References. Then select the service application to be added to the application package.

Figure 2-7 shows the contents of the combined hybrid application package. (See Chapter 19 for more information on hybrid application development.)

A hybrid application enables you to develop a highly portable web application and still take advantage of the performance and deep platform integration of a native application.

Figure 2-8 shows the output of the HybridWebApp when it executes.

When you click the START button, the HybridWebApp starts to talk to and display messages from the HybridServiceApp. The HybridWebApp sends the "start" command to the service application, which sends "timer expired" messages to the web application until it's requested to "stop." This is a simple example of a hybrid application, but it does show the concepts and can be used as the basis for your own more advanced applications.

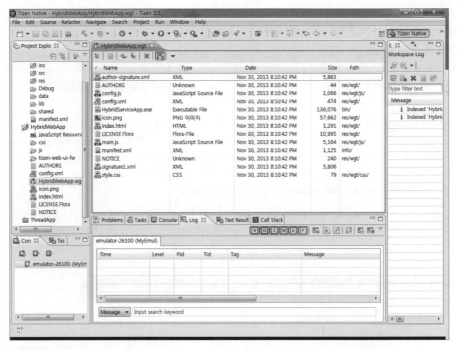

FIGURE 2-7

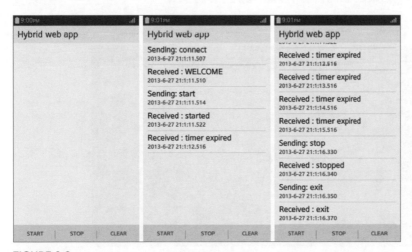

FIGURE 2-8

USING OPTIONAL FEATURES

Among the elements in the `config.xml` or `manifest.xml` files you should give special attention to the `<feature>` or `<Requirements>` element. Features can be specified in the Tizen IDE — using the configuration editor for web apps, and the manifest editor for native applications. Features refers to optional capabilities that are dependent on some software or hardware. Optional means that a feature may not be present on some Tizen devices. Applications which are dependent on optional features may not run properly on Tizen devices which do not have these features.

An application distribution channel, such as the Tizen Store, can use features to filter applications so that only those which will run properly on a particular device are made available to download. If an application depends on a feature that the device doesn't support, that application will not be shown to the user.

You can access the list of optional features in the Tizen IDE from the Help ➪ Help Contents ➪ Tizen Native App Programming ➪ Programming Guide ➪ System: Getting System Information and the Using Alarms ➪ System Information ➪ Feature keys section. Each optional feature is represented by a corresponding URL which provides more information about the feature. The Tizen Web framework and Tizen native framework features share the same URLs.

For example, the camera is optional hardware and is represented by the URL `http://tizen.org/feature/camera`. If you browse to this URL you will see the documentation for this feature, as shown in Figure 2-9.

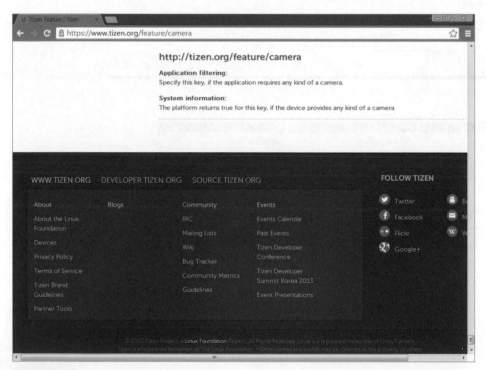

FIGURE 2-9

Some features have a feature hierarchy. For example, using the preceding URL on its own requires only that any kind of camera is present on the device. You can be more specific by adding features for the front camera (`http://tizen.org/feature/camera.front`) and the back camera (`http://tizen.org/feature/camera.back`).

If your application requires a camera flash you add further subfeatures, `http://tizen.org/feature/camera.front.flash` and `http://tizen.org/feature/camera.back.flash`.

Most features are simply present or not, but some features are a little bit more complex. For example, when specifying the `http://tizen.org/feature/multi_point_touch.point_count` feature, you include a specific value for the minimum number of touch points required in a multi-point touch.

If your application cannot run properly without an optional feature, you should specify the feature in the `<feature>` element in `config.xml` (in a web application) or the `<Requirements>`/ `<Feature>` element in `manifest.xml` (in a native application). Figures 2-10, 2-11, and 2-12 show every API which is dependent on an optional feature, including the W3C APIs, device APIs, and native APIs.

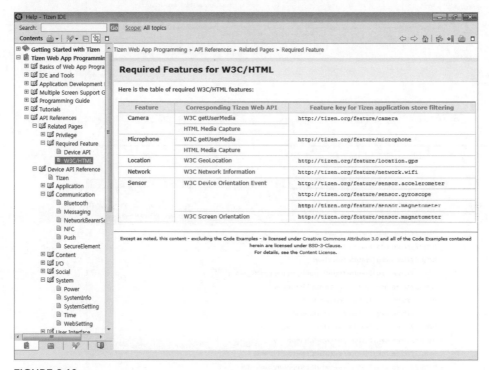

FIGURE 2-10

You can check the availability of an optional feature within a web or native application as follows:

➤ **Web API** — The `SystemInfoDeviceCapability` interface defines read-only attributes for all optional features. You can obtain this object by calling `tizen.systeminfo` `.getCapabilities()`.

➤ **Native API** — The `Tizen::System::SystemInfo::GetValue(key, value)` method returns values for the specified feature URL key argument.

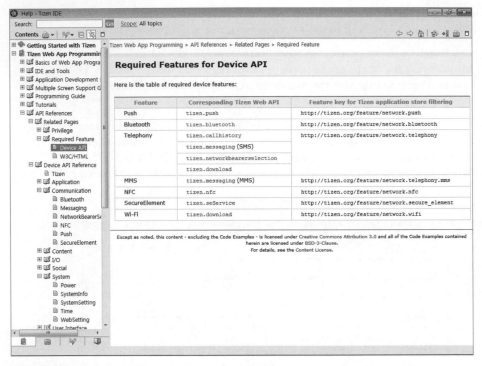

FIGURE 2-11

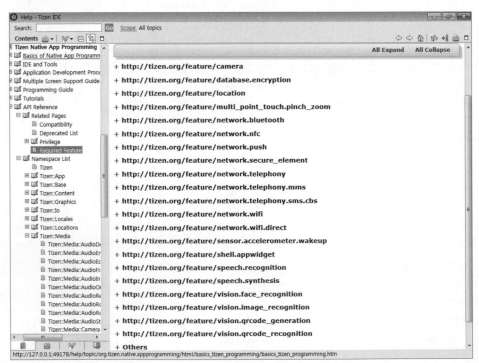

FIGURE 2-12

Each Web Device API and Native API which is dependent on an optional feature throws the `WebAPIException` with error type `NotSupportedError` or returns the `E_UNSUPPORTED_OPERATION` exception, respectively, if the feature is not available. The behaviour of W3C/HTML APIs when an optional feature is not supported is dependent on the W3C specification.

You should pay particular attention to the screen size and resolution-related features because these features are conceptually different from other features. An application should declare a feature for the screen size and resolutions it supports, using the URL starting with `http://tizen.org/feature/screen.size`.

The application may declare multiple screen sizes and resolutions, or specify that it supports all sizes and resolutions. Currently only the `normal` screen size is defined, which refers to the smartphone and phablet form factor, including screens of up to around 6.5 inches. The application can declare `http://tizen.org/feature/screen.size.normal` if it can support all possible current and future resolutions at the normal screen size, and `http://tizen.org/feature/screen.size.all` if it can support all possible current and future screen sizes and resolutions. Hosted web apps are likely to use this feature setting.

For details about feature-based application filtering, select Help ➪ Help Contents ➪ Getting Started with Tizen ➪ Overview ➪ Application Filtering.

USING PRIVILEGED APIS

Tizen provides API-level access control to protect the system and sensitive user data from malicious or insecure apps.

A privilege is defined for security-sensitive operations which, if not used correctly, can harm user privacy and system security. Such APIs are called *privileged APIs*. Applications that use privileged APIs must declare the required privileges in the `config.xml` or `manifest.xml` files, for web and native applications, respectively.

Each privilege belongs to a privilege level, either public, partner, or platform, depending on its security risk. The platform level is assigned to privileges with the highest security risk, while the public level is used for the least risky privileged APIs. For example, the package install/uninstall privilege is a platform-level privilege because a malicious application may install another application without user intervention. Typically the package install/uninstall privileges are granted only to a limited set of application store–type applications. Partner-level privileges can only be accessed by developers who are registered as partners on the Tizen Store, while public privileges are open to all developers.

Each privilege is represented by a corresponding URL. The Tizen Web framework and Tizen Native framework share the same URL for the same privilege. For example, the privilege to read contact information is represented by the URL `http://tizen.org/privilege/contact.read`. You can find documentation on a privilege by browsing to the privilege URL, as shown in Figure 2-13.

FIGURE 2-13

You can find documentation on all privileges by selecting Help ⇨ Help Contents ⇨ Tizen Web App Programming ⇨ API References ⇨ Related Pages ⇨ Privilege or Help ⇨ Help Contents ⇨ Tizen Native App Programming ⇨ API References ⇨ Related Pages ⇨ Privilege, in the Tizen IDE. The help description of each API also includes any privilege required to use it, as shown in Figures 2-14 and 2-15.

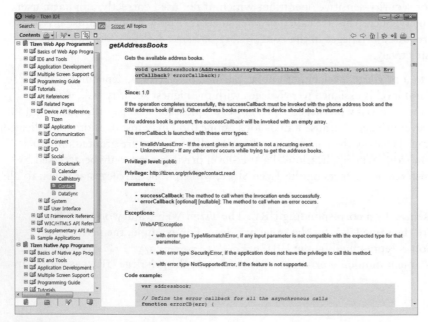

FIGURE 2-14

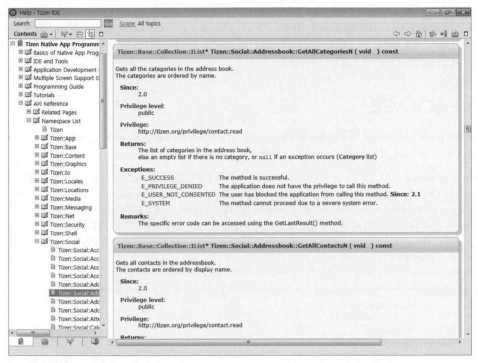

FIGURE 2-15

All privileged APIs may throw a SecurityError exception (in a web application) or return an E_PRIVILEGE_DENIED exception (in a native application) when your application does not declare a required privilege in config.xml or manifest.xml. It's also possible for a previously nonprivileged API to become a privileged API in a later release due to security reasons. Therefore, it's always wise to check for the SecurityError or E_PRIVILEGE_DENIED exceptions after calling an API.

There are special privileges related to user privacy. Tizen handles privacy-related privileges to protect the user's sensitive data in the following ways:

➤ The Tizen platform provides the user with access to privacy settings on a per-application basis (Settings ➪ Privacy ➪ [ApplicationName]) through the preinstalled settings application.

➤ The Tizen platform may show a privacy setting pop-up to give the user a chance to adjust privacy-related privileges when the application is first launched, as shown in Figure 2-16.

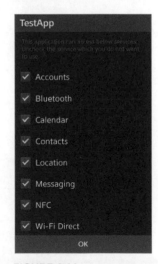

FIGURE 2-16

Users can allow or disallow privacy-related privileges of installed applications when the application is first launched or using the settings menu. If a user disallows a privacy-related privilege, then the related APIs will throw a `SecurityError` exception (in a web application) or return a `E_USER_NOT_CONSENTED` exception (in a native application).

SIGNING A PACKAGE

Tizen application packages must be signed with author and distributor signatures, following the W3C recommendations for XML digital signatures for widgets:

➤ **Author signature** — An author signature determines the integrity of an application package as intended by the developer and confirms that all applications signed with the same author certificate are trustworthy. The author certificate, which is used for signing an author signature, can be generated from the Security Profiles dialog in the Tizen IDE, as shown in Figure 2-17. You can access the Security Profiles dialog from Windows ⇨ Preferences ⇨ Tizen SDK ⇨ Security Profiles.

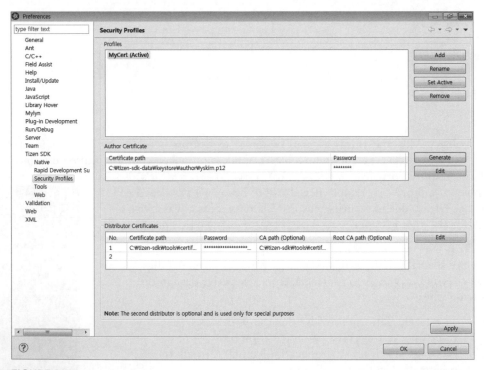

FIGURE 2-17

For more details on how to generate and register an author certificate, in the Tizen IDE select Help ⇨ Help Contents ⇨ Development Environment ⇨ Tizen SDK ⇨ Certificate Generator.

> ➤ **Distributor signature** — A distributor signature is generated by an application publisher, such as the Tizen Store, to confirm that the publisher has distributed the application package and to prove its integrity.

The package is signed automatically by the Tizen IDE after you register your author certificate.

You can see the `author-signature.xml` file for an author signature and the `signature1.xml` file for a distributor signature in Figure 2-7, which shows the package for a hybrid application. The Tizen application installer will accept only application packages with both signatures. The Tizen IDE prepares a temporary distributor certificate and automatically adds a distributor signature so that your application package is installed without problems during application development. This temporary distributor signature will be replaced by the real application distribution channel — for example, the Tizen Store or your local telecom operator's application store.

The Tizen distributor signature determines the privilege levels granted to your application. For example, if an application is signed with the public-level certificate for the distributor signature, the application is limited to public-level privileges. If you want to use partner-privileged APIs on the Emulator or developer devices, rather than commercial devices, you first need to patch the Tizen IDE using the following steps:

1. cd `$TIZEN_SDK_HOME/tools/certificate-generator/patches`.

2. Execute the following command:

   For Windows:

   `patch.bat partner [$TIZEN_SDK_HOME]`

   For Linux or Mac OS X:

   `./patch.sh partner [$TIZEN_SDK_HOME]`

If `$TIZEN_SDK_HOME` is omitted, the patch installs the certificates at the default SDK location. If you want to install public certificates again, specify `public` instead of `partner`.

If you want to use the platform-privileged APIs on the Emulator or developer devices, follow these steps:

1. Open the `http://goo.gl/ojuuaC` URL in your browser. This URL redirects you to the git directory for the temporary platform-level certificate.

2. Download the `tizen-distributor-partner-manufacturer-signer.p12` file.

3. Rename the file to **`tizen-distributor-signer.p12`**.

4. Replace `$TIZEN_SDK_HOME/tools/certificate-generator/certificates/distributor/tizen-distributor-signer.p12` with the file from step 3.

You cannot install applications which are signed with the preceding temporary certificates onto commercial devices.

SUMMARY

In this chapter you learned about some of the key concepts of the Tizen application development process, including packaging, features, privileges, and signing. You learned about the three types of applications and the corresponding packages: wgt packages for web and hybrid apps, and tpk packages for native applications. You should now be familiar with the contents of the `config.xml` and `manifest.xml` files which describe the application itself, and understand how Tizen protects access to certain APIs using privileges. You've also taken your first step to app store immortality by learning about signing application packages.

The skills you learned in this chapter for finding your way around configuration and manifest files will be important in the next few chapters as you become more familiar with the Tizen IDE and start creating applications that take advantage of Tizen's many features.

3

Tizen Development Tools

WHAT'S IN THIS CHAPTER?

➤ The Tizen IDE

➤ The Tizen Emulator

➤ The Tizen Web Simulator

➤ Debugging and testing tools

➤ Creating UIs for native applications

This chapter is your Tizen development primer, providing you with hints, tips, and techniques to get the most out of the developer tools, including the Emulator, Web Simulator, and Event Injector. You'll learn how to configure the Emulator for the best performance, how to access advanced features, and how to test and debug both web and native applications.

THE TIZEN IDE

The tool you will use the most during your development is probably the Tizen IDE. In Chapter 1, "An Introduction to Tizen," you learned how to install the SDK and IDE, and how to use the New Project wizard to create the simple Hello World project. In this section, you'll look at the IDE in more detail.

Because the Tizen IDE is based on Eclipse, its layout is very similar to other Eclipse-based IDEs, such as the Android Development Tools (ADT) and the Samsung bada IDE. Figure 3-1 shows the Tizen IDE, including the Project Explorer window and source code editor.

On the top of the IDE window is a set of toolbars containing project- and file-related tools — for building, debugging, running, and profiling the project. On the left side of the main window is the Project Explorer panel, while the window in the bottom-left corner is the Connection Explorer. The Project Explorer provides you with quick access to all projects, files, and resources in your current workplace. The Connection Explorer provides information and quick access to the Tizen Emulator and connected Tizen devices.

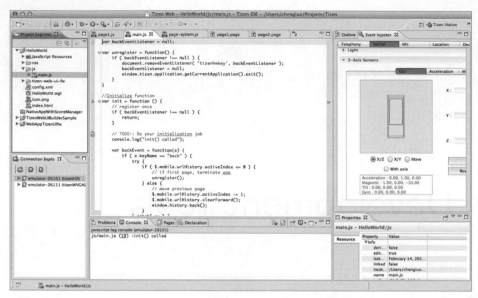

FIGURE 3-1

The code editor is shown in the middle of the main window, with the Problems, Tasks, and Console panels located at the bottom. These windows provide information related to compilation errors, logs, and debugging messages. The right side of the main window shows the Outline, Event Injector, or other panels, such as CSS Preview and HTML Preview, according to the perspective you choose.

This chapter doesn't spend time explaining common Eclipse IDE features such as compiling and running projects. We assume you are already very familiar with using the Eclipse environment. Instead we focus on explaining how to use the Tizen-specific tools that are integrated into the Eclipse IDE.

TIZEN EMULATOR

The Tizen SDK comes with a very powerful and comprehensive emulator. You can think of the Tizen Emulator as a strict implementation of a Tizen specification, matching the features of a real Tizen reference device. The Tizen Emulator is based on the open-source QEMU project, and comprises the virtual CPU, memory, and other peripherals, including some of the hardware features such as sensors and cameras.

There are two different ways to start the Emulator depending on your requirements: using the command line or using the Emulator Manager. You can use the command line to start the Emulator if you need more control over the options passed to it. Detailed information about the command-line options can be found in the Tizen SDK documentation at Getting Started with Tizen ⇨ Development Environment ⇨ Tizen SDK ⇨ Emulator ⇨ Emulator Start-up options. You can specify two types of options using the command line: skin options and QEMU options. Using skin options, you can make changes to the Emulator skin settings such as the resolution and skin images. Using QEMU options, you can change the settings of the QEMU virtual machine, to use your own customized virtual image, or to change the memory size and other settings to fine-tune the Emulator according to your own needs.

Most of you will probably use the Emulator Manager which is integrated into the Tizen IDE and can be opened from the Emulator Manager icon in the Connection Explorer window. Using the Emulator Manager, you can easily customize the settings for your Tizen virtual machine. The options available from the Emulator Manager are very similar to those provided by the command line. For example, you can choose the resolution, pixel density, skin images, and other settings, as shown in Figure 3-2.

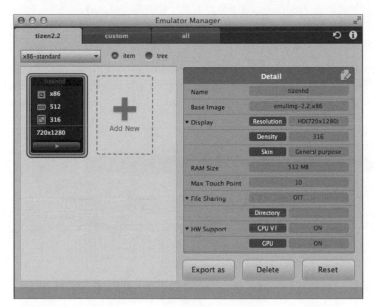

FIGURE 3-2

The Emulator Manager manages all your Tizen virtual machines. To create a standard Tizen virtual machine, follow these steps:

1. From the "tizen2.2" tab (refer to Figure 3-2), name the virtual machine—for example, "tizenhd".

2. Choose the standard Tizen 2.2 image (emulimg-2.2.x86) which comes with the Tizen SDK 2.2.1. This is the default image for the standard Tizen virtual machine.

3. There are two preset skin images from which you can choose: a general-purpose skin for Tizen apps using profiles, such as IVI or laptop, and an HD phone skin for developing applications using the Tizen mobile profile.

4. Set the RAM size. Remember to choose a reasonable size for the virtual machine. This RAM size is shared from the physical host's memory. If it is too large, your virtual machine may not be able to launch.

5. Turn on the File Sharing option and choose a file path from the host if you need to share data between the virtual machine and host. We explain the details of file sharing later in this chapter.

6. If your host environment supports hardware acceleration, such as CPU and GPU acceleration, you will be able to enable the HW Support options. We will show you how to enable hardware acceleration for your virtual machine later in the "Enabling Hardware Acceleration" section.

> **NOTE** *Tizen only supports a host with the X86 architecture. Other CPU architectures are not supported at the time of writing.*

In some cases, you might want to create a customized virtual machine using your own image. You can do this from the "custom" tab. The steps are very similar to creating the standard Tizen virtual machine. The only difference is that you have to choose your customized image file using the Base Image option (see Figure 3-3).

FIGURE 3-3

A custom image is useful when testing apps that are built with nonstandard Tizen stacks. For example, if you download the Tizen source code and modify or add new components to the platform, you then can build your own Tizen customized image and select it using the Base Image option. The other steps will be exactly the same as creating the standard virtual machine.

Once the virtual machine is created, you can launch it by clicking the play icon on the image.

> **NOTE** *When you run the virtual machine for the first time, it will probably take quite a long time to launch because it is doing some initial setup. Fortunately, the next time the Emulator image will launch a lot faster.*

Enabling Hardware Acceleration

Enabling hardware acceleration will give you a great boost in terms of Emulator performance, especially if you are testing calculation-heavy or graphically intensive apps. Enabling hardware acceleration is easy; if HAMX is not installed, you just need to install the Intel HAXM package that is provided with the SDK download. You can find HAXM in [SDK Install Folder]/tools/ emulator/etc/IntelHaxmTizen.dmg or .exe, depending on whether you are using Mac OS X or Windows. If you're using Linux, then hardware acceleration is provided by Kernel-based Virtual Machine (KVM), which requires no additional installation.

Because the software providing hardware acceleration for the virtual image depends on the chipset vendor — in this case, Intel — there is no guarantee that it is available for the host environment you are using. For example, there are compatibility issues with the Intel HAXM package and the latest version of Mac OS X Mavericks.

> **NOTE** *If you use the latest Mac OS Mavericks, you need to install the hot fix provided by Intel. The link of the hot fix is* http://software.intel.com/ en-us/articles/intel-hardware accelerated-execution-manager/.

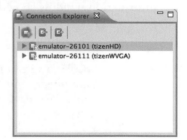

FIGURE 3-4

Once the Emulator is launched, you will see that it appears in the Tizen IDE under the Connection Explorer panel, as shown in Figure 3-4.

Tizen supports multiple instances of the Emulator, which is quite useful when you want to compare multiple versions of your application running with different resolutions and other Emulator settings, or if you want to test peer-to-peer communication between two or more emulators.

Using the Tizen Emulator

Once the Emulator appears in the Connection Explorer, you are ready to run or debug your application. As mentioned earlier in the "Tizen Emulator" section, there are two types of skin you can choose for the Emulator. If you choose the phone image, the first time you launch the Emulator you will see the screen shown in Figure 3-5.

FIGURE 3-5   **FIGURE 3-6**

The text on the screen shows the booting process of the Linux virtual machine. For the first launch, it might take few minutes. After the virtual machine is booted, you will see the Tizen logo and the home screen.

The phone skin mimics a standard Tizen reference phone. It consists of a volume up key, volume down key, and power key on the side; and a menu key, home key, and back key on the bottom of the phone. Operating the Emulator is straightforward. The Emulator picks up touch events and key press click events from the mouse. You can access more features from the context menu by right-clicking the mouse in the Emulator, as shown in Figure 3-6.

You can get Emulator details by clicking the Emulator name in the menu. This brings up the information window showing details such as CPU architecture, resolution, pixel density, SD card path, and RAM size.

> **NOTE** *You can find more information about the Emulator by going to the Documentation ⇨ Dev Guide ⇨ Getting Started with Tizen ⇨ Development Environment ⇨ Emulator section on the Tizen developer website (*`http://developer.tizen.org`*).*

The Advanced menu provides some useful features, such as taking a snapshot of the Emulator, as well as specifying whether to use the host keyboard or the soft keyboard from the Emulator itself. This is extremely handy if you are testing an input-extensive application.

Another very useful feature is the Emulator Shell. This feature opens the Smart Development Bridge (SDB) shell command window shown as Figure 3-7. We explain more about SDB in the section "Smart Development Bridge."

```
●○○          ⌂ tongwu — emulator-26101 — sdb — 66×20          ⤢

sh-4.1$ ls
bin    csa    etc    lost+found   opt    run      smack   system   var
boot   data   home   media        proc   sbin     srv     tmp
cache  dev    lib    mnt          root   sdcard   sys     usr
sh-4.1$ ▊
```

FIGURE 3-7

That covers the basic features of the Tizen Emulator, but it supports other extended features you should also become familiar with. For example, you can test multi-touch features using the Tizen Emulator as well. To use multi-touch, press and hold the Ctrl key (or the Command key in Mac OS X) while mouse-clicking on the Emulator screen area to add the touch point. An example of using the multi-touch feature is to use two touch points to zoom in and zoom out of an image in the Gallery application. To add the second touch point, hold down the Ctrl key (or Command key in Mac OS X) and click the left button of the mouse. To emulate the two-finger pinch to zoom out gesture, use the mouse to move the second touch point towards the first touch point, and the image will be zoomed out (see Figure 3-8).

You can also use the webcam as the extended device camera in the Emulator. There is a detailed explanation about how to use the webcam for the Emulator in the "Using Extended Emulator Features" section of the SDK help. Using the extended features, the Emulator is able to communicate with the host OS. The Tizen Emulator is based on the QEMU virtual machine. It uses QEMU user networking using the SLIRP protocol as the network back end. By default, the Emulator IP address is set to 10.0.2.16, the default gateway is 10.0.2.2, and the DNS is 10.0.2.3.

The Emulator is able to send outbound TCP packages to the host OS without any problems; but if the Emulator needs to receive incoming TCP connections, it is not possible to route the TCP/UDP package to the guest OS without setting up port redirection, which you can set up by editing the QEMU configuration file located at `~/tizne_vms/x86/ [Your VM name]/vm_config.xml`. The following is an example of the configuration file that redirects TCP packages from the host OS port

FIGURE 3-8

1202 to the guest OS port 22. Using port redirection, you can also set up a connection between two Emulators:

```
<usability>
    <logging>
        <level>NONE</level>
    </logging>
    <filesharing/>
    <hwVirtualization>true</hwVirtualization>
    <advancedOptions>-redir tcp:1202:10.0.2.16:22</advancedOptions>
</usability>
```

Another important extended feature of the Tizen Emulator is file sharing. The File Sharing feature enables you to transfer large files between the host and guest OS. For example, if you have a large user-data file that you want to transfer to the guest OS for testing purposes, you can set up the host OS file-sharing path in the Emulator Manager. When you want to transfer files from the host OS to the Emulator, you need to mount the host file-sharing folder in the Emulator guest OS using the SDB shell. The following SDB command is used to mount a Windows folder:

```
# mount -t cifs //10.0.2.2/emulator-26100 /mnt/host
-o unc=//10.0.2.2\\emulator-26100,user=sdk,pass=test,noperm,rw
```

This command mounts the host file system folder /mnt/host to the Emulator share path, which in this case is the path with the Emulator name.

The -t option indicates the local file system type; in this case the Emulator file system type is CIFS (Common Internet File System). The -o flag lists all the options used for the mount command; in this example it specifies the UNC (Universal Naming Convention) name of the server and share path. The options also include the username and password of the Emulator to authenticate the connection.

TIZEN WEB SIMULATOR

The Tizen Emulator is a powerful tool, especially when you develop native applications and web apps using Tizen-specific features. Web developers can use another tool — the Web Simulator. The Simulator is perfect for debugging the UI and standard HTML5 features of your web application. You can choose to run your web application in the Simulator by right-clicking the project in the Project Explorer and choosing Run As ➪ Tizen Web Simulator Application, as shown in Figure 3-9.

FIGURE 3-9

The Web Simulator is based on the Ripple-UI framework and runs in a Google Chrome window, so in order to use the Simulator you must have Google Chrome installed.

When you use the Simulator, there are some settings you need to consider. The default Chrome browser blocks cross-domain requests and access to local files for security reasons. To enable these options, you need to set following flags while launching the Chrome browser:

➤ `--allow-access-from-files` — Allows the Simulator JavaScript APIs to access files on the disk (such as `config.xml` and the application icon)

➤ `--disable-web-security` — Allows the Simulator to perform cross-domain requests (such as access map locations on another server)

On Linux or Mac OS X, you can set these flags from the command line like this:

```
$ google-chrome --allow-file-access-from-files
--disable-web-security
```

On Windows, you can set the flags in the properties of the Google Chrome browser, as shown in Figure 3-10.

Once the Simulator is launched, you are able to simulate a lot of device-related events. The menus (see Figure 3-11) displayed on the left side of the Simulator window, such as Notification, Sensors, Communication, Geolocation, Network Management, and Power Management, enable you to specify device settings and simulate particular features.

FIGURE 3-10

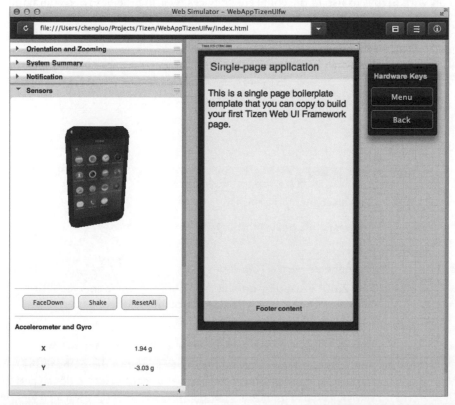

FIGURE 3-11

For example, you can simulate the device orientation event from the Sensors menu by dragging the virtual device in different orientations. Similarly, you can simulate GPS data using the Geolocation menu.

Debugging in the Simulator and Emulator is explained in more detail in the "Debugging and Testing" section later in this chapter.

SMART DEVELOPMENT BRIDGE

We mentioned the SDB shell earlier in the chapter, but the SDB provides many more functions than just the shell. It manages Tizen development devices, including the Emulator.

> **NOTE** *If you have Tizen developer devices, remember to turn the USB debugging option on to connect with SDB. You'll find the option on the device in Settings ➪ More System Settings ➪ Developer Options ➪ USB Debugging.*

SDB is all command-line based. To use the SDB, you need to launch the command-line terminal from your host machine. Adding the path of the `sdb` executable to your system environment will make your job much easier because you won't have to navigate to the SDB folder each time.

The first thing to do with SDB is to list all the connected devices by using the `devices` command:

```
$ sdb devices
List of devices attached
emulator-26100 device myemulator1
emulator-26200 device myemulator2
$
```

Table 3-1 shows the full list of `sdb` commands.

TABLE 3-1: SDB Commands

COMMAND	DESCRIPTION
`sdb devices`	Lists all connected devices.
`sdb connect <host>[:<port>]`	Connects to a device through TCP/IP.
`sdb disconnect <host>[:<port>]`	Disconnects from a TCP/IP device. Port 26101 is used by default if no port number is specified. Using this command with no additional arguments disconnects from all connected TCP/IP devices.
`sdb push <local> <remote> [-with-utf8]`	Copies a file or directory recursively to the device's data file. The `<local>` and `<remote>` parameters refer to the paths to the target files or directories on the development machine (local) and the device instance (remote). The following command shows an example:

	`$ sdb push data.txt /opt/apps/org.tizen.hellotizen/data/data.txt` The `[-with-utf8]` parameter creates the remote file with the UTF-8 character encoding.
`sdb pull <remote> [<local>]`	Copies a file or directory recursively from the device's data file. The `<remote>` and `<local>` parameters refer to the paths to the target files or directories on the device instance (remote) and the development machine (local). The following command shows an example: `$ sdb pull /opt/apps/org.tizen.hellotizen/data/data.txt data.txt`
`sdb shell`	Runs a remote shell interactively by dropping into a remote shell on an Emulator or device instance. To exit the remote shell, press Ctrl+D or use the `exit` command to end the shell session.
`sdb shell <command>`	Runs a remote shell command without entering the SDB remote shell on the device. The following commands are available: `ls`, `rm`, `mv`, `cd`, `mkdir`, `cp`, `touch`, `echo`, `tar`, `grep`, `cat`, `chmod`, `rpm`, `find`, `uname`, `netstat`, and `killall`.
`sdb dlog [option] [<filter-spec>]`	Views and follows the content of the device log buffers. To view the log output in your development computer or from a remote SDB shell, use the `sdb dlog` or `dlogutil` commands, respectively. The `[<filter-spec>]` parameter defines the tag of interest (the system component from which the message originates) and the minimum level of priority to report for that tag. The format is `tag:priority`, and multiple filters must be separated with a space. The available priorities (from lowest to highest) are `V` (Verbose), `D` (Debug), `I` (Info), `W` (Warning), `E` (Error), and `F` (Fatal). For example, to view all log messages of the info priority in addition to the MyApp tag messages of the debug priority, use the following command: `$ sdb dlog MyApp:D *:E` For more information about the command options, go to Document ⇨ Dev Guide ⇨ Getting Started with Tizen ⇨ Development Environment ⇨ Tizen SDK ⇨ Smart Development Bridge ⇨ Controlling Log Output on the Tizen developer site (`http://developer.tizen.org`).

continues

TABLE 3-1 *(continued)*

COMMAND	DESCRIPTION
sdb install <path_to_tpk>	Pushes the tpk package file to the device and installs it. The <path_to_tpk> parameter defines the path to the tpk file. The following command shows an example: `$ sdb install /home/tizen/ko983dw33q-1.0.0-i386.tpk`
sdb uninstall <appid>	Uninstalls the application from the device. The <appid> parameter defines the application ID of the application. The following command shows an example: `$ sdb uninstall ko983dw33q`

sdb forward <local> <remote>	Sets up arbitrary port forwarding of requests from a specific host port to a different port on a device instance.
	
	The format for the <local> and <remote> parameters is tcp:<port>. The following example shows how to forward requests from host port 26102 to device port 9999:
	
	`$ sdb forward tcp:26102 tcp:9999`
	
	After you set up port forwarding, development tools between the device and host can work remotely. For example, gdb in a host/gdbserver in a device, and gdbserver in a device open with the tcp:9999 port:
	
	`$ sdb shell gdbserver:9999 hellotizen`
	
	`gdb in a host connects to localhost:26102`
	
	`$ gdb hellotizen ... (gdb) target remote localhost:26102`

sdb help	Shows the help message.
sdb version	Shows the version number.
sdb start-server	Starts the server if it is not running.
sdb kill-server	Stops the server if it is running.
sdb get-state	Prints the target device connection status.
sdb get-serialno	Prints the serial number of the target device.
sdb status-window	Continuously prints the connection status for a specified device.
sdb root <on|off>	Switches between the root and developer account mode. The on value sets the root mode and the off value sets the developer account mode.

Other handy commands SDB commands are `kill-server` and `start-server`. If a connected device can't be seen from SDB, you can try to restart the SDB daemon by using the `kill-server` and `start-server` commands.

DEBUGGING AND TESTING

The Tizen IDE is based on Eclipse, so if you've used other Eclipse-based IDEs you should be familiar with how to use testing and debugging features such as setting breakpoints, and step in and step out. The Tizen IDE takes debugging and testing features to the next level by integrating the Remote Inspector JavaScript debugger and the powerful Event Injector.

To debug your web application in the Web Simulator, launch the Remote Inspector by pressing the F12 key. The inspector will be opened in a new Google Chrome window, as shown in Figure 3-12.

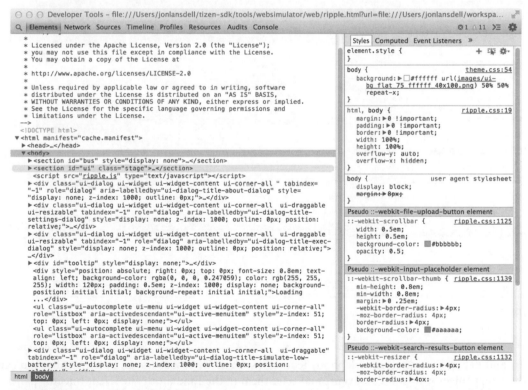

FIGURE 3-12

To debug your web application in the Emulator, right-click your project in the Project Explorer and choose Debug As ⇨ Tizen Web Application, or alternatively you can click the Debug icon in the toolbar at the top of the IDE window.

Once your application is copied, installed, and launched in the Emulator, the Remote Inspector will be launched in a new Chrome window. The inspector is based on the WebKit Web Inspector and has been enhanced to support remote debugging. When debugging with the Emulator, the Emulator communicates with Chrome using HTTP.

You can debug the JavaScript by clicking the Source icon. All JavaScript code in your project will be listed on the left side of the Web Inspector window. After you open the JavaScript file you want to debug, you can then right-click the line number and choose Add Breakpoint.

Debugging a native application in the Tizen IDE is very similar to other Eclipse-based IDEs. Right-click your project in the Project Explorer and choose Debug As ⇨ Tizen Native Application. The application will be launched in the Emulator or on the device, and the GNU Project Debugger (GDB) will be open in the IDE, as shown in Figure 3-13.

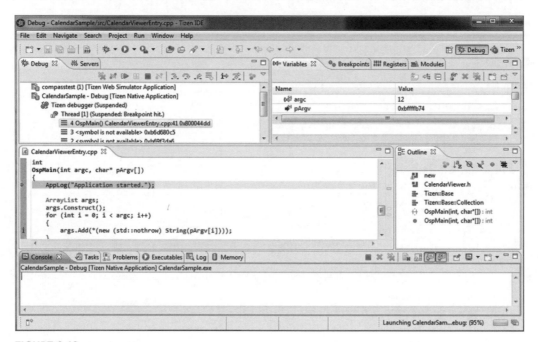

FIGURE 3-13

To test and debug hardware and telephony features, such as GPS, sensors, and phone calls, you can use the Event Injector to simulate events and send them to the Emulator. The Event Injector panel has five tabs: Telephony, Sensor, NFC, Location, and Device, as shown in Figure 3-14. Using the Event Injector is quite simple; just choose the feature you want to test.

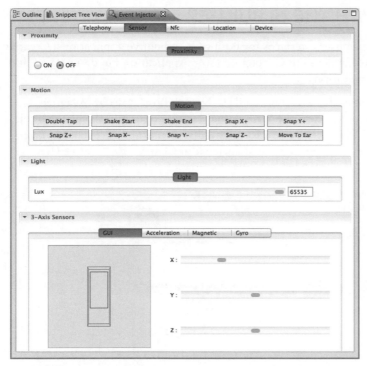

FIGURE 3-14

For example, to test how your application interacts with an incoming SMS, click the Telephony tab, expand the Telephony Messaging section, type the text message in the Message field, and click the Send Msg button. The Emulator will pick up this event and respond accordingly, as shown in Figure 3-15 and Figure 3-16.

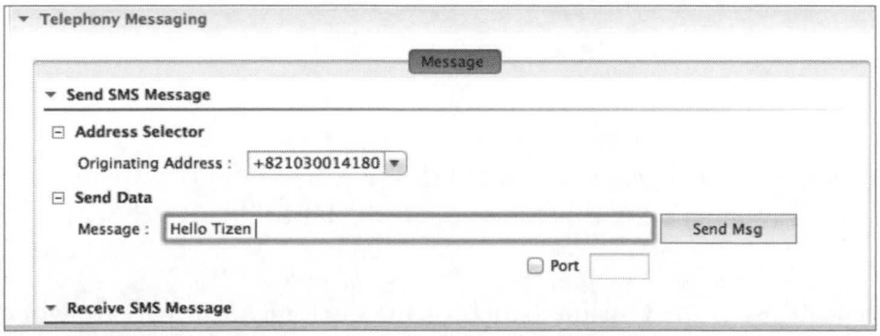

FIGURE 3-15

FIGURE 3-16

> **NOTE** *The Event Injector works with the Tizen Emulator for both native and web applications.*

DESIGNING THE UI WITH THE UI BUILDER

The UI Builder is used for designing user interfaces for both web and native applications. Creating UIs for web applications is covered in detail in Chapter 4, "Web Application Fundamentals," so this section concentrates on native applications.

To get started with the UI Builder, in the IDE choose File ⇨ New ⇨ Project ⇨ Tizen Native Project ⇨ Form-based Application and select the With SceneManager option in the Native Project Wizard, as shown in Figure 3-17. This will create a form-based application with SceneManager features. You can find out much more about scene management in Chapter 10, "Native UI Applications."

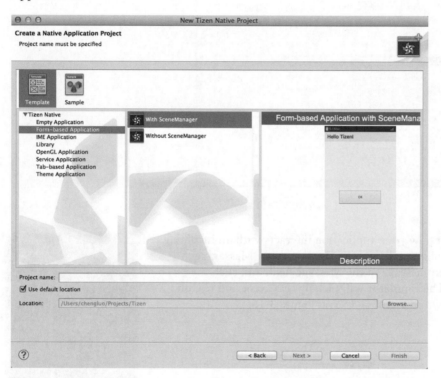

FIGURE 3-17

When the project is created, the Project wizard generates an XML file called `IDL_FORM.xml` inside the `res/screen-size-normal` folder. Double-click this file to open the UI Builder as shown in Figure 3-18.

On the left side of the UI Builder window is the Outline panel for the current Form you are working on. Below the Outline panel is the overview of the entire Form. In the middle of the UI Builder is the design window and the Toolbox containing all the available UI elements.

On the right side of the UI builder window is the Resource panel showing the hierarchy of each form and any containers inside it. This is particularly useful when you have multiple forms in your application, as you can double-click the form name in the Resource panel to start working on the selected form.

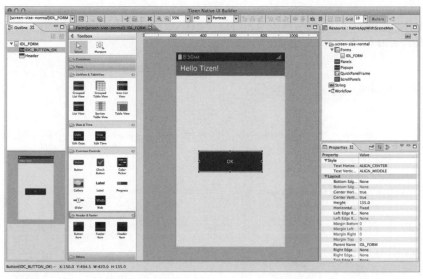

FIGURE 3-18

When you drag and drop a UI element onto the form, you can also change the properties of the element from the Properties panel.

Sometimes it is tricky to select a UI element on a Form directly, so you can also highlight the element you want to select from the Outline view.

The top-most UI element is the Form (or Frame) that occupies the full screen, and it contains other elements arranged in a hierarchy within it. Some elements, such as panels, can also contain child elements. To add child elements to a panel, double-click the panel in the Resource view and the selected panel will be opened in the design window. Then you can drag and drop a child element to the panel, as shown in Figure 3-19.

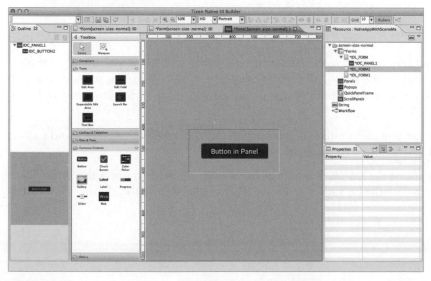

FIGURE 3-19

From the UI Builder, you can also add event handlers to some controls, such as Buttons and ListViews. Right-click the control and choose the Add Event Handler option. The Tizen Event Handler wizard window will be displayed, as shown in Figure 3-20.

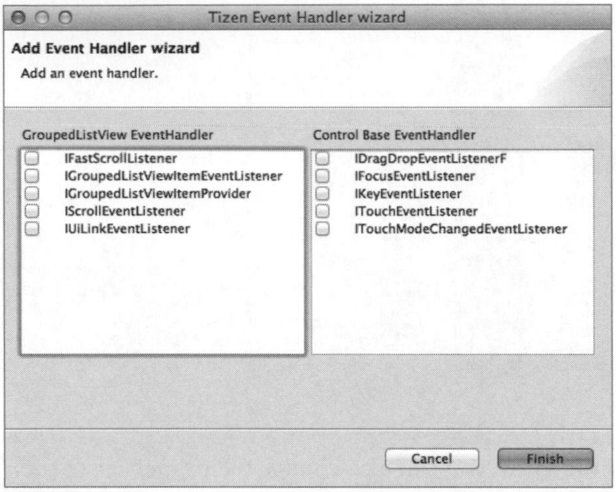

FIGURE 3-20

In the Event Handler wizard, you can choose from event handlers that are specific to the type of control, as well as those common to all controls. For example, GroupedListView has its own event handlers, including IFastScrollListener and IScrollEventListener, but you can also add event handlers from the base Control class, such as IKeyEventListener or IFocusEventListener.

Once you select the event handler and click the Finish button, you are returned to an auto-generated code stub in the Tizen IDE. You can then start to implement the control's event-handling code.

SUMMARY

After working through this chapter, you should now be familiar with the most important tools provided by the Tizen SDK. You should also understand how to run web applications in the Web Simulator and how to run and debug both web and native applications in the Emulator and on a device.

Using the Event Injector, you can simulate events such as location and SMS messages and test out device features, even if you don't have access to a device.

Chapter 4 explains some of the low-level details of the Web Runtime, introduces the Tizen device APIs, and shows how to use the UI Builder to create UIs for your web applications.

PART II
Tizen Web APIs

Web Application Fundamentals

WROX.COM CODE DOWNLOADS FOR THIS CHAPTER

The wrox.com code downloads for this chapter are found at www.wrox.com/go/ professionaltizen on the Download Code tab. The code is in the Chapter 4 download. After decompressing the downloaded Zip file you will have a TizenWebUIBuilder directory with the finished application.

In this chapter we start by going behind the scenes and looking at the roles of the various components which make up the Tizen Web Runtime, implementing tasks such as application installation and launching and enforcing security. While you don't have to know these details in order to write Tizen applications, the material covered here builds on some of the concepts introduced in Chapter 2, "Tizen Application Packages," such as privileges, the configuration file, and application signing.

The Tizen Device APIs enable web developers to access features in their applications not supported by W3C APIs, such as NFC, messaging, and calendars. This chapter includes a brief summary of each of the APIs, some of which are covered in code-level detail in the following chapters.

The last part of the chapter shows you how to create a UI for your web application, making use of the features of the Tizen Web UI framework and the UI Builder.

THE WEB RUNTIME

The Web Runtime is the environment within which all web applications run on Tizen. It provides web applications with the capability to access local device and platform resources, such as the hardware, network, and file systems. The Web Runtime not only extends the capabilities of web applications, but also manages the installation, execution, and security of web applications on Tizen. Services of the Runtime are accessible through the application programming interface (API), which is explained in the "Tizen Device APIs" section later in this chapter.

Figure 4-1 shows the internal components of the Tizen Web Runtime.

Tizen Web Runtime

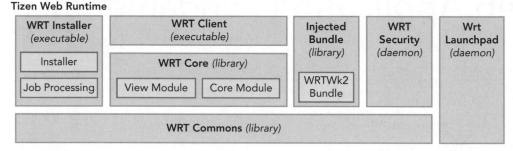

FIGURE 4-1

The Web Runtime Installer component is an executable that is called when the system installs a web application on Tizen. After the download from a store or website is finished, the Web Runtime Installer installs the web application on the device. The application is registered in the Web Runtime database using the information supplied in the application's configuration file, including the application ID, the package ID, and the name of the app.

During installation, the contents of the package file are extracted, the configuration file is checked, the resources are installed to the appropriate directories on the device, and a manifest file is generated for interacting with native applications. The Simplified Mandatory Access Control Kernel (SMACK) policy rules are updated for the application, based on the privileges requested in the application's `config.xml` file, and any privileges the user allowed or disallowed.

The configuration file, privileges, and application signing are covered in detail in Chapter 2, while the security model is explained below.

The second component inside the Web Runtime is the Web Runtime Core, which consists of two shared libraries: the core module and the view module.

The core module is responsible for initialising the database that is used by other Web Runtime components, and preparing information for web application launching. An important class inside the core module is the `RunnableWidgetObject` class. This class is responsible for running and controlling the web application in a given window, and its methods run when the web application's state changes. The core module also checks the network access setting of web applications.

> **NOTE** *If you are interested in how the Web Runtime Core is implemented on Tizen, you can find the source code from the Tizen git repository at* `https://review.tizen.org/gerrit/framework/web/wrt`. *The core module is under the* `src/api_new/` *directory, and the view module is under the* `src/view/` *directory.*

The view module is responsible for controlling web views which contain a web application's content. The view module contains an interface class called `IViewModule`, which includes the methods to control the web application view layer, including the capability to show, hide, and suspend the web application. The view module also contains classes such as `ViewLogic` that uses WebKit and the EFL Evas canvas library for the view layer. It enables web applications to use geolocation, web notifications, and other plugins.

The Web Runtime Client component is an executable running on top of the Runtime Core. It implements callbacks related to the application life cycle, such as launch, resume, pause, and terminate. These callbacks are common for both native and web applications on Tizen. The Web Runtime rendering engine is based on WebKit2. Every time a new web application is launched, the system spawns two processes: a UI process, which manages the life cycle of an app, and a web process, which is responsible for rendering the web content.

The injected bundle library is a WebKit2 component that builds a process management mechanism inside the WebKit API layer. The Tizen Web Runtime uses the injected bundle to load the Tizen Device API object on demand, functioning like a plugin.

The Web Runtime Security component is a daemon running in the background. It provides a sandbox environment for web applications, enforcing the SMACK rules for each application so that an application cannot access the files of another application, read system files such as the contacts database, or make use of particular system features unless it has been granted permission to do so.

The last Web Runtime component shown in the diagram is Launchpad. Launchpad's role is to pre-load WebKit and Web Runtime libraries, such as `libewebkit2.so` and `wrt-client`. Launchpad forks a new process, the UI process, when a web application is launched and registers application configuration information.

TIZEN DEVICE APIS

This section provides a high-level overview of the Tizen Device APIs provided by the Tizen Web Runtime. While Tizen provides comprehensive support for the HTML5 features in the W3C APIs, such as location-based services and audio and video, some device-specific functions aren't included in the W3C specifications. To fill these gaps, you use the following Tizen Device APIs to implement features that would otherwise only be available to native applications:

➤ **Tizen** — The `tizen` JavaScript object is the base object used to access other APIs such as Contact, Calendar, and NFC.

To access the default address book, for example, you use the following code:

```
var addressBook = tizen.contact. getDefaultAddressBook();
```

The `contact` object is a property of the `tizen` object and contains a `ContactManager` object, which provides access to the Contact API, including the `getDefaultAddressBook()` function. The same pattern is used with the other Device APIs.

➤ **Alarm** — The Alarm API enables you to set an alarm to run an application at a specified time and launch it if it's not already running.

➤ **Application** — The Application API enables you to retrieve a list of running applications and launch other apps by using an application control. For example, you might launch the Camera application to take a picture or record video, or use the media player to play music files. You can also provide services to other applications.

➤ **Bookmark** — The Bookmark API provides access to the device's bookmarks. You can use it to retrieve bookmarks, as well as add and remove both bookmarks and bookmark folders.

➤ **Bluetooth** — The Bluetooth API provides access to the Bluetooth protocol, which can be used for transmitting files over short distances between devices.

➤ **Calendar** — The Calendar API enables you to manage events and tasks, such as handling your schedule or to-do list.

➤ **CallHistory** — The CallHistory API provides access to the call history functionality, such as finding and removing call history entries.

➤ **Contact** — You use the Contact API to manage contacts and handle multiple address books. Chapter 9, "Contacts and Calendars," provides a practical introduction to handling contacts and calendars.

➤ **Content** — The Content API enables you to search for content on the device, stored either locally or on a memory card. Chapter 6, "Multimedia," covers this API in detail, complete with code examples.

➤ **DataControl** — The DataControl API is used to access data exported by other applications — for example, native applications. You can use the functionality provided by the DataControl API on both SQL and key-value databases.

➤ **DataSynchronization** — The DataSynchronization API, supported beginning with Tizen 2.1, enables you to synchronise device data with a server using the OMA Data Synchronization 1.2 protocol.

➤ **Download** — The Download API is used to download files from the Internet and monitor the download status.

➤ **Filesystem** — The Filesystem API provides access to the device's file system. The SDK includes more information, including tutorials.

➤ **MessagePort** — The MessagePort API enables you to exchange data with another web application or native application. Data is sent using the RemoteMessagePort, and data is received from the LocalMessagePort.

➤ **Messaging** — The Messaging API enables you to send SMS, MMS, and e-mail messages and search messages on the device. The Messaging API is discussed in Chapter 8, "Messaging Services."

➤ **NetworkBearerSelection** — The NetworkBearerSelection API, new to Tizen 2.1, enables you to specify a particular network connection to be used from your web applications to connect a given domain or host.

➤ **NFC** — Near field communication (NFC) is used for short-range wireless communication. NFC-enabled devices can be used for multiple purposes, such as for mobile payments and various other applications. More information on NFC can be found in Chapter 7, "Sensors and other Hardware."

➤ **Notification** — The Notification API, introduced in Tizen 2.0, provides a way of alerting the user to events happening in your app. You can find details about how to create and manage notifications in the SDK help.

➤ **Package** — The Package API, new to Tizen 2.1, enables you to install and uninstall packages, retrieve information about the packages installed on the device, and monitor any changes to installed packages.

➤ **Power** — Another new API introduced in Tizen 2.0, this provides access to a device's power state and enables you to control settings such as display dimming and brightness, for example. More information, including a tutorial, is included in the SDK.

➤ **Push** — The Push API, new in Tizen 2.1, enables web applications to receive push notifications from the push server.

➤ **SecureElement** — The SecureElement API, introduced in Tizen 2.1, provides access to secured elements on the device, such as a UICC/SIM, embedded security element, or secure SD card.

➤ **SystemInfo** — This API provides access to device-specific information, such as local storage, battery levels, cellular network, and so on. More information and a tutorial are included in the SDK.

➤ **SystemSetting** — The SystemSetting API, introduced in Tizen 2.0, enables you to get and set various device properties. At the time of writing, you can get and set the following device properties: the device and lock screen wallpaper, the ringtone for incoming calls, and the e-mail message notification sound.

➤ **Time** — This API provides date and time functions, including working with the current date and time and locale-specific date and time handling.

In addition to the information in subsequent chapters, tutorials and sample code demonstrating the features of these APIs can be found in the SDK help.

TIZEN WEB UI FRAMEWORK

While the Tizen Device APIs can be used to create a web application which can access device features, the Tizen Web framework enables you to create a web application with the look and feel of a native app. In this section you'll learn how the Tizen UI framework is based on standard technologies and adds features unique to the platform. Then you'll discover how to use the Tizen SDK Web UI Builder to create a UI and add functionality to it.

Overview of the Tizen Web UI Framework

The Tizen Web UI framework is based on open-source JavaScript libraries, including jQuery Mobile, jQuery, and Globalize. It provides a large set of widgets that have the same look and feel as the native UI controls.

The Tizen UI framework also provides two reference themes, black and white, which are used on development devices.

The internal components of Web UI framework are shown in Figure 4-2.

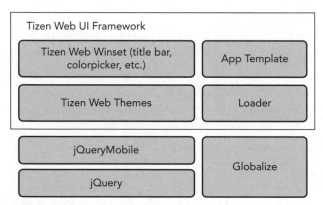

FIGURE 4-2

The Tizen Web widgets provide UI controls for building a web application's UI. Table 4-1 shows the full list of available widgets provided by the Tizen UI framework in Tizen 2.1.

Many of these widgets are implemented by jQuery Mobile, while some are provided by the Tizen Web UI service. See Tizen Web App Programming ➪ API References ➪ UI Framework Reference in the SDK help for more details on each widget.

TABLE 4-1: Widgets in the Tizen UI Framework

WIDGET	DESCRIPTION
Autodividers	Automatically creates dividers for a list view
Button	Shows a control on the screen that can be used to generate an action event
Checkbox	Shows a list of options on the screen from which one or more can be selected
Context popup	Shows a small pop-up list of application options
Date picker, Time picker, and Date Time picker	Shows a control that you can use to enter date and time values

Extendable list	Used to display a list of data elements that can be extended
Fast scroll	Shows a shortcut list that is bound to its parent scroll bar and respective list view
Flip toggle switch	Shows a two-state switch on the screen
Gallery	Shows images in a gallery on the screen
Gallery 3D	Enables three-dimensional arranging and handling of images
Handler	Provides a touch-friendly scroll bar
Header and footer	Shows the default header and footer bar on the screen
HTML block	Treats custom HTML as a widget
List	Displays a list view
List divider	A list separator used for grouping lists
Multimedia view	Displays the audio and video player
Notification	Displays a small pop-up indicating accidental events
Popup	Displays a pop-up window
Progress	Shows that an operation is in progress
Progress bar	Shows a control that indicates the progress percentage of an ongoing operation
Search filter bar	Used to search for page content
Slider	Used to change a value by dragging a handle
Split view	Separates content into different areas
Swipe	Shows a list view on the screen which can be swiped vertically
Tabbar	Shows an unordered list of buttons on the screen wrapped together in a single group
Token text area	Enables the user to enter text and convert it to a button
Virtual grid	Used to display the data elements in a grid format with dynamic data management
Virtual list	Used to display the data elements in a list format with dynamic data management

The two Tizen reference themes are referred to using the values: `tizen-white` and `tizen-black`. Each theme consists of a set of CSS files and images. The application template provides the template to generate web apps using the Tizen Web UI framework. You can find this template from the Eclipse New Project wizard.

The only component you might not be familiar with is the loader, which is responsible for theme loading, viewport setting, and loading the Globalize library.

VISUAL VIEWPORT VS. LAYOUT VIEWPORT

It's worth discussing the viewport in more detail here. The viewport is an area showing the web content on the browser contained in the `<html>` element. Unlike desktop browsers, mobile browsers support the logical viewport setting, which means that an application can set viewport width, height, and zoom level by itself. In a mobile browser, there are two viewports: *visual viewport* and *layout viewport*. For more details about the difference between the two viewports, you can refer to the blog `www.quirksmode.org/mobile/viewports2.html` from Peter Paul Koch.

Note that the viewport resolution in pixels is `logical`, unlike the device pixels, which are left unchanged. For example, if the viewport width is set to 480 pixels on a mobile device with a screen width of 720 pixels, the viewport width is considered to be 480 pixels logically. All elements added to the right of a 480px horizontal position will not be shown on the viewport. That's why most websites that are optimized for mobile devices always set the viewport width to the device width:

```
<meta name="viewport" content="width=device-width, ...">
```

The Basics of jQuery Mobile

Because much of the functionality of the Tizen Web UI framework is provided by jQuery Mobile, this section provides a quick recap of some key jQuery Mobile concepts before moving on to the Tizen-specific features.

Embedded Custom Data Attributes

In the HTML5 specification, custom data attributes are intended to be used to store custom data private to a web page or application. The jQuery Mobile framework makes heavy use of custom data attributes to embed data into HTML5 markup. These data attributes are used to initialise and configure UI widgets, such as buttons, lists, headers, and footers.

Page Structure

The page widget is responsible for managing a single item in jQuery Mobile's page-based architecture. It is designed to support either single-page or multiple-page web applications within an HTML document. To use jQuery Mobile, you just need to create one HTML file. The HTML file must start with a `doctype` to make use of the jQuery Mobile library. In the `head` tag, you can specify a meta data tag `viewport` for the initial scale and screen size of your mobile web app. Under the `body` tag, you can create a single or multiple jQuery Mobile `page` by using `data-role= "page"` inside the `div`. This creates a view that uses the full screen of your mobile device if the status bar area is hidden.

Inside the page `div`, you can also add the header, content, and footer sections, as shown in Figure 4-3.

The Tizen Web UI framework allows you to use the existing features of the jQuery Mobile framework, such as page transitions, touch events, and the flexible theme design, and adds Tizen-specific features. The next section shows how easy it is to create a fully functional Tizen UI with the UI Builder.

FIGURE 4-3

USING THE UI BUILDER

The UI Builder in the Tizen IDE enables you to build your UI visually by dragging and dropping, rather than manually coding HTML and CSS.

To use the UI Builder, you first need to create a new Tizen web project in the IDE (choose File ➪ New ➪ Tizen Web Project) and select Tizen Web UI Builder from the list of templates. Go through the steps to create the new project, and you will see that a file called `page1.page` has been created inside your project's page folder. You use this file with the UI Builder to create your UI.

You'll notice that there are two very similar-sounding templates listed in the New Tizen Web Project wizard: Tizen Web UI Framework and the one you chose, Tizen Web UI Builder. Both of these templates include the code for the Tizen Web UI framework, which provides the widgets, transitions, and animations for the Tizen UI, but the Web UI Builder framework adds some extra features.

The Web UI Builder framework includes an `app` object for handling application life cycle events, and page and page manager objects that work together with the UI Builder to make it easier to manage widgets and pages. The information in the following section refers to an application created using the Web UI Builder template and makes use of the features of the UI Builder framework (select Creating a UI Builder Project ➪ UI Builder Framework in the SDK help for more information).

Choosing Your Widgets

Getting to grips with the UI Builder is easy, especially if you've used similar tools for desktop or mobile development. Figure 4-4 shows the UI Builder interface, while Figure 4-5 shows the page folder and page files in the Project Explorer.

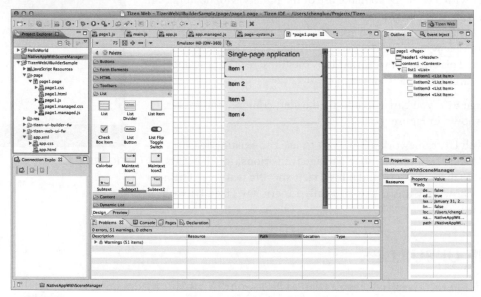

FIGURE 4-4

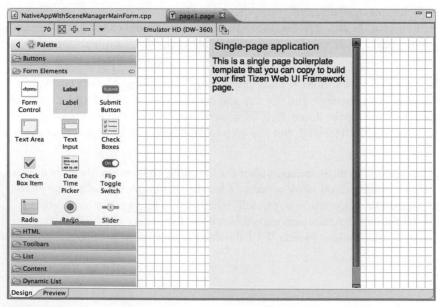

FIGURE 4-5

The Palette, which is shown on the left of the Design view in Figure 4-5, contains all the widgets and elements that are available for use in your app. These widgets are grouped into different categories, such as Buttons, HTML, and Form Elements. You drag and drop widgets from the Palette to the Design view to construct your UI.

Two tabs appear at the bottom of the Design view:

➤ **Design** — Select this tab while you're building the UI.

➤ **Preview** — Select this tab to see the result as your design develops.

The Outline and Properties views, which are shown on the right-hand side of Figure 4-5, are used a lot during the UI design process. The Outline view shows the hierarchy of `div` elements within the page. This view provides easy access to elements on the page, particularly in the case of widget nesting. In the example shown in Figure 4-6, which was generated using the Navigator UI template, you can see that the `List Item` elements appear within the `List` element.

After you drag the UI widget to the page, you can adjust its default properties from the Properties view. In the example shown in the Figure 4-7, the text of the List Item is highlighted, ready to be updated.

FIGURE 4-6

FIGURE 4-7

Implementing Events in the UI Builder

The UI Builder can also generate code to handle the events supported by Tizen's predefined UI widgets. For example, a list item supports the SwipeLeft event, and you can generate the skeleton JavaScript code to handle this event from within the UI Builder.

Highlight the list item in the UI Builder and click the Event Handler tab in the Properties panel. You will see a drop-down menu which lists all the events the List Item widget supports. Choose SwipeLeft to assign this event to the List Item and click the triangle that appears below the menu, as shown in Figure 4-8. Clicking the triangle will generate the code to handle this event.

FIGURE 4-8

The UI Builder generates the skeleton code to handle this event and adds it to the JavaScript file `page1.js`:

PAGE1.JS

```
/**
* @param {Object} event * @base _page1_page
* @returns {Boolean}
*/
_page1_page.prototype.listitem3_onswipeleft = function(event) {
        this.listitem3.remove(); //(1)
};
```

 (1) In this case, we remove list item 3 from the list when it is swiped to left.

Handling Page Events

When you create a web application using the UI Builder, the UI Builder generates the file named with the postfix `page`. You can use the UI Builder to edit the content and layout of the page, and assign event handlers to the page or to the widget inside the page.

The page file is very similar to the page widget in jQuery Mobile using the `data-role` attribute. It contains the layout information and event handlers of the page. Accordingly, each page file has three corresponding files: an HTML file and a CSS file for the widget layout, and a JavaScript file for the event handlers.

The JavaScript file is responsible for handling events related to the page. The Tizen Web UI Builder framework creates the `page` object when the page is being loaded. The `page` object is defined in the JavaScript file called `page-system.js`, which can be found within the `tizen-ui-builder-fw` folder in the Project Explorer.

You can access the corresponding page object with the `this` keyword. The `page` object provides some of the event handlers that the jQuery Mobile page widget does, including `pagebeforecreate`, pagebeforehide, pagebeforeshow, pagecreate, pagehide, pageinit, and pageremove. However, the pagechange event is handled by the pageManager object, which is also defined in the page-system.js file under the tizen-ui-builder-fw folder.

Here is an example of how to handle the pagecreate event using the UI Builder template project. Highlight the page item in the Outline view of the UI Builder, and click the Event Handler tab in the Properties panel. You will see a drop-down menu which lists all the events that the page widget supports. Choose PageCreate to assign this event to the page and click the triangle that appears below the menu, as shown in Figure 4-9.

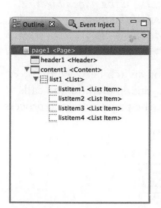

FIGURE 4-9

This process leads you to the JavaScript file page1.js, which contains the skeleton code the UI Builder has generated to handle this event:

PAGE1.JS

```
/**
 * @param {Object} event
 * @base _page1_page
 * @returns {Boolean}
 */
_page1_page.prototype.onpagecreate = function(event) {
        console.log("Page1 is created!");
};
```

The Tizen Web UI Builder framework provides a page manager object to handle interactions and navigations between pages. The page manager object is a global object, meaning it can be accessed anywhere from JavaScript files. This handy object is unique to the Tizen Web UI Builder framework; it is not part of jQuery Mobile.

For example, our example project has two pages: Page1 and Page2. Here's how you can switch to page 2 when you tap the button:

PAGE1.JS

```
/**
 * @param {Object} event
 * @base _page1_page
 * @returns {Boolean}
 */
_page1_page.prototype.button1_ontap = function(event) {
      pageManager.changePage("page2");
};
```

> **NOTE** *In the preceding code, you access the Button widget from the page object. The button is treated as a member variable of the* `page` *class. If the member widget is a jQuery Mobile type, you can also use the jQuery Mobile APIs.*

Figure 4-10 shows the sequence of event callbacks that occur when you switch between two pages. When you tap the button on the Page1, it triggers the `button1_ontap` method and calls the `changePage` method from the page manager object. At this point, the page-switching process starts.

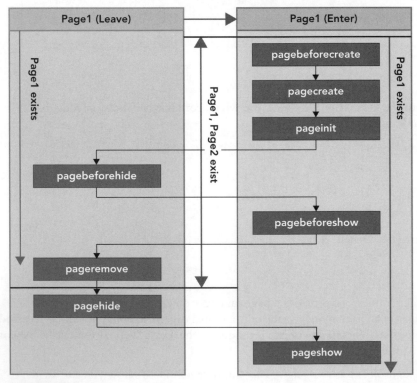

FIGURE 4-10

The first method called is pagebeforecreate, followed by the pagecreate and pageinit methods of Page2. Right after Page2 is initialised and about to be shown on the screen, the pagebeforehide method of Page1 is called. Once the pagebeforehide method of Page1 is finished, it then calls the pagebeforeshow method of Page2. When Page2 is eventually displayed on the screen, Page2 will be removed from the Document Object Model (DOM). Before it's removed from the DOM, the pageremove method is called, followed by the pagehide method of Page1. The final method called is the pageshow method of Page2. At this point, the process of switching between two pages is done.

To summarise the life cycle of a page, it starts from the pagebeforecreate method and ends at the pageremove method.

SUMMARY

This chapter gave you a behind the scenes glimpse into how the Tizen Web Runtime is structured, building on some of the concepts introduced in Chapter 2 such as privileges and the security model. Then the Tizen Device APIs were introduced, some of which, such as Content, Messaging, Contacts, and Calendar, you'll find out much more about, with practical examples, in the following chapters.

The second half of the chapter introduced the Web UI framework and how to use the UI Builder to create the UI for your Tizen web applications. To get a closer look at some of Tizen's UI widgets, build and explore the TizenWinset sample in the Tizen SDK.

5

Location-Based Services

WHAT'S IN THIS CHAPTER?

➤ Using the Google Maps API

➤ Finding and tracking location

➤ Geocoding

WROX.COM CODE DOWNLOADS FOR THIS CHAPTER

The wrox.com code downloads for this chapter are found at www.wrox.com/go/professionaltizen on the Download Code tab. The code is in the Chapter 5 download and the code snippets in this chapter gradually build up to form the complete application. After decompressing the downloaded Zip file you will have a tizen-lbs directory that contains the finished application.

This chapter looks at location-based services that run during the Tizen Web Runtime environment. Tizen's Access and Privileges configuration enables you to create an application that displays a map, which you can build upon by implementing markers and making geocoding requests.

For the geolocation example application in this chapter, you will use the Google Maps v3 API, which provides a feature-rich interface that is easy to learn, fun to use, and quick to implement, facilitating rapid application development.

Along the way, you'll discover and learn about the W3C Geolocation API and how it is used within the Tizen Web Runtime. You'll use this API to detect a user's location and make changes to the map so that it responds by updating its display when the user's location has changed.

DISPLAYING A MAP

In a Tizen project you are free to use any map provider that you wish. However, whichever provider you want to use, you will more than likely need to make network requests for things like static assets that are necessary to display map tiles, and you will also need to interact with online APIs. Making network requests inside a Tizen application is disabled by default. This behaviour complies with the W3C Widget Access Requests Policy (WARP, see `www.w3.org/TR/widgets-access/` for more information), and in order to make network requests your application must explicitly ask for permissions to use the network resource. In a Tizen application this is achieved by modifying the `config.xml` file.

Under the Access tab of the `config.xml` screen in the IDE, you can list the domains to which your application needs access (see Figure 5-1). Our demo application makes use of the Google Maps API, so add the following domains to the list and be sure to set `Allow subdomain` to `true` for each of them:

➤ http://gstatic.com

➤ http://googleapis.com

➤ http://google.com

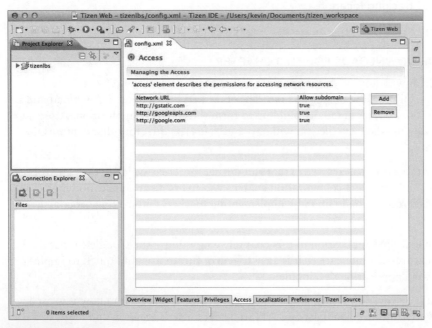

FIGURE 5-1

The first thing you need to do is to add the necessary `<script>` tag that references the Google Maps API script to your `index.html` page. The query string has two parameters: `key` (your API key) and `sensor`. You can obtain your API key from `https://code.google.com/apis/console`. On the console page, under API Access, look for the API key which is referenced under the Simple API Access section. The sensor parameter should be true; it denotes that your application is using a sensor to detect the user's location.

With the <script> tag in place, add an empty div element that will hold the map and all its necessary markup. Make the width and height of this 100% by adding the necessary style declarations in the CSS file:

HTML

```html
<!-- inside <head> -->
<script type="text/javascript"
src="http://maps.googleapis.com/maps/api/js?key=
    <YOUR_API_KEY>&sensor=true"></script>

<!-- inside <body> -->
<div id="map"></div>
```

CSS

```css
#map {
    width: 100%;
    height: 100%;
}
```

Inside your application's JavaScript file, create a new instance of a Google Map object. The first parameter should be an HTMLElement and the second parameter is a set of options passed as a JavaScript object. The map will be centred over the United Kingdom by default, with a zoom level of 6:

JAVASCRIPT

```javascript
var map, mapOptions, longitude, latitude;

latitude = 54.482;
longitude = -3.087;

mapOptions = {
    center: new google.maps.LatLng(latitude, longitude),
    zoom: 6,
    mapTypeId: google.maps.MapTypeId.ROADMAP,
    disableDefaultUI: true,
    zoomControl: true
};

map = new google.maps.Map(
    document.getElementById("map"),
    mapOptions
);
```

For mobile applications, you have to consider the size and scale of the display when choosing what controls you want to place on the map. Some controls included with Google Maps do not provide a great user experience for mobile devices, so you want to choose sensible controls that offer the best mobile experience.

In the map options, the default UI controls are not shown. Instead, the only control that is shown is the zoom control (specified with the `zoomControl` property).

Now, when you run the Web Simulator (Run ⇨ Run As ⇨ Tizen Web Simulator Application) you will see a map that occupies 100% of the screen, as shown in Figure 5-2.

DETECTING A USER'S LOCATION

FIGURE 5-2

Mobile devices naturally make great platforms for location-based applications due to the GPS capabilities of the device. A common feature that you will want to include is detecting the device's current location.

The Tizen Web Runtime fully implements the W3C Geolocation API specification, and as such it can be used inside the JavaScript implementation of your Tizen web application.

However, before your application can obtain the device location, you need to make another configuration change. This time, under the Privileges tab of the `config.xml` screen, add the following URL: `http://tizen.org/privilege/location`.

This change tells the Web Runtime that your application requires the user to grant privileges that allow the application to determine the user's location. When the application next loads, you will be prompted to grant access to the application to use the device location.

In the example application, include the jQuery library to make it easier and quicker to implement many of the common JavaScript tasks. Download the latest jQuery version from `www.jquery.com/download` and place it inside your application's `js` folder. At the time of writing, the latest version of jQuery is 2.0.2. Now add the necessary `<script>` tag to the `<head>` section of the `index.html` page:

JAVASCRIPT

```
<script src="js/jquery-2.0.2.min.js"></script>
```

The application also needs some kind of button so that when the user touches it, the application will retrieve the device's current coordinates and then use them to centre the map. Make the following changes to the markup in `index.html` so that a button is displayed, along with placeholders for what will be the longitude and latitude coordinates of the geolocation query:

HTML

```
<div id="controls">
    <ul>
        <li><button id="geolocate">My Location</button></li>
        <li>Latitude: <span id="lat-display"></span></li>
        <li>Longitude: <span id="lon-display"></span></li>
    </ul>
</div>
```

The JavaScript implementation uses the W3C Geolocation API to query the current location of the device. The API call that needs to be made is `navigator.geolocation.getCurrentPosition` and it takes two parameters: The first is a callback function that handles the results and the second, optional parameter is a function to handle any errors. The success handler will be passed a position object as the first parameter.

The event listener that is bound to the button's `touchstart` event triggers a call to the Geolocation API and uses the position result to centre the map:

JAVASCRIPT

```javascript
function updateCoordinateDisplay(latitude, longitude) {
    $('#lat-display').text(latitude);
    $('#lon-display').text(longitude);
}

updateCoordinateDisplay(latitude, longitude);

$('#geolocate').on('touchstart', function(e){
    e.preventDefault();
    navigator.geolocation.getCurrentPosition(function(position){
        var lat, lon;
        lat = position.coords.latitude;
        lon = position.coords.longitude;
        updateCoordinateDisplay(lat, lon);
        map.setCenter(new google.maps.LatLng(lat, lon));
    }, function(){
        alert("Sorry, we're unable to detect your location");
    });
});
```

Notice that the event being listened to is `touchstart`. This is one of four different touch events available on mobile devices:

➤ `touchstart`

➤ `touchend`

➤ `touchmove`

➤ `touchcancel`

> **NOTE** *Tizen partially implements the W3C Touch Events version 1. See* `www.w3.org/TR/2013/WD-touch-events-20130124/` *for more information on the touch specification.*

Now when you next run the application in the Tizen Emulator, you will be prompted to grant permission to allow the application to use the device location (see Figure 5-3).

If you are using the Web Simulator to test the application, you will need to enable touch events in order for the button to work with your mouse clicks. Open the developer tools, click the settings icon, and then click the "Emulate touch events" check box (at the bottom-right of Figure 5-4). Note that touch event emulation will work only while the developer tools window remains open.

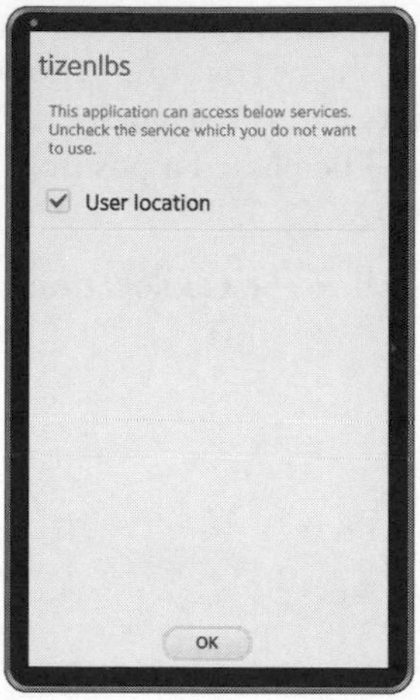

FIGURE 5-3

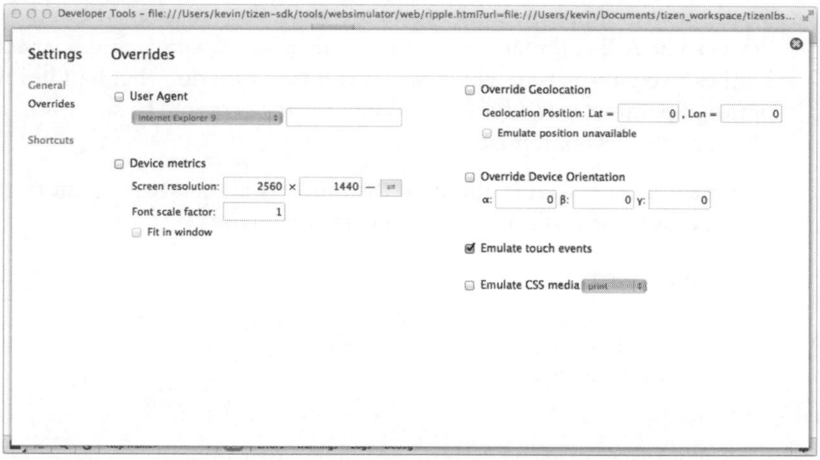

FIGURE 5-4

NOTE *In the new version of the Google Chrome developer tools, the Emulate Touch Event has been moved and renamed. To access this option, open the developer tools window, click the settings icon and choose the Overrides section. Tick the box that says "Show 'Emulation' view in console drawer" and close the settings window.*

Show the console drawer by clicking the icon to the left of settings. Select the Emulation tab at the top of the console drawer and from the Sensors section tick the box labeled "Emulate touch screen" (see Figure 5-5).

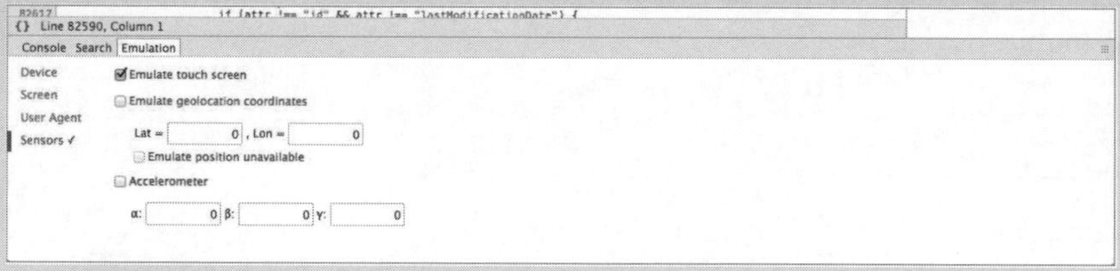

FIGURE 5-5

For more details, see the Emulate Touch Events section of this article on the Google developer site: `http://developers.google.com/chrome-developer-tools/docs/mobile-emulation`.

Now when you run the application and click the Detect Location button, the map will be centred on the device coordinates and the longitude and latitude will be displayed below the button.

The Web Simulator provides a way to set the device's location to any part of the world. You can adjust the device's location, along with a range of other location settings, in the Geolocation settings tab of the Web Simulator (see Figure 5-6).

To simulate the device being in another location, centre the map in the Geolocation tab to a different location or explicitly set the longitude and latitude values using the input boxes. Once you have done this, you can test the location detection functionality again by clicking the Detect Location button (see Figure 5-7).

FIGURE 5-6

FIGURE 5-7

Monitoring the User's Position

You could improve the functionality a step further by automatically updating the display when the user's location has changed so that they never have to touch a button. This approach is ideal for an application that needs to send live data back to the user, such as a routing application. The watchPosition function of the W3C Geolocation API specification (www.w3.org/TR/geolocation-API/) provides this functionality. Modify the existing code to offer this capability as follows:

JAVASCRIPT

```javascript
var watchID = navigator.geolocation.watchPosition(function(position) {
    var lat, lon;
    lat = position.coords.latitude;
    lon = position.coords.longitude;
    updateCoordinateDisplay(lat, lon);
    map.setCenter(new google.maps.LatLng(lat, lon));
});
```

Now when you run the application in the Web Simulator, you can observe the display updating every time you change the user's position by modifying the location setting in the Web Simulator. Notice that the return value of `watchPosition` is assigned to a variable; this enables you to stop watching for position changes later.

A Word of Caution

If your application executes a lot of calculations for each update, you need to be mindful of how much resource your application uses and optimise accordingly, as the `watchPosition` handler may be called multiple times over a short period. If you need to stop watching the user's position at any time, use `geolocation.clearWatch`:

JAVASCRIPT

```javascript
navigator.geolocation.clearWatch(watchID);
```

ADDING MARKERS TO A MAP

A marker represents a point of interest on the map. In the Google Maps v3 API, the default red pinpoint represents a marker. Although it is quite easy to change the marker to a different graphic, the default icon is used in this example to show how you can use markers with the least amount of code.

Add the following required markup and JavaScript that will render a marker on the map using the map's current centre position:

HTML

```html
<li>
    <button id="geolocate">Detect Location</button>
    <button id="drop-marker">Add Marker</button>
</li>
```

JAVASCRIPT

```javascript
$('#drop-marker').on('touchstart', function(e){
    e.preventDefault();
    var marker = new google.maps.Marker({
        map: map,
        position: map.getCenter()
    });
});
```

FIGURE 5-8

This simple addition of a button element combined with an event listener that is called on `touchstart` will create a new marker on your map instance using the map's current centre coordinate (see Figure 5-8).

> **NOTE** *More information about the touch events and the entire W3C Touch Events specification can be found at* www.w3.org/TR/touch-events/.

GEOCODING AND REVERSE GEOCODING

Geocoding is the process of taking a place name and converting it to a coordinate. *Reverse geocoding*, as you would expect, is the process of taking a coordinate and converting it into a meaningful place name. Our example application will demonstrate how this can be done using the Google Geocoding API.

First, add an input field to the application so that you can capture some user input. The value for this input will be used to query the Geocoding API and if the place can be found, the map will update to centre on that location.

HTML

```
<form method="post" action="#">
    <div id="controls">
        <ul>
          <li>
                <button id="geolocate">Detect Location</button>
                <button id="drop-marker">Add Marker</button>
          </li>
          <li>Latitude: <span id="lat-display"></span></li>
          <li>Longitude: <span id="lon-display"></span></li>
          <li><input type="text" id="placename"
    placeholder="Search for a location..." /></li>
        </ul>
    </div>
</form>
```

Note that the whole control's container is now wrapped in a `form` tag. This enables binding the geocode request to the form's default submit action. Next, add the necessary JavaScript to make all this work:

JAVASCRIPT

```
var geocoder = new google.maps.Geocoder();

$('form').on('submit', function(e){
    e.preventDefault();
    var placename = $('#placename').val();
    geocoder.geocode({ address: placename }, function(results, success){
        if (success === google.maps.GeocoderStatus.OK) {
            map.setCenter(results[0].geometry.location);
            updateCoordinateDisplay(
                results[0].geometry.location.lat(),
                results[0].geometry.location.lng()
            );
        } else {
```

```
                    alert('Unable to find "' + placename + '"');
                }
        });
    });
```

The hook here is in the `form` element's `submit` action. The event listener that is bound to that event first prevents the default action of the form (to submit), and then sends the value of the place name input field to the Geolocation API. When a result is handled, a check is made to determine whether the status is OK; if so, the centre of the map is set and then the coordinate display is updated with the new latitude and longitude values. If no results are returned, then the application opens an alert window with a default message stating that the place name could not be found.

If you run the Web Simulator with this additional code, enter a place name in the input field and press return; you'll notice the display update accordingly. To be thorough, try searching for an invalid place and verify that the alert box is shown.

> **NOTE** *If the Web Simulator is not updating the application when making source code changes, this may be because Google Chrome is caching static assets. To disable this behaviour, open the Developer Tools settings page and ensure that the Disable cache check box is ticked.*

Reverse geocoding is no more complicated than the previous example. The first thing to do is to create a new function that will make the geocode request:

JAVASCRIPT

```
geocoder = new google.maps.Geocoder();
//..

function reverseGeocode(point, fn) {
    geocoder.geocode({latLng: point}, function(results, status){
    var address = '';
    if (status === google.maps.GeocoderStatus.OK) {
        if (results.length > 2) {
                address = results[1].formatted_address;
            }
        }
        fn(address);
    });
}
```

The new `reverseGeocode` function takes a point object as the first parameter (an instance of `google.maps.LatLng`) and a callback function that will be called with a formatted address string when a successful geocode request has been made.

Now, rather than create a completely new control in the example application, modify the event listener for the marker button so that when the touch event is fired, the marker has an info window attached to it that displays the reverse geocoded place name. The new code is highlighted in the following snippet:

JAVASCRIPT

```
$('#drop-marker').on('touchstart', function(e){
    e.preventDefault();
    var marker = new google.maps.Marker({
        map: map,
        position: map.getCenter()
    });
    reverseGeocode(map.getCenter(), function(address){
        var infoWindow = new google.maps.InfoWindow();
        infoWindow.setContent(address);
        infoWindow.open(map, marker);
    });
});
```

This piece of code introduces a new feature of the Google Maps API: the info window. You can use the info window as a simple way of displaying some content on the map that is associated with a marker — in this case, the formatted address of a reverse geocode result (see Figure 5-9).

FIGURE 5-9

SUMMARY

That concludes your look at using location-based services within the Tizen runtime environment. You saw that once you enable the correct privileges and access settings within the `config.xml` file, you can implement a simple yet feature-rich mapping application in a familiar HTML5 environment. Then, with minimal code, you were up and running with a map, markers, info windows, and geocoding requests.

Don't be afraid to explore the Google Maps API further by using the example application as a starting point. You will be pleasantly surprised at how easily and quickly you can implement your own ideas to run within the Tizen runtime environment.

Multimedia

WHAT'S IN THIS CHAPTER?

➤ Discovering multimedia content

➤ Accessing the device's camera

➤ HTML5 multimedia features

WROX.COM CODE DOWNLOADS FOR THIS CHAPTER

The wrox.com code downloads for this chapter are found at www.wrox.com/go/professionaltizen on the Download Code tab. The code is in the Chapter 6 download. After decompressing the downloaded Zip files, you will have two project folders containing the full code for the Content Manager and Camera applications.

In this chapter you will discover the multimedia capabilities available to you in the Tizen Web Runtime. You will first take a look at discovering content using the Tizen Content Manager API, then you will look at a simple three-page application that lists media directories, the contents of a selected directory, and then an overview and preview page for a single piece of content. This covers the majority of cases you are likely to encounter when developing your own applications.

From there you will take a look at using the HTML5 Media Capture API to control a device's camera, including how to take a still image from a camera stream and save it to the file system. Along the way you'll learn about the HTML5 audio and video elements and get to know the creative possibilities those APIs provide.

DISCOVERING MULTIMEDIA CONTENT

Retrieving information about media files from the device's file system is achieved through using the ContentManager. In order to do this function, the application needs the correct privileges. Adding the following URIs to the Privileges section of the config.xml file will grant both read and write access for your application:

➤ http://tizen.org/privilege/content.read

➤ http://tizen.org/privilege/content.write

With those set, you can start working with the API to access media files on the device. The JavaScript and HTML listings in this section build up into the full Content Manager sample included in the code downloads accompanying this chapter.

You can list all the public media directories through the `getDirectories` function:

```
var success = function(directories) {
    directories.forEach(function(directory){
        console.log(directory.directoryURI);
    });
};
var error = function(e) {
    alert('Error: ' + e.message);
};
tizen.content.getDirectories(success, error);
```

Here, the success handler takes an array of `ContentDirectory` objects as its first parameter. It then iterates over each directory and then simply logs to the console the directory's URI on the file system. The error callback in this example just alerts you to the fact that something went wrong, but this is where you would put your error-handling logic. The error callback is passed an instance of `WebAPIError`.

You can quickly build a content page that lists the directories using the following HTML:

```
<div data-role="page" id="directory-listing">
    <div data-role="header" data-position="fixed">
        <h1>Media Directories</h1>
    </div>
    <div data-role="content">
        <ul data-role="listview" id="directory-list"></ul>
    </div>
</div>
```

The following JavaScript snippet adds the required logic to render a list of directory contents onto the page:

```
$(document).delegate('#directory-listing', 'pagebeforeshow', function(){

    var listView = $('#directory-list');

    listView.children().remove();

    tizen.content.getDirectories(function(directories){
        directories.forEach(function(directory){
            var item = $('<li />'),
            link = $('<a />', {
                'href': '#directory-contents',
                'text': directory.title
            });
```

```
                        link.on('vclick', function(){
                            selectedDirectory = directory;
                        });
                        item.append(link).appendTo(listView);
                    });
                    listView.listview('refresh');
                }, errorCallback);

            });
```

In the preceding example, a new page has been defined whose content element has a single empty unordered list. This unordered list element has been declared as having the role of a `listview`. In JavaScript, the contents of the unordered list are removed before making a call to the `getDirectories` function of the Content Manager API. Then the callback function iterates over the directories array and for each directory in that array, and updates the list so that the directory title and link to another page is appended to it.

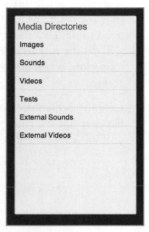

You'll also notice that an event handler has been bound to each newly created link so that when a `vclick` event is fired, the `selectedDirectory` variable is assigned the value of the directory in that iteration. This ensures that the next page, `#directory-contents`, knows which directory has been selected and can render its view accordingly.

After the unordered list has been updated with all the directories, the list view is refreshed so that all the relevant Web UI Framework styles are applied (see Figure 6-1).

FIGURE 6-1

WHAT IS A VCLICK?

The `vclick` event is supplied by jQuery Mobile. It is an attempt to abstract away the differences between mouse events (`mousedown`, `mouseup`, and `click`) and touch events. This means that when your application needs to work with both mouse clicks and touch events, you only need to register for the one type of event, and then underneath the hood jQuery will work out the rest.

The following example builds on the previous code by displaying a page that lists the contents of the selected directory. The first thing that is needed is some more HTML markup:

```
<div data-role="page" data-add-back-btn="true" id="directory-contents">
    <div data-role="header" data-position="fixed">
        <h1>
            <strong>Directory</strong>: <span id="directory-name"></span>
        </h1>
    </div>
</div>
```

```
    <div data-role="content" data-scroll="y">
        <ul data-role="listview" id="directory-contents-
list"></ul>
    </div>
    <div data-role="footer"></div>
</div>
```

FIGURE 6-2

The first thing you'll notice is that a new `div` element is defined with the familiar page role. One thing that you may be wondering about is the relevance of the `data-add-back-btn` attribute. This attribute specifies that the page has a back button. In order for this to work, however, you need to define a `div` that has the role of footer. The Web UI Framework will do the rest to insert the required back button (see Figure 6-2); and its action, when clicked or touched, will return the user to the previous screen.

Like the previous example, the content section has an empty unordered list that has the role of `listview`, as shown in the following code. This will be where the directory listing is displayed.

```
$(document).delegate('#directory-contents', 'pagebeforeshow', function(){

    var listView = $('#directory-contents-list');

    listView.children().remove();

    $('#directory-name').text(selectedDirectory.title);

    tizen.content.find(function(contents){
        contents.forEach(function(content){
            var item = $('<li class="ui-li-has-multiline" />'),
                link = $('<a />', {
                    'href': '#content-info',
                    'text': content.title
                }).appendTo(item);

            var sizeKb = Math.ceil(content.size / 1024);

            link.append('<span class="ui-li-text-sub">'
                    + content.contentURI + '</span>');
            link.append('<span class="ui-li-text-sub2"> ('
                    + content.type + ') ' + sizeKb + 'KB</span>');

            link.on('vclick', function(){
                selectedContent = content;
            });
            listView.append(item);
        });
        listView.listview('refresh');
    }, errorCallback, selectedDirectory.id);
});
```

There is a little bit more going on in the preceding JavaScript code, but when broken down, you can see that it is quite simple.

Again, before the directory listing is displayed, the contents of the unordered list are removed. This enables return visits to the page to be refreshed with new data. The directory title is assigned as the text value of the span placeholder in the header section on the page.

A call is then made to the find function of the Content Manager API. There is a rich set of parameters to this function that enable filtering, sorting, and pagination, but for simplicity the example simply defines a success handler, passes the error callback function name, and, more importantly, the directory ID as the third parameter.

The success handler accepts one parameter, contents, which is an array of Content objects; it iterates over each one, appending a new list item to the list view each time.

The structure of each list item is slightly different on this page compared to the previous one. You may notice that each list item has the class ui-li-has-multiline assigned to it. This allows additional lines to be displayed for each item, and that style is then applied by the Web UI Framework so that it is legible and in keeping with the current theme. For this to work properly, each sub-line must be wrapped in additional span elements with the classes ui-li-text-sub and ui-li-text-sub2.

When each item is clicked or touched, the current Content object is assigned as the value of selectedContent. This is then used in the third page, where details about the selected content will be displayed (see Figure 6-3).

The #content-info page is straightforward and the steps to create it will feel familiar to you by now. The following code starts with the HTML:

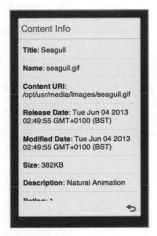

FIGURE 6-3

```html
<div data-role="page" data-add-back-btn="true" id="content-info">
    <div data-role="header" data-position="fixed">
        <h1>Content Info</h1>
    </div>
    <div data-role="content" data-scroll="y">
        <ul id="content-info" data-role="listview"></ul>
    </div>
    <div data-role="footer"></div>
</div>
```

Nothing new is going on here; the example simply defines a new page that has a back button and an empty unordered list with the role of listview so that information about the content to be displayed will be formatted using the Web UI Framework.

The following JavaScript code adds the necessary logic to display detailed information about a selected file:

```javascript
$(document).delegate('#content-info', 'pagebeforeshow', function(){

    var listView = $('#content-info', this),
```

```
        content = $('*[data-role="content"]', this);

    listView.children().remove();

    listView.append('<li><strong>Title</strong>: '
                + selectedContent.title + '</li>');
    listView.append('<li><strong>Name</strong>: '
                + selectedContent.name + '</li>');
    listView.append('<li><strong>Content URI</strong>: '
                + selectedContent.contentURI + '</li>');
    listView.append('<li><strong>Release Date</strong>: '
                + selectedContent.releaseDate + '</li>');
    listView.append('<li><strong>Modified Date</strong>: '
                + selectedContent.modifiedDate + '</li>');
    listView.append('<li><strong>Size</strong>: '
                + Math.ceil(selectedContent.size / 1024) + 'KB</li>');
    listView.append('<li><strong>Description</strong>: '
                + selectedContent.description + '</li>');
    listView.append('<li><strong>Rating</strong>: '
                + selectedContent.rating + '</li>');

    if (selectedContent.type === 'VIDEO') {
        var video = $('<video data-contols="true" style="width: 100%;" />');
        video.append('<source src="' + selectedContent.contentURI
                + '" type="' + selectedContent.mimeType + '" />');
        content.prepend(video);
    } else if (selectedContent.type === 'IMAGE') {
        var img = $('<img src="' + selectedContent.contentURI
                + '" style="width: 100%" />');
        listView.prepend(img);
    } else if (selectedContent.type === 'AUDIO') {
        var audio = $('<audio data-controls="true" style="width: 100%;" />');
        audio.append('<source src="' + selectedContent.contentURI
                + '" type="' + selectedContent.mimeType + '" />');
        content.prepend(audio);
    }

    listView.listview('refresh');
});
```

Quite a bit is going on in the preceding example, so let's break it down. The goal is to display a page with details about the selected content file and try to render a preview for it. The start of the code defines the steps to remove any previous markup that exists for the list view. Then, new list items are appended to the list view with details about the content file. This is done by using the values of a number of properties defined in the Content interface.

There are a number of properties of the Content object that provide information about the file. You can find a full list of properties in the Tizen API documentation, but for now Table 6-1 shows the ones that are of interest to us.

TABLE 6-1: Content Object Properties

NAME	TYPE	SINCE	DESCRIPTION
title	String	2.0	Content title
name	String	2.1	Name of the content
contentURI	String	2.0	URI that can be used to access the content
releaseDate	Date	2.0	Release date of the content
modifiedDate	Date	2.0	Date the content was last modified
size	Number	2.0	Size of the content file in bytes
description	String	2.0	Content description
rating	Number	2.0	A rating between 0 and 10
mimeType	String	2.0	MIME type of the content file

Using the values of these properties, the page can now display a list of useful information about the file.

To render a preview, the application code first needs to know what type of file it is. This is ascertained by evaluating the property type that will be one of VIDEO, IMAGE, AUDIO, or OTHER. The preceding example uses this value combined with the MIME type and content URI to render the appropriate HTML tag and this tag is prepended to the content container.

Embedding HTML5 Audio and Video

This section covers audio and video support in HTML5 and the level of support provided by the Tizen Web Runtime.

HTML5 uses the `<audio>` and `<video>` tags to embed audio and video media, respectively, in a web page. You can define a single source through the src attribute of the tag or alternatively provide multiple `<source>` tags defined as child elements of the parent tag. If for any reason the media cannot be played, you can add regular markup to display a useful message to the user.

The following HTML shows how to add a video element to a page. The first `<video>` element defines a single video source as part of the element attribute. The second shows how to define multiple sources. When multiple sources are defined, the browser will play the first one in that list that it supports. If it cannot play any of the ones defined, the paragraph message is displayed.

```
<!-- source as attribute of tag -->
<video src="/path/to/video.mp4" controls />

<!-- source defined as child <source> elements of parent tag -->
<video controls>
    <source src="/path/to/video.mp4" type="video/mp4" />
    <source src="/path/to/video.webm" type="video/webm" />
    <p>Sorry, but we are unable to play this video</p>
</video>
```

As you already know, the runtime environment is based on the WebKit browser engine and as such has full support for the audio and video specifications.

Multimedia in a Tizen web application that uses the UI Framework must have the necessary data attributes defined in order for them to be displayed and functional. Table 6-2 lists the range of widget options for a multimedia element in a Tizen application.

TABLE 6-2: Multimedia View Widget Options

OPTION	TYPE	DESCRIPTION
data-controls	Boolean	The default is true. When set to false the widget uses the browser's default controls.
data-full-screen	Boolean	When set to true, the media will be displayed in full screen mode. The default is false.
data-theme (optional)	String	Select the widget's theme. Defaults to the parent control's theme.

Therefore, in your Tizen web applications, you need to define your multimedia elements accordingly. The following HTML shows how to set up audio widget options:

```
<audio data-controls="true" style="width: 100%;">
    <source src="/path/to/audio.mp3" type="audio/mp3" />
</audio>
```

CAPTURING IMAGES

To make use of the device's camera and microphone hardware, your application can use the HTML5 Media Capture and Streams feature. This is a working draft specification that defines a JavaScript API that enables local media (including audio and video) to be requested by a platform.

The main function you will use when working with the device camera is getUserMedia. However, at the time of writing, the JavaScript API in the Web Runtime uses a vendor-prefixed version of the function name (webkit). Future releases will deprecate the vendor prefix and eventually the prefix will be removed altogether from the function name. To make your code work with both the prefixed and unprefixed versions, you can assign them back to the navigator object. The following JavaScript code shows how to do this:

```
navigator.getUserMedia = navigator.getUserMedia || navigator.webkitGetUserMedia;
```

The current getUserMedia API accepts three parameters, as shown in Table 6-3.

TABLE 6-3: Navigator.getUserMedia Parameters

PARAMETER	TYPE	DESCRIPTION
constraints	Object	The media types that should support the LocalMediaStream interface (used in the success callback).
successCallback	Function	A function handler invoked when a request for a media device is successful. An instance of LocalMediaStream is passed as the first parameter.
errorCallback	Function	A function handler invoked when a request for the media device fails.

Using this API, you can build a multimedia application that utilises the device camera and microphone.

> **NOTE** *You can read more about the Media Capture specification at* http://www.w3.org/TR/mediacapture-streams/.

Creating a Simple Camera Application

In this section you will create a simple application that uses the camera to create and save images, and then enhance this application by capturing video.

The JavaScript and HTML listings in this section are part of the Camera sample that is included in website downloads for this chapter. See the beginning of the chapter for more details.

First, create a new Tizen single-page web application that uses the UI Framework:

```
<div data-role="page" id="camera-page">
    <div data-role="header" data-position="fixed">
        <h1>Camera App</h1>
    </div><!-- /header -->
    <div data-role="content">
        <div id="video-container"></div>
        <div id="control-buttons">
            <div data-role="button" data-inline="true"
                id="picture-button">Take Picture</div>
            <div data-role="button" data-inline="true"
                id="video-button">Capture Video</div>
        </div>
    </div><!-- /content -->
</div><!-- /page -->
```

Now add some JavaScript that defines a new object (Camera) that first requests access to the media stream and handles the success and error callbacks:

```javascript
function Camera() {

    var constraints = {
        video: true,
        audio: true
    };

    navigator.getUserMedia(
        constraints,
        this.cameraSuccessCallback.bind(this),
        this.cameraErrorCallback.bind(this)
    );
}

Camera.prototype.cameraSuccessCallback = function(mediaStream) {

    this.cameraIsSupported = true;

    this.video = $('<video />', {
        autoplay: 'autoplay',
        id: 'camera-viewport',
        css: {
            height: '100%',
            width: '100%'
        },
        src: window.webkitURL.createObjectURL(mediaStream)
    });

    $('#video-container').append(this.video);
    $('#picture-button').on('vclick', this.takePicture.bind(this));
};

Camera.prototype.cameraErrorCallback = function(code) {

    this.cameraIsSupported = false;

    if (code.PERMISSION_DENIED) {
        alert('You must grant permission for this application to use your camera');
    } else if (code.NOT_SUPPORTED_ERROR) {
        alert('This application requires a camera in order to work');
    } else if (code.MANDATORY_UNSATISFIED_ERROR) {
        alert('Your device does not support all the '
                + 'features this application needs to run')
    }
};

Camera.prototype.takePicture = function() {};
Camera.prototype.takeVideo = function() {};
```

Breaking down the preceding example, in the `Camera` constructor, a request is made to `navigator`
`.getUserMedia`, which is passed references to the success and error callback functions attached to
the current `Camera` instance. Notice that a call to `bind` is made to each callback function, with `this`
passed as the only parameter. This ensures that when each of the functions is called, it retains the
same context as the `Camera` instance.

In order to output the stream to a web page, you need to create an element that can happily contain it. The HTML5 `<video>` tag fits the bill perfectly and that is what is initially happening inside the `cameraSuccessCallback`. Notice that the `src` property is assigned the value of `window .webkitURL.createObjectURL`, which is a reference to the file object of the stream. Once the element has been created it is appended to the video container. Lastly, event listeners are bound to the two control buttons.

The error callback is quite simple. It is passed an instance of `NavigatorUserMediaError` containing the type of error generated. The error is evaluated and an appropriate alert message is shown. In your production-ready applications, you'll obviously handle errors better than simply displaying an alert message.

When you run the application, the user will be asked to grant camera access to the application (see Figure 6-4). Once this access is granted, the video stream will be rendered on the page.

FIGURE 6-4

> **NOTE** *You can test the application on a Tizen device or by running it in the Web Simulator or Emulator on a computer with a webcam.*

Capturing an Image

In order to capture the image and save it to the file system, the application needs the correct privileges. Add the following URLs to the Privileges section of the `config.xml` file:

➤   `http://tizen.org/privilege/filesystem.read`

➤   `http://tizen.org/privilege/filesystem.write`

Now you can access the file system through the `tizen.filesystem` interface.

The application needs a way to turn the video stream into a still image. This can be achieved by drawing the current video frame on a `<canvas>` element. The following JavaScript code demonstrates how to capture a picture:

```
Camera.prototype.takePicture = function() {

    var canvas = $('<canvas id="canvas" />', {
        css: {
            width: this.video.width(),
            height: this.video.height()
        }
    });

    canvas[0].getContext('2d').drawImage(
```

```
        this.video[0],
        0,
        0,
        this.video.width(),
        this.video.height()
    );

    var data = canvas[0].toDataURL()
                        .replace('data:image/png;base64,', '')
                        .replace('data:,', '');

    var fileName = 'IMAGE_' + Date.now().toString() + '.png';

    tizen.filesystem.resolve('images', function(dir){
        var file = dir.createFile(fileName);
        file.openStream('w', function(stream){
            stream.writeBase64(data);
            stream.close();
            alert('Image saved to "' + file.toURI() + '"');
        }, function(e){
            alert('Error: ' + e.message);
        }, 'UTF-8');
    }, function(e){ alert('Error: ' + e.message); });
};
```

The first part of the preceding code creates a new <canvas> element with width and height properties matching the <video> element's dimensions. If you're not familiar with the syntax of creating
elements, it uses the jQuery function, passing a string of the element tag as the first parameter and
a JavaScript object full of options as the second parameter. The return value is a jQuery object containing the newly created element.

Using the raw <canvas> element, the code gets the two-dimensional drawing context and calls the
drawImage function to create the still image. An image is then rendered using the video element
specified at the top-left corner of the rectangle, with the same dimensions as the video element itself.
You could now if you wished append the canvas element to the document and view the still image —
this would be a great way to display a thumbnail of the recently taken photo.

In order to obtain the raw image data, the function proceeds to get the base64-encoded version of
the image. Then it creates a new filename in the format of IMAGE_[TIMESTAMP].png and continues
to use the file system API to save the new file.

The first thing the code does is to resolve the destination directory path to an images folder inside
the current working directory. Inside the success handler for this call, a new file is created inside the
directory, and then, finally, the base64-encoded image data is written to that stream. To confirm
that this has worked correctly, a message is displayed containing the absolute path to the captured
image (see Figure 6-5).

FIGURE 6-5

CAPTURING VIDEO

At the time of writing, the current release of the Tizen SDK (2.2.1) does not have support for native video capture using the Media Capture API, although there are plans to support it in a future release. When it is officially supported, it will enable streaming and other video media-related capabilities. For more information on the use of HTML5 video, you can read the W3C specification at `www.w3.org/wiki/HTML/Elements/video`.

SUMMARY

The examples in this chapter used the Content Manager API to access the device's file system. This API will become second nature to you once you start developing your own Tizen web applications, as you will undoubtedly write feature-rich apps that need to both read content from and write content to the device. At the beginning of the chapter, you saw that it is possible to list the contents of a directory and discover content as you go. You also saw that these files contain a great deal of metadata, which you can use to both display the information and make logical decisions in your application.

HTML5 video and audio is a huge topic, and one worthy of its own book let alone a chapter, but the material provided here has demonstrated that with a modest amount of code you can get up and running quickly to obtain control over a device's camera. The Media Capture API, along with the canvas and video HTML elements, gives you great power to create fully functional multimedia applications. As more support is added to the Tizen SDK for this API, you will have more power to build a richer set of creative applications that utilise video and even video streaming.

It really is an exciting time to discover the multimedia possibilities that HTML5 and the Tizen web platform provide you. What are you waiting for? Go discover other fantastic things that you can do with them!

7

Sensors and Other Hardware

WHAT'S IN THIS CHAPTER?

- ➤ Using sensors in your web applications
- ➤ Testing your sensor code in the Simulator
- ➤ Near field communication (NFC)

WROX.COM CODE DOWNLOADS FOR THIS CHAPTER

The wrox.com code downloads for this chapter are found at www.wrox.com/go/ professionaltizen on the Download Code tab. The code is in the Chapter 7 download section, and after decompressing the downloaded Zip files, you will have a project folder containing the full code for the Leveller sample.

In this chapter you'll create a fully functional code sample in order to learn how to use sensors in your Tizen web applications. By building an application step by step, you'll learn how to use the W3C DeviceOrientation Event API to monitor and respond to sensor data and discover how to test sensor functionality in the Web Simulator before running your application on a device.

Near field communication (NFC) is a technology for short-range wireless communication which is exploding in popularity and is well supported by the Tizen Device APIs. The second part of the chapter shows you how to use NFC in your Tizen applications.

DEVICE ORIENTATION

Sometimes your application needs to know the device's orientation so that it can respond to it accordingly. For example, if you were writing a spirit level application, the application itself would only be useful if it knew the device's orientation. Another obvious example would be a compass. Without some way for your application to access the motion sensor hardware, these ideas couldn't be turned into reality.

Thankfully, there is a W3C specification for this specific purpose: the DeviceOrientation Event Specification. As the name suggests, it is based on events that tell registered listeners that the orientation of the device has changed. The Tizen Web Runtime has full support for this specification, providing a wide range of creative possibilities for application developers.

The syntax for responding to a change in device orientation is simple enough, as outlined in the following example:

JAVASCRIPT — REGISTERING A LISTENER FOR DEVICE ORIENTATION CHANGES

```
window.addEventListener('deviceorientation', function(event) {
    //.. Update the application state based on the new orientation values
});
```

Before looking at a working example application, it is important to understand three new properties of the event object whose values are unique to device orientation:

➤ Alpha

➤ Beta

➤ Gamma

As shown in Table 7-1, these values represent the three dimensions of orientation and express the motion in degrees. We are assuming here that you are familiar with the x- and y- values to express a two-dimensional surface, and that you are likely familiar with the z-value to express a third dimension.

TABLE 7-1: Device Orientation Values

ORIENTATION	AXIS	VALUES
Alpha	Z	0° to 360°
Beta	X	-180° to 180°
Gamma	Y	-90° to 90°

The orientation properties are related to these three dimensions. The Alpha property expresses the value of the motion around the z-axis, the Beta property is the value of the motion around the x-axis, and the Gamma property is the value of motion around the y-axis (see Figure 7-1).

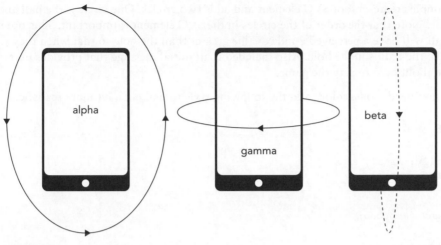

FIGURE 7-1

A Working Example

In this section you'll put the theory into practice. The application discussed in this section demonstrates how easy it is to listen to the device orientation event and update the display accordingly. As shown in Figure 7-2, the application simulates a putting green in golf. The aim of the game is to putt the ball by tilting the green — or, more accurately, the device.

The HTML, CSS, and JavaScript shown in the rest of this section are part of the Leveller example which is included in the downloads for this chapter.

To get started, the application needs some graphics. Rather than head to your favorite graphics application to create the scene, you can use SVG, as shown in the following code:

FIGURE 7-2

CREATING THE GREEN USING SVG

```
<section id="info">
    <p id="initial-message">Tilt the device to put the ball in the hole.</p>
</section>
<section id="canvas">
    <svg xmlns="http://www.w3.org/2000/svg" version="1.1" id="root">
        <circle cx="160" cy="440" r="12" fill="black" id="hole" />
        <circle cx="160" cy="40" r="10" fill="white" id="ball" />
    </svg>
</section>
```

The preceding example creates a root SVG element and adds two circles. One circle is the ball and the other is the hole. Note that the order of the circles in the SVG element is important. This order ensures that the ball will have a perceived *z*-index value greater than the hole so that when they overlap, it looks like the ball is in the hole. Also included is an initial message that provides users with a helpful hint about how to play the game.

Now your application needs some color. Add the following style to make it a bit more realistic:

PUTTER STYLE

```css
body {
    font-family: Arial, sans;
    background: green;
}
#info {
    background: #ebebeb;
}
#info p {
    text-align: center;
    padding: 4px 10px;
}
```

All the application now needs is some JavaScript to bring the game alive. As outlined earlier, you do this using the DeviceOrientation Event Specification:

PUTTER JAVASCRIPT LOGIC

```javascript
(function () {

    var ball, hole, startX, startY, holeX, holeY;

    ball = document.getElementById('ball');
    hole = document.getElementById('hole');
    holeX = parseInt(hole.attributes.cx.value, 10);
    holeY = parseInt(hole.attributes.cy.value, 10);

    /**
     * Listener for the deviceorientation event
     *
     * @param {Event} event
     */
    function orientationChanged(event) {

        var x, y;

        startX = startX || event.gamma;
        startY = startY || event.beta;

        x = 160 + (startX - event.gamma) * 5;
        y = 90 + (startY - event.beta) * 5;
```

```
        ball.attributes.cx.value = x;
        ball.attributes.cy.value = y;
    }

    window.addEventListener('deviceorientation', orientationChanged);
}());
```

Looking at the preceding JavaScript snippet in more detail, you will first notice that a few variables are declared at the top of the self-executing function. The `ball` and `hole` variables hold references to the SVG circle elements. Then a reference to the hole's *x*- and *y*-coordinates are held in the `holeX` and `holeY` variables. This enables detecting a collision later on.

Then the main body of the logic is held in the `orientationChanged` function. The listener function takes one parameter, the event object. The purpose of this function is to redraw the golf ball based on the device orientation values.

The `startX` and `startY` values are used to calculate the new *x*- and *y*-values of the ball on the screen. When the event is first fired, they are assigned the value of Gamma and Beta.

Following that, the new *x*- and *y*-values are calculated accordingly. Then the ball's `cx` and `cy` values are updated. This causes the ball to be redrawn, giving the impression that the ball is moving along in response to the device orientation change.

The last bit of the code binds the function to the `deviceorientation` event.

Putter Improvements

Those of you who were paying attention earlier will have noticed that variables were defined to contain the hole's position and we said these would be used to detect a collision. The following updates the example so that the application knows if the user has indeed putted the ball:

PUTTER MARK-UP CHANGES

```
<section id="info">
    <p id="initial-message">Tilt the device to put the ball in the hole.</p>
    <p id="success-message">Well done, nice putt!</p>
</section>
```

PUTTER STYLE UPDATES

```
body {
    font-family: Arial, sans;
    background: green;
}
#info {
    background: #ebebeb;
}
#info p {
    text-align: center;
    padding: 4px 10px;
```

```
    }
    #success-message {
        display: none;
        color: green;
        font-weight: bold;
    }
```

PUTTER JAVASCRIPT LOGIC UPDATE

```
function orientationChanged(event) {

    var x, y;

    startX = startX || event.gamma;
    startY = startY || event.beta;

    x = 160 + (startX - event.gamma) * 5;
    y = 90 + (startY - event.beta) * 5;

    ball.attributes.cx.value = x;
    ball.attributes.cy.value = y;

    if ((holeX === x) && (holeY === y)) {
        document.getElementById('initial-message').style.display = 'none';
        document.getElementById('success-message').style.display = 'block';
        window.navigator.vibrate(1000); // vibrate for one second
    }
}
```

The preceding examples add some additional logic to detect whether the ball has entered the hole. To accomplish this, the hole's *x*- and *y*-values are used in combination with the *x*- and *y*-values of the ball. If they match, then the initial message is hidden and the success message is shown.

You may be wondering what `window.navigator.vibrate` is doing, although you can probably tell by the name of the API call. This line of code introduces another W3C specification: the Vibration API. This API provides an interface to the hardware vibration mechanism. The interface is pretty simple:

VIBRATION API USAGE

```
window.navigator.vibrate(pattern); // {Number|Array}
```

The pattern can be either a number or an array. If it is a number, then the vibration will last for the duration specified, in milliseconds. If an array of numbers is provided, then each value alternates the vibration and pause lengths. Take a look at the following examples to understand the call:

VIBRATION API TYPICAL EXAMPLES

```
window.navigator.vibrate(2000); // single vibration lasting 2 seconds
window.navigator.vibrate([2000, 400, 2000]); // 2 vibrations lasting 2
                                              // seconds with a 400
                                              // milisecond pause in between
```

The Vibration API provides a great way to offer feedback in games where a collision is detected.

> **NOTE** *You can find more details about the W3C specifications used in this chapter at the following locations:*
>
> ➤ *The DeviceOrientation Event Specification*
>
> > ➤ http://dev.w3.org/geo/api/spec-source-orientation .html
> >
> > ➤ https://developer.mozilla.org/en-US/ docs/Web/Guide/API/DOM/Events/ Orientation_and_motion_data_explained
>
> ➤ *The Vibration API*
>
> > ➤ http://www.w3.org/TR/vibration/
> >
> > ➤ https://developer.mozilla.org/en-US/docs/Web/API/ Navigator.vibrate

Testing the Application Using the Web Simulator

To run the full application using the Web Simulator, right-click on the project and select Run As ➪ Tizen Web Simulator Application. You can simulate device movements and see how the application responds by opening the Sensors tab (see Figure 7-3) and then click and drag the mobile image until you get the ball in the hole.

If everything turned out correct and you putted the ball, then the Simulator will shake the screen and you'll get the success message at the top of it.

The Device Motion Event

The devicemotion event is a superset of the deviceorientation event used in the putter example and provides acceleration data as well as orientation data.

The acceleration data is returned in three axes: x, y, and z. These are measured in meters per second squared (m/s²).

FIGURE 7-3

To get the motion data, you need to add the `devicemotion` event listener to your window object as shown in the following code:

```
window.addEventListener("devicemotion",
    function(data)
      {
        var acceleration = data.accelerationIncludingGravity;
      }
```

If the device supports hardware, such as a gyroscope, to exclude the effect of gravity from the acceleration data, then you can access the acceleration property directly:

```
function motionHandler(data){
var  acceleration  =  data.acceleration;
}
```

The difference between these two properties is shown in Table 7-2. This shows the values for a device face-up and then moved upwards, forward, left, and up and to the right.

TABLE 7-2: Acceleration Data Sample

	NOT ACCELERATING	ACCELERATING UP	ACCELERATING FORWARD	ACCELERATING LEFT	ACCELERATING UP AND TO THE RIGHT
Acceleration	{0, 0, 0}	{0, 0, 5}	{0, 2, 0}	{3, 0, 0}	{5, 0, 9}
Acceleration, Including Gravity	{0, 0, 9.81}	{0, 0, 15}	{0, 2, 9.81}	{3, 0, 9.81}	{5, 0, 11}

> **NOTE** *The Compass, SensorBall, and DeviceMotionCapture web samples in the Tizen SDK demonstrate how to use the* `deviceorientation` *and* `devicemotion` *events.*

NEAR FIELD COMMUNICATION (NFC)

NFC is a standard for secure short-range wireless communication. It enables contactless communication between devices that are within a few centimeters of each other. NFC can be used to exchange information between an NFC-enabled device and an NFC tag, which is a chip that can securely store data, including personal information such as credit card numbers, contact details, or device configuration information. NFC can also be used to exchange data between two devices or make a payment by holding a device close to a point-of-sale terminal instead of swiping a smart card.

Compared to other networking technologies such as Bluetooth, NFC is low power, does not need to be paired, and is quicker to set up.

In this section, you'll learn how to use the Tizen NFC Device API to support the following NFC operating modes:

➤ **Read/write mode** — NFC devices can read or write small amounts of information to NFC-compatible tags. Possible uses include getting information from an NFC tag on a smart poster or creating your own personal NFC sticker.

➤ **Peer-to-peer mode** — Two NFC devices exchange data. This data could include Bluetooth or Wi-Fi link setup parameters, virtual business cards, or digital photos.

Using NFC in Your Web Applications

To use NFC features in your application, you first need to add the required privileges to the `config` `.xml` file. For example, if you use the tag feature, add the following:

```
<tizen:privilege name="http://tizen.org/privilege/nfc.tag" />
```

The full list of NFC privileges is as follows:

➤ `http://tizen.org/privilege/nfc.tag` — Allows the application to read and write NFC tag information

➤ `http://tizen.org/privilege/nfc.p2p` — Allows the application to push NFC messages to other devices

➤ `http://tizen.org/privilege/nfc.common` — Allows the application to manage common NFC features

➤ `http://tizen.org/privilege/nfc.admin` — Allows the application to change NFC status, such as turning NFC on or off

You can also add the NFC feature to your `config.xml` file to filter out devices that do not support NFC when your application is shown in the Tizen Store:

```
http://tizen.org/feature/network.nfc
```

At runtime, you can find out if the device supports NFC by using the SystemInfo Device API:

```
var deviceCapabilities;
 deviceCapabilities = tizen.systeminfo.getCapabilities();
 if (deviceCapabilities.nfc)
 {
     console.log("NFC is supported");
 }
```

> **NOTE** *For more information about SystemInfo, consult the help documentation at Tizen Web App Programming ➪ API References ➪ Device API Reference ➪ System.*

Turning on NFC

To use NFC, you have to create the `NFCAdapter` object. It is fairly simple to create the adapter by just calling the following:

```
var nfcAdapter = tizen.nfc.getDefaultAdapter();
```

This code returns the default NFC adaptor on the device. Because there is no error callback for this method, you can also check the error message by using a try and catch block:

```
try { nfcAdapter = tizen.nfc.getDefaultAdapter(); }
catch(error){
console.log(error.name + ":" + error.message);
  }
```

Next, you need to turn the NFC adapter on by calling `setPowered()`. This function takes three parameters: a Boolean value indicating on/off, a callback function for successful completion, and an error-handling callback:

```
nfcAdapter.setPowered(
  true,
  function(){
      //SuccessCallback
  },
  function(){
      //ErrorCallback
      //e.g. ServiceNotAvailableError: NFC service is busy
  }
);
```

Detecting Tags and Peers

After you successfully enable the adapter, you need to set the appropriate listeners to communicate with other devices. A *tag listener* allows the device to detect attaching and detaching of NFC tags, while a *peer listener* allows the device to detect another available peer when using peer-to-peer mode.

To set the tag listener, you need to set up at least one `NFCTagDetectCallback` function to handle the tag events `onattach` and `ondetach`:

```
nfcAdapter.setTagListener(
      function(){
            //handle the onattach and ondetach events
      }
);
```

To set the peer listener, you call the `NFCPeerDetectCallback` function:

```
nfcAdapter.setPeerListener(
        function(){
                //handle onattach or ondetach events
        }
);
```

Reading from a Tag

When a tag is detected by the device, it calls the `NFCTagDetectCallback` function that was specified when you called `setTagListener()`. At this point, you can carry out an operation on the detected tag.

For example, to read data from the tag, use the `readNDEF` method, as shown in the following code:

```
var onTagDetect = {
    onattach: function(tag){
        if(tag.isSupportedNDEF){
            tag.readNDEF(
                function(message){
                    for(var i=0; i < message.recordCount; i++){
                        switch(message.records[i].tnf){
                        case tizen.nfc.NFC_RECORD_TNF_EMPTY:
                            //go through different records
                        }
                    }
                },
                function(){
                    //error callback of readNDEF()
                }
            );
        }
    }
};
```

The preceding code shows a typical example of how to read an NFC data exchange format (NDEF) message. The `readNDEF` function takes two parameters: a compulsory `NDEFMessageReadCallback` and an optional `ErrorCallback`.

An NDEF message may contain multiple records. Each NDEF record contains a Type Name Format (TNF) field that specifies how to interpret the data in the rest of the record, including the record type and payload.

Tizen defines three types of `NDEFRecord`: `NDEFRecordText`, `NDEFRecordURI`, and `NDEFRecordMedia`. For a known type of record, instead of using the general payload property from the `NDEFRecord`, you can use the more specific property according to the type of record. For example, you can use the `text` property if you know the record type is `text`:

```
if( record instanceof tizen.NDEFRecordText)
    document.getElementById("Payload").innerText = record.text;
```

Otherwise, you can use the `payload` property of an unknown type record, which is a buffer.

Writing to a Tag

The implementation of writing to a tag is similar to the code required to read a tag. After the `NFCTagDetectCallback` is triggered, you can use the `writeNDEF()` method of the tag object to write information to the tag:

```
var onTagDetect = {
  onattach: function(tag){
    if(tag.isSupportedNDEF){
      tag.writeNDEF(
        ndefMessage,
        function(){
          //handle success case
        },
        function(){
          //handle failure case
        }
      );
    }
  }
};
```

The `writeNDEF` method takes three parameters. The first parameter is the NDEF message needed to write to the tag. The optional second and third parameters are the success and error callback functions.

To create the NDEF message, create an `NDEFMessage` object, contained in the `ndefMessage` variable in the following code. An `NDEFMessage` object has two properties, a record count and a record array:

```
var ndefRecord = new tizen.NDEFRecordText(
'Text Payload', 'en-US', 'UTF16');
var recordArray = new Array(ndefRecord);
var ndefMessage = new tizen.NDEFMessage(recordArray);
```

After you create the NDEF message, you can pass it to the `writeNDEF` method.

Peer-to-Peer Mode

Peer-to-peer mode always involves two NFC devices (*peers*), and it's a two-way communication. Tizen provides both send and receive NDEF message functionality for peer-to-peer mode. One peer can send an NDEF message proactively, but it can only receive an incoming NDEF message if the receive listener is set.

To implement peer-to-peer mode, you first need to detect the peer. After setting the `NFCPeerDetectCallback`, you receive an attached event when a peer is detected, and a detached event when a peer is lost.

The second step is to connect the `setReceiveNDEFListener` to the adapter itself to enable the application to receive incoming messages from another peer.

When a peer is detected, you always need to check whether the peer is connected or not. If it's connected, then you can send the message to that peer. The following code shows how to set up the listeners for peer-to-peer communication:

```
nfcAdapter.setPeerDetectListener({
  onattach: function(peer){
    if(peer.isConnected){
      var ndefMessage;
      var recordArray = new Array(new tizen.
        NDEFRecordText( 'test', 'en-US', 'UTF16'));
      ndefMessage = new tizen.NDEFMessage(recordArray);
      sendNDEF(ndefMessage);
      peer.setReceiveNDEFListener({
        onsuccess: function(message){
          for(var i = 0; i < message.recordCount;
          i++){
              switch(message.records[i].tnf ){
                  case tizen.nfc.NFC_RECORD_TNF_
          EMPTY:
                  }
              }
          }
      });
    }
    // read the record
    else{
      //peer not connected
    }
  },
  ondetach:function(){
    //peer lost }
});
```

Testing NFC in the Simulator and Emulator

You can test NFC features before you run your application on a real device by using the Web Simulator or the Emulator. To use the Web Simulator, launch your application and select the Network Management section on the left-hand side of the window. Turn the NFC switch to On and use the options provided to simulate reading from and writing to a tag and peer-to-peer mode. Figure 7-4 shows the NFC section of the Web Simulator.

In the Emulator you can use the Event Injector to test NFC functionality, as shown in Figure 7-5.

FIGURE 7-4

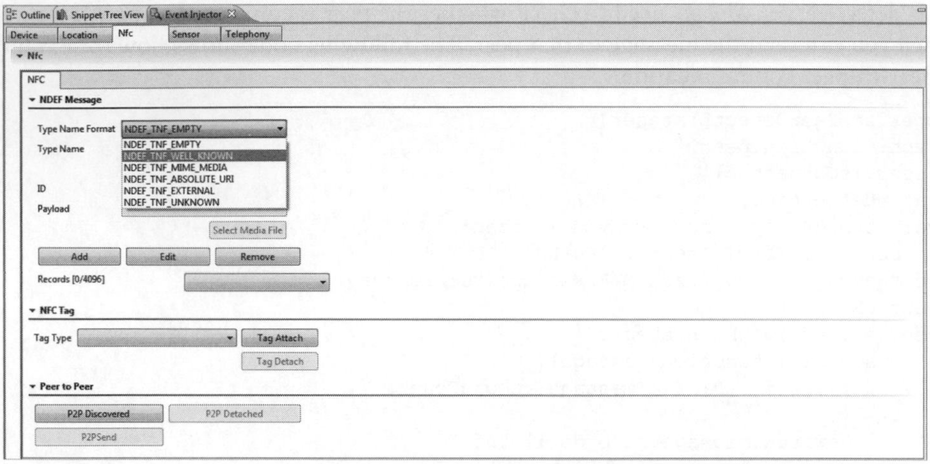

FIGURE 7-5

SUMMARY

In this chapter you developed a putter game to show off the capabilities of the `deviceorientation` event. Now that you have the full source code, it's a good opportunity to test out your newly acquired Tizen web programming skills by adding support for the `devicemotion` event to the game and responding to the acceleration data.

While Tizen's sensor support makes use of the W3C APIs, in order to use NFC you need to use the Device APIs. You should now know how to read from and write to an NFC tag and transfer data between devices using peer-to-peer mode. For a practical example of what NFC can do, take a look at the ContactsExchanger sample web application in the Tizen SDK. This sample application shows you how to exchange contacts between devices using NFC; and together with the introduction in this chapter, it is a good starting point for creating your own apps. To learn how to implement NFC functionality in native applications, see Chapter 14, "Telephony and Networking."

8

Messaging Services

➤ Creating and sending messages

➤ Receiving messages

➤ The message storage

➤ Building an e-mail client

This chapter introduces the Messaging API, the Tizen device API which enables web app developers to create, send, and receive SMS (Short Message Service), MMS (Multimedia Message Service), and e-mail messages from within their applications. While you can send messages using the sms and mailto attributes in HTML5, Tizen's Messaging API goes far beyond this, providing convenient access to a range of messaging operations. By the end of this chapter, you will not only be familiar with Tizen's messaging features, you will also have built a fully functional e-mail client.

MESSAGING SERVICE

The messaging service handles the transmission of messages — which consist of text, multimedia data, and attachments — between mobile devices.

The Messaging API includes functions to create, send, read, store, and manage messages and attachments for SMS, MMS, and e-mail messages, and enables the web app developer to do the following:

➤ Create and send messages

➤ Add and retrieve attachments specified by MIME type (such as image/png or text/pdf)

➤ Receive messages

➤ Access the user's inbox, sent items box, and outbox, and search for messages

➤ Create and send MMS messages containing image, video, audio, vCard (business card standard format), and iCalendar (calendar item standard format) attachments

➤ Set the body text, subject, recipient list, and attachments for an e-mail message

The capability to send and receive messages involves access to the user's private data and is protected by privileges. To use the features of the Messaging API, your application needs to set the following privileges:

➤ `http://tizen.org/privilege/messaging.write` — Allows the application to send SMS, MMS, and e-mail messages

➤ `http://tizen.org/privilege/messaging.read` — Allows the application to receive messages

The privileges must be specified in `config.xml` as follows:

```
<!--Configuration file content-->
<widget …>
  <!--Other configuration details-->
  …
  <tizen:privilege name="http://tizen.org/privilege/messaging.read"/>
  <tizen:privilege name="http://tizen.org/privilege/messaging.write"/>
</widget>
```

These are basic privileges which are available to all application developers. However, the user may choose to prevent certain applications from being able to access messages. See Chapter 2 for more details about privileges and user settings.

The Messaging API is accessed from the `tizen.messaging` object. It supports two objects: `MessageService` and `MessageStorage`.

`MessageService` provides methods to manipulate and send messages and supports message creating, sending, and fetching features. The functions provided by `MessageService` are defined as follows:

➤ `sendMessage()` — Sends a message.

➤ `loadMesageBody()` — Loads the body of a specified message.

➤ `loadMessageAttachment()` — Loads an attachment from a message.

➤ `sync()` — Synchronizes the service content with an external mail server.

➤ `syncFolder()` — Synchronizes the folder contents to an external mail server.

➤ `stopSync()` — Stops `sync()` and `syncFolder()` operations.

`MessageStorage` stores messages in conversations and folders (inbox, drafts, outbox, and sent items box), and provides functions to query, update, and delete messages. The functions provided by the `MessagingStorage` object are defined as follows:

➤ `addDraftMessage()` — Adds a message as a draft to the Drafts folder of the message storage.

➤ `findMessages()` — Finds messages in the message storage.

➤ `removeMessages()` — Removes messages from the message storage.

➤ `updateMessages()` — Updates messages in the message storage.

➤ `findConversations()` — Finds conversations in the message storage.

➤ `removeConversations()` — Removes conversations from the message storage.

➤ `findFolders()` — Finds folders in the message storage.

➤ `addMessagesChangeListener()` — Adds a listener to be notified of message storage changes.

➤ `addConversationsChangeListener()` — Adds a listener to be notified of conversation updates.

➤ `addFoldersChangeListener()` — Adds a listener to be notified of changes to the message folder.

➤ `removeChangeListener()` — Removes and unsubscribes the specified listener from further change notifications. The three add listener functions above each return a subscription identifier that is passed as a parameter to `removeChangeListener()` to specify the listener to be removed.

To use the message service APIs, you need to retrieve the message service that corresponds to the required message type, such as SMS, MMS, and e-mail. The following code snippet shows how to retrieve the e-mail messaging service:

```
tizen.messaging.getMessageServices("messaging.sms", onMessageServiceFound, onError);
```

`getMessageServices()` gets the messaging service for the specified service type. (SMS, MMS, and e-mail are supported in the current release.) Because `getMessageServices()` is called asynchronously, you should set a success callback to receive the return values, and an error callback to report any errors.

If the request succeeds, an array of available `MessageService` objects is returned via the success callback, shown in the `onMessageServiceFound()` function:

```
var gSmsService = null;
function onMessageServiceFound(services)
{
    var gSmsService = services[0];
}
```

In this case, we requested the SMS service, `"messaging.sms"`, and `services[0]` is the first retrieved message service.

`onError` is called if the function fails. For debugging purposes, it's good to write the error message to the console:

```
function onError(err) {
    console.log("Error: " + err.message);
}
```

Writing and Sending Messages

Now that you have retrieved the `MessageService` object for the SMS messaging service, you can use it to create and send SMS messages.

You use the `Message` interface to define the content and attributes of the message, and then send the message using the `sendMessage()` method of the `MessageService` interface:

```
try
{

    /* Construct SMS */
    var msg = new tizen.Message("messaging.sms",
        {
          plainBody: "Hello World."},
          to: ["+1234567890", "+0987654321"]
        });

    // send message
    gSmsService.sendMessage(msg, onMessageSent, function(e)
        {
          /* Error handling */
          gSmsService.messageStorage.addDraftMessage(msg,
                              onDraftAdded, onError);
        });
}
```

`tizen.Message()` returns an SMS message with the content and sender information as shown in the preceding code. This `Message` object is then passed as the first parameter to `sendMessage()`, while the second and third parameters specify the success and error callbacks.

If sending the message fails, the code saves the message into the Draft folder of the message storage. The error callback should handle all possible errors and exceptions that could cause message delivery to fail.

The success callback will be invoked if the message was sent successfully. In the case of an SMS, the success callback could be invoked several times, depending on the number of recipients:

```
function onMessageSent(recipients)
{
    for (var i = 0; i < recipients.length; i++)
    {
        console.log("The SMS has been sent to " + recipients[i]);
    }
}
```

If you want to send MMS or e-mail messages with attachments, add the attachments as an array of `MessageAttachment` objects:

```
var msg = new tizen.Message("messaging.email");
msg.attachments = [new tizen.MessageAttachment("images/myimage.png", "image/png"),
                   new tizen.MessageAttachment("docs/mydoc.pdf","text/pdf")];
```

Receiving Messages

The Tizen platform stores incoming messages in the message storage, which you need to monitor to receive the incoming messages. In the case of the e-mail service, your application might support a synchronisation button or auto-sync feature. When your application synchronises the service storage with the external e-mail server, the entire message is downloaded to the device. To monitor the message storage changes, register event listeners to get message storage change notifications for a particular conversation or message folder. In this example, we will monitor the message storage.

The addMessagesChangeListener(), addConversationsChangeListener(), and addFoldersChangeListener() methods of the MessageStorage interface register an event listener, which starts asynchronously once the method returns the subscription identifier for the listener. You can use the MessagesChangeCallback, MessageConversationsChangeCallback, and MessageFoldersChangeCallback interfaces to define listener event handlers for receiving notifications about the changes.

The following code gets notifications for changes in message storage:

```
var onMessageChanged =
{
    /* When messages are updated */
    messagesupdated: function(messages)
    {
        console.log(messages.length + " message(s) updated");
    },

    /* When messages are added */
    messagesadded: function(messages)
    {
        console.log(messages.length + " message(s) added");
    },

    /* When messages are deleted */
    messagesremoved: function(messages)
    {
        console.log(messages.length + " message(s) removed");
    }
};
var id = gSmsService.messageStorage.addMessagesChangeListener(onMessageChanged);
```

The event handler onMessageChanged() is called when messages are updated, added, or removed. To stop the notifications, use the removeChangeListener() method of the MessageStorage interface:

```
gSmsService.messageStorage.removeChangeListener(id);
```

Searching Messages

To manage messages, you need to search for messages by using the findMessages() method of the MessageStorage object with a tizen.AttributeFilter:

```
function onMessageFound(messages) {
   for (var i=0; i < messages.length; i++)
   {
       console.log("From: " + messages[i].from
            + "When: " + messages[i].timestamp.toLocaleString());
   }
}

// searches for all SMS messages
var typeFilter = new tizen.AttributeFilter("type", "EXACTLY", "messaging.sms");
gSmsService.messageStorage.findMessages(typeFilter, onMessageFound, onError);
```

The attribute filter shown in the preceding example narrows down your search to SMS messages
only. If you want to find other message types, change `messaging.sms` to `messaging.mms` or
`messaging.email` for MMS and e-mail, respectively.

Like other methods in the messaging service, the `findMessages()` method is asynchronous,
and an array containing the matched messages is returned through the callback function,
`onMessageFound()`. If no SMS messages are found, the success callback is invoked with an empty
array. If any errors occur while searching for contacts, the `onError` callback is called.

The first parameter of `AttributeFilter` is the attribute name, the second is a match flag, and the
third is a value.

The match flags are specified as follows:

➤ `EXACTLY` — Match exactly (case sensitive)

➤ `FULLSTRING` — Match exactly (case insensitive)

➤ `CONTAINS` — Contains the specified string (case insensitive)

➤ `STARTSWITH` — Starts with the specified string (case insensitive)

➤ `ENDSWITH` — Ends with the specified string (case insensitive)

➤ `EXISTS` — The specified attribute exists

In addition to message types, you can search messages based on other attributes such as ID,
timestamp, from, to, body, attachment, and so on:

```
var bodyFilter = new tizen.AttributeFilter("body", "CONTAINS", str);
var nameFilter = new tizen.AttributeFilter("from", "FULLSTRING", name);
var attachmentFilter = new tizen.AttributeFilter("hasAttachment", "EXACTLY", true);
```

The filter attributes of messages include id, conversationId, folderId, type, timestamp, from,
to, cc, bcc, body.loaded, body.plainBody, body.htmlBody, body.inlineAttachments, isRead,
hasAttachment, isHighPriority, subject, isResponseTo, messageStatus, and attachments.
You must use `AttributeRangeFilter` instead of `AttributeFilter` for timestamp:

```
var begin = new Date(2013, 1, 1, 0, 0, 0);
var end = new Date(2013, 1, 2, 0, 0, 0);
var timeFilter = new tizen.AttributeRangeFilter("timestamp", begin, end);
```

If you need to search based on two or more filters, combine the filters by using `CompositeFilter`:

```
var searchFilter = new tizen.CompositeFilter("INTERSECTION",
        [bodyFilter, nameFilter, timeFilter]);
```

The `CompositeFilter` provides two combine options: the `INTERSECTION` option matches all specified filters, and the `UNION` option matches any of the specified filters.

The search result does not contain the actual body of the messages. To load the message body, call the `loadMessageBody()` method of the `MessageService` interface:

```
function onMessageFound(messages)
{
    for (var i = 0; i < messages.length; i++)
    {
        var message = messages[i];
        if (!message.body.loaded)
        {
            tizen.messaging.loadMessageBody(message, onMessagedLoaded, onError);
            tizen.messaging.loadMessageAttachment(message.attachments[0],
                                     onAttachmentLoaded, errorCb);
        }
    }
}
```

The preceding code also downloads the message attachments using the `loadMessageAttachment()` method with an array of attachments (with valid file paths) as a parameter.

Managing Messages

To update a message in the storage, use the `updateMessages()` method. The method takes an array of `Message` objects as a parameter. You'll pass in the array of objects that were returned by `findMessage()`:

```
function onMessageFound(messages)
{
    messages[0].isRead = true;
    emailService.messageStorage.updateMessages(messages, onMessageUpdated, onError);
}
```

The `isRead` attribute of the first `Message` object in the given array is updated to true.

To delete a message from the message storage, use the `removeMessages()` method:

```
function onMessageFound(messages)
{
    smsService.messagingStorage.removeMessages(messages, onMessageRemoved, onError);
}
```

In the case of e-mail, you need to synchronize e-mail messages to an e-mail server. To synchronize all account folders, use the `sync()` method:

```
var gEmailService = null;
function onServiceFound(services)
{
    gEmailService = services[0];
    gEmailService.sync(serviceSynced, null, 30);
}

tizen.messaging.getMessageServices("messaging.email", onServiceFound);
```

To synchronize a specific folder, use the `syncFolder()` method. In the following example, only folders containing `"INBOX"` in their name are synchronized:

```
function onFolderFound(folders)
{
    for (var i = 0; i < folders.length; i++)
    {
        emailService.syncFolder(folders[i], onFolderSync, null, 30);
    }
};

var filter = new tizen.AttributeFilter("name", "CONTAINS", "INBOX");
emailService.messageStorage.findFolders(filter, onFolderFound));
```

E-MAIL CLIENT EXAMPLE

In this section, you'll learn how to write a simple e-mail client that sends and receives e-mail messages. Before creating a Tizen Web project, start the Emulator or your device and set the e-mail configuration in the Settings Menu as shown in Figure 8-1. The e-mail settings menu can be reached from Tizen Home ➪ Settings ➪ Accounts. You can check your settings with the preloaded e-mail client application.

FIGURE 8-1

Create a single-page application after selecting Tizen Web UI Framework as shown in Figure 8-2. The name of the project is **EmailClient.**

The first thing you need to do is set your app's privileges. Add the message read and write privileges to `config.xml` as discussed at the beginning of this chapter (see Figure 8-3).

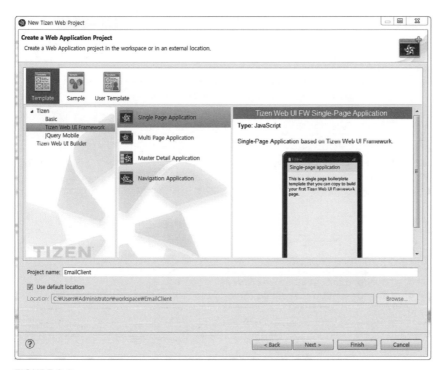

FIGURE 8-2

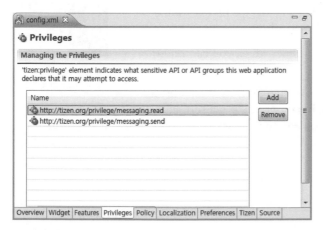

FIGURE 8-3

The first screen of the EmailClient shows some buttons on the header and e-mail lists. Open `index.html` and add the following code within the `<body></body>` tags, replacing the HTML that was automatically generated by the template:

```html
<div data-role="page" id="main">
 <div data-role="header" data-position="fixed" id="header">
  <h1>
   <span id="title">Inbox</span> <a href="#folders" data-rel="popup"
    data-role="button" data-icon="arrow-d"></a>
  </h1>
   <div data-role="button" data-icon="rename" class="naviframe-button"
    id=btn_compose></div>
   <div data-role="button" data-icon="refresh" class="naviframe-button"
                        onclick="getEmailMessages()"></div>
 </div>
 <!-- /header -->

 <div data-role="content">
  <ul data-role="listview" id="listview">
  </ul>
 </div>
 <!-- /content -->

 <!-- context popup -->
 <div id="folders" data-role="popup">
  <ul data-role="listview">
    <li><a href="#" id="cp_inbox">Inbox</a></li>
    <li><a href="#" id="cp_drafts">Drafts</a></li>
    <li><a href="#" id="cp_sentbox">Sentbox</a></li>
  </ul>
 </div>

</div>
<!-- /page -->
```

Save the `index.html` file and run the application. You will see a screen like the one shown in Figure 8-4. If you click the down arrow button next to Inbox, a context pop-up appears. The HTML file invokes some JavaScript functions that you haven't implemented yet.

You'll add the JavaScript code to the `main.js` file, which you can find in the `/js` folder of your project.

First, implement the `getEmailMessages()` function for the refresh button. To get e-mail messages, you should get the Email service, synchronise folders, and retrieve e-mail messages, as shown in the following code:

```javascript
var gEmailService = null;
var gMessages = null;
var gFolderId = 1;
var gSyncOpId = null;

function onError(err) {
    console.log("Error: " + err.message);
}
```

FIGURE 8-4

```javascript
function makeListItem(id, mainText, subText) {
    return '<li class="ui-li-has-multiline" id="' + id
        + '"><a href="#details">' + mainText
        + '<span class="ui-li-text-sub">' + subText + '</span></a></li>';
}

function onMessageFound(messages) {
    var str = "";

    gMessages = messages;
    console.log("onMessageFound");

    for ( var i = 0; i < messages.length; i++) {
      str += makeListItem(i, messages[i].subject, messages[i].from
          + " email(s)");
    }

    $("#listview").html(str).trigger("create").listview("refresh");
    $('#listview').delegate('li', 'click', function() {
      showEmailDetail($(this).attr("id"));
    });
}

function onSync() {
    console.log("Synchronisation succeeded");
    gSyncOpId = null;
    var filter = new tizen.AttributeFilter("folderId", "EXACTLY", gFolderId);
    gEmailService.messageStorage.findMessages(filter, onMessageFound, onError);
}

function getEmailMessages() {
    if (gSyncOpId) {
      console.log("Sync stop");
      gEmailService.stopSync(gSyncOpId);
      gSyncOpId = null;
    }

    console.log("Sync all started");
    gSyncOpId = gEmailService.sync(onSync, onError, 20);
    console.log("Waiting new messages");

}

function initEmailService() {

    function onMessageServiceFound(services) {
if (services.length == 0) {
        alert("No Email MessageServices found. Check Privileges.");
        return;
      }

      gEmailService = services[0];
      console.log("Email service retrieved");
    }
```

```
    try {
      tizen.messaging.getMessageServices("messaging.email",
        onMessageServiceFound);
    } catch (exc) {
      alert("getMessageServices exc: " + exc.name + ":" + exc.message);
    }
  }
```

`onError()` is an error callback for messaging service function calls. For simplicity, one error callback is shared between functions and it just writes error messages out to the console. `makeListItem()` adds the e-mail subject and sender as items of the list view in the HTML file.

The `onMessageFound()` callback is called when e-mail messages are successfully retrieved. `onSync()` is called when synchronisation between the external e-mail server and the local e-mail message storage has completed.

`getEmailMessages()` is called when the refresh icon in the header is clicked as specified in the HTML file. Because `getEmailMessages()` uses the e-mail message service, `initEmailService()` must be called at the beginning of application execution:

```
//Initialise function
var init = function () {
    …
    initEmailService();
    …
}
```

The preceding function is called when the application starts, and you can add it to the initialisation code which is already in `main.js`. Now if you execute the EmailClient application and click the refresh button, you'll see the screen shown in Figure 8-5.

To see details of e-mail content, add the following HTML code to the `<body></body>` section of `index.html`:

FIGURE 8-5

```
<div data-role="page" id="details" data-add-back-btn="true">
 <div data-role="header" data-position="fixed">
  <h1>Details</h1>
 </div>
 <div data-role="content">
  <ul data-role="listview">
  <li><label for="detail-from">From</label> <label
      id="detail-from"></label></li>
  <li><label for="detail-sub">Subject</label> <label
      id="detail-sub"></label></li>
  <li><label>Body</label> <textarea readonly cols="40" rows="8"
      id="detail-body" style="height: 300px"></textarea></li>
  </ul>
 </div>
 <div data-role="footer" data-position="fixed"></div>
</div>
```

The following JavaScript code shows the details of the selected e-mail when a list view item is clicked, as shown in Figure 8-6. For simplicity, it is implemented to show the body of the message as plaintext:

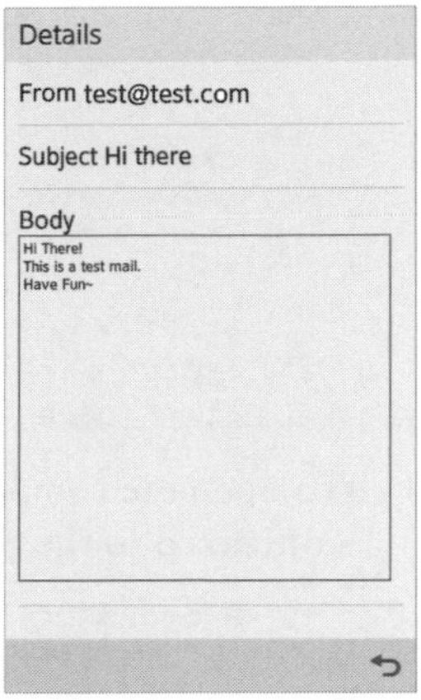

```javascript
function showEmailDetail(id) {
    function onEmailFindMessagesSuccess(messages) {
        if (messages.length == 0) {
            alert("The last email of the message not found");
            return;
        }

        var email = messages[0];

        $("#detail-from").text(email.from);
        $('#detail-sub').text(email.subject);

        try {
            console.log("email.body.loaded:" + email.body.loaded);
            if (email.body.loaded) {
                console.log("email body already loaded");
                console.log("plain:" + email.body.plainBody);
                $("#detail-body").val(email.body.plainBody);
            } else {
                console.log("email body about to load");
                gEmailService.loadMessageBody(email, function(message) {
                    console.log("email body just loaded");
                    console.log("plain:" + message.body.plainBody);
                    $("#detail-body").val(message.body.plainBody);
                }, onError);
            }
        } catch (exc) {
            alert("showEmailDetail failed: " + exc.message);
        }
    }

    console.log("lastMessageId = " + gMessages[id].id);
    gEmailService.messageStorage.findMessages(new tizen.AttributeFilter("id",
                    "EXACTLY", "" + gMessages[id].id), onEmailFindMessagesSuccess,
                    onError);
}
```

Details

From test@test.com

Subject Hi there

Body

Hi There!
This is a test mail.
Have Fun~

FIGURE 8-6

The e-mail compose page is very similar to the details page. The compose page has a destination e-mail address, subject and body fields, and send/save buttons on the footer:

```html
<div data-role="page" id="compose" data-add-back-btn="true">
 <div data-role="header" data-position="fixed">
  <h1>Compose</h1>
 </div>
 <div data-role="content">
  <ul data-role="listview">
   <li><label for="new-mail">Email</label> <input type="text"
    style="color: black;" id="new-mail" value="your@email.com" /></li>
   <li><label for="new-sub">Subject</label> <input type="text"
    style="color: black;" id="new-sub" value="Test Subject" /></li>
```

```
      <li><label for="new-body">Body</label> <textarea cols="40"
        rows="8" id="new-body" style="height: 150px"></textarea></li>
     </ul>
    </div>
    <div data-role="footer" data-position="fixed">
     <div id="send" data-role="button" onclick="sendMessage()">Send</div>
     <div id="save" data-role="button" onclick="saveMessage()">Save</div>
    </div>
   </div>
   <!-- /page -->
```

To open the compose page, shown in Figure 8-7, the page needs to be
connected to the compose icon in the first list view page in main.js:

```
$(document).one("pagecreate", "#main", function() {
        $("#header").on("vclick", "#btn_compose", function() {
                console.log("compose page");
                $.mobile.changePage('#compose', {
                        transition : "flip"
                });
        });
});
```

FIGURE 8-7

The following functions send and save the composed messages. The
sendMessage() function sends the e-mail message and saveMessage()
saves the message as a draft:

```
function sendMessage() {
    function onMessageSent(recipients) {
      alert("EMAIL sent successfully");
      console.log("The EMAIL has been sent");
      history.back();
    }

    console.log("email compose:" + $("#new-mail").val() + " "
      + $("#new-sub").val() + " " + $("#new-body").val());

    var mailIds = new Array();
    mailIds[0] = $("#new-mail").val();
    var msg = new tizen.Message("messaging.email", {
            subject : $("#new-sub").val(),
            plainBody : $("#new-body").val(),
            to : mailIds
    });

    try {
      gEmailService.sendMessage(msg, onMessageSent, onError);
    } catch (exc) {
      alert("sendMessage exc: " + exc.name + ":" + exc.message);
    }
}

function saveMessage() {
    function onMessageSaved(recipients) {
```

```
        alert("EMAIL saved successfully");
        console.log("The EMAIL has been saved");
        history.back();
    }

    console.log("email save:" + $("#new-mail").val() + " "
            + $("#new-sub").val() + " " + $("#new-body").val());
    var msg = new tizen.Message("messaging.email", {
            subject : $("#new-sub").val(),
            plainBody : $("#new-body").val(),
            to : $("#new-mail").val()
    });
    gEmailService.messageStorage.addDraftMessage(msg, onMessageSaved, onError);
}
```

Finally, the following code snippet shows the other folders in the content pop-up:

```
$(document).one("pagecreate", "#main", function() {
    ...
    $("#folders").on("vclick", "#cp_inbox", function() {
      $("#header h1 #title").text("Inbox");
      gFolderId = 1;
      getEmailMessages();
    });

    $("#folders").on("vclick", "#cp_sentbox", function() {
      $("#header h1 #title").text("Sentbox");
      gFolderId = 4;
      getEmailMessages();
    });

    $("#folders").on("vclick", "#cp_drafts", function() {
      $("#header h1 #title").text("Drafts");
      gFolderId = 3;
      getEmailMessages();
    });
});
```

SUMMARY

In this chapter you learned how to use the features of the Tizen Messaging API in your web applications. You now know how to create, send, and receive e-mail, SMS, and MMS messages in your code, how to add attachments to e-mail and MMS messages, and how to search the message storage. The second half of the chapter presented a complete example, taking you step by step through the creation of an e-mail application that can create, send, and receive messages. Now that you've built a fully functional e-mail client, you're all set to use this as the basis for your own messaging application.

Contacts and Calendars

➤ Mastering the address book

➤ Managing contacts

➤ Calendar events and tasks

➤ Alarms and recurring events

WROX.COM CODE DOWNLOADS FOR THIS CHAPTER

The wrox.com code downloads for this chapter are found at www.wrox.com/go/professionaltizen on the Download Code tab. The code is in the Chapter 9 download and named according to the names throughout the chapter.

In this chapter you'll learn how Tizen supports two of the most essential features of a mobile device: contacts and calendars. The W3C APIs don't provide the functionality to manipulate address books, contacts, and calendars, but Tizen web application developers can use the Contact and Calendar Device APIs to use these features in their applications.

You can write web applications to add, update, delete, and search for contacts in any of the device's address books, set up events and tasks in the calendar, create recurring events and alarms, and import and export in standard formats, such as vCard for events and iCalendar for calendar items. All of this, together with a lot of sample code, is included in this chapter.

SETTING PRIVILEGES

Accessing the address book and calendar on a device involves reading and writing the user's private data, and as such this functionality is protected by privileges. To use the Contact API to read from and write to address books, you need to add the following privileges to your config.xml file:

➤ `http://tizen.org/privilege/contact.write` — Allows the application to add, update, and delete contacts

➤ `http://tizen.org/privilege/contact.read` — Allows the application to read contacts

To use the Calendar API to read, write, update, and delete schedule and task information, the following privileges are required:

➤ `http://tizen.org/privilege/calendar.write` — Allows the application to create, update, and delete schedule and task information

➤ `http://tizen.org/privilege/calendar.read` — Allows the application to read schedule and task information

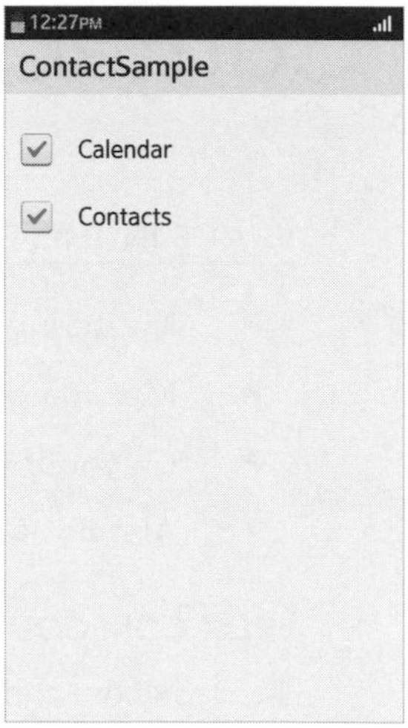

As shown in Figure 9-1, users can choose to allow or prevent the application from accessing their calendar and address book, either when the application is first launched or by selecting Settings ➪ Privacy ➪ [ApplicationName] on the device, if you added related privileged in the `config.xml` file. If the required privacy setting is not checked, the API will throw a `SecurityError` exception when you try to access the related privilege-protected API, even though the privilege is included in the `config.xml` file. More information about privileges can be found in Chapter 2.

THE CONTACT API

The Contact API is responsible for managing contacts and address books and enables you to add, delete, update, and search for contacts, manage groups of contacts, and import and export contact information in vCard format. You can monitor the address book for changes and take advantage of the `Person` object, which makes it easy to manage multiple contact entries that refer to the same person. You'll find sample code to demonstrate all of this functionality in the following sections.

FIGURE 9-1

Address Book

An address book is a container of contacts. Contact information can be accessed through the `AddressBook` interface. Tizen provides a default address book, and other address books are generally created for different services, such as Facebook or cloud-based e-mail providers. You can retrieve address books using the `ContactManager` interface, which is accessed from the `tizen.contact` object. The following address book information can be retrieved:

➤ The default address book

➤ All address books, including the default and other address books

➤ The unified address book, which contains all contacts in all address books

> **NOTE** *You can create a new address book only with the native framework APIs, not by using the Contact API in a web application. Therefore, if your web application needs to create a new address book, you will need to build a hybrid application, combining web and native applications, and use the* Tizen::Social::AddressbookManager *API in the native application to create a new address book. Full source code for an example hybrid application can be found in Chapter 19.*

Getting Address Books

The default address book, provided for the device's preloaded contact application, is the one that most applications will make use of. Retrieving the default address book is simple, as shown in Listing 9-1.

LISTING 9-1: Getting the default address book (addressbook-sample.js)

```
function getDefaultAddressbooks()
{
        addressBook = tizen.contact.getDefaultAddressBook();
}
```

To get all address books, use the getAddressBooks() function and define a success callback, which will be passed an array of AddressBook objects. As Listing 9-2 shows, you should also define an error callback, which in our sample logs any errors to the console.

LISTING 9-2: Getting all address books (addressbook-sample.js)

```
var addressBook;

function allAddressBooksCallback(addressBooks)
{
        if (addressBooks.length > 0)
        {
           for(i = 0; i < addressBooks.length; i++)
           {
                   addressBook = addressBooks[i];
                   console.log(addressBook.id);
                   console.log(addressBook.name);
                   console.log(addressBook.readOnly);
           }
        }
}

function errorCallback(error)
{
        console.log(error.name + ": " + error.message);
}

function getAllAddressbooks()
{
        tizen.contact.getAddressBooks(allAddressBooksCallback, errorCallback);
}
```

You can get all contacts on the device, regardless of which address book contains them, by calling getUnifiedAddressBook(). This returns all contacts from all address books combined into one logical address book as shown in Listing 9-3.

LISTING 9-3: Getting the unified address book (addressbook-sample.js)

```
function getUnifiedAddressbook()
{
        addressBook = tizen.contact.getUnifiedAddressBook();
}
```

The AddressBook interface defines the attributes shown in Table 9-1 and contains methods to add, update, or remove contact information.

TABLE 9-1: Attributes of the AddressBook Interface

ATTRIBUTE	DATA TYPE	DESCRIPTION
id	AddressBookId	Address book ID
name	DOMString	Address book name
readOnly	boolean	True if the address book is read-only

Contact groups are also managed with the methods defined in the AddressBook interface, and each address book maintains its own list of groups.

Contacts

A Contact object is used to contain a person's contact information, including addresses, phone numbers, e-mail addresses, and other personal information such as birthdays and anniversaries. Contacts can be imported and exported in vCard format, as defined in the RFC 2426 vCard MIME Directory Profile for exchanging contacts. Contacts are managed by the AddressBook interface and each contact has an ID which is assigned to it after it has been successfully added to the specified address book. The defined Contact attributes are shown in Table 9-2.

TABLE 9-2: Attributes of the Contact Interface

ATTRIBUTE	DATA TYPE	DESCRIPTION
id	ContactId	Contact ID
personId	PersonId	Person ID
addressBookId	AddressBookId	ID of the address book ID that includes the contact

`lastUpdated`	`Date`	Last updated timestamp
`isFavorite`	`boolean`	True if the contact is in the favourites This is associated with the `isFavorite` attribute of the `Person` interface
`name`	`ContactName`	Contact name
`addresses`	`ContactAddress[]`	Multiple addresses
`photoURI`	`DOMString`	URI of the contact's picture
`phoneNumber`	`ContactPhoneNumber[]`	Multiple phone numbers
`emails`	`ContactEmailAddress[]`	Multiple e-mail addresses
`birthday`	`Date`	Birthday
`anniversaries`	`ContactAnniversary[]`	Multiple anniversaries
`organizations`	`ContactOrganization[]`	Multiple organisations
`notes`	`DOMString`	Notes
`Urls`	`ContactWebSite[]`	URLs such as the contact's blog or related web pages
`ringtoneURI`	`DOMString`	Specified ringtone for the contact
`groupIds`	`ContactGroupId[]`	Group IDs for the groups that contain this contact; the contact can be included in multiple groups

Adding Contacts

Adding a contact to an address book is shown in the following code. After creating a new `Contact` object with the name and phone number information, call the `add()` method of the `AddressBook` interface as shown in Listing 9-4.

LISTING 9-4: Adding contacts (contact-sample.js)

```
var contact1 = new tizen.Contact({
            name: new tizen.ContactName ({firstName: 'John', lastName: 'Smith'}),
            phoneNumbers: [new tizen.ContactPhoneNumber('0123456789')]
```

continues

LISTING 9-4 *(continued)*

```
                });

var contact2= new tizen.Contact({
                name: new tizen.ContactName ({firstName: 'Joan', lastName: 'Snow'}),
                phoneNumbers: [new tizen.ContactPhoneNumber('1234567890')]
            });

function addContact()
{
        addressBook = tizen.contact.getDefaultAddressBook();
        addressBook.add(contact1);
        addressBook.add(contact2);
}
```

The `AddressBook` interface provides a batch method for adding multiple contacts at the same time. The success callback passed to the `addBatch()` method will be sent an array of contacts successfully added to the address book, as Listing 9-5 shows.

LISTING 9-5: Adding contacts with a batch method (contact-sample.js)

```
function contactBatchAddedCallback(contacts)
{
        console.log('addBatch() is successful! '
           + contacts.length + 'contacts are added.');

        searchContactList();
}

function addBatchContact()
{
        addressBook = tizen.contact.getDefaultAddressBook();
        try    {
                addressBook.addBatch([contact1, contact2],
                   contactBatchAddedCallback, errorCallback);
        } catch (error) {
                console.log('The error is occured while adding batch contacts. '
                   + error.name + ": " + error.message);
        }
}
```

Searching for Contacts

Searching is a frequently used function in applications that manage contacts. You can search for contacts in a specific group or with a specified name using filters, a feature enabled by the `AbstractFilter` interface. The attributes defined in the `AbstractFilter` interface are shown in Table 9-3.

TABLE 9-3: Attributes of the AbstractFilter Interface

ATTRIBUTE	DATA TYPE	DESCRIPTION
attributeName	DOMString	Name of the object attribute to be used for filtering (e.g., `'name.firstname'`).
matchFlag	FilterMatchFlag	Comparison operator for filtering: `EXACTLY` (default value, case sensitive) — The attribute value matches exactly. `FULLSTRING` (case insensitive) — The attribute value is matched with the whole string, but case is irrelevant. `CONTAINS` (case insensitive) — The attribute value contains the specific string. `STARTSWITH` (case insensitive) — The attribute value starts with the specific string. `ENDSWITH` (case insensitive) — The attribute value ends with the specific string. `EXISTS` — The specific attribute exists.
matchValue	any	Value to be used for filtering.

By using a match flag, you retrieve exactly the range of values you want. If you don't set a match flag, EXACTLY will be used by default.

The example shown in Listing 9-6 searches for contacts with "Jo" in the first name. Note that you set the abstract filter with the firstname attribute, the match flag to "CONTAINS", and the search keyword to "Jo." The search result is retrieved in the success callback as an array of contacts.

LISTING 9-6: Searching for contacts which contain "Jo" (contact-sample.js)

```
var contactResult;
function contactListSuccessCallback(contacts)
{

        console.log('Number of searched contacts: ' + contacts.length);
        if (contacts.length > 0)
        {
                for(i = 0; i < contacts.length; i++)
                {
                        contactResult = contacts[i];
                        console.log('contact [' + contactResult.id + ']: '
                                        + contactResult.name.firstName + ' '
                                        + contactResult.name.lastName);
```

continues

LISTING 9-6 *(continued)*

```
            }
        }
    }

function searchContactList()
{
        var filter = new tizen.AttributeFilter('name.firstName', 'CONTAINS', 'Jo');
        var sortMode = new tizen.SortMode('name.firstName', 'ASC');
        addressBook.find(contactListSuccessCallback, errorCallback, filter, sortMode);
    }
```

Updating Contacts

You can update contacts in the address book synchronously or asynchronously. A simple contact update is shown in Listing 9-7. The address book updates the name of the specified contact.

LISTING 9-7: Updating a contact (contact-sample.js)

```
function updateContact(contact)
{
        contact.name.firstName = "Johnson";
        addressBook.update(contact);
        console.log('updated contact [' + contact.id + ']: '
                        + contact.name.firstName + ' ' + contact.name.lastName);
    }
```

When you need to update several contacts, use the updateBatch() method of the AddressBook interface and define success and error callbacks. Contacts can also be removed from an address book synchronously using the remove() method or asynchronously using removeBatch().

> **NOTE** *These batch operations don't provide any progress information, and the success and error callbacks will be invoked only when the operation is complete. For that reason, it's better to perform batch adding, updating, and removal in batches of around 10 contacts for each operation. However, you should use the batch methods wherever possible, so that your application continues to be responsive while these operations are being processed.*

Managing Groups of Contacts

Organising contacts into groups makes them easier to manage and is more convenient for users. Groups are added, updated, or removed from a specific address book and referred to using a group ID. The addGroups() function in Listing 9-8 shows how to add three groups, named Family, Work, and Friend, to the default address book and log the group ID of each new group to the console when it's added successfully. The removeGroups() function shows how to remove each group.

LISTING 9-8: Adding and removing groups (contact-sample.js)

```javascript
var groups = ['Family',
              'Work',
              'Friend'];

function addGroups()
{
      addressBook = tizen.contact.getDefaultAddressBook();

      for (i = 0, j = 0; i < groups.length; i++, j++)
      {
            try {
                  var group = new tizen.ContactGroup(groups[i]);
                  addressBook.addGroup(group);
                  console.log("Group[" + group.id + ']: ' + group.name);
                  groupIds[j] = group.id;
                  console.log("Group Id[" + j + ']: ' + groupIds[j]);
            } catch (error) {
                  console.log(error.name + ": " + error.message);
            }
      }

      var currentGroups = addressBook.getGroups();
      console.log('Number of the current group: ' + currentGroups.length);
      }

function removeGroups()
{
      addressBook = tizen.contact.getDefaultAddressBook();
      var currentGroups = addressBook.getGroups();

      for (i = 0; i < currentGroups.length; i++)
      {
            try {
                  addressBook.removeGroup(currentGroups[i].id);
                  console.log("Removed group[" + currentGroups[i].id + ']: '
                        + currentGroups[i].name);
            } catch (error) {
                  console.log(error.name + ": " + error.message);
            }
      }

      var currentGroups = addressBook.getGroups();
      console.log('Number of the current group: ' + currentGroups.length);
}
```

Importing and Exporting Contacts in vCard Format

The Contact API provides methods to import or export contacts in the vCard 3.0 format. You can create a `Contact` instance from a vCard using the code shown in Listing 9-9.

LISTING 9-9: Adding a vCard format contact (contact-sample.js)

```
function importingVcard()
{
        addressBook = tizen.contact.getDefaultAddressBook();
        var currentGroups = addressBook.getGroups();
        var vcardContact = null;

        try
        {
                vcardFormatContact = new tizen.Contact("BEGIN:VCARD\n"+
                                      "VERSION:3.0\n"+
                                      "N:Rollence;Julia\n"+
                                      "FN:Julia Rollence\n"+
                                      "ORG:ABCD Co.\n"+
                                      "TITLE:Writer\n"+
                                      "TEL;WORK:(111) 234-5678\n"+
                                      "TEL;HOME:(111) 876-5432\n"+
                                      "EMAIL;WORK;PREF:julia.rollence@abcd.com\n"+
                                      "END:VCARD");

                addressBook.add(vcardFormatContact);
                console.log("Contact was added with ID " + vcardFormatContact.id);
        } catch (error) {
                console.log(error.name + ": " + error.message);
        }
}
```

A `Contact` can also be exported as a vCard string. Listing 9-10 shows how a list of contacts can be converted to vCard format.

LISTING 9-10: Exporting contacts as the vCard format (contact-sample.js)

```
function exportingVcard(tempContacts)
{
        var vcards = [];
        for(i = 0; i < tempContacts.length; i++)
        {
                try {
                        vcards[i] = tempContacts[i].convertToString("VCARD_30");
                } catch (error)     {
                        console.log(error.name + ": " + error.message);
                }
        }

}
```

Monitoring Address Book Changes

To be notified when another application makes a change to an address book, such as adding a contact or changing contact information, you can register to receive address book change notifications by adding an address book change listener. Call the `addChangeListener()` method of the address book you want to watch, and pass an `AddressBookChangeCallback` object containing the callback functions to be invoked when contacts are added, updated, or removed. Listing 9-11 shows how to start watching for changes in the default address book.

LISTING 9-11: Monitoring the address book changes (contact-sample.js)

```
var listenerId = 0;

var listener = {
        // If contacts are added
        oncontactsadded: function (contacts)
        {
                console.log('Added contacts: ' + contacts.length);
        },

        // If contacts are updated
        oncontactsupdated: function (contacts)
        {
                console.log('Updated contacts: ' + contacts.lenqth);
        },

        // If contacts are deleted
        oncontactsremoved: function (ids)
        {
                console.log('Removed contacts:' + ids.length);
        }
};

function addListener()
{
        addressBook = tizen.contact.getDefaultAddressBook();
        listenerId = addressBook.addChangeListener(listener, errorCallback);
        console.log('Listener ID: ' + listenerId);
}
```

To stop monitoring the specific address book, call `removeChangeListener()` as shown in Listing 9-12.

LISTING 9-12: Unmonitoring the address book (contact-sample.js)

```
function removeListener()
{
        addressBook = tizen.contact.getDefaultAddressBook();
        try {
                addressBook.removeChangeListener(listenerId);
        } catch (error) {
                console.log(error.name + ": " + error.message);
        }
}
```

Person Objects

The person concept in the Contact API may be unfamiliar to you and it should not be confused with a contact. For example, suppose that you have added several contacts to the address book and you realise that two of the contacts actually contain information for the same friend, "Tom". There's only one "Tom" but he has two contact entries in the address book. The functionality of the Person object is designed to handle this; it's an aggregation of one or more contacts associated with the same person.

Figure 9-2 shows the relationship between Contact and Person objects. In this figure, there is some information, perhaps an e-mail address, which is common to both Contact2 and Contact3, and this diagram indicates that both these contacts relate to Person2.

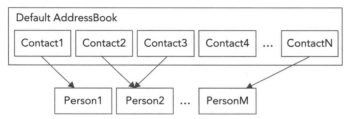

FIGURE 9-2

A Person cannot be created directly. It is created automatically by the Tizen platform when a new Contact is added to the address book. A Contact and a Person are linked to each through the PersonId of the Contact.

Getting Persons

Person information is accessed using the ContactManager interface. You can get the current person list by calling the find() method and supplying a success callback function. Results can be filtered based on a specified search filter or you can retrieve all Person objects. Listing 9-13 shows how to retrieve all Person objects from the contact database

LISTING 9-13: Getting persons (contact-sample.js)

```
function personListSuccessCallback(persons)
{
        console.log('Number of persons: ' + persons.length);
        for (i = 0; i < persons.length; i++)
        {
                console.log('Person id: ' + persons[i].id);
        }
}

function getPersons()
{
        tizen.contact.find(personListSuccessCallback, errorCallback);
}
```

Updating Persons

You can change the favourite flag, photo URI, ringtone URI, and `displaycontactId` for a `Person`. After updating `Person` information, call the `update()` method of the `ContactManager` interface as shown in Listing 9-14.

LISTING 9-14: Updating person information (contact-sample.js)

```
function updatePerson(person)
{
        person.displayName = true;
        try
        {
                tizen.contact.update(person);
        } catch (error)
        {
                console.log(error.name + ": " + error.message);
        }
}
```

Merging Persons

Whenever a new `Contact` is added to the address book, `Person` information is created at the same time. Each `Contact` has a related `personID` and each `Person` is linked to one or more contacts. If each `Person` is linked to only one `Contact`, then the `Person` list will be the same as the contact list in the address book.

If some contacts are thought to relate to the same person, you can merge those related persons into one. Listing 9-15 shows how to merge the `Person` information of two contacts: `contacts[0]` and `contacts[1]`. The `personId` related to `contacts[1]` is merged with the `personId` connected to `contacts[0]`. The `Person` with the `personId` which was previously related to `contacts[1]` is deleted automatically because there is no longer a contact related to it.

LISTING 9-15: Merging contacts as a person (contact-sample.js)

```
function mergePerson(contacts)
{
        originPerson = tizen.contact.get(contacts[0].personId);
        originPerson.link(contacts[1].personId);
}
```

Figure 9-3 shows the relationship between contacts and persons and should make the concept easier to understand.

➤ You start with the same number of contact and person records.

➤ If Person4 is merged with Person2, Person4 is deleted and the related person ID of Contact4 is changed to Person2.

➤ If Contact1 is removed, Person1 is removed too because there is no longer a contact with a person ID of Person1.

➤ If Contact8 is added, Person8 is created.

➤ If Contact4 is removed, Person2 remains because its related contact, Contact2, still exists.

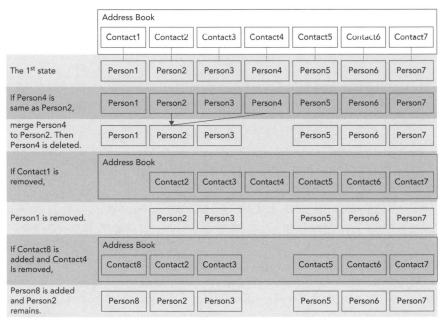

FIGURE 9-3

To receive change events for person information, register a callback with the addChangeListener() method of the ContactManager interface.

THE CALENDAR API

The calendar is an essential feature for scheduling applications, and you can use it in Tizen web applications through the Calendar Device API. Tizen provides default event calendars and task calendars, and other calendars can be created from within native applications using the Tizen::Social::Calendarbook class. To create a new calendar from within a web application, you need to create a hybrid application, combining a web application and native application, and get the native application to do the work.

The Calendar object contains a set of events or tasks depending on the calendar type. Figure 9-4 shows the two calendar types.

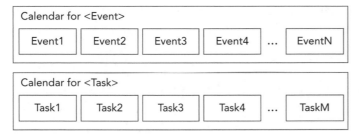

FIGURE 9-4

Each event or task can be added, updated, removed, and searched using the methods defined in the `Calendar` interface. To retrieve the default calendar, use the `getDefaultCalendar()` method, as shown in Listing 9-16. In this code the default event calendar is returned.

LISTING 9-16: Getting the default calendar (calendar-sample.js)

```
function getDefaultCalendar()
{
    var eventCalendar = tizen.calendar.getDefaultCalendar('EVENT');
    console.log('Calendar ID: ' + eventCalendar.id);
    console.log('Calendar name: ' + eventCalendar.name);
}
```

You can check the calendar's ID and name in the console view. You can also retrieve a calendar by specifying the calendar ID:

CONSOLE VIEW

```
js/calendar-sample.js (4) :Calendar ID: 1
js/calendar-sample.js (5) :Calendar name: Default event calendar
```

If you want to access all events or tasks regardless of which calendar they're in, you can use `getUnifiedCalendar()`. This returns a `Calendar` instance containing all events and tasks in all calendars on the device as shown in Listing 9-17.

LISTING 9-17: Getting the unified calendar (calendar-sample.js)

```
function getUnifiedCalendar()
{
    var eventCalendar = tizen.calendar.getUnifiedCalendar('EVENT');
    console.log('Calendar ID: ' + eventCalendar.id);
    console.log('Calendar name: ' + eventCalendar.name);
}
```

The `Calendar` API provides the `CalendarItem` interface, which defines a set of attributes that are common to both events and tasks. Some of these attributes are used differently depending on whether the item is an event or a task. See Table 9-4 for more information about how these attributes are used for events and tasks.

`CalendarItem` is a parent of `CalendarEvent` and `CalendarTask`, which define attributes that are specific to events and tasks, respectively.

TABLE 9-4: Attributes of the CalendarItem Interface

ATTRIBUTE	DATA TYPE	DESCRIPTION
id	CalenderItemId	ID of the calendar item. It indicates the event or task item ID
calendarId	CalendarId	ID of the calendar in which the calendar item is included
lastModificationDate	TZDate	Last modified date and time
description	DOMString	Detailed description of the event or task
summary	DOMString	Summary or subject for the event or task
isAllDay	boolean	Set to true for an all-day event or task
startDate	TZDate	Start date and time for the event or task
duration	TimeDuration	Duration of the event or task; the millisecond unit is ignored
location	DOMString	The event or task location
geolocation	SimpleCoordinates	Longitude and latitude of the location for the event or task
organizer	DOMString	Organiser name
visibility	CalendarItemVisibility	Visibility level for the event or task: PUBLIC, PRIVATE, CONFIDENTIAL
status	CalendarItemStatus	Status for the event or task: For the event — TENTATIVE, CONFIRMED, CANCELLED For the task — NEEDS_ACTION, IN_ PROCESS, COMPLETED, CANCELLED
priority	CalendarItemPriority	Priority level for the event or task: HIGH, MEDIUM, LOW
alarms	CalendarAlarm[]	Alarm list for the event or task
categories	DomString[]	Category list for the event or task; it can be used as a search condition
attendees	CalendarAttendee[]	Attendee list for the event. It includes the following: URI — Often used to store an e-mail of the form mailto:name@domain.com

		Attendee name
		Role — `REQ_PARTICIPANT`, `OPT_PARTICIPANT`, `NON_PARTICIPANT`, `CHAIR`
		Attendee status — `PENDING`, `ACCEPTED`, `DECLINED`, `TENTATIVE`, `DELEGATED`, `COMPLETED`, `IN_PROCESS`
		RSVP — Attendee's participation status reply
		Type — `INDIVIDUAL`, `GROUP`, `RESOURCE`, `ROOM`, `UNKNOWN`
		Group — Participant's group
		DelegatorURI — URI of the person who has delegated his or her participation to this attendee
		DelegateURI — URI of the attendee to whom the person has delegated his or her participation
		ContactRef — Participant's reference

Calendar Events

A `CalendarEvent` occurs at a specified time of day for a given duration and has attributes, including its subject, description, end date, and location name. In addition to the attributes inherited from `CalendarItem`, the `CalendarEvent` interface includes some attributes that are specific to an event. One of these attributes is the `recurrenceRule` that is used to define recurring events. You'll find out more about recurring events later in this chapter. We'll also demonstrate how to add an alarm to an event or task.

Table 9-5 shows these additional attributes.

TABLE 9-5: CalendarEvent-specific Attributes

ATTRIBUTE	DATA TYPE	DESCRIPTION
`isDetached`	`boolean`	Flag if the event recurs and is saved to the calendar
`endDate`	`TZDate`	End date and time for the event
`availability`	`EventAvailability`	Availability status: `BUSY`, `FREE`
`recurrenceRule`	`CalendarRecurrenceRule`	Recurrence rule for the event

Calendar Tasks

Tasks are similar to events but have some attributes specific to them. Table 9-6 shows these additional attributes.

TABLE 9-6: CalendarTask-specific Attributes

ATTRIBUTE	DATA TYPE	DESCRIPTION
dueDate	TZDate	Due date and time for the task. Milliseconds are ignored.
completedDate	TZDate	Date and time that the task is completed. The default value is null, meaning the task is not completed yet.
progress	Unsigned short	Completion percentage for the task (0–100).

Listing 9-18 shows how to get the default task calendar and add a task.

LISTING 9-18: Adding a task (task-sample.js)

```
var task1 = new tizen.CalendarTask({description: "Prepare for guests",
    summary: "Home Party",
    startDate: new tizen.TZDate(2014, 5, 1, 17, 0),
    visibility: 'PUBIC',
    priority: 'HIGH',
    categories: ['Home'],
    dueDate: new tizen.TZDate(2014, 5, 5, 9, 0)
});

function taskResultListCallback(tasks)
{
    console.log('taskResultListCallback() is called.');
    var taskCalendar = tizen.calendar.getDefaultCalendar('TASK');

    for(i = 0; i < tasks.length; i++)
    {
        console.log('Task[' + tasks[i].id + ']: ' + tasks[i].summary);
    }
}

function getTasks()
{
    var taskCalendar = tizen.calendar.getDefaultCalendar('TASK');
    taskCalendar.find(taskResultListCallback, errorCallback);
}

function addTask()
{
    var taskCalendar = tizen.calendar.getDefaultCalendar('TASK');
    try {
        taskCalendar.add(task1);
    } catch (error){
        console.log(error.name + ': ' + error.message);
    }
    console.log('Added task ID: ' + task1.id);
    getTasks();
}
```

The usage of events and tasks in the Calendar API is very similar except for a few attributes such as the `recurrenceRule`. The following section concentrates on calendar events, but much of the information can also be applied to tasks.

Adding Events

Events are added to a calendar using the `add()` method of the `Calendar` interface. Listing 9-19 shows how to add two events to the default event calendar. The first event is for a birthday; the second one is for a team meeting and includes some attendee information. A unique calendar event ID is assigned if the event is added successfully.

LISTING 9-19: Adding events (event-sample.js)

```javascript
var event1 = new tizen.CalendarEvent({description: "Joan's Birthday",
        summary: "Joan's Birthday",
        startDate: new tizen.TZDate(1990, 2, 27),
        isAllDay: true,
        visibility: 'PRIVATE',
        priority: 'HIGH',
        categories: ['Anniversary']
});

var attendee1 = new tizen.CalendarAttendee("mailto: grace@domain.com",
            {name: 'Grace', role: 'CHAIR'}
);

var attendee2 = new tizen.CalendarAttendee("mailto: joy@domain.com",
            {name: 'Joy', role: 'REQ_PARTICIPANT'}
);

var attendee3 = new tizen.CalendarAttendee("mailto: tom@domain.com",
            {name: 'Tom',
            role: 'OPT_PARTICIPANT'}
);

var event2 = new tizen.CalendarEvent({description:"Team meeting",
        summary:"Team meeting",
        startDate: new tizen.TZDate(2014, 6, 2),
        duration: new tizen.TimeDuration(1, 'HOURS'),
        visibility: 'CONFIDENTIAL',
        priority: 'HIGH',
        location:"Idea meeting room",
        categories: ['Work'],
        attendees: [attendee1, attendee2, attendee3]
});

function addEvent()
{
        var eventCalendar = tizen.calendar.getDefaultCalendar('EVENT');
        try {
```

continues

LISTING 9-19 *(continued)*

```
                eventCalendar.add(event1);
        } catch (error1){
                console.log(error1.name + ": " + error1.message);
        }
        console.log('Added event ID: ' + event1.id.uid);
        try {
                eventCalendar.add(event2);
        } catch (error2){
                console.log(error2.name + ": " + error2.message);
        }
        console.log('Added event ID: ' + event2.id.uid);
}
```

Rather than add events to the calendar one at a time, as shown in Listing 9-19, several events can be added at once using a batch method. Listing 9-20 shows how to add two events at once with the `addBatch()` method of the `Calendar` interface. When the batch operation is complete, either the success callback or the error callback will be invoked. If the events are successfully added, the success callback will be sent an array of the newly added events.

LISTING 9-20: Adding events with the batch method (event-sample.js)

```
function calendarAddBatchListCallback(calendarItems)
{
        var eventCalendar = tizen.calendar.getDefaultCalendar('EVENT');

        for(i = 0; i < calendarItems.length; i++)
        {
                console.log('Event[' + calendarItems[i].id.uid + ']: '
                    + calendarItems[i].summary);
        }
}

function errorCallback(error)
{
        console.log(error.name + ": " + error.message);
}

function addBatch()
{
        var eventCalendar = tizen.calendar.getDefaultCalendar('EVENT');
        try {
                eventCalendar.addBatch([event1, event2], calendarAddBatchListCallback,
                    errorCallback);
        } catch (error){
                console.log(error.name + ": " + error.message);
        }
}
```

You can also update and delete calendar events using the appropriate batch methods.

Getting Events

You can retrieve all events in a specified calendar by calling the find() method of the Calendar interface without setting a filter condition. Listing 9-21 shows you how.

LISTING 9-21: Getting all events (event-sample.js)

```
function calendarResultListCallback(calendarItems)
{
        var eventCalendar = tizen.calendar.getDefaultCalendar('EVENT');

        for(i = 0; i < calendarItems.length; i++)
        {
                console.log('Event[' + calendarItems[i].id.uid + ']: ' +
                    calendarItems[i].summary);
        }
}

function getEvents()
{
        var eventCalendar = tizen.calendar.getDefaultCalendar('EVENT');
        eventCalendar.find(calendarResultListCallback, errorCallback);
}
```

If you want to find events based on a specific condition, set an attribute filter. Listing 9-22 shows how to find events for which the priority is high. The search results will be sent to the success callback.

LISTING 9-22: Finding events with high priority (event-sample.js)

```
function findHighPriorityEvents()
{
        var eventCalendar = tizen.calendar.getDefaultCalendar('EVENT');
        var filter = new tizen.AttributeFilter('priority', 'CONTAINS', 'HIGH');
        var sortMode = new tizen.SortMode('summary', 'ASC');
        eventCalendar.find(calendarResultListCallback, errorCallback, filter, sortMode);
}
```

Updating Events

Calendar events can be updated using the update() method of the Calendar interface. To do so, you need to retrieve the calendar event, change the event information, and then call the update() method, as shown in Listing 9-23.

LISTING 9-23: Changing the event priority (event-sample.js)

```
function meetingEventCallback(meetingEvents)
{
        for(i = 0; i < meetingEvents.length; i++)
```

continues

LISTING 9-23 *(continued)*

```
        {
                console.log('Event[' + meetingEvents[i].id.uid + ']: ' +
                    meetingEvents[i].summary);
        }

        meetingEvents[0].priority = 'LOW';

        var eventCalendar = tizen.calendar.getDefaultCalendar('EVENT');
        eventCalendar.update(meetingEvents[0]);

        getEvents();
    }

    function updateEvent(event)
    {
        addEvent();

        var eventCalendar = tizen.calendar.getDefaultCalendar('EVENT');
        var filter = new tizen.AttributeFilter('summary', 'CONTAINS', 'meeting');
        eventCalendar.find(meetingEventCallback, errorCallback, filter);

    }
```

Creating Recurring Events

To create a recurring event you use the `CalendarRecurrenceRule` interface, whose attributes are shown in Table 9-7. The attributes of `CalendarRecurrenceRule` allow you to specify information such as the frequency with which the event recurs, the interval, and the end date. You can only create recurring events, not tasks.

TABLE 9-7: Attributes of the CalendarRecurrenceRule Interface

ATTRIBUTE	DATA TYPE	DESCRIPTION
frequency	RecurrenceRuleFrequency	Frequency of the recurrence: DAILY, WEEKLY, MONTHLY, YEARS.
interval	unsigned short	Interval for the frequency. The default value is 1 — e.g., if the frequency is WEEKLY and the interval is 2, the event will recur every two weeks.
untilDate	TZDate	End date for the recurrence event.
occurrenceCount	Long	Number of occurrences of the event.

daysOfTheWeek	ByDayValue[]	Days in the week on which the event will recur: MO, TU, WE, TH, FR, SA, SU.
setPositions	short[]	List of ordinal numbers for occurrences. It can be expressed as a positive or negative number (1–365 or -365–1) — e.g., if the frequency is MONTHLY, daysOfTheWeek is MO through FR, and setPosition is 1 and -1, then the event will recur the first week and the last week of the month.
exceptions	TZDate[]	List of dates and times when the event should not recur. Milliseconds are ignored.

Listing 9-24 shows how to set the recurrence of an event to once a year, such as a birthday.

LISTING 9-24: Setting a recurrence rule (event-sample.js)

```javascript
var recurrenceRule1 = new tizen.CalendarRecurrenceRule("YEARLY");

function birthdayEventCallback(birthdayEvents)
{
        var eventCalendar = tizen.calendar.getDefaultCalendar('EVENT');

        for(i = 0; i < birthdayEvents.length; i++)
        {
                console.log('Event[' + birthdayEvents[i].id.uid + ']: ' +
                    birthdayEvents[i].summary);
        }

        birthdayEvents[0].recurrenceRule = recurrenceRule1;
        eventCalendar.update(birthdayEvents[0]);
}

function addBirthdayRecurrence()
{
        addEvent();

        var eventCalendar = tizen.calendar.getDefaultCalendar('EVENT');
        var filter = new tizen.AttributeFilter('summary', 'CONTAINS', 'birthday');
        eventCalendar.find(birthdayEventCallback, errorCallback, filter);
}
```

Listing 9-25 shows how to make the event occur five times with weekly frequency. If this recurrence rule is added successfully, five instances of the event will exist internally.

LISTING 9-25: Setting a recurrence rule (event-sample.js)

```javascript
var recurrenceRule2 = new tizen.CalendarRecurrenceRule("WEEKLY", {occurrenceCount: 5});

var event2 = new tizen.CalendarEvent({description:"Team meeting",
    summary:"Team meeting",
    startDate: new tizen.TZDate(2014, 6, 2, 9, 0),
    duration: new tizen.TimeDuration(1, 'HOURS'),
    visibility: 'CONFIDENTIAL',
    priority: 'HIGH',
    location:"Idea meeting room",
    categories: ['Work'],
    attendees: [attendee1, attendee2, attendee3],
    recurrenceRule: recurrenceRule2
});

function addEvent()
{
    var eventCalendar = tizen.calendar.getDefaultCalendar('EVENT');
    eventCalendar.add(event2);
    console.log('Added event ID: ' + event2.id.uid);
}
```

When you need to change only some specific instances of a recurring event, use the
`expandRecurrence()` method of the `CalendarEvent` interface.

In the preceding example, `event2` starts on June 2, 2014, and repeats five times at weekly frequency.
If you only need to change the event information for those events scheduled between the June 8 and
June 17, find the recurrence event instances in the callback of `expandRecurrence()` and update
their information as required. Listing 9-26 shows you how.

LISTING 9-26: Changing the existing recurrence event for the specific period (event-sample.js)

```javascript
function someRecurrenceEventResult(events)
{
    console.log('Event count: ' + events.length);
    for(i = 0; i < events.length; i++)
    {
        console.log('Event[' + events[i].id.uid + ']: ' + events[i].summary);
    }
}

function meetingEventCallback(meetingEvents)
{
    var eventCalendar = tizen.calendar.getDefaultCalendar('EVENT');

    for(i = 0; i < meetingEvents.length; i++)
    {
        console.log('Event[' + meetingEvents[i].id.uid + ']: ' +
            meetingEvents[i].summary);
```

```
        }

        meetingEvents[0].expandRecurrence(new tizen.TZDate(2014, 6, 8),
            new tizen.TZDate(2014, 6, 17), someRecurrenceEventResult, errorCallback);
}

function updateThisMeeting()
{
        addEvent();

        var eventCalendar = tizen.calendar.getDefaultCalendar('EVENT');
        var filter = new tizen.AttributeFilter('summary', 'CONTAINS', 'meeting');
        eventCalendar.find(meetingEventCallback, errorCallback, filter);
}
```

Setting Alarms

Setting an alarm helps the user not to forget events or tasks. The alarm information is part of the `CalendarItem` attributes and is defined in the `CalendarAlarm` interface, whose attributes are described in Table 9-8. Multiple alarms can be attached to the same event or task, so you could show a reminder a few days before an event and then another a few hours before, for example.

TABLE 9-8: Attributes of the CalendarAlarm Interface

ATTRIBUTE	DATA TYPE	DESCRIPTION
absoluteDate	TZDate	The absolute date that the alarm should be triggered.
before	TimeDuration	Duration between when the event or task starts and when the alarm should be triggered. Note that `absoluteDate` and `before` are mutually exclusive.
method	AlarmMethod	Notification method: SOUND, DISPLAY.
description	DOMString	Alarm description. This should be defined if the alarm method is DISPLAY.

To add an alarm to play a sound 15 minutes before an event, see Listing 9-27.

LISTING 9-27: Setting an alarm (event-sample.js)

```
    var alarm1 = new tizen.CalendarAlarm(new tizen.TimeDuration(15, "MINS"), "SOUND");

    var event2 = new tizen.CalendarEvent({description:"Team meeting",
            summary:"Team meeting",
            startDate: new tizen.TZDate(2014, 6, 2, 9, 0),
            duration: new tizen.TimeDuration(1, 'HOURS'),
            visibility: 'CONFIDENTIAL',
```

continues

LISTING 9-27 *(continued)*

```
            priority: 'HIGH',
            location:"Idea meeting room",
            categories: ['Work'],
            attendees: [attendee1, attendee2, attendee3],
            recurrenceRule: recurrenceRule2,
            alarms:[alarm1]
});

function addEvent()
{
        var eventCalendar = tizen.calendar.getDefaultCalendar('EVENT');
        eventCalendar.add(event2);
        console.log('Added event ID: ' + event2.id.uid);
}
```

Converting Events to iCalendar Format

The `Calendar` API supports the iCalendar format 2.0 (RFC 5545) and you can convert calendar items to and from this format. Listing 9-28 shows you how to add a calendar event specified as an iCalendar format string. You can also convert and add items asynchronously using the `addBatch()` method.

LISTING 9-28: Converting events to the iCalendar format (event-sample.js)

```
var iCal = new tizen.CalendarEvent(
        "BEGIN:VCALENDAR\r\n" +
        "BEGIN:VEVENT\r\n" +
        "DTSTAMP:20140901T1500Z\r\n" +
        "DTSTART:20140903T150000Z\r\n" +
        "DTEND:20140903T190000Z\r\n" +
        "SUMMARY:Task check\r\n" +
        "CATEGORIES:BUSINESS\r\n" +
        "END:VEVENT\r\n" +
        "END:VCALENDAR", "ICALENDAR_20"
);

function convertEventResult(events)
{
        for(i = 0; i < events.length; i++)
        {
                console.log('Event[' + events[i].id.uid + ']: ' + events[i].summary);
        }

        var iCalEvent = events[0].convertToString("ICALENDAR_20");
        console.log(iCalEvent);

}

function convertEvent()
```

```
      {
                 var eventCalendar = tizen.calendar.getDefaultCalendar('EVENT');
                 eventCalendar.add(iCal);
                 eventCalendar.find(convertEventResult, errorCallback);
      }
```

SUMMARY

In this chapter you learned how your web application can make use of Tizen's Contact and Calendar APIs. Using code examples, you discovered how to manage contacts and address books using the Contact API and wrote code to add, delete, update, and find contacts based on a wide range of search criteria. You should now understand the `Person` object and how it differs from a `Contact`, and be able to export contact information in vCard format for use in other platforms and applications. If you're writing an application that manages contacts, you're well on your way.

The second half of the chapter discussed calendars and explained how to manage events and tasks. You walked through code for setting up recurring events and now know how to set up alarms for both events and tasks.

While this chapter contains a lot of code, you can find more in the web application samples that are part of the Tizen SDK. `Chatter` and `Contacts Exchanger` demonstrate the Contact API, while the Calendar API is used in the `Event Manager` sample. Take some time to explore the sample code, and together with what you've learned in the last few chapters you'll have a great grounding in Tizen web application development.

We now move to Part III, which focuses on the APIs for creating Tizen native applications.

PART III
Tizen Native APIs

10

Native UI Applications

WHAT'S IN THIS CHAPTER?

➤ UI application architecture

➤ The building blocks of a great UI

➤ The application life cycle

➤ Creating form-based applications

➤ Handling events

This chapter explains the basic building blocks of native UI applications, including frames, forms, events, and the application life cycle. The key namespaces and classes are introduced and you'll learn about the anatomy of a form-based application, before you dive into the code and create your own application using the New Project Wizard. You'll then build up the application to handle UI events and support more advanced features like hardware keys and gestures.

By the end of the chapter, you will have the broad foundation necessary to start building your own native UI applications.

UI FRAMEWORK ARCHITECTURE

A Tizen native UI application is built using the Tizen native application framework and UI framework. The native application framework is implemented by the classes and methods in the `Tizen::App` namespace. This namespace contains the `Tizen::App::App` class, the base class for all Tizen native applications, which contains methods for accessing basic application information such as name, ID, and version, as well as pure virtual functions for initialisation and termination. The `Tizen::App::UiApp` class, which inherits from `Tizen::App::App` is the base class for all native UI applications. The native UI framework provides the `Tizen::Ui` namespaces that contain UI controls.

Native UI applications can be launched from the main menu, from the task manager, from other applications, or by registering a launch condition for your application, so it launches at a specified time, for example. All native UI applications must be shown in the main menu and the task manager.

Figure 10-1 shows the architecture of the native UI and graphics framework.

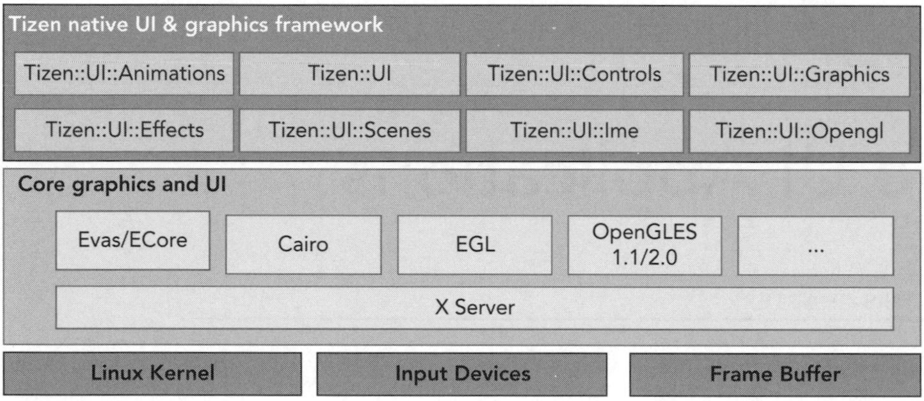

FIGURE 10-1

Tizen uses the Enlightenment Foundation Libraries (EFL) as a core UI framework. EFL is a collection of libraries supporting 2D and 2.5D UI rendering for the Tizen platform. EFL provides common GUI widgets, handling and routing of input, data management, and communications. The native UI framework uses the EFL Evas canvas scene-graph library and ECore for the main event loop and other core tasks.

> **NOTE** *The Enlightenment open-source project is not just a window manager for Linux/X11 and others, but also a whole set of libraries to help you create beautiful user interfaces with much less work than doing it the old-fashioned way and fighting with traditional toolkits, not to mention a traditional window manager. The official website of Enlightenment is* `http://www.enlightenment.org/`*.*

For graphics, the native UI framework uses Cairo (`https://code.google.com/p/cairogles`), a vector graphics-based, device-independent 2D graphics library. Cairo and EFL internally use EGL (OpenGL) (`www.khronos.org/registry/egl`) and OpenGL-ES (`www.khronos.org/opengles`). EGL is an interface between the OpenGL ES APIs and the underlying native platform windowing-system for 2D and 3D rendering. OpenGL-ES is a subset of the OpenGL 3D graphics API designed for embedded systems.

The Tizen native framework provides the `Ui` namespaces, as described in Table 10-1.

TABLE 10-1: Tizen::Ui Namespaces

NAMESPACE	DESCRIPTION
Tizen::Ui	The basic foundation for constructing UI controls and UI applications
Tizen::Ui::Controls	Buttons, lists, and advanced controls
Tizen::Ui::Animations	Animation capabilities for the UI controls
Tizen::Ui::Scenes	UI flow navigation
Tizen::Ui::Ime	The basic interface for creating IME (input method editor) applications

SERVICE APPLICATIONS

The Tizen native application framework also supports service applications, which have no user interface and run in the background. These applications can run periodically or continuously, performing tasks that require no user intervention, such as processing sensor data.

Service applications can be explicitly launched by a web or native UI application or registered to launch when a specified condition is met — at a given time or when certain data is received via a serial connection or near field communication (NFC).

A user cannot launch service applications in the same way as UI applications and they are not shown on the main menu. A service application can be shown in the task switcher, but it is not selectable.

UI and service applications can be packaged together, but the combined package must contain only one UI application, although it can contain multiple service applications. Applications in the same package follow the same installation process, while each application follows its own application life cycle.

THREAD SAFETY IN THE UI FRAMEWORK

EFL is not thread-safe. Therefore, all EFL callbacks must be registered to the main thread, which is also called the UI thread. The native framework has the same limitation, which means that all UI handling should be done in the main thread. This is because only the main thread dispatches events to UI controls.

This limitation does not mean that the UI needs to be blocked when it does processor-intensive tasks that might otherwise cause the UI to be unresponsive. You can create a thread for a particular task and in this new thread, call SendUserEvent() to send a message to the main thread. The OnUserEventReceivedN() callback will be invoked in the main thread and the UI can be safely updated.

TYPES OF NATIVE UI APPLICATIONS

As described in Table 10-2, there are several different types of native UI applications: form-based, theme, IME, OpenGL, and tab-based. A form-based application is the most basic native UI application. Form-based applications can be built with or without scene management features, which are described in more detail in Chapter 16. Theme, IME, and tab-based applications are other variations of form-based applications, whereas OpenGL applications can be either form- or frame-based, the latter taking up the entire screen, with no UI controls.

TABLE 10-2: Native UI Application Types

APPLICATION TYPE	DESCRIPTION
Form-based Application With SceneManager	This template is suitable for creating a form based on the scene management feature. The template contains the basic application functionality as well as the functionality for drawing a form on the device screen.
Form-based Application Without SceneManager	This template is suitable for creating a simple project based on a form. The template contains the basic application functionality as well as the functionality for drawing a form on the device screen.
IME Application	This template is suitable for creating a form-based IME application project, which requires partner-level privileges to run. The template contains the basic application functionality as well as the functionality for drawing a form on the device screen.
Form-based OpenGL Application	This template is suitable for creating a simple form-based project based on the `Tizen::Graphics::Opengl::GlPlayer` and `Tizen::Graphics::Opengl::IGlRenderer` classes, which make it easier to create OpenGL ES applications. The template contains an IGlRenderer instance that draws a rotating triangle on a GL window surface on the form. You must override this instance to draw each scene. Use this template if you want to render scenes onto a form and mix them with other UI controls.
Frame-based OpenGL Application	This template is suitable for creating a simple frame-based project based on the `GlPlayer` and `IGlRenderer` classes, which make it easier to create OpenGL ES applications. The template contains an IGlRenderer instance that draws a rotating triangle on a GL window surface on the frame. You must override this instance to draw each scene. Use this template if you need no UI controls, since the frame-based template needs less memory and causes less overhead than the form-based template.

Tab-based Application With SceneManager	This template is suitable for creating a tab-based application using the scene management feature. The template contains the basic tab-switching functionality.
Tab-based Application Without SceneManager	This template is suitable for creating a tab-based application. The template contains the basic tab-switching functionality.
Theme Application	The Home application template is suitable for creating a home screen. The Lock application template is suitable for creating a lock screen application.

Figure 10-2 shows the window hierarchy of a form-based application, which consists of a frame, a form, and controls. A frame is a top window that is automatically generated for each application. The major role of a frame is to contain and show a form on the screen. `Frame` is the root object of all UI controls that are created when an application is initialised. It can contain only `Form` instances inside it.

A form is a full screen control that you can use to display an indicated area, header, footer, and other UI controls on the screen. A form is the only control that can contain other UI controls as child controls. A header and footer are placed on top and bottom, respectively, and other UI components are also placed on the form. These UI elements are described in more detail in Chapter 12.

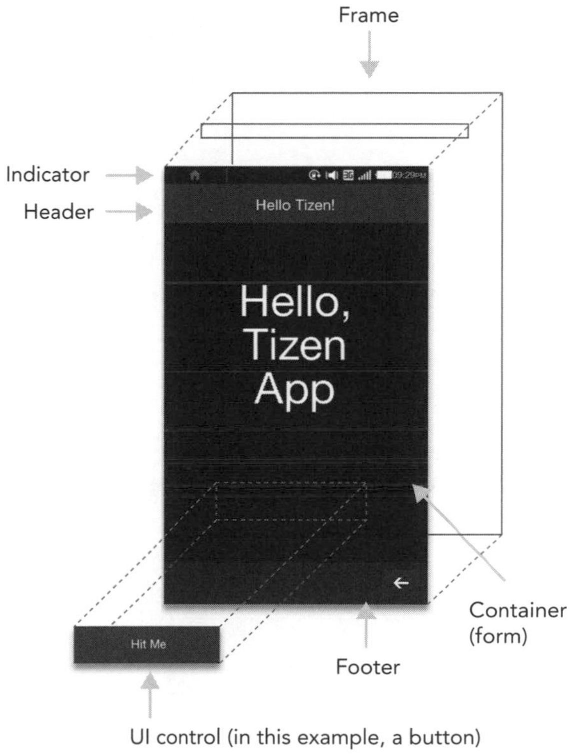

FIGURE 10-2

NATIVE UI APPLICATION LIFE CYCLE

The native application framework provides application management features, including the capability to launch other applications, and access to predefined system services, such as the system dialer application. The framework also notifies applications of common events, such as low memory or battery events, changes in screen orientation, and push notifications. The Tizen native framework provides these features through the `Tizen::App` namespace.

The `App` namespace also provides the means for Tizen native applications to interact with each other through launching applications with parameters and providing operations and data to other applications with an appropriate level of access control.

Figure 10-3 illustrates the basic life cycle of a native UI application, including launching and terminating an application, and perspective shifts between background and foreground.

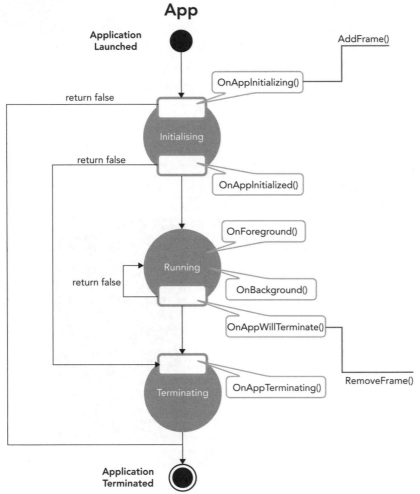

FIGURE 10-3

State Transition Flow

A native application has the following four states (with corresponding event handlers):

➤ **Initialising** — In the initialising state, the framework initialises the application. Previously saved application data is restored and the application frame is created.

➤ **Running** — In the running state, a user can interact with the UI application. The UI application can switch between the background and foreground.

➤ **Terminating** — In the terminating stage, the application removes its resources and saves its preferences.

➤ **Terminated** — In the terminated state, the framework removes the application from memory.

Figure 10-4 shows how a Tizen native application transits these states.

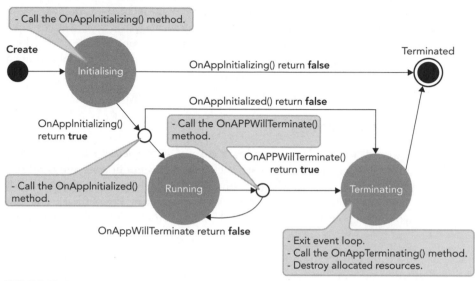

FIGURE 10-4

Initialisation and Termination

Users access native UI applications through the device's main menu, the task switcher, or through another application. The main menu displays the icons of all native and Web UI applications installed on the device, while the task switcher displays the icons for currently running applications to provide the user with quick access to them.

If the user selects an application in the main menu that is not currently running, the application is launched. If the user selects an already running application in the main menu or task switcher, the application is simply moved to the foreground.

When a native UI application is launched, the native application framework initialises the application and creates the application's frame. The user interface is constructed, and the application data saved on the previous run is restored.

The entry point of the application is the OspMain() method. In the application initialisation phase, the OnAppInitializing() event handler of the Tizen::App::App class is called. In the OnAppInitializing() event handler, the previous application states can be loaded through the Tizen::App::AppRegistry class and any required processing is done. If the OnAppInitializing() event handler returns false, the application state changes to Terminating and exits. If the event handler returns true, the application enters the Running state and can instantiate its resources, such as UI controls and state.

When the application's initialisation is finished, the App::OnAppInitialized() event handler is called. Before the OnAppInitialized() event handler returns, a frame must be created and added by the AddFrame() method of Tizen::App::UiApp. If no frame is created, the application state changes to Terminating.

A running application can be terminated when the Tizen native application calls the `Terminate()` method of `Tizen::App::App`. The system can also terminate the application when memory or battery power is extremely low. Application termination is handled in the `OnAppTerminate()` event handler of the `App` class. When the event handler is called, the application has to free its resources and terminate. The allocated UI controls, such as the form and its child controls, are released in the `OnTerminating()` event handler of the `Tizen::Ui::Controls::Frame` class. The application has to remove its own resources and save its preferences through the `Osp::App::AppRegistry` class. The framework removes the application from memory.

Application and Frame States

A UI application has a frame, its top-level main window has three states: activated, deactivated, and minimized. When a frame is activated, it can receive events from input devices and is fully visible. When a frame is deactivated, such as when a visible window is shown, it no longer receives events and the frame is partially shown. The frame state is minimized when the frame is completely covered, which occurs when the application is moved to the background and the frame becomes invisible.

Figure 10-5 shows the transition between these states. To respond to frame state changes, implement the event handlers defined in the `Ui::Controls::IFrameEventListener` that are displayed in Figure 10-5.

The `GetAppUiStates()` method of `Tizen::App::UiApp` returns the UI state of the application, which is either foreground, partial background, or background. The frame state will also change as the application UI state changes.

An application moves to the foreground and the frame of the application is activated when:

➤   The application is selected from the task switcher.

➤   The application icon in the main menu is pressed when the application is either in the background or not running.

➤   A system window that covered the application is closed.

An application transitions to the background state when system windows, such as incoming calls or alarms, are displayed and will move back to the foreground state once the windows are dismissed. In this state the application frame state is deactivated.

When the Home key is pressed or another application is launched, a running application moves to the background. In the background state, applications are invisible and the frame state will be set to minimized.

When the application moves to the background, it is best practice to stop graphic processing, such as 3D or animations, release unnecessary resources, and stop media processing and monitoring sensors. The foreground application has the focus and must resume any graphic processing operations that were paused when it moved to the background.

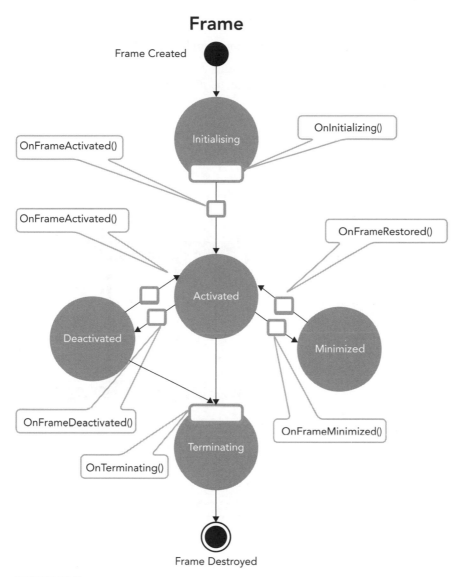

FIGURE 10-5

CREATING A FORM AND HANDLING EVENTS

You can use the Project Wizard in the Tizen IDE to easily create new projects from templates, including form-based, theme, IME, OpenGL, and tab-based applications.

This example uses the Empty Application template to create a form-based application. The following sections then show how to add code to the application to handle UI events, hardware keys, and gestures.

1. In the IDE, select File ➪ New ➪ Tizen Native Project.

2. In the New Tizen Native Project window, select the Template tab and choose Empty Application.

3. Type **FormAndEvent** in the Project name text field, as shown in Figure 10-6, and click Finish.

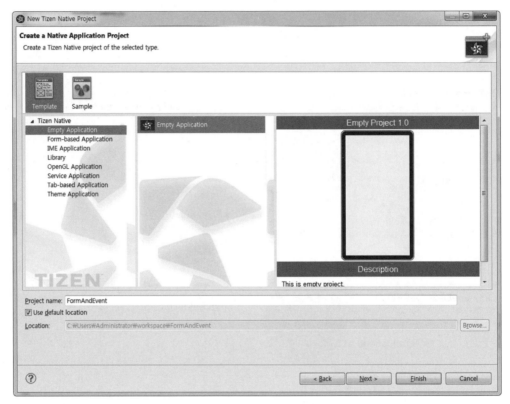

FIGURE 10-6

The Tizen::Ui namespace is used to construct graphical user interfaces. It contains classes and interfaces for handling UI-related events. To create a form, you need a class inherited from the Form class, adding it to the frame:

1. Right-click the TestApp project in Project Explorer.

2. Select New ➪ Class.

3. Type **MyForm** as a class name and select Form as a base class, as shown in Figure 10-7.

4. MyForm.cpp and MyForm.h can now be seen in Project Explorer. To make the form functional, add the form to a frame and set it as the current form. Add the following highlighted code to FormAndEventFrame.cpp:

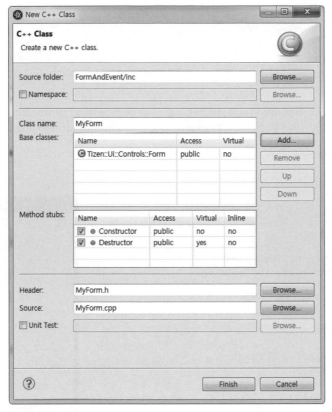

FIGURE 10-7

```cpp
#include "MyForm.h"
#include "FormAndEventFrame.h"

...

result
FormAndEventFrame::OnInitializing(void)
{
    result r = E_SUCCESS;
    // Create a form in the heap, no need to delete explicitly later
    MyForm* pForm = new MyForm();

    // Construct the form
    pForm->Construct(FORM_STYLE_INDICATOR | FORM_STYLE_HEADER
                                          | FORM_STYLE_FOOTER);

    // Add the form to the frame
    AddControl(pForm);

    // Set your form as the current form
```

```
    SetCurrentForm(pForm);

    // Draw
    Invalidate(true);

    return r;
}
```

5. To handle the `OnInitializing` and `OnTerminating` events, you need to implement `Form::OnInitializing()` and `Form::OnTerminating()`. Add the following highlighted code to `MyForm.h`:

```
class MyForm
: public Tizen::Ui::Controls::Form
{
public:
    MyForm() {};
    virtual ~MyForm() {};
public:
    virtual result OnInitializing(void);
    virtual result OnTerminating(void);
```

6. Add the method implementation into `MyForm.cpp`:

```
result
MyForm::OnInitializing(void)
{
        AppLog("Initializing MyForm");
        return E_SUCCESS;
}

result
MyForm::OnTerminating(void)
{
        AppLog("Terminating MyForm");
        return E_SUCCESS;
}
```

FIGURE 10-8

7. Build the project and run it in the emulator or a device. You will see the empty form shown in Figure 10-8.

8. You cannot close the application because you didn't provide a way to do so yet. To close the application, long press the Home button to bring up the task switcher and click the End button next to TestApp (see Figure 10-9).

Because you put a call to `AppLog()` in `OnInitializing()` and `OnTerminating()`, you can see the logs in the Log window, shown in Figure 10-10. You need to filter logs using a tag with the same name as your application name.

FIGURE 10-9

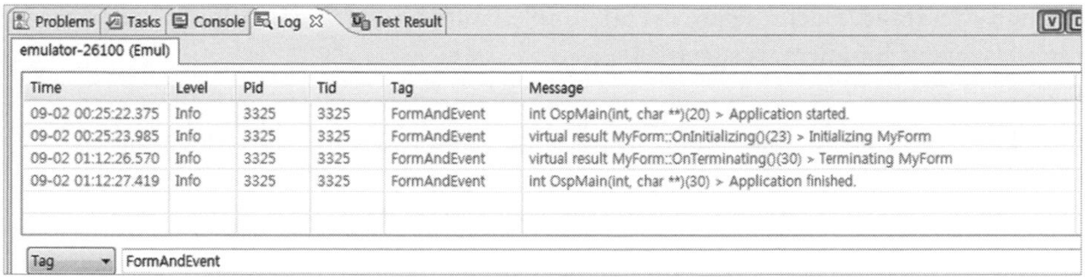

FIGURE 10-10

Handling UI Events

In the Tizen native framework, UI events such as touch, key presses, and drag events are handled by implementing event listeners. For example, ITouchEventListener is for touch, IKeyEventListener is for key inputs, and so on.

To receive touch events, inherit the ITouchEventListener interface:

```
#include <FUiCtrlForm.h>
#include <FUi.h>

class MyForm
    : public Tizen::Ui::Controls::Form
    , public Tizen::Ui::ITouchEventListener
{
public:
        MyForm();
        virtual ~MyForm();
public:
        virtual result OnInitializing(void);
        virtual result OnTerminating(void);

        // Touch events
        virtual void OnTouchPressed(const Tizen::Ui::Control &source,
                const Tizen::Graphics::Point &currentPosition,
                const Tizen::Ui::TouchEventInfo &touchInfo);
        virtual void OnTouchReleased(const Tizen::Ui::Control &source,
                const Tizen::Graphics::Point &currentPosition,
                const Tizen::Ui::TouchEventInfo &touchInfo);
        virtual void OnTouchFocusIn (const Tizen::Ui::Control &source,
                const Tizen::Graphics::Point &currentPosition,
                const Tizen::Ui::TouchEventInfo &touchInfo) {};
        virtual void OnTouchFocusOut (const Tizen::Ui::Control &source,
                const Tizen::Graphics::Point &currentPosition,
                const Tizen::Ui::TouchEventInfo &touchInfo) {};
        virtual void OnTouchMoved (const Tizen::Ui::Control &source,
                const Tizen::Graphics::Point &currentPosition,
                const Tizen::Ui::TouchEventInfo &touchInfo) {};

};
```

To handle the touch press and touch release events, implement the `OnTouchPressed()` and `OnTouchReleased()` event handlers, respectively:

```cpp
#include <FApp.h>
#include "MyForm.h"

...

result
MyForm::OnInitializing(void)
{
        AppLog("Initializing MyForm");
        AddTouchEventListener(*this);
        return E_SUCCESS;
}

result
MyForm::OnTerminating(void)
{
        AppLog("Terminating MyForm");
        return E_SUCCESS;
}


void
MyForm::OnTouchPressed(const Tizen::Ui::Control &source,
                 const Tizen::Graphics::Point &currentPosition,
                     const Tizen::Ui::TouchEventInfo &touchInfo)
{
        AppLog("TouchPressed [%d,%d]", currentPosition.x, currentPosition.y);
}

void
MyForm::OnTouchReleased(const Tizen::Ui::Control &source,
                 const Tizen::Graphics::Point &currentPosition,
                     const Tizen::Ui::TouchEventInfo &touchInfo)
{

        AppLog("TouchReleased [%d,%d]", currentPosition.x, currentPosition.y);
        if (currentPosition.x < 200 && currentPosition.y < 200)
        {
            // Terminates the application
            Tizen::App::App::GetInstance()->Terminate();
        }
}
```

When you run the example, you will see that `OnTouchPressed` and `OnTouchReleased` are logged whenever you touch the application form area. If you touch the upper-left corner of this application, it will be terminated. The following log shows that the application has been started, many touch events were generated, and the application finished:

```
INFO / FormAndEvent ( 3808 : 3808 ) : int OspMain(int, char **)(20) > Application
started.
INFO / FormAndEvent ( 3808 : 3808 ) : virtual result MyForm::OnInitializing()(23) >
Initializing MyForm
```

```
INFO / FormAndEvent ( 3808 : 3808 ) : virtual void MyForm::OnTouchPressed(const
Tizen::Ui::Control &, const Tizen::Graphics::Point &, const Tizen::Ui::TouchEventInfo
&)(40) > TouchPressed [454,356]
INFO / FormAndEvent ( 3808 : 3808 ) : virtual void MyForm::OnTouchReleased(const
Tizen::Ui::Control &, const Tizen::Graphics::Point &, const Tizen::Ui::TouchEventInfo
&)(48) > TouchReleased [454,356]
INFO / FormAndEvent ( 3808 : 3808 ) : virtual void MyForm::OnTouchPressed(const
Tizen::Ui::Control &, const Tizen::Graphics::Point &, const Tizen::Ui::TouchEventInfo
&)(40) > TouchPressed [388,250]
INFO / FormAndEvent ( 3808 : 3808 ) : virtual void MyForm::OnTouchReleased(const
Tizen::Ui::Control &, const Tizen::Graphics::Point &, const Tizen::Ui::TouchEventInfo
&)(48) > TouchReleased [386,262]
INFO / FormAndEvent ( 3808 : 3808 ) : virtual void MyForm::OnTouchPressed(const
Tizen::Ui::Control &, const Tizen::Graphics::Point &, const Tizen::Ui::TouchEventInfo
&)(40) > TouchPressed [208,498]
INFO / FormAndEvent ( 3808 : 3808 ) : virtual void MyForm::OnTouchReleased(const
Tizen::Ui::Control &, const Tizen::Graphics::Point &, const Tizen::Ui::TouchEventInfo
&)(48) > TouchReleased [208,498]
INFO / FormAndEvent ( 3808 : 3808 ) : virtual void MyForm::OnTouchPressed(const
Tizen::Ui::Control &, const Tizen::Graphics::Point &, const Tizen::Ui::TouchEventInfo
&)(40) > TouchPressed [28,424]
INFO / FormAndEvent ( 3808 : 3808 ) : virtual void MyForm::OnTouchReleased(const
Tizen::Ui::Control &, const Tizen::Graphics::Point &, const Tizen::Ui::TouchEventInfo
&)(48) > TouchReleased [28,424]
INFO / FormAndEvent ( 3808 : 3808 ) : virtual void MyForm::OnTouchPressed(const
Tizen::Ui::Control &, const Tizen::Graphics::Point &, const Tizen::Ui::TouchEventInfo
&)(40) > TouchPressed [126,318]
INFO / FormAndEvent ( 3808 : 3808 ) : virtual void MyForm::OnTouchReleased(const
Tizen::Ui::Control &, const Tizen::Graphics::Point &, const Tizen::Ui::TouchEventInfo
&)(48) > TouchReleased [126,318]
INFO / FormAndEvent ( 3808 : 3808 ) : virtual void MyForm::OnTouchPressed(const
Tizen::Ui::Control &, const Tizen::Graphics::Point &, const Tizen::Ui::TouchEventInfo
&)(40) > TouchPressed [56,258]
INFO / FormAndEvent ( 3808 : 3808 ) : virtual void MyForm::OnTouchReleased(const
Tizen::Ui::Control &, const Tizen::Graphics::Point &, const Tizen::Ui::TouchEventInfo
&)(48) > TouchReleased [56,258]
INFO / FormAndEvent ( 3808 : 3808 ) : virtual void MyForm::OnTouchPressed(const
Tizen::Ui::Control &, const Tizen::Graphics::Point &, const Tizen::Ui::TouchEventInfo
&)(40) > TouchPressed [6,178]
INFO / FormAndEvent ( 3808 : 3808 ) : virtual void MyForm::OnTouchReleased(const
Tizen::Ui::Control &, const Tizen::Graphics::Point &, const Tizen::Ui::TouchEventInfo
&)(48) > TouchReleased [6,178]
INFO / FormAndEvent ( 3808 : 3808 ) : virtual result MyForm::OnTerminating()(31) >
Terminating MyForm
INFO / FormAndEvent ( 3808 : 3808 ) : int OspMain(int, char **)(30) > Application
finished.
```

Handling Hardware Keys

In this section you learn how to interact with the Menu and Back hardware keys provided by all Tizen devices. You will add code to terminate the application when a user presses the hardware Back key and to display an option menu control when the user presses the hardware Menu key.

To receive Menu and Back key events, make the `Form` class inherit the `Tizen::Ui::Controls::IFormBackEventListener` and `Tizen::Ui::Controls::IFormMenuEventListener` interfaces. In addition, declare an OptionMenu control for the Menu key:

```
class MyForm
    : public Tizen::Ui::Controls::Form
    , public Tizen::Ui::ITouchEventListener
    , public Tizen::Ui::Controls::IFormBackEventListener
    , public Tizen::Ui::Controls::IFormMenuEventListener
{
...

public:
    // IFormBackEventListener
    virtual void OnFormBackRequested(Tizen::Ui::Controls::Form& source);

    // IFormMenuEventListener
    virtual void OnFormMenuRequested(Tizen::Ui::Controls::Form& source);

private:
    Tizen::Ui::Controls::OptionMenu* __pOption;

};
```

Then create an OptionMenu and set the event listeners:

```
#define ID_CONTEXT_ITEM 0

result
MyForm::OnInitializing(void)
{
    AppLog("Initializing MyForm");


    __pOption = new (std::nothrow) Tizen::Ui::Controls::OptionMenu();
    __pOption->Construct();
    __pOption->AddItem(L"item 0", ID_CONTEXT_ITEM);
    __pOption->SetShowState(false);

    // set HW key listeners
    SetFormBackEventListener(this);
    SetFormMenuEventListener(this);

    return E_SUCCESS;
}
```

Implement `OnFormBackRequested()` and `OnFormMenuRequested()` with the following code:

```
void
MyForm::OnFormBackRequested(Tizen::Ui::Controls::Form& source)
{
    // React to key press
    Tizen::App::App::GetInstance()->Terminate();
}

void
```

```
MyForm::OnFormMenuRequested(Tizen::Ui::Controls::Form& source)
{
    __pOption->SetShowState(true);
    __pOption->Show();
}
```

If the Back key is pressed, the application will be terminated. In response to a Menu key press, the OptionMenu will be displayed, as shown in Figure 10-11.

Handling Gestures

Let's extend the application a little more by adding gesture support. In this section, you will write the code to draw a rectangle on the form and change the size of the rectangle in response to the pinch gesture.

To implement a pinch gesture, you need to implement the pinch gesture event listener and a pinch gesture detector. Here's how to add this functionality to our application.

FIGURE 10-11

Declare the listener event methods, the pinch gesture detector, and some member variables in MyForm.h., as follows:

```
#include <FGraphics.h>
#include <FUi.h>

class MyForm
    : public Tizen::Ui::Controls::Form
    ...
    , public Tizen::Ui::ITouchPinchGestureEventListener
{
public:
    MyForm();
    virtual ~MyForm();
public:
    virtual result OnInitializing(void);
    virtual result OnTerminating(void);
    virtual result OnDraw(void);

    ...

    // Pinch Gesture
    virtual void OnPinchGestureStarted(
                Tizen::Ui::TouchPinchGestureDetector &gestureDetector);
    virtual void OnPinchGestureChanged(
                 Tizen::Ui::TouchPinchGestureDetector &gestureDetector);
    virtual void OnPinchGestureCanceled(
                Tizen::Ui::TouchPinchGestureDetector &gestureDetector) {};
    virtual void OnPinchGestureFinished(
                Tizen::Ui::TouchPinchGestureDetector &gestureDetector) {};

private:
    Tizen::Ui::Controls::OptionMenu* __pOption;
    Tizen::Ui::TouchPinchGestureDetector* __pPinchGesture;
```

```
    float __startingPinchScale;
    float __pinchScaleRatio;
};
```

Initialise the member variables in the initialisation list of the form's constructor:

```
MyForm::MyForm()
    : __pOption(null)
    , __pPinchGesture(null)
    , __startingPinchScale(0)
    , __pinchScaleRatio(1)
{
}
```

In the `OnInitializatizing()` method of `MyForm`, create a `TouchPinchGestureDetector` and add it as a gesture detector for your form class. To ensure that the form class receives pinch gesture events, add the form as a listener to the `TouchPinchGestureDetector`:

```
result
MyForm::OnInitializing(void)
{
    AppLog("Initializing MyForm");

    …

    // create a pinch gesture detector
    __pPinchGesture = new (std::nothrow)
                  Tizen::Ui::TouchPinchGestureDetector;
    if (__pPinchGesture != null)
    {
        __pPinchGesture->Construct();

        // add the gesture detector to our form
        AddGestureDetector(__pPinchGesture);

        // add our form (the listener) to the gesture detector
        __pPinchGesture->AddPinchGestureEventListener(*this);
    }

    return E_SUCCESS;
}
```

Remember to clean up the gesture detector when the application terminates:

```
result
MyForm::OnTerminating(void)
{
    AppLog("Terminating MyForm");

    if (__pPinchGesture != null)
    {
        __pPinchGesture->RemovePinchGestureEventListener(*this);
        delete __pPinchGesture;
    }

    return E_SUCCESS;
}
```

To handle pinch gesture events, you need to implement the event listener methods:

```
void
MyForm::OnPinchGestureStarted(Tizen::Ui::TouchPinchGestureDetector &gestureDetector)
{
    __startingPinchScale = gestureDetector.GetScaleF();
    AppLog("starting scale %d", __startingPinchScale);
}

void
MyForm::OnPinchGestureChanged(Tizen::Ui::TouchPinchGestureDetector &gestureDetector)
{
    float scale = gestureDetector.GetScaleF();
    __pinchScaleRatio = scale / __startingPinchScale;

    // update screen
    Invalidate(true);
    AppLog("scale ratio %f", __pinchScaleRatio);
}
```

The `OnPinchGestureStarted()` and `OnPinchGestureChanged()` methods are passed as a parameter, a reference to the gesture detector that was created earlier in the code — in this case, a `TouchPinchGestureDetector`. Through the `TouchPinchGestureDetector` instance, you can get information like the centre point of the pinch and the scale factor among the touched points. In this example, you save the first scale factor and calculate the scale ratio with a changed scale factor. Since you will draw a rectangle based on this scale ratio, you update the screen by calling `Invalidate()`.

DRAW() VS. INVALIDATE()

You can update a control, such as the form in this example, using either the `Invalidate()` method or the `Draw()` method. The difference between the methods is that `Draw()` synchronously draws on a rendering buffer, whereas `Invalidate()` draws asynchronously. This does not mean that `Draw()` immediately updates the screen; the update timing depends on the platform configuration and implementation.

The following code draws a rectangle based on the pinch scale factor:

```
result
MyForm::OnDraw(void)
{
        Tizen::Graphics::Canvas* pCanvas = GetCanvasN();

        if (pCanvas != null)
        {
                // calculate a rectangle size and position based on scale
                // and client area.
                const Tizen::Graphics::Rectangle clientRect =
```

```
GetClientAreaBounds();

            int width = static_cast< int >
                    (clientRect.width / 2 * __pinchScaleRatio);
            int height = static_cast< int >
                    (clientRect.height / 2 * __pinchScaleRatio);

            pCanvas->SetLineWidth(10);
            pCanvas->SetForegroundColor(Tizen::Graphics::Color(0xFF,
0x00, 0x00));
            pCanvas->DrawRectangle(Tizen::Graphics::Rectangle(20, 200,
width, height));
            delete pCanvas;
        }

        return E_SUCCESS;
    }
```

GetCanvasN() is a method of Tizen::Ui::Control, which creates and returns a canvas equal to the bounds of the control. A canvas is implemented by the Tizen::Graphics::Canvas class and is a background for drawing graphic elements on controls. On a canvas, you can draw a line, text, polygon, bitmap, rectangle, and so on. In this example, you create a canvas with the bounds of your form control and use it to draw a rectangle. The width and height of the rectangle is changed based on the pinch scale ratio.

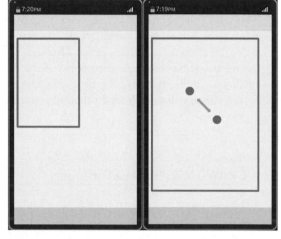

As you see in Figure 10-12, the application shows a small rectangle when it is launched. If you pinch it the rectangle is changed.

FIGURE 10-12

That's it. You've now built an application which supports pinch gestures, and you can run the application on the emulator or a Tizen device. If you're running the application in the emulator, you can simulate multi-touch by Ctrl-clicking twice.

SUMMARY

At this point you probably can't wait to take your native application development to the next level. The following chapters will show you how. Now you know your way around the architecture of a typical native UI application, understand the application life cycle, and can create a simple form-based application using the Project Wizard. You learned how to add code to support touch and key events and how to handle some of the more advanced events like gestures. Now it's time to put this knowledge into action.

11

Native Application Fundamentals

WHAT'S IN THIS CHAPTER?

➤ Handling errors and exceptions

➤ Debugging macros and logging

➤ Native programming idioms

➤ Smart pointers for smarter code

➤ Strings and collections

WROX.COM CODE DOWNLOADS FOR THIS CHAPTER

The wrox.com code downloads for this chapter are found at www.wrox.com/go/
professionaltizen on the Download Code tab. The code is in the Chapter 11 download and
named according to the names throughout the chapter. After decompressing the downloaded
Zip file, you will have a tizen-fundamentals directory that contains the sample code.

This chapter explains the essential idioms and programming styles used by the Tizen native
APIs that you should follow in your own code. Time spent becoming familiar with these
concepts now will pay off later in your development efforts; so while these may not be the
most glamorous topics, they're arguably the most important.

If you design your code with proper error handling, log information to help with debugging, and understand the object ownership rules, your code will be easier to maintain and
debug. By becoming familiar with manipulating Tizen's core data types, such as strings,
collections, and date and time, you can spend more of your development time on the details
of your applications. This chapter will help you start to master these Tizen development
essentials.

BASIC IDIOMS AND STYLES

In this section, you'll learn how the Tizen approach to error handling compares with standard C++ exceptions and how to use debugging and logging macros for testing and tracking down those hard to find bugs. The Tizen approach to object ownership is also explained, an important concept when it comes to preventing memory leaks, especially when combined with the `unique_ptr` smart pointer implementation. By following these guidelines, your code should be cleaner, more consistent, and work well with the Tizen native APIs.

Error Handling

No matter how carefully you write your code, errors will always happen; but it's how your application handles and recovers from these errors that counts. An application which terminates without warning, not providing users with a chance to save their data, will lose the user's trust and may generate negative feedback on the Tizen app store. A detailed knowledge of the error-handling features of Tizen is essential for creating a well-behaved application, and that's what this section provides you with.

The Tizen native APIs return a result code from a function or set a global error value for the last function called, rather than use C++ exceptions. The two styles of returning error codes take the following forms:

➤ **Return value style**

> ➤ Signature — `result SomeClass::SomeMethod(...)`. A variable of `result` type contains the error code.

➤ **Global last return value style**

> ➤ Signature — `SomeClass::SomeMethod(...)`. `GetLastResult()` is used to access the last error code or result set with the `SetLastResult()` function. This is used to check for errors from methods that do not return an error code.

The `result` type is defined by the Tizen native framework as follows:

```
typedef unsigned long result;
```

Various error codes are defined by the framework; and the possible error codes returned by each method, or returned by `GetLastResult()`, are shown in the API reference in the SDK help. For example, the Exceptions section of the `Tizen::Base::String::IndexOf(...)` API reference lists three error codes and explains when each error occurs (see Figure 11-1).

Figure 11-2 shows the SDK help description for a function which does not return an error code.

As you can see in the Remarks section, the `GetLastResult()` function is used to check the error code after the method has been called.

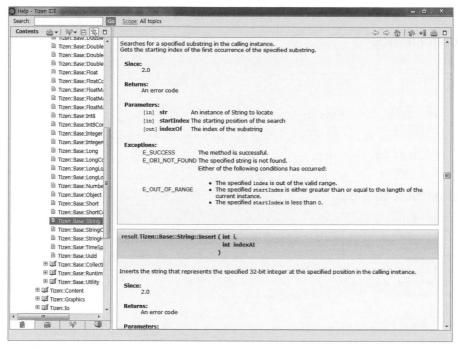

FIGURE 11-1

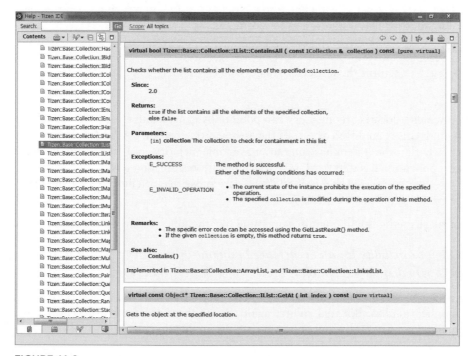

FIGURE 11-2

The following code examples show the two styles of checking for errors:

RESULT RETURN METHOD

```
#include <FBase.h>

String str = ...;
int pos = 0;
result r = str.IndexOf(L"search_string", 0, pos);
if (r != E_SUCCESS)    // if (IsFailed(r))
{
    // error handling
}
```

LAST RESULT RETURN METHOD

```
#include <FBase.h>

IList* pList1 = ..., pList2 = ...;
ClearLastResult();
bool contained = pList1->ContainsAll(*pList2);
result r = GetLastResult();
if (r != E_SUCCESS)    // if (IsFailed(r))
{
    // error handling
}
```

➤ E_SUCCESS is a result code which indicates that the method executed successfully.

➤ IsFailed(r) tests whether r is not equal to E_SUCCESS, and will return true if the method failed for any reason. This is equivalent to writing if (r != E_SUCCESS).

➤ ClearLastResult() resets the global last result to E_SUCCESS.

➤ GetLastResult() returns the last error result, which will be E_SUCCESS if no error occurred.

Any Tizen method which allocates any memory can potentially generate an E_OUT_OF_MEMORY exception, even though this is not listed as one of the errors in the method's API help description. In these cases it's likely that the system has run out of available memory, and all you can do is free any resources your application has allocated, save the application state, and terminate. The methods for which E_OUT_OF_MEMORY is listed as a potential error are those that attempt to allocate a large amount of memory, such as an image buffer.

The description of these methods will contain something like the following in the Remarks section:

> *"There is a high probability for an occurrence of an out-of-memory exception. If possible, check whether the exception is* E_OUT_OF_MEMORY *or not."*

If you get an out-of-memory error when attempting to call such a method, you may choose to free up memory your application has allocated and try again, or ask the user how to proceed. In any case you should handle the error gracefully and not terminate the application.

Figure 11-3 shows an example of a method which is likely to return an E_OUT_OF_MEMORY error.

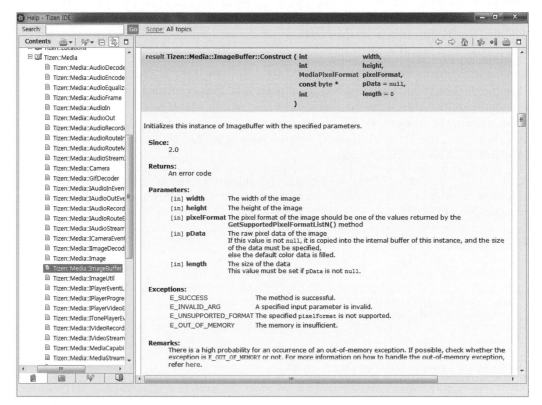

FIGURE 11-3

Comprehensive log information from the native framework is available to help you identify and fix the cause of errors. Figure 11-4 illustrates the information shown in the log window of the Tizen IDE when an error occurs.

FIGURE 11-4

The Timestamp field is in the format of month-day hours:minutes:seconds.milliseconds. The Prefix for log type field represents the type of log and can have the value of Error, Info, or Debug. The Tag field represents a tag for each module. The default tag for an application is the application's name, and the tag for a framework module is its namespace. The Fully-qualified name field is the fully scoped name for the function or method from which the exception occurs. The Exception name field is the "stringified" name of each exception.

The Tizen native framework does not support C++ exceptions at the platform level and as a result uses new (std::nothrow) internally instead of plain new. This is because new (std::nothrow) returns a null pointer when it cannot allocate memory, whereas plain new throws a std::bad_alloc exception. Due to the lack of C++ exception support, avoid the use of plain new in any of your code which makes use of the Tizen framework, as throwing a std::bad_alloc exception could leave your application in an inconsistent state.

If you have code which makes use of C++ exceptions, implement an *exception fence* to ensure that no exceptions leave your code. To do so, define a class from which all your exception classes are derived. Here's an example:

BASE EXCEPTION CLASS

```
#include <exception>   // for 'std::exception' type
#include <FBase.h>   // for 'result' type

class YourExceptionBase
    : public std::exception
{
public:
    virtual const char* what() const;
    virtual result GetResult() const;
};
```

You can catch user-defined and standard exceptions and map to Tizen error results as follows:

EXCEPTION FENCE

```
void
YourClass::OnSomeEventReceived(result r)
{
    try
    {
        // your code
        char* pBuf = new char[MAX_BUF_SZ]; // use of plain new
        SomeMethodThrowingYourException();
        // other code
    }
    catch (const YourExceptionBase& yourEx)
    {
        // exception handling
        SetLastResult(yourEx.GetResult());
    }
    catch (const std::bad_alloc& oomEx)
    {
        // exception handling
```

```
            SetLastResult(E_OUT_OF_MEMORY);
    }
    // You can map each standard exception into Tizen native framework's
    // exception
    catch (const std::exception& stdEx)
    {
        // uncaught standard exception, which can not be mapped to
        // Tizen native framework's exception, reaches here
        SetLastResult(E_UNKNOWN);
    }
    catch (...)
    {
        // absorbs other unknown exceptions
        SetLastResult(E_UNKNOWN);
    }
}
```

If you are not familiar with C++ exceptions, follow the Tizen native framework error handling approach and use `new (std::nothrow)` instead of plain `new`, as shown in the following code:

TIZEN NATIVE-STYLE ERROR HANDLING

```
#include <new>    // for 'std::nothrow'

void
YourClass::OnSomeEventReceived(result r)
{


    // your code
    char* pBuf = new (std::nothrow) char[MAX_BUF_SZ];
    if (!pBuf)
    {
        SetLastResult(E_OUT_OF_MEMORY);
        return;
    }
    result ret = SomeMethod();
    // other code
}
```

Debugging Macro Functions

The native framework provides you with various debugging macro functions that help you to handle errors and log runtime information in a consistent and concise way. There are four categories of debugging macros:

➤ **Try macros** — For error handling

➤ **Log macros** — For logging information while debugging

➤ **Assert macros** — For checking conditions and killing the process if it's false

➤ **Secure log macros** — For logging information if the application is compiled with the _SECURE_LOG definition

Try Macros

The native framework conveniently gathers error-handling code into a well-defined set of try macro functions:

➤ `TryReturnTag(tag, condition, resultValue, message, ...)` — If `condition` is not `true`, log `message` and return immediately with `resultValue` through the return statement. You can use this function with a result return-style function.

➤ `TryReturnVoidResultTag(tag, condition, resultValue, message, ...)` — If `condition` is not `true`, log `message` and return immediately with `resultValue` through the `SetLastResult()` function. Use this function with a method that sets the global error result, rather than return a result code.

➤ `TryReturnResultTag(tag, condition, returnValue, resultValue, message, ...)` — If `condition` is not `true`, log `message` and return immediately with both `returnValue` and `resultValue`. Use this function to return both a value through the return statement and a value of `result` type through the last result.

➤ `TryCatchTag(tag, condition, statements, message, ...)` — If `condition` is not `true`, evaluate `statements`, log `message`, and go to the `CATCH:` label. Typically you use this function when logic for error handling is relatively complex. This function can handle all the scenarios that the other try macro functions can handle.

➤ `TryReturnVoidTag(tag, condition, message, ...)` — If `condition` is not `true`, log `message` and return immediately without any error value. You can use this function when your function does not define any error codes.

➤ `TryLogTag(tag, condition, message, ...)` — If `condition` is not `true`, log `message` and proceed to the next line of code; do not abort the execution of the current function. You can use this function when you want to ignore the error but still log it.

As you can see, `tag`, `condition`, and `message` are common arguments but the others are specific to each macro function. The arguments are used as follows:

➤ `tag` — A user-defined identifier of the current module. This tag can be used when you want to use tag-based log filtering in Tizen IDE log view.

➤ `condition` — Any expression can be evaluated to a `bool` value.

➤ `Message` — A `printf`-like message.

➤ `resultValue` — The value of `result` type. This is typically an application-defined error, but error codes predefined by the native framework can be used, too.

➤ `returnValue` — This should be the same type as the return value of the function inside which the macro function is used.

➤ `statements` — A sequence of any valid C++ statements. Each statement should be separated by a semicolon (;). Typically, resource clean-up statements are specified.

The `tag` argument can be omitted for relatively simple applications, in which case you can use another series of try macro functions, including the following:

➤ `TryReturn(condition, resultValue, message, ...)`

➤ `TryReturnVoidResult(condition, resultValue, message, ...)`

➤ `TryReturnResult(condition, returnValue, resultValue, message, ...)`

➤ `TryCatch(condition, statements, message, ...)`

➤ `TryReturnVoid(condition, message, ...)`

➤ `TryLog(condition, message, ...)`

The tag field of each log message entry is filled with the application's executable name when you use the preceding functions.

Log Macros

All the logging macros will display output in the log view of the Tizen IDE, like the error log messages shown earlier in Figure 11-4. To show the log view, choose Show View from the Window menu in the IDE and then select Log. Each entry shown in the log window will show the app name, the fully qualified function name, the line number, and the message. Because the log view can fill up fast, particularly if you have a complex application which logs a lot of entries, use the `TryXxxTag` series of macros so that you can use the filtering function of the log view to see only those entries marked with a particular tag.

There are various logging levels — for example, the log level of information logged by the try macro functions is Error — but other macros log information in the Debug or Info levels. You can choose which levels are displayed in the log view:

➤ `AppLogTag(tag, message, ...)` — Logs messages in the Info level

➤ `AppLogDebugTag(tag, message, ...)` — Logs messages in the Debug level

➤ `AppLogExceptionTag(tag, message, ...)` — Logs messages in the Error level

The preceding log macro functions are enabled only when running a debug build of the application.

There are also versions of these AppLog macros without the tags:

➤ `AppLog(message, ...)` — Logs messages in the Info level

➤ `AppLogDebug(message, ...)` — Logs messages in the Debug level

➤ `AppLogException(message, ...)` — Logs messages in the Exception level

Assert Macros

Assert macros are used to test that your application is working as it is designed to and that assumptions made by certain functions are true. The assert function is passed a condition which should be true if the program is working correctly; and if it isn't, then this means that a serious error has occurred and the program should print out a message and exit immediately. Two assert macros are available, each of which is only compiled in to an application built in debug mode:

➤ `AppAssert(condition)` — If `condition` is not `true`, prints assertion point and exits immediately

➤ `AppAssertf(condition, message, ...)` — If `condition` is not `true`, prints assertion point with `message` and exits immediately

Secure Log Macros

The last set of macro functions are the secure log macro functions. These functions are only compiled into a debug version of the application with the `_SECURE_LOG` definition set; they are not included in a release build of the application. Messages logged by the secure log macro functions are prefixed with `[SECURE_LOG]` and can be easily filtered in the log view.

The main objective of the secure log macro functions is to ensure that a user's private data is not logged on a real device when using a published app, and simultaneously provide you with debugging aids for such information at development time.

There is a secure macro function corresponding to each try macro function or log macro function, as follows:

➤ `AppSecureLogTag(tag, message, ...)`

➤ `AppSecureDebugLogTag(tag, message, ...)`

➤ `AppSecureExceptionLogTag(tag, message, ...)`

➤ `SecureTryReturnTag(tag, condition, resultValue, message, ...)`

➤ `SecureTryReturnVoidResultTag(tag, condition, resultValue, message, ...)`

➤ `SecureTryReturnResultTag(tag, condition, returnValue, resultValue, message, ...)`

➤ `SecureTryCatchTag(tag, condition, statements, message, ...)`

➤ `SecureTryReturnVoidTag(tag, condition, message, ...)`

➤ `SecureTryLogTag(tag, condition, message, ...)`

Two-Phase Construction

In C++, a constructor does not return a result, so the only way of indicating that construction of a complex object has failed is to throw an exception. Tizen, as you discovered earlier in this chapter, does not use C++ exceptions for error handling, instead uses a two-phase construction pattern for constructing complex objects. In this pattern, the construction is divided into two methods, the constructor and a `Construct()` method that returns a result and in which anything that can fail, such as memory allocation, takes place.

Construct() methods report an error through the result return value and have a signature similar to the following method:

```
result SomeClass::Construct(arg1, arg2, ...)
```

The two-phase construction pattern is used only for framework classes that may return an error during construction. The Construct() method must be called only once for an object; otherwise, an assert failure will be generated.

> **NOTE** *Calling* Construct() *more than once for the same object can lead to memory leaks and other errors at runtime, so catching this error early is important.*

The following code shows how you can use two-phase construction, in this case to construct an object of the File class. The file object is only safe to use when it has been successfully constructed.

TWO-PHASE FILE INSTANCE CONSTRUCTION

```
File file;
String filePath(L"data/list.txt");
result r = file.Construct(filePath, "r");         // open the file in read-only
                                                  // mode
TryReturnTag("PTAD", r == E_SUCCESS,
            "[%ls] Failed to open file(%ls)",
            GetErrorMessage(r), filePath.GetPointer());
// Now you can use 'file' object
```

The RAII Idiom

Resource Acquisition Is Initialization (RAII) is a fundamental C++ programming idiom used to automate resource management. It is recommended that the RAII idiom be used throughout an application and even during exception handling.

Using the RAII idiom means acquiring resources during initialisation (using the C++ constructor) and releasing resources symmetrically during de-initialisation (using the C++ destructor). The idiom factors all repetitive resource clean-up code out and moves it to the destructor. Because the destructor is called on stack objects when they go out of scope, the idiom simplifies resource management, and as a result prevents resource leaks.

The following three examples highlight the advantage of using the RAII idiom over other ways of performing resource cleanup.

In the following code snippet, the delete keyword and fclose(pFile) method are used to perform resource cleanup. Even though only two resources, a file and a memory chunk, are being used, the resource clean-up code is complicated, as the fclose(pFile) method is called repetitively. The clean-up process becomes even more complicated when more resources are used.

TRADITIONAL RESOURCE CLEANUP

```
char*
ReadFile(const char* pFilePath)
{
   FILE* pFile = fopen(pFilePath, "r");
   if (!pFile)
   {
      return null;
   }

   fseek(pFile, 0L, SEEK_END);
   long sz = ftell(pFile);
   fseek(pFile, 0L, SEEK_SET);

   char* pData = new (std::nothrow) char[sz];
   if (!pData)
   {
      fclose(pFile); // For pFile
      return null;
   }

   fread(pData, sizeof(char), sz, pFile);
   if (ferror(pFile))
   {
      delete [] pData; // For pData
      fclose(pFile); // For pFile
      return null;
   }

   fclose(pFile); // For pFile
   return pData;
}
```

You can simplify the preceding code snippet using try macro functions, but the problem of repeated resource clean-up code remains:

TIZEN NATIVE-STYLE RESOURCE CLEANUP

```
char*
ReadFile(const char* pFilePath)
{
   FILE* pFile = fopen(pFilePath, "r");
   TryReturnTag("PTAP", pFile,
               null, "Failed to open file %s", pFilePath);

   fseek(pFile, 0L, SEEK_END);
   long sz = ftell(pFile);
   fseek(pFile, 0L, SEEK_SET);

   char* pData = new (std::nothrow) char[sz];
   TryCatchTag("PTAP", pData, , "Memory allocation failure");

   fread(pData, sizeof(char), sz, pFile);
   TryCatchTag("PTAP", !ferror(pFile),
```

```
                        delete [] pData, "Failed to read file");

    fclose(pFile); // For pFile
    return pData;

CATCH:
    fclose(pFile); // For pFile
    return null;
}
```

The following code snippet demonstrates the use of RAII. In this approach, the RAII-style `File` (for file resources) and `unique_ptr` class (for memory resources) are used to release the owned resources. The `TryReturnTag()` method can be used instead of the `TryCatchTag()` method because resource cleanup will be handled by the destructors of the stack-based objects:

RAII-STYLE RESOURCE CLEANUP

```
char*
ReadFile(const char* pFilePath)
{
    File file; // (1)
    result r = file.Construct(pFilePath, "r"); // (1)
    TryReturnTag("PTAP", r == E_SUCCESS,
                 null, "Failed to open file %s", pFilePath);

    file.Seek(FILESEEKPOSITION_END, 0L);
    int sz = file.Tell();
    file.Seek(FILESEEKPOSITION_BEGIN, 0L);

    unique_ptr< char[] > pData(new (std::nothrow) char[sz]); // (2)
    TryReturnTag("PTAP", pData, null, "Memory allocation failure");

    file.Read(pData[0], sz);
    TryReturnTag("PTAP", GetLastResult() == E_SUCCESS,
                 null, "Failed to read file"); // (3)

    // fclose(pFile);  (4)
    return pData.release();  // (5)

// CATCH:  (3)
// fclose(pFile);
    // return null;
} // (6)
```

(1) `File` is an RAII-style class for a file resource. `file` will have the ownership of the allocated file resource internally.

(2) `unique_ptr` is an RAII-style class for a memory resource. `pData` will take ownership of the newly allocated `char` array.

(3) You can use `TryReturnTag()` instead of `TryCatchTag()` because the memory resource will be automatically released by `unique_ptr`, and the file resource by `File`.

(4) You need not call `fclose()` on the file resource because it will be released automatically by `File`.

(5) `release()` will release ownership of the char array as a return value.

(6) The `File` and `unique_ptr` destructors will be called when stack objects go out of scope.

Using the unique_ptr Class

The RAII-style `unique_ptr` is a smart pointer class used to uniquely save a pointer of an owned object. No other `unique_ptr` can own this object and the object will be destroyed when the `unique_ptr` is destroyed. The object can be moved to another `unique_ptr` instance but cannot be copied.

The following example shows the basic usage of the `unique_ptr` class:

BASIC UNIQUE_PTR USAGE

```
#include <cassert>
#include <iostream>
#include <unique_ptr.h>      // (1)

// A basic class
class Foo
{
    public:
        Foo()
        {
            std::cout << "Foo() called" << std::endl;
        }

        ~Foo()
        {
            std::cout << "~Foo() called" << std::endl;
        }
};

void
SomeFunction(void)
{
    // Declare and allocate the Foo class with a unique pointer
    std::unique_ptr< Foo > foo(new (std::nothrow) Foo());

    // Dynamic array with a unique pointer
    std::unique_ptr< Foo[] > foo(new (std::nothrow) Foo[2]());

    ...

} // Before leaving this function, the destructor of each unique_ptr instance is
  // called and the objects allocated by the Foo() and Foo[2] are released
```

The version of `unique_ptr` provided by the Tizen native framework is an open-source implementation that conforms to the C++ 11 standards. To use `unique_ptr` in your code, include the `<unique_ptr.h>` header.

If the `unique_ptr` class is no longer required to own the memory resource, use the `release()` method to release ownership. `release()` resets its internal pointer to a null pointer, so the `unique_ptr` will not release the resource even when it moves out of scope:

RELEASING UNIQUE_PTR'S RESOURCE

```
IEnumerator*
ArrayList::GetEnumeratorN(void) const
{
    unique_ptr< _ArrayListEnumerator > pEnum(
        new (std::nothrow) _ArrayListEnumerator(*this, __modCount));
    TryReturnTag("PTAD", pEnum != null,
                  null, E_OUT_OF_MEMORY, "[E_OUT_OF_MEMORY]");
    SetLastResult(E_SUCCESS);
    return pEnum.release();
}
```

If a class contains a member pointer variable, this variable can be a defined `unique_ptr` class instance,

A CLASS WITH A UNIQUE_PTR MEMBER VARIABLE

```
class ExampleClass
{
```

as a `unique_ptr` class instance:

A CLASS WITH A UNIQUE_PTR MEMBER VARIABLE

```
class ExampleClass
{
    public:

        ...

    private:
        // Declaration with unique_ptr instead of
        // "Index* __pRootIndex;"
        unique_ptr< Index > __pRootIndex;
};
```

In the case of one-phase construction classes, a `unique_ptr` member variable must be initialised by RAII and acquire memory in the constructor initialisation list. You should check whether allocation is successful or not in the body of the constructor:

CONSTRUCTOR FOR A CLASS WITH A UNIQUE_PTR MEMBER VARIABLE

```
ExampleClass::ExampleClass(void)
    : __pRootIndex(new (std::nothrow) Index)
{
        TryReturnVoidTag("PTAD", __pRootIndex.get(),
                          "[%s] Memory allocation failed.",
                          GetErrorMessage(E_OUT_OF_MEMORY))
};
```

Whenever an instance of `ExampleClass` is destroyed, the destructor for `__pRootIndex`, which is a `unique_ptr`, is called and the object is automatically released. It is not necessary to release the memory inside the `ExampleClass` destructor:

DESTRUCTOR FOR A CLASS WITH A UNIQUE_PTR MEMBER VARIABLE

```
ExampleClass::~ExampleClass(void)
{
    // delete __pRootIndex; // This statement can be removed
    // __pRootIndex = null; // This statement can be removed
};
```

To move a resource owned by a `unique_ptr` to another instance, use the `std::move()` function. This will transfer ownership of the object managed by the `unique_ptr` from one instance to another. For example, assume that `ExampleClass::Update()` needs to alter `__pRootIndex`. Inside the `Update()` method, you need to delay modification of `__pRootIndex` until you can be sure all necessary work is done. So, you introduce a temporary variable `pTmpRootIndex`, do all necessary work with `pTmpRootIndex`, and, finally, move the resource owned by `pTmpRootIndex` into `__pRootIndex`:

MOVING A RESOURCE OF UNIQUE_PTR

```
void
ExampleClass::Update(void)
{
    unique_ptr< Index > pTmpRootIndex(new (std::nothrow) Index);

    // do all necessary work with pTmpRootIndex

    // take ownership of the object managed by pTmpRootIndex.
    __pRootIndex = std::move(pTmpRootIndex);
}
```

Because `unique_ptr` does not support copy, add an explicit method to implement move-semantics for classes that have `unique_ptr` member variable(s) instead of implementing a copy constructor or copy assignment operator. A copy constructor or copy assignment operator with move-semantics will be quite confusing to use.

The object owned by `unique_ptr` can also be released by a custom deleter. A custom deleter is quite useful when you need to call special functions or additional methods other than a simple `delete`. You can register the custom deleter during the `unique_ptr` variable declaration. If a custom deleter is not specified, the default deleter is used, which uses `delete` for a single object or `delete[]` for an array of objects.

The following snippet shows a custom deleter for the `FILE` object of the standard C library and how it is invoked:

CUSTOM DELETER FOR UNIQUE_PTR

```
// Using a custom deleter
struct
CFileDeleter
```

```
{
    void operator()(FILE* pFile)
    {
        fclose(pFile);
    }
};
unique_ptr< FILE, FileDeleter > pCFile(fopen("data/list.txt", "r"));
```

Transferring Object Ownership

A method that has an N postfix returns a new instance with ownership transferred, meaning that the caller is responsible for deleting the returned object when it is no longer required. The following code snippet shows an example:

A METHOD TRANSFERRING OBJECT OWNERSHIP

```
class Searcher
{
    public:
        IList* SearchN(const String& criteria) const;

    // Other methods declared here
};

IList*
Searcher::SearchN(const String& criteria)
{
    // Stores search results matched to criteria to the list
    ArrayList* pList = new (std::nothrow) ArrayList();

    // Add the search results to the list

    return pList;
}

void
MyClass::SomeMethod(void)
{
    Searcher searcher;
    IList* pList = searcher.SearchN(L"Most popular");
    // Delete the list in the caller side
    delete pList;
}
```

You can use a unique_ptr to automate freeing of memory as follows:

```
void
MyClass::SomeMethod(void)
{
    Searcher searcher;
    unique_ptr< IList > pList(searcher.SearchN(L"Most popular"));
    // Use pList
} // unique_ptr's destructor will release IList instance
```

Event handling methods can also have the N postfix. In this case, ownership of one or more arguments is transferred. The event-handling method must delete the object before returning, as shown in the following example:

A CALLBACK TRANSFERRING OBJECT OWNERSHIP

```
void
SampleUiApp::OnUserEventReceivedN(RequestId requestId, IList* pArgs)
{
    // pArgs has been passed with ownership
    result r = E_SUCCESS;

    ... // Use pArgs

    // Delete the object
    delete pArgs;
}
```

You can use unique_ptr to automate memory release in the same way that you do in the Searcher::SearchN() function:

```
void
SampleUiApp::OnUserEventReceivedN(RequestId requestId, IList* pArgs)
{
    // pArgs has been passed with object ownership
    unique_ptr< IList > pList(pArgs);
    result r = E_SUCCESS;

    ...  // Use pArgs
} // unique_ptr's destructor will release IList instance
```

FUNDAMENTAL DATA TYPES

Certain data types are essential to any type of application, whether you're writing a game, a contact manager, a multimedia player, or a to-do list. The Tizen::Base namespace is the home to these application building blocks, from the Object that all Tizen classes derive from, to classes for handling strings, collections, byte buffers, and date and time. This section explains these data types and provides code showing you how to use them in your own applications.

Object

The Tizen::Base::Object class is the most fundamental class of the Tizen native API and the parent class of most Tizen native API classes. It defines a common interface, including the Equals(), GetHashCode(), and ~Object() methods.

➤ Equals() — Should return true if the Object instance is equivalent to the given instance. The default implementation of this method just checks pointer equivalence. You should implement your own algorithm if this behaviour is not appropriate for your class.

➤ GetHashCode() — Should return the unique hash code for the instance. The default implementation of this method returns the object pointer as an integer value. Implement your own hashing algorithm if this behaviour is not appropriate for your class.

➤ ~Object() — This is a polymorphic destructor which you override to implement the destructor for your own class.

It is recommended that your own classes derive from the Object class and override the three methods described above. For example, you should make your class derive from Object if you want to store instances of the class in collections, which are explained later in this section.

String

The Tizen::Base::String class is the most commonly used class within Tizen native applications and deserves a section of its own. String is defined as a mutable, or modifiable, sequence of 32-bit Unicode characters, and Tizen provides methods to make it easy to create, compare, convert, and manipulate strings within your application.

Listing 11-1 shows how to create a String instance.

LISTING 11-1: Creating string instances

```
#include <FBase.h>

using namespace Tizen::Base;

void
CreateString()
{
    String str1(L"ABC");        // (1)
    String str2("DEF");         // (2)
    String str3(str2);          // (3)

    AppLogTag("PTAP", "str1 = %ls", str1.GetPointer());    // (4)
    AppLogTag("PTAP", "str2 = %ls", str2.GetPointer());    // (4)
    AppLogTag("PTAP", "str3 = %ls", str3.GetPointer());    // (4)
}
```

(1) Normally a String instance is created with a pointer to a wchar_t (wide-char) string. The L preceding the string indicates that it is a wchar_t Unicode string literal.

(2) A String instance can be created with a plain string literal. This will be converted to a wchar_t Unicode string.

(3) A String instance can be copy-constructed.

(4) The GetPointer() method returns a pointer to the wchar_t internal buffer of the String instance, which can then be printed using the %ls formatting option. The returned pointer can also be used with the wchar_t string C functions, such as wcslen(), wcscmp(), and wcscat().

If you have a String instance constructed, you can perform various comparison, searching, and extraction tasks with it. Listing 11-2 demonstrates some of these features.

LISTING 11-2: Comparing and searching strings

```
void CompareAndSearchString()
{
    String s1(L"ABCD");
    String s2(L"abcd");

    // (1)
    TryLogTag(
        "PTAP",
        !s1.Equals(s2, false),
        "%ls == %ls in case-insensitive comparison",
        s1.GetPointer(), s2.GetPointer()
        );

    // (1)
    TryLogTag(
        "PTAP",
        s1.Equals(s2, true),
        "%ls != %ls in case-sensitive comparison",
        s1.GetPointer(), s2.GetPointer()
        );

    // (2)
    TryLogTag(
        "PTAP",
        s1 == s2,
        "comparision with operator==() : %ls != %ls",
        s1.GetPointer(), s2.GetPointer()
        );

    // (3)
    TryLogTag(
        "PTAP",
        s1.CompareTo(s2) <= 0,
        "comparision with CompareTo() method : %ls > %ls",
        s1.GetPointer(), s2.GetPointer()
        );

    // (3)
    TryLogTag(
        "PTAP",
        String::Compare(s2, s1) >= 0,
        "comparision with Compare() method : %ls < %ls",
        s2.GetPointer(), s1.GetPointer()
        );

    String str(L"String can be used to do various searching tasks");
    AppLogTag("PTAP", "str = %ls", str.GetPointer());

    // (4)
    if (str.Contains(L"various"))
    {
        AppLogTag("PTAP", "str contains \"various\"");
```

```
    }
    else
    {
        AppLogTag("PTAP", "str does not contain \"various\"");
    }

    // (5)
    if (str.StartsWith(L"String", 0))
    {
        AppLogTag("PTAP", "str starts with \"String\"");
    }
    else
    {
        AppLogTag("PTAP", "str does not starts with \"String\"");
    }

    // (6)
    if (str.EndsWith(L"tasks"))
    {
        AppLogTag("PTAP", "str end with \"tasks\"");
    }
    else
    {
        AppLogTag("PTAP", "str does not end with \"tasks\"");
    }

    // (7)
    int prevIdx = 0;
    int curIdx = 0;
    result r = str.IndexOf(L' ', 0, prevIdx);
    TryReturnVoidTag("PTAP", r == E_SUCCESS, "can't find space");
    String word;
    while (str.IndexOf(L' ', prevIdx + 1, curIdx) == E_SUCCESS)
    {
        AppAssert(str[curIdx] == L' ');
        int wl = curIdx - prevIdx - 1;
        if (wl >= 1)
        {
            // (8)
            str.SubString(prevIdx + 1, curIdx - prevIdx - 1, word);
            AppLogTag("PTAP", "word = %ls", word.GetPointer());
        }
        prevIdx = curIdx;
    }
    AppLogTag("PTAP", "str = %ls", str.GetPointer());
}
```

(1) You can check whether two String instances are equivalent in case-sensitive or insensitive mode with the Equals() method. The second argument of the Equals() method specifies case sensitivity.

(2) You can check whether two String instances are equivalent in case-sensitive mode with the == operator.

(3) You can determine the ordering of two `String` instances using the `CompareTo()` method or the `String::Compare()` static method. If you have two `String` instances `s1` and `s2`, you can get the same result for both `s1.CompareTo(s2)` and `String::Compare(s1, s2)`.

(4) The `Contains()` method returns `true` if and only if the `String` instance contains the given substring at any position. In this example, the `str` `String` instance definitely contains `L"various"`.

(5) The `StartsWith()` method returns `true` if and only if the `String` instance starts with the given substring at the given position. In this example, `str` starts with `L"String"` at position 0.

(6) The `EndsWith()` method returns `true` if and only if the `String` instance ends with the given substring at the end. In this example, `str` ends with `L"tasks"`.

(7) The last portion of the code snippet shows how to use the `IndexOf(wchar_t ch, int startIndex, int& indexOf)` method. This method searches the string for the character passed into the function — in this case, a space — and returns the index of the first occurrence. You can also use the version of `IndexOf(...)` which takes a `String` to search for or `LastIndexOf(...)` which returns the index of the last occurrence of a character or string.

(8) `str.SubString(prevIdx + 1, curIdx - prevIdx - 1, word)` returns the substring of `str`, which starts from the position `prevIdx + 1` with length `curIdx - prevIdx - 1` in the `word` output argument. If you get `word` by `str.SubString(0, str.GetLength(), word)`, then `str == word` is always `true`. If you want just one character, use the expression `str[i]`.

In addition to the tasks explained so far, you can also modify a `String` instance in place, as demonstrated in Listing 11-3.

LISTING 11-3: Modifying strings

```
void ModifyString()
{
    String str;                 // Initialised to empty string L""

    str.Append(L'A');           // (1) str becomes L"A"
    AppLogTag("PTAP", "str = %ls", str.GetPointer());
    str.Append('=');            // (1) str becomes L"A="
    AppLogTag("PTAP", "str = %ls", str.GetPointer());
    str.Append(10);             // (1) str becomes L"A=10"
    AppLogTag("PTAP", "str = %ls", str.GetPointer());
    str.Append(L',');           // (1) str becomes L"A=10,"
    AppLogTag("PTAP", "str = %ls", str.GetPointer());
    str.Append(L"B=20");        // (1) str becomes L"A=10,B=20"
    AppLogTag("PTAP", "str = %ls", str.GetPointer());
    String str2(L",C=30");
    str.Append(str2);           // (1) str becomes L"A=10,B=20,C=30"
```

```
    AppLogTag("PTAP", "str = %ls", str.GetPointer());

    str.Insert(L'a', 5);          // (2) str becomes L"A=10,aB=20,C=30"
    AppLogTag("PTAP", "str = %ls", str.GetPointer());
    str.Insert('=', 6);           // (2) str becomes L"A=10,a=B=20,C=30"
    AppLogTag("PTAP", "str = %ls", str.GetPointer());
    str.Insert(12, 7);            // (2) str becomes L"A=10,a=12B=20,C=30"
    AppLogTag("PTAP", "str = %ls", str.GetPointer());
    str.Insert(L',', 9);          // (2) str becomes L"A=10,a=12,B=20,C=30"
    AppLogTag("PTAP", "str = %ls", str.GetPointer());
    str.Insert(L"b=22,", 15); // (2) str becomes L"A=10,a=12,B=20,b=22,C=30"
    AppLogTag("PTAP", "str = %ls", str.GetPointer());
    str2 = L",c=32";
    str.Insert(str2, str.GetLength());  // (2) str becomes
// L"A=10,a=12,B=20,b=22,C=30,c=32"
    AppLogTag("PTAP", "str = %ls", str.GetPointer());

    str.Replace(L"C=30", L"D=45");        // (3) str becomes
// L"A=10,a=12,B=20,b=22,D=45,c=32"
    AppLogTag("PTAP", "str = %ls", str.GetPointer());

    // (4)
    int dpos = 0;
    str.IndexOf(L",D=45", dpos);
    str.Remove(dpos, wcslen(&str[dpos]));// str becomes L"A=10,a=12,B=20,b=22"
    AppLogTag("PTAP", "str = %ls", str.GetPointer());

    // (3) str becomes L"A=10/a=12/B=20/b=22"
    str.Replace(L',', L'/');
    AppLogTag("PTAP", "str = %ls", str.GetPointer());
    // (5) str becomes L"A=10/A=12/B=20/B=22"
    str.ToUpperCase();
    AppLogTag("PTAP", "str = %ls", str.GetPointer());
    // (6) str becomes L"a=10/a=12/b=20/b=22"
    str.ToLowerCase();
    AppLogTag("PTAP", "str = %ls", str.GetPointer());

    // (7)
    String str3(str);                       // str3 is same to str
    // str3 becomes L"a=10,a=12,b=20,b=22"
    str3.Replace(L'/', L',');
}
```

(1) You can append one wide character (wchar_t), one char (char), a numeric value, a wide character string, or a String instance. The numeric value is converted into a String instance first and then appended. '+=' behaves in the same way as the Append() method.

(2) You can insert one wide character (wchar_t), one char (char), a numeric value, a wide character string, or a String instance at the given position. The numeric value is converted into a String instance first and then inserted. str.Append(arg) can be thought as a convenient alternative function to str.Insert(arg, str.GetPointer()).

(3) You can replace one substring (`str1`) with another substring (`str2`) by calling `Replace(str1, str2)`, or one character (`ch1`) with another character (`ch2`) by calling `Replace(ch1, ch2)`.

(4) You can remove a substring at the position *pos* with the length *len* by calling `Remove(pos, len)`. In this example, you can remove the substring `L",D=45"`. `&str[dpos]` returns the pointer at the `dpos` position.

(5) Make all characters uppercase letters by calling `ToUpperCase()`.

(6) Make all characters lowercase letters by calling `ToLowerCase()`.

(7) If you want to get a new `String` instance to modify, create it by using the copy constructor and then call the desired modification method.

Collection

Collections are probably the most commonly used data structure after `String`. The collection classes are essential when developing any of the following types of applications:

➤ **Contacts** — Creates a contact group and treats the group as if it were one entity

➤ **Email** — Sorts searched e-mails by their sent date and time

➤ **File browser** — Shows users the list of files inside a directory

In these scenarios, the contact group, searched e-mails, and list of files are all collections, a concept that is used in many other types of applications.

The `Tizen::Base::Collection` namespace defines three different forms of list, provided by the `IList`, `IMap`, and `IMultiMap` interfaces (see Figure 11-5).

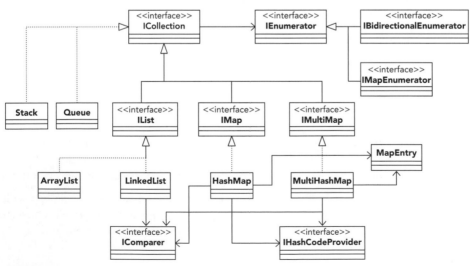

FIGURE 11-5

`IList` represents an ordered list of elements and defines a common interface, including the following methods:

➤ `IsRandomAccessible()`

➤ `GetBidirectionalEnumeratorN()`

➤ `Add(Object* pObj)`

➤ `GetAt(int idx)`

➤ `IndexOf(const Object& obj)`

➤ `InsertAt(Object* pObj, int idx)`

➤ `SetAt(Object* pObj, int idx)`

➤ `Remove(const Object& obj)`

➤ `Sort()`

Both `ArrayList` and `LinkedList` implement the `IList` interface.

The main difference between `ArrayList` and `LinkedList` is how they are implemented. An `ArrayList` is stored in a contiguous area of memory, whereas the `LinkedList` is implemented as a doubly linked list in which each item stores a pointer to the next and previous items. The `ArrayList` is faster to access but slower to modify, because when new elements are added, the entire block of memory used to store the array may need to be resized. The `LinkedList` is slower to access and sort but faster to add elements to. Therefore, if you have a list which won't change that much and for which speed of access is important, use an `ArrayList`; but if you will be adding and removing items frequently, use a `LinkedList`.

`IList` provides the `IsRandomAccessible()` method, which enables differentiating between a `LinkedList` and an `ArrayList`, each of which has different characteristics in terms of performance and efficiency, as shown in Table 11-1.

TABLE 11-1: ArrayList vs LinkedList

COMPARISON ITEM	ARRAYLIST	LINKEDLIST
Addition	Mostly constant except when expanding	Always constant
Retrieval	Constant	Linear
Insertion	Linear	Always constant
Removal	Linear	Always constant
Sorting	nlogn	2n + nlogn See (8) explanation

Listing 11-4 shows how to use `ArrayList`.

LISTING 11-4: Using IList

```cpp
#include <unique_ptr.h>
#include <FBase.h>

using namespace Tizen::Base;
using namespace Tizen::Base::Collection;

void
YourClass::ArrayListSample(void)
{
    ArrayList list(SingleObjectDeleter);  // (1)

    list.Add(new Integer(1));    // (2) 1
    list.Add(new Integer(2));    // (2) 1,2
    list.Add(new Integer(3));    // (2) 1,2,3

    Integer* pInt = static_cast< Integer* >(list.GetAt(0));  // (3)

    if (pInt->Equals(Integer(1)))
    {
        AppLogTag("PTAP", "Apparently Integer(1) is stored at index 0");
    }
    else
    {
        AppAssertf(false, "Cannot reach here!");
    }

    list.InsertAt(new Integer(4), 1);   // (4) 1,4,2,3
    list.Remove(Integer(3));            // (5) 1,4,2
    list.RemoveAt(0);                   // (6) 4,2
    if (list.IsRandomAccessible())      // (7)
    {
        list.Sort(IntegerComparer());   // (8) 2,4
    }

    // Uses an enumerator to access elements in the list
    std::unique_ptr< IEnumerator > pEnum = list.GetEnumeratorN();   // (9)
    Object* pObj = null;
    while (pEnum->MoveNext() == E_SUCCESS)    // (10)
    {
        Integer* pInt2 = static_cast< Integer* >(pEnum->GetCurrent());   // (11)
        AppLogTag("PTAP", "Integer value = %d", pInt2->value);
    }
} // (12)
```

(1) You can specify a deleter when you create an instance of `ArrayList`. The deleter is called whenever an element is about to be removed. There are two predefined deleters:

➤   `SingleObjectDeleter` — Destroys the element by calling `delete`. Specifying this deleter will create an owning collection, which has ownership of the elements and is responsible for destroying the elements.

➤ NoOpDeleter — Does nothing with the given Object pointer. When this deleter is specified, a non-owning collection is created, which will not own the elements and will not destroy them.

NoOpDeleter is declared as the default deleter:

```
ArrayList::ArrayList(DeleterFunctionType deleter = NoOpDeleter);
```

The list instance is an owning collection in the preceding example. This deleter concept is also applied to LinkedList, HashMap, and MultiHashMap.

(2) Add() can take a pointer to an instance of classes that derive from Object. If the collection is an owning one, then ownership is transferred to the collection. You can add any instance of a class that derives from the Object class, so it is possible to store heterogeneous elements in one ArrayList. Other collections support this concept too.

(3) GetAt() returns a pointer to the element at the given index. The returned pointer should be cast to a class deriving from Object before use. The index is zero-based.

(4) InsertAt() inserts a new element at the given index.

(5) Removes the first occurrence of an element with the value specified. Equality is checked with the Equal() method. The deleter will be called on the element to be removed. SingleObjectDeleter will be called in the preceding sample code.

(6) Removes the element at the specified position. The deleter will be called to delete this element.

(7) IsRandomAccessible() always returns true for ArrayList and false for LinkedList.

(8) Sort() sorts elements using a given criteria. The criteria can be any class that implements the Tizen::Base::Collection::IComparer interface. The given criteria is IntegerComparer in the preceding sample code. IntegerComparer can be used to sort integer values in ascending order. Note that you can call Sort() on a LinkedList but its implementation first copies all elements into an ArrayList, calls Sort() on the ArrayList, and then copies the elements back into the original LinkedList. Therefore, you should be cautious when using Sort() on a LinkedList.

(9) You need to get an IEnumerator instance to iterate through elements in a collection. The initial position of the IEnumerator instance is before the first element in the collection. You can get an IBidirectionalEnumerator instance too which also supports MovePrevious() and ResetLast() operations.

The following code snippet shows how to use the IBidirectionalEnumerator to iterate through the elements of an ArrayList in reverse order:

```
unique_ptr< IBidirectionalEnumerator > pEnum(list.
  GetBidirectionalEnumeratorN());
while (pEnum->MovePrevious() == E_SUCCESS)
{
    // do your job
}
```

(10) `MoveNext()` moves the `IEnumerator` to the next element in the collection. The first call to `MoveNext()` positions the enumerator at the first element. The `MoveNext()` method returns `E_INVALID_OPERATION` when there are no more elements.

(11) `GetCurrent()` returns the current element. The returned pointer should be cast to a class derived from `Object` before use.

(12) The `ArrayList` destructor removes all elements and calls the deleter on each element. This behaviour is the same for all other collections.

`IMap` represents a collection of key value pairs and defines a common interface, including the following methods:

➤   `GetMapEnumeratorN()`

➤   `Add(Object* pKey, Object* pValue)`

➤   `ContainsKey(const Object& key)`

➤   `GetKeysN()`

➤   `GetValue(const Object& key)`

➤   `SetValue(const Object& key, Object* pValue)`

➤   `Remove(const Object& key)`

`HashMap` implements the `IMap` interface. Listing 11-5 shows `HashMap` in use.

LISTING 11-5: Using IMap

```
#include <unique_ptr.h>
#include <FBase.h>

using namespace Tizen::Base;
using namespace Tizen::Base::Collection;

void
MyClass::HashMapSample(void)
{
    HashMap map(SingleObjectDeleter);    // (1)

    // Constructs a HashMap instance with default capacity,
    // load factor, hash code provider, and comparer
    map.Construct();              // (2)

    map.Add(new String(L"Zero"),
            new Integer(0));      // (3) ({Zero:0})
    map.Add(new String(L"One"),
            new Integer(1));      // (3) ({Zero:0},{one:1})
```

```
map.Add(new String(L"Two"),
        new Integer(2));      // (3) ({Zero:0},{one:1},{Two:2})

// (4) Gets a value with the specified key
Integer* pValue = static_cast< Integer* >(map.GetValue(String(L"Zero")));

// (5) Removes the value with the specified key
map.Remove(String(L"Zero")); // ({one:1},{Two:2})

// (6) Uses a map enumerator to access elements in the map
std::unique_ptr< IMapEnumerator > pMapEnum = map.GetMapEnumeratorN();
String* pKey = null;
while (pMapEnum->MoveNext() == E_SUCCESS)      // (7)
{
    pKey = static_cast< String* >(pMapEnum->GetKey());        // (8)
    pValue = static_cast< Integer* >(pMapEnum->GetValue());   // (9)
    AppLogTag("PTAP", "%ls = %d", pKey->GetPointer(), pValue->value);
}
}  // (10)
```

(1) The HashMap instance is an owning collection because it is created with a SingleObjectDeleter.

(2) HashMap is constructed using two-phase construction.

(3) The first argument of Add() is a key and the second a value. Their ownership is transferred when you add them to an owning collection.

(4) Gets the value associated with the specified key.

(5) Removes the specified key value pair.

(6) The IMap interface provides a GetMapEnumerator() in addition to GetEnumerator(). The IMapEnumerator interface enables you to access the key and value using the GetKey() and GetValue() methods, whereas IEnumerator does not. When you use the IEnumerator interface with HashMap, you should type-cast the returned Object pointer into a MapEntry pointer as follows:

```
MapEntry* pElem = static_cast< MapEntry* >(pEnum->GetCurrent);
String* pKey = static_cast< String* >(pElem->GetKey());
Integer* pValue = static_cast< Integer* >(pElem->GetValue());
```

(7) MoveNext() moves the enumerator to the next element in the HashMap and behaves in the same way as the ArrayList enumerator described above.

(8) GetKey() returns the key of the current element as an Object pointer. You should type-cast it into the concrete type.

(9) GetValue() returns the value of the current element as an Object pointer. You should type-cast it into the concrete type.

(10) The HashMap destructor removes all elements and calls the deleter on each element.

IMultiMap represents a collection of keys and values, with each key mapped to one or multiple values. IMultiMap defines a common interface that includes the following methods:

➤ GetMapEnumeratorN()

➤ Add(Object* pKey, Object* pValue)

➤ ContainsKey(const Object& key)

➤ GetKeysN()

➤ GetValuesN(const Object& key)

➤ SetValue(const Object& key, const Object& value, Object* pNewValue)

➤ Remove(const Object& key)

➤ Remove(const Object& key, const Object& value)

➤ Remove(const Object& key)

Note that because IMultiMap supports multiple values per key, it also includes some additional methods:

➤ GetValuesN(const Object& key)

➤ Remove(const Object& key, const Object& value)

➤ SetValue(const Object& key, const Object& value, Object* pNewValue)

MultiHashMap implements the IMultiMap interface, as demonstrated in the Listing 11-6.

LISTING 11-6: Using IMultiMap

```
#include <unique_ptr.h>
#include <FBase.h>

using namespace Tizen::Base;
using namespace Tizen::Base::Collection;

void
MyClass::MultiHashMapSample(void)
{
    MultiHashMap map(SingleObjectDeleter);   // (1)

    // Constructs a MultiHashMap instance with default values for
    // capacity, load factor, hash code provider, and comparer
    map.Construct();   // (2)

    map.Add(new String(L"Zero"),
            new Integer(0));     // (3) {Zero:0}
    map.Add(new String(L"One"),
            new Integer(1));     // (3) {Zero:0},{One:1}
    map.Add(new String(L"Two"),
            new Integer(2));     // (3) {Zero:0},{One:1},{Two:2}
    map.Add(new String(L"Two"),
            new Integer(20));    // (3) {Zero:0},{One:1},{Two:2,20}
```

```
    Integer* pValue = null;
    // (4) Gets values with the specified key
    unique_ptr< IEnumerator > pValueEnum(map.GetValuesN(String(L"Two")));
    while(pValueEnum->MoveNext() == E_SUCCESS)
    {
        pValue = static_cast< Integer* > (pValueEnum->GetCurrent());
        AppLogTag("PTAP", "Two ==> %d", pValue->value);
    }

    // (5) Removes values with the specified key
    map.Remove(String(L"Two"));     // {Two:2,20} removed

    // (6) Uses an enumerator to access elements in the map
    unique_ptr< IMapEnumerator > pMapEnum(map.GetMapEnumeratorN());
    String* pKey = null;
    while (pMapEnum->MoveNext() == E_SUCCESS)    // (7)
    {
        pKey = static_cast< String* > (pMapEnum->GetKey());        // (8)
        pValue = static_cast< Integer* > (pMapEnum->GetValue());   // (9)
        AppLogTag("PTAP", "%ls ==> %d", pKey->GetPointer(), pValue->value);
    }
} // (10)
```

(1) The `MultiHashMap` instance is an owning collection because it is created with a `SingleObjectDeleter`.

(2) `MultiHashMap` is constructed using a two-phase construction.

(3) The first argument of `Add()` is a key and the second a value. Their ownership is transferred when you add them to an owning collection.

(4) You can get an enumerator for the list of values corresponding to a key using the `GetValuesN(const Object& key)` method. Note that the `GetValuesN()` method returns an enumerator because there may be multiple values for a key.

(5) You can remove all values corresponding to a key by using `Remove(const Object& key)`. If you want to remove a specific key and value pair, use the `Remove(const Object& key, const Object& value)` method instead.

(6) The `IMultiMap` interface also provides a `GetMapEnumerator()` in addition to `GetEnumerator()`.

(7) `MoveNext()` moves the enumerator to the next element in the `MultiHashMap` and behaves in the same way as the `ArrayList` enumerator described above.

(8) `GetKey()` returns the key of the current element as an `Object` pointer. You should type-cast it into a concrete type.

(9) `GetValue()` returns the value of the current element as an `Object` pointer. You should type-cast it into a concrete type.

(10) The `MultiHashMap` destructor removes all elements and calls the deleter on each element.

STLConverter

The Standard Template Library (STL) is one of the core tools for C++ programmers. The Tizen native APIs use collections, as described in the previous section, but they don't make use of STL containers. If you have existing code using STL and don't want to rewrite it to use collections, use the `Tizen::Base::Collection::StlConverter` class, which is a bridge between two different worlds: STL containers and Tizen native collections.

The `StlConverter` can convert Tizen native collections into STL containers and vice versa. It enables these conversions through iterators. The conversion from Tizen native collections to STL containers is enabled by `IteratorT`, `PairIteratorT`, and `RandomIteratorT`. You can obtain these iterators by calling the following methods defined in the `Tizen::Base::Collection::StlConverter` class:

➤ `IteratorT< T > GetBeginIterator(const IList* pList)`

➤ `IteratorT< T > GetEndIterator(const IList* pList)`

➤ `PairIteratorT< K, V > GetBeginIterator(const IMap* pMap)`

➤ `PairIteratorT< K, V > GetEndIterator(const IMap* pMap)`

➤ `PairIteratorT< K, V > GetBeginIterator(const IMultiMap* pMultiMap)`

➤ `PairIteratorT< K, V > GetEndIterator(const IMultiMap* pMultiMap)`

➤ `RandomIteratorT< T > GetBeginRandomIterator(const IList* pList)`

➤ `RandomIteratorT< T > GetEndRandomIterator(const IList* pList)`

These APIs model the STL container `begin()` and `end()` methods. Conversion from STL containers to Tizen native collections can be done using iterators as well. You can use the following APIs for this purpose:

➤ `std::unique_ptr< ArrayList > GetArrayListN(FwdIter begin, FwdIter end, DeleterFunctionType deleter)`

➤ `std::unique_ptr< LinkedList > GetLinkedListN(FwdIter begin, FwdIter end, DeleterFunctionType deleter)`

➤ `std::unique_ptr< HashMap > GetHashMapN(PairedFwdIter begin, PairedFwdIter end, DeleterFunctionType deleter)`

➤ `std::unique_ptr< MultiHashMap > GetMultiHashMapN(PairedFwdIter begin, PairedFwdIter end, DeleterFunctionType deleter)`

Conversion is done using iterators because too many APIs would need to be defined if there were one API to convert between each container and collection. For example, the `HashMap` collection can be converted to `std::vector<MapEntry*>`, `std::list<MapEntry*>`, `std::map<K*, V*>`, and `std::unordered_map<K*, V*>`. Four separate APIs would be required to support all these conversions, but only two APIs are required when using iterators.

Listing 11-7 shows how to use `StlConverter`.

LISTING 11-7: Using STLConverter

```cpp
#include <vector>
#include <tr1/unordered_map.h>
#include <algorithm>
#include <unique_ptr.h>
#include <FBase.h>

using namespace std;
using namespace std::tr1;
using namespace Tizen::Base;
using namespace Tizen::Base::Collection;

bool IsOdd(Integer* pInt)
{
   return (pInt->ToInt() % 2) == 1;
}

void InitializeList(IList& list, int elemCnt)
{
   for (int i = 0; i < elemCnt; ++i)
   {
      list.Add(new Integer(i));
   }
}

// (3)
void PrintVec(const vector< Integer* >& v1)
{
   for(vector< Integer* >::const_iterator i = v1.begin();
       i != v1.end(); ++i)
   {
      AppLogTag("PTAP", "%d", (*i)->ToInt());
   }
}

// (7)
void PrintList(const IList* pList)
{
   unique_ptr< IEnumerator > pEnum(pList->GetEnumeratorN());
   while (pEnum->MoveNext() == E_SUCCESS)
   {
      AppLogTag(
         "PTAP", "%d",
         static_cast< Integer* >(pEnum->GetCurrent())->ToInt()
         );
   }
}

// (9)
template <>
struct hash<String *>
{
    size_t operator()(String* pStr) const
```

continues

LISTING 11-7 *(continued)*

```
        {
            return static_cast< size_t >(pStr->GetHashCode());
        }
};

// (10)
void PrintMap(const IMap* pMap)
{
    unique_ptr< IMapEnumerator > pEnum(pMap->GetMapEnumeratorN());
    while (pEnum->MoveNext() == E_SUCCESS)
    {
        AppLogTag(
            "PTAP", "%ls = %d",
            static_cast< String* >(pEnum->GetKey())->GetPointer(),
            static_cast< Integer* >(pEnum->GetValue())->ToInt()
            );
    }
}

void
MyClass::StlConverterSample()
{
    // (1) Initialise a LinkedList
    LinkedList list;
    InitializeList(list, 10);   // {0,1,2,...,9}

    // (2) vector can be created through IteratorT
    vector< Integer* > v1(
        StlConverter::GetBeginIterator< Integer* >(&list),
        StlConverter::GetEndIterator< Integer* >(&list)
        );

    // (3)
    PrintVec(v1);

    // (4)
    vector< Integer* >::iterator pos =
        find_if(
            StlConverter::GetBeginIterator< Integer* >(&list),
            StlConverter::GetEndIterator< Integer* >(&list),
            IsOdd
            );
    AppAssert(IsOdd(*pos));

    // (4)
    int cnt =
        count_if(
            StlConverter::GetBeginIterator< Integer* >(&list),
            StlConverter::GetEndIterator< Integer* >(&list),
            IsOdd
            );
    AppAssert(cnt == 5);
```

```
    // (5) The case of conversion from STL Container to Collection
    vector< Integer* > v2;

    v2.push_back(new Integer(1));
    v2.push_back(new Integer(2));
    v2.push_back(new Integer(3));

    // (6)
    unique_ptr< ArrayList > pList(
        StlConverter::GetArrayListN(
            v2.begin(), v2.end(), NoOpDeleter
            )
        );

    // (7)
    PrintList(pList.get());

    // (8)
    for (vector< Integer* >::iterator i = v2.begin();
         i != v2.end(); ++i)
    {
        delete *i;
    }

    // (9)
    unordered_map< String*, Integer* > m1;
    m1.insert(make_pair(new String(L"One"), new Integer(1)));
    m1.insert(make_pair(new String(L"Two"), new Integer(2)));
    m1.insert(make_pair(new String(L"Three"), new Integer(3)));
    unique_ptr< HashMap > pMap(
        StlConverter::GetHashMapN(
            m1.begin(), m1.end(), SingleObjectDeleter
            )
        );

    // (10)
    PrintMap(pMap.get())
}
```

(1) Initialises the `LinkedList` instance with 10 elements from 0 to 9.

(2) Constructs a vector instance with iterators obtained from `GetBeginIterator()` and `GetEndIterator()`. The element type of the vector should be same as the template parameter type given to `GetBeginIterator()` and `GetEndIterator()`.

(3) Prints all elements of the vector using the STL iterator.

(4) You can call standard nonmutating algorithms such as `find_if()` and `count_if()`, but you cannot call standard mutating algorithms such as `sort()` and `remove()` because `IteratorT`, `PairIteratorT`, and `RandomIteratorT` do not support the `OutputIterator` concept. This means that you cannot modify elements inside Tizen collections using these iterators.

(5) Initialises a vector with `Integer` instances.

(6) Obtains a new copy of `ArrayList` by calling `GetArrayListN()`. In this case, `NoOpDeleter` is given as the `deleter` argument. Therefore, conceptually, the ownership of `Integer` instances is not transferred to the `ArrayList` instance. If you specify the `SingleObjectDeleter` for the `deleter` argument, consider that you are transferring the ownership of the `Integer` instance. You should always be careful about element ownership.

(7) Prints all elements of the `ArrayList`.

(8) You should delete all elements of the `v2` vector to avoid memory leaks because ownership of elements is not transferred to `ArrayList` as mentioned in (6).

(9) If you want to use `String*` as a key in an `unordered_map`, define a special hasher for the type. The default hasher of the C++ standard library will generate a hash value based only on the pointer value, not the content of the object pointed to. `struct hash< String* >` defines such a hasher.

(10) Prints all elements of the `HashMap` using the `IMapEnumerator` interface.

In addition to the collection APIs explained so far, there are additional template collection APIs, including the following classes:

➤ `ArrayListT`

➤ `LinkedListT`

➤ `HashMapT`

➤ `MultiHashMapT`

The interfaces of the preceding collections mostly correspond to the non-template versions, except that they do not support the `deleter` concept. Implementation of the template collection APIs assumes that every element is of a primitive type. If you want to store non-primitive types, then use a non-template collection API.

DateTime and TimeSpan

Now that you're familiar with Tizen's fundamental coding idioms and core data types such as strings and collections, this section examines the classes for manipulating date and time: `Tizen::Base::DateTime` and `Tizen::Base::TimeSpan`.

The `DateTime` class represents a specific date and time ranging from 00:00:00 A.M. (midnight), January 1, 1 A.D., to 11:59:59 P.M., December 31, 9999 A.D. in the Gregorian calendar. The `TimeSpan` class represents the interval between two `DateTime`s. Both `DateTime` and `TimeSpan` measure time in ticks. A tick may vary between platforms, but on Tizen one tick equals one millisecond. The exact value can be obtained by calling `DateTime::GetTicksPerSecond()`, which for Tizen returns 1,000.

`DateTime` encapsulates the date and time with years, months, days, hours, minutes, seconds, and milliseconds. The class also provides methods to set and retrieve each element, together with various comparison methods and overloaded operators.

`TimeSpan` represents a time with days, hours, minutes, seconds, and milliseconds and provides corresponding access methods.

The `DateTime` and `TimeSpan` classes are best explained through examples, as shown in Listing 11-8.

LISTING 11-8: Using DateTime and TimeSpan

```
void
DateTimeTimeSpanExample()
{
    // (1)
    DateTime dt;
    AppAssert(dt.GetYear() == 1 && dt.GetMonth() == 1 &&
              dt.GetDay() == 1 && dt.GetHour() == 0 &&
              dt.GetMinute() == 0 && dt.GetSecond() == 0 &&
              dt.GetMillisecond() == 0);
    // (2)
    dt.SetValue(2013, 8, 4);
    AppAssert(dt.GetYear() == 2013 && dt.GetMonth() == 8 &&
              dt.GetDay() == 4 && dt.GetHour() == 0 &&
              dt.GetMinute() == 0 && dt.GetSecond() == 0 &&
              dt.GetMillisecond() == 0);

    // (3)
    DateTime dt2(dt);
    if (dt == dt2)
    {
        AppLogTag("PTAP", "dt2 is definitely the same as dt");
    }

    // (4)
    dt.AddHours(13);
    dt.AddMinutes(29);
    dt.AddSeconds(13);
    dt.AddMilliseconds(300);
    if (dt > dt2)
    {
        AppLogTag("PTAP", "dt is definitely greater than dt2)
    }

    // (5)
    dt.SetValue(dt.GetTicks() + 60 * DateTime::GetTicksPerSecond());

    // (6)
    TimeSpan ts = dt.GetTimeOfDay();
    dt.Subtract(ts);
    if (dt == dt2)
    {
        AppLogTag("PTAP", "dt is the same as dt2");
    }

    // (7)
```

continues

LISTING 11-8 *(continued)*

```
        DateTime dt3;
        DateTime::Parse(dt.ToString(), dt3);
        AppAssert(dt == dt3);

        // (8)
        TimeSpan ts2(0, 13, 30, 13, 300);
        AppAssert(ts2.GetDays() == 0 && ts2.GetHours() == 13 &&
                  ts2.GetMinutes() == 30 && ts2.GetSeconds() == 13 &&
                  ts2.GetMilliseconds() == 300);
        if (ts == ts2)
        {
            AppLogTag("PTAP", "ts is definitely same to ts2");
        }

        // (9)
        TimeSpan oneDay(TimeSpan::NUM_OF_TICKS_IN_DAY);

        // (10)
        ts2 = oneDay + ts;
        AppAssert(ts2.GetDays() == 1 && ts2.GetHours() == 13 &&
                  ts2.GetMinutes() == 30 && ts2.GetSeconds() == 13 &&
                  ts2.GetMilliseconds() == 300);
        AppAssert(ts2 > ts);
        AppAssert(ts2 - ts == oneDay);
}
```

(1) The `DateTime` dt instance is initialised to 00:00:00 A.M. (midnight), January 1, 1 A.D. which is the value returned by `DateTime::GetMinValue()` after default construction. You can retrieve the maximum value from `DateTime::GetMaxValue()`.

(2) The `DateTime` dt instance is set to 00:00:00 A.M. (midnight), August 4, 2013 A.D. The `SetValue()` method takes additional optional arguments for the hour, minute, and second elements, but these will default to 0 if not specified. `dt.SetValue(2013, 8, 4)` has the same effect as `dt.SetValue(2013, 8, 4, 0, 0, 0, 0)`.

(3) The `DateTime` class supports copy construction and various comparison operators, including `operator==`.

(4) `DateTime` dt is set to 13:29:13.0300 P.M., August 4, 2013 A.D. when the preceding code is executed and dt is now greater than dt2.

(5) This code gets the number of ticks represented by dt and adds to it the number of ticks representing one minute (`60 * DateTime::GetTicksPerSecond()`).

`dt.AddTicks(60 * DateTime::GetTicksPerSecond())` has exactly the same effect as the preceding code.

(6) `GetTimeOfDay()` returns a `TimeSpan` object representing the time interval since midnight on the date specified by dt. In the example, ts is initialised to 13:30:13.0300 P.M. You can subtract ts from dt by calling `dt.Subtract(ts)`. After this subtraction, dt and dt2 are now equal.

(7) The `DateTime` class also provides a `ToString()` method to convert a date and time to a string, and a `Parse()` static method to retrieve date and time elements from a string.

(8) A `TimeSpan` instance can be created with various constructors. One of them enables you to specify days, hours, minutes, seconds, and milliseconds individually, as shown in the preceding code. The `ts2` instance should be the same as the `ts` instance retrieved by `dt.GetTimeOfDay()`.

(9) A `TimeSpan` instance can also be constructed from a number of ticks, and `NUM_OF_TICKS_IN_DAY` represents the number of ticks per day.

(10) `TimeSpan` provides various operators, such as `operator+`, `operator-`, `operator==`, and so on. You can also perform timespan arithmetic and comparisons just as you would with any primitive type.

ByteBuffer

The `ByteBuffer` class encapsulates a sequence of bytes in memory and provides methods for reading and writing all built-in primitive types, with the exception of `bool`. Listing 11-9 shows how to use `ByteBuffer`.

LISTING 11-9: Using ByteBuffer

```
void
MyClass::ByteBufferSample()
{
    // (1)
    const int BUFFER_SIZE_MAX = 1024;
    ByteBuffer buf;
    buf.Construct(BUFFER_SIZE_MAX);

    // Copies five values from 'A' to 'E' into the buf
    for (int i = 0; i < 5; i++)
    {
        byte b = 'A' + i;

        // (2) Writes byte b to the current position of the buf
        buf.SetByte(b);
    }

    // (3) Flips the buf
    buf.Flip();

    // Reads bytes from the buf using "relative access method"
    while (buf.HasRemaining())
    {
        byte b;

        // (4)
        buf.GetByte(b); // The position is incremented by one
        AppLogTag("PTAP", "%c", b);
```

continues

LISTING 11-9 *(continued)*

```
    }

    // (5)
    buf.Clear();

    // Writes int values to the buf
    for (int i = 0; i < 5; i++)
    {
        // (6)
        buf.SetInt(i);
    }

    // Flips the buf
    buf.Flip();

    // (7) Creates a new view, IntBuffer.
    // Capacity of pIntBuf = 5
    // The content of pIntBuf is from the buf's position to the buf's limit
    unique_ptr< IntBuffer > pIntBuf(buf.AsIntBufferN());

    // (8)
    pIntBuf->Set(4, 9);

    // Reads int values from the buf using "absolute access method"
    for (int i = 0; i < 5; i++)
    {
        int out;

        // (9)
        pIntBuf->Get(i, out);
        AppLogTag("PTAP", "%d = %d", i, out);
    }
}
```

(1) Initialises a `ByteBuffer` instance `buf` with reserved memory for the specified capacity —
that is, `BUFFER_SIZE_MAX`.

(2) `SetByte()` writes a byte and advances to the next position to write or read a value.
Therefore, the position is moved to 5 after the loop. This access mode is referred to as the
relative access method.

(3) `Flip()` sets the current position to 0.

(4) `GetByte()` reads byte `b` from the current position of `buf` and advances the next position
by one byte.

(5) `Clear()` clears the contents of `buf`, which resets `buf` to its initial state.

(6) `SetInt()` writes a four-byte integral value and advances the position by four bytes.

(7) `buf` contains only four-byte integral values. Therefore, you can treat the `ByteBuffer`
instance as an `IntBuffer` by calling `AsIntBufferN()` to retrieve the `IntBuffer` view for
this instance. `AsIntBufferN()` will just return a view, not a copy, of the buffer.

(8) `IntBuffer::Set(index, val)` sets the value at the given index without advancing the position. This access mode is called the *absolute access method*.

(9) The `IntBuffer::Get(index, out)` method reads a value at the specified index.

SUMMARY

This chapter covered a lot of ground, but you should now be familiar with the essentials of Tizen native development. You learned how Tizen handles errors and how you can use your existing exception handling code. Your code will be more reliable and easier to debug as a result of using the logging and debugging macros and following the rules of object ownership. The Tizen implementation of `unique_ptr` was also explained, giving you a key weapon to use against memory leaks.

Tizen's fundamental data types were also introduced, together with sample code demonstrating useful tricks and techniques. Strings, collections, and date and time classes will find a home in just about any application, and you now know how to use these features in your own code. The essentials you learned in this chapter will give you a good grounding for what's to come.

12

Native UI Controls

WHAT'S IN THIS CHAPTER?

➤ UI controls

➤ Container controls

➤ Event handlers and listeners

➤ Headers, footers, and forms

➤ Lists and tables

Tizen provides more than 40 native UI controls, from simple controls, such as push buttons and labels, to sliders, split panels, and icon lists. These controls provide you with the tools to create an efficient, well-designed, and great-looking UI for your Tizen applications.

In this chapter you learn how to work with the different types of UI controls and some of the key concepts, such as containers, the coordinate system, layout, and listeners. You will discover how to handle editable text items, create groups of check buttons, build a simple slide show, and use advanced lists and table views. Each section is accompanied by code snippets to show you how to make use of a control in your own code.

AN OVERVIEW OF UI CONTROLS

UI controls are the user interface elements, such as forms, buttons, lists, and edit fields, that serve as the visual building blocks used to create an application's layout. Some platforms refer to these user interface elements as widgets. The Tizen native environment provides around 40 controls, some of which are shown in Figure 12-1.

FIGURE 12-1

In the class hierarchy, all control classes are derived from an abstract base class `Tizen::Ui::Control`. This class provides the following:

➤ Control properties such as size and position

➤ Draw and show functions

➤ Interfaces to respond to user input

➤ The structure to process and dispatch events, including key, focus, touch, gesture, and drag-and-drop events

Note that controls need to be bound to a window in order to be displayed on the device screen. Therefore, an instance derived from `Tizen::Ui::Control` should be added to an instance derived from `Tizen::Ui::Window`.

The Tizen platform automatically handles the control's life cycle. All controls are deleted when an application terminates, as the platform deletes the frame control and all controls within the frame.

Note two important points about a control's life cycle:

➤ Controls not added to a container must be deleted explicitly. Use the `RemoveControl()` or `RemoveAllControls()` methods to delete these controls.

➤ If the application performs custom resource allocation and cleanup, implement the control's `OnInitializing()` and `OnTerminating()` event handlers to allocate and clean up these resources.

Displaying a control, changing its size and position, and ensuring that an editable control can respond to text input is relatively straightforward:

➤ You can change the size and position of controls by using `SetSize()` and `SetPosition()`, respectively.

➤ To display a control, use the `Invalidate(true)` method. It will recursively invalidate child controls and force the control and all its children to be redrawn.

➤ You can hide a control by calling `SetShowState(false)` and `Invalidate()` sequentially.

➤ To get key input events, you need to set focus on the control. Call the `SetFocus()` method to ensure that the control responds to key input.

USING CONTAINERS

Containers are controls that contain other controls. A container can even contain other containers — for example, a Window can contain a Panel control within it.

The one basic container is the `GroupContainer`, which provides a grouped look for the controls added to it, including a configurable grid-line color and background color. Child controls can be added in corresponding cells relative to the cell's top-left corner x, y position based on the index passed. `GroupContainer` allows merging the cells from left to right (see Figure 12-2) or from top to bottom. A child control can be added only to the parent cell in the case of merged cells. Rows and columns can be set as stretchable, which means that Container control is resized, any changes to height/width will be applied only to those rows or columns set as stretchable.

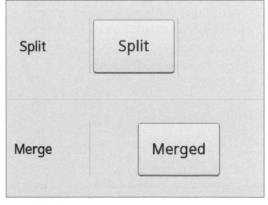

FIGURE 12-2

The rest of this section covers pop-up containers and panels. The `TableView` control is also a container, but it is discussed later in this chapter.

Popups

`Popup`, `MessageBox`, and `ProgressPopup` controls are displayed in the top centre of the screen as a modal or modeless dialog box. A modal dialog requires either user interaction or a specified amount of time to elapse before it can be closed, while a modeless dialog allows other processing to continue while it is on-screen.

Examples of `Popup`, `MessageBox`, and `ProgressPopup` controls are shown in Figure 12-3.

FIGURE 12-3

`MessageBox` provides a subset of `Popup` functionality but is less configurable and easier to set up. `Popup` supports both modal and modeless, whereas `MessageBox` supports only modal.

The following code snippet shows how to display a message box dialog and get the user's response. Notice that the last parameter sent to the `Construct()` method is `3000`, which is the timeout value in milliseconds, after which time the `MessageBox` will be closed:

```
// Creates a MessageBox instance
MessageBox messageBox;
messageBox.Construct(L"MessageBox Title",
        L"MessageBox Sample Code.", MSGBOX_STYLE_OKCANCEL, 3000);

int modalResult = 0;

// ShowAndWait() shows the message box and gets a user response
messageBox.ShowAndWait(modalResult);

switch (modalResult)
{
case MSGBOX_RESULT_OK:
```

```
      // ....
      break;
  case MSGBOX_RESULT_CANCEL:
      // ....
  default:
      break;
  }
```

Panels

The Panel control is a general-purpose rectangular container that you can use to group UI controls, or even other panels. Panel can be used to create a custom background for a defined area, or to organize and align UI controls. Without setting any layout properties, the look and feel of a panel do not differ from the basic Form control. The following code snippet shows how to create a Panel:

```
  // Creates an instance of Panel
  __pPanel = new Panel();
  __pPanel->Construct(GetClientAreaBounds());

  // Adds the panel to the form
  AddControl(__pPanel);

  // Add child controls to __pPanel
```

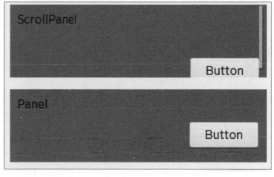

FIGURE 12-4

ScrollPanel, shown in Figure 12-4, is a specialised type of panel that automatically handles scrolling and displays the scroll bar. You can add items to the ScrollPanel and the platform automatically adds scroll bars as required.

SplitPanel, shown in Figure 12-5, is a UI control that can manage a set of individual panes. Generally, the second pane in the SplitPanel is used to show detailed information about the selected item on the first pane.

FIGURE 12-5

When you create an instance of `SplitPanel`, you need to specify whether the panel is divided vertically or horizontally:

```
__pSplitPanel = new (std::nothrow) SplitPanel();
__pSplitPanel->Construct(Rectangle(0, 0, 800, 400),
        SPLIT_PANEL_DIVIDER_STYLE_MOVABLE,
        SPLIT_PANEL_DIVIDER_DIRECTION_VERTICAL);
```

Next, set two panels to panes of the `SplitPanel`:

```
__pFirstPanel = new (std::nothrow) Panel();
__pFirstPanel->Construct(Rectangle(0, 0, 400, 480));

__pSecondPanel = new (std::nothrow) Panel();
__pSecondPanel->Construct(Rectangle(0, 0, 400, 480));

//Sets the divider position to the slit panel
__pSplitPanel->SetDividerPosition(400);

//Sets panes to the split panel
__pSplitPanel->SetPane(__pFirstPanel, SPLIT_PANEL_PANE_ORDER_FIRST);
__pSplitPanel->SetPane(__pSecondPanel, SPLIT_PANEL_PANE_ORDER_SECOND);
```

Layout

If you group controls by using containers, you can align several controls to a specific layout easily. For example, if the upper side of a form contains labels and the bottom side has buttons, containers make specifying this layout easy. For example, OK and Cancel buttons can be placed horizontally inside a container and the container placed on the bottom side of a form with right alignment.

You can use the `Tizen::Ui::RelativeLayout` class to automatically align the controls within a container. That means the size and position of each child control is relative to the size and position of the other child controls in the container. To apply a layout to a container, you pass an instance of `RelativeLayout` to the container's `Construct()` method when you create the container:

```
RelativeLayout layout;
layout.Construct();
Panel* pRelativePanel = new Panel;
pRelativePanel->Construct(layout, Rectangle(0, 0, 100, 100));
```

`RelativeLayout` provides methods such as `SetHeight()`, `SetCenterAligned()`, `SetMargin()`, `SetRelation()`, and `SetWidth()`. Using these methods, you can align the controls horizontally or vertically or set the position of one control to the horizontal or vertical centre of the container:

```
// Sets relations between the pUpButton and pMiddleButton
layout.SetRelation(*pUpButton, pMiddleButton,
    RECT_EDGE_RELATION_LEFT_TO_LEFT);
layout.SetRelation(*pUpButton, pMiddleButton,
    RECT_EDGE_RELATION_BOTTOM_TO_TOP);
layout.SetMargin(*pUpButton, 0, 0, 0, 10);

// Sets the middle button
layout.SetCenterAligned(*pMiddleButton, CENTER_ALIGN_HORIZONTAL);
```

```
layout.SetCenterAligned(*pMiddleButton, CENTER_ALIGN_VERTICAL);
layout.SetMargin(*pMiddleButton, 10, 10, 10, 10);

// Sets relations between the pDownButton and the pMiddleButton
layout.SetRelation(*pDownButton, pMiddleButton,
    RECT_EDGE_RELATION_RIGHT_TO_RIGHT);
layout.SetRelation(*pDownButton, pMiddleButton,
    RECT_EDGE_RELATION_TOP_TO_BOTTOM);
layout.SetMargin(*pDownButton, 0, 0, 10, 0);
```

There are other layout classes too, such as `CardLayout`, which is used to position the child controls to fit within the bounds of the parent container, and `HorizontalBoxLayout` and `VerticalBoxLayout`, which are used to align controls in a linear horizontal/vertical layout. `GridLayout` is used to align the child controls in a two-dimensional rectangular grid.

You can see `RelativeLayout`, `VerticalBoxLayout`, and `GridLayout` in Figure 12-6.

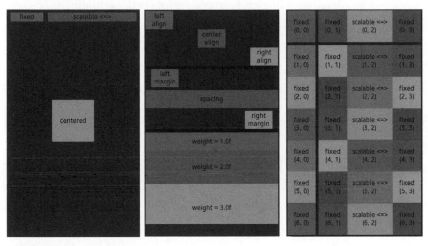

FIGURE 12-6

Coordinate System

Tizen uses a relative coordinate system. Each control's position is defined relative to the the top-left corner of its immediate parent container. In the case of a form, this will be the top-left corner of the form's client area.

The client area of a form — that is, the area within which other controls can be added — varies in size depending on whether the form contains a header, footer, or indicator.

Figure 12-7 shows a form with an indicator and header area.

To get the client area bounds of a form, use the `GetClient AreaBoundsF()` method.

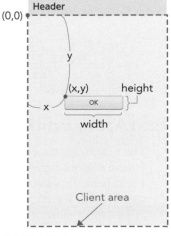

FIGURE 12-7

To get the control bounds, use the `GetBoundsF()`, `GetPositionF()`, `GetSizeF()`, `GetWidthF()`, and `GetHeightF()` methods. In Figure 12-7, the location of the button control is relative to the form's client area.

USING UI CONTROLS

You can use a variety of UI controls in your application. This section explains the basic controls, including the `Button` and `EditField`, as well as selectable controls, including the `CheckBox` and `ColorPicker`. Also covered are the `Header` and `Footer` controls and creating custom controls.

Button

The `Button` control is a rectangular UI control that generates an action event when it is pressed and released. The appearance of a button, including its label text and alignment, background image, color, and text color, as well as its appearance in each button state (normal, highlighted, pressed, or disabled), can be customized.

To listen for and handle events that are generated when a button is pressed, you use the `OnActionPerformed()` event handler:

```
// IActionEventListener implementation
void
YourForm::OnActionPerformed(const Control& source, int actionId)
{
    switch (actionId)
    {
    case ID_BUTTON:
    {
        // ....
    }
    break;
    // ....

}
```

> **NOTE** *You can find more information about event listeners in Chapter 10, "Native UI Applications."*

EditArea, EditField, Textbox, and ExpandableEditArea

The `EditArea`, `EditField`, `Textbox`, and `ExpandableEditArea` controls can be configured to receive various types of text, from simple numbers to URLs. Users enter text in an application via a text field. Tapping the text field activates the keypad and reveals a cursor automatically. When a user touches the `EditArea`, it gets the focus and shows a preconfigured keypad. It supports both full screen and overlay styles. You can control the appearance of the edit control, including its background image and color and the color of its text.

`EditArea` supports multi-lines, whereas `EditField` supports only a single line of text. `ExpandableEditArea` displays a multi-line text editor, the height of which is automatically adjusted according to the number of lines currently visible in the text box. `TextBox` displays a non-editable text field. These controls are shown in Figure 12-8.

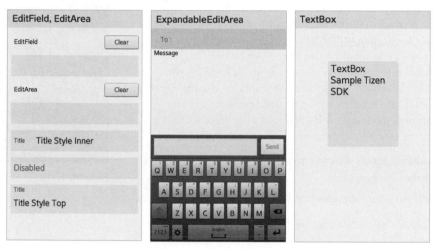

FIGURE 12-8

Keypad

As shown in Figure 12-9, the `Keypad` control provides a full-screen form to input or edit text with the Input Method Editor (IME). The `Keypad` automatically appears when `EditField` or `EditArea` gets the focus. If you want to show the keypad manually, you must create an instance of `Keypad` by yourself. You can show different styles of keypad such as `NORMAL`, `PASSWORD`, `EMAIL`, `URL`, `NUMBER`, `PHONE_NUMBER`, or `IP_V4`.

To get keypad events, use the `Tizen::Ui::ITextEventListener`. There are two events: `OnTextValueChanged()`, which is called when the Done button of the keypad is pressed, and `OnTextValueChangeCanceled()`, which is called when the user cancels the change they have made by tapping the Back hardware key.

FIGURE 12-9

Gallery

The Gallery control, as shown in Figure 12-10, is a UI control that is used to display a set of still images one at a time, so that the user can scroll through each image in turn, or automatically as a slide show. Gallery also supports zooming in or out of an image using the pinch gesture or by double-clicking.

FIGURE 12-10

You can add or delete images from the Gallery, or retrieve a count of the number of images. An item in the Gallery is represented by the GalleryItem class; and to add a GalleryItem to the Gallery control, you need to implement the methods defined by the IGalleryItemProvider interface. This interface contains the pure virtual functions, CreateItem(), DeleteItem(), and GetItemCount(). In the CreateItem() method, an image is loaded and used to construct a GalleryItem object.

The following code snippet shows an example of the CreateItem() method implementation:

```
// IGalleryItemProvider implementation
GalleryItem*
GalleryItemProviderImpl::CreateItem(int index)
{
    // Gets an instance of Bitmap
    AppResource* pAppResource
            = Application::GetInstance()->GetAppResource();
    Bitmap* pImageTemp = pAppResource->GetBitmapN(L"Image.jpg");

    // Creates an instance of GalleryItem and
    // registers the bitmap to the gallery item
    GalleryItem* pGalleryItem = new GalleryItem();
    pGalleryItem->Construct(*pImageTemp);

    // Deallocates the bitmap
    delete pImageTemp;

    // The returned item is added to the gallery.
    return pGalleryItem;
}
```

You must set up your instance of the IGalleryItemProvider when you create the gallery:

```
_pGallery->SetItemProvider(*pGalleryItemProviderImpl);
```

SearchBar

FIGURE 12-11

The SearchBar control provides an interface to type search keywords and display the results. Initially SearchBar shows a single-line text field, and if the SearchBar has the focus, by the user tapping inside it, the display changes to input mode as shown on the right in Figure 12-11. In input mode, the search bar's content area is changed to semi-transparent and the overlay keyboard appears. In its basic form, SearchBar provides a Cancel button, which is configurable in terms of text, color, and so forth.

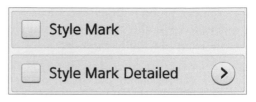

FIGURE 12-12

CheckButton

The CheckButton control displays a button with a label, and it can be either checked or unchecked. The following check button styles are available:

➤ Mark style (a check box), with or without a detailed button, which allows multiple selections (see Figure 12-12).

➤ Radio style (a check box), with or without a detailed button, which allows only a single selection (see Figure 12-13).

➤ On/off sliding style, which is used to indicate the state of each button (on or off), as shown in Figure 12-14.

FIGURE 12-13

FIGURE 12-14

Tapping the check box or the label toggles the check status, while tapping the detail button generates a separate action ID. For example, the following code snippets set action IDs for checked, unchecked, and detailed button click actions:

```
__pCheckButton->SetActionId(ID_BUTTON_CHECKED, ID_BUTTON_UNCHECKED, ID_BUTTON_DETAIL);
__pCheckButton->AddActionEventListener(*this);
```

In OnActionPerformed(), the different action IDs will be passed based on action types:

```
void
MyTestButtonApp::OnActionPerformed(const Control& source, int actionId)
{
    switch (actionId)
    {
        case ID_BUTTON_CHECKED:
            __pLabelLog->SetText(L"Selected.");
            break;
        case ID_BUTTON_UNCHECKED:
            pLabelLog->SetText(L"Unselected.");
            break;
        case ID_BUTTON_DETAIL:
            pLabelCheck->SetText(L"Detail button clicked.");
         break;
    }
    __pLabelLog->Invalidate(false);
}
```

You can group multiple check boxes together so that only one check box in the group can be selected. Use the `Tizen::Ui::Controls::RadioGroup` class to implement this functionality, as shown in the following code:

```
// Creates instances of CheckButton
CheckButton *pCheckButton1 = new CheckButton();
pCheckButton1->Construct(
            Rectangle(50, 50, GetClientAreaBounds().width - 100, 100),
            CHECK_BUTTON_STYLE_RADIO,
            BACKGROUND_STYLE_DEFAULT,
            false,
            L"Radio1");
pCheckButton1->SetActionId(ID_BUTTON1_CHECKED, ID_BUTTON1_UNCHECKED);
pCheckButton1->AddActionEventListener(*this);

CheckButton *pCheckButton2 = new CheckButton();
pCheckButton2->Construct(
            Rectangle(50, 160, GetClientAreaBounds().width - 100, 100),
            CHECK_BUTTON_STYLE_RADIO,
            BACKGROUND_STYLE_DEFAULT,
            false,
            L"Radio2");
pCheckButton2->SetActionId(ID_BUTTON2_CHECKED, ID_BUTTON2_UNCHECKED);
pCheckButton2->AddActionEventListener(*this);

// Adds check buttons to the form
AddControl(pCheckButton1);
AddControl(pCheckButton2);

// Creates an instance of RadioGroup
__pRadioGroup = new RadioGroup();
__pRadioGroup->Construct();

// Adds the check buttons to the radio group
__pRadioGroup->Add(pCheckButton1);
__pRadioGroup->Add(pCheckButton2);
```

Slider and Progress

The `Slider` control enables the user to change values by dragging a slideable button, which can also have icons and title text added to it. To listen for and respond to drag button input events, use the `Tizen::Ui::IAdjustmentEventListener` interface and the `OnAdjustmentValueChanged()` event handler.

The `Progress` control is very similar to `Slider`, but `Progress` has no event listeners for user input. Both controls are shown in Figure 12-15.

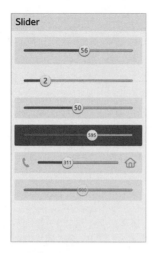

FIGURE 12-15

To create an instance of `Tizen::Ui::Controls::Progress`, you need to set the range of the progress in `Construct()` and set the current value in that range:

```
// Creates an instance of Progress
__pProgress = new Progress();
__pProgress->Construct(
            // display region
            Rectangle(50, 50, GetClientAreaBounds().width - 100, 100),
             // range
            0, 100);
             // current value
__pProgress->SetValue(0);
```

Don't forget to call `Invalidate(true)` to update your screen after changing the current value:

```
__pProgress->SetValue(__pValue);
__pProgress->Invalidate(true);
```

EditTime and EditDate

EditTime and EditDate are used to display and modify the time and date, respectively (see Figure 12-16). To modify the date and time, users can touch the values, and a bar with date/time values will be displayed, allowing them to choose the date and time.

EditDate and EditTime provide the `OnDateChanged()` and `OnTimeChanged()` event handlers, respectively. Adding code to enable the user to set the date and time is fairly straightforward, as the bar with date/time values is displayed automatically:

```
// Creates an instance of EditTime
__pEditTime = new EditTime();
__pEditTime->Construct(Point(100, 100));
```

FIGURE 12-16

```
    __pEditTime->AddTimeChangeEventListener(*this);

    // Creates an instance of EditDate
    __pEditDate = new EditDate();
    __pEditDate->Construct(Point(100, 100));
    __pEditDate->AddDateChangeEventListener(*this);
```

ContextMenu and OptionMenu

A `ContextMenu` control enables users to select from a set of options. The context menu displays further options that appear when the parent object is pressed (see Figure 12-17).

FIGURE 12-17

When you create an instance of `ContextMenu`, you need to specify a coordinate of the anchor (▲). You can choose the direction of the context menu with the anchor position or let the platform choose the best option:

```
    __pContextMenuIconText = new ContextMenu();
    __pContextMenuIconText->Construct(Point(100,240), CONTEXT_MENU_STYLE_LIST);
```

The `ContextMenu` has two types of styles. It can be set to a `CONTEXT_MENU_STYLE_LIST` or `CONTEXT_MENU_STYLE_ICON` in the parameters of the `Construct()` method. You can add items like this:

```
    // Add list style items
    __pContextMenuIconText->AddItem(L"Item 1", ID_CONTEXT_ITEM1,
            *pNormalBitmap1, pPressedBitmap1);
    __pContextMenuIconText->AddItem(L"Item 2", ID_CONTEXT_ITEM2,
            *pNormalBitmap2, pPressedBitmap2);
```

To show the context menu, you need to call SetShowState(true):

```
__pContextMenu->SetShowState(true);
__pContextMenu->Show();
```

The OptionMenu control (Figure 12-18) is provided to display a menu when the hardware menu key is pressed. Note that all Tizen devices must have a hardware menu key. The OptionMenu is displayed at a fixed position, can show two levels of menu items, and includes items related to the entire application, whereas the ContextMenu will typically contain items specific to a particular form or feature.

FIGURE 12-18

TabBar

The TabBar control displays horizontally placed tabs to enable users to navigate between multiple layouts. This does not mean that TabBar automatically changes a layout; instead, TabBar provides the UI interface and corresponding UI events. The height of the TabBar is fixed, but its width and the position can be set. As shown in Figure 12-19, TabBar is scrollable if the items contained within it exceed its width. To specify the TabBar's items, you need to use the TabBarItem class:

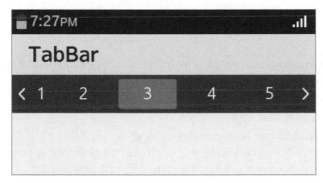

FIGURE 12-19

```
// Creates an instance of TabBar
__pTabBar = new TabBar();
__pTabBar->Construct(0, 0, GetClientAreaBounds().width);

// Creates instances of TabBarItem
TabBarItem tabBarItem1;
TabBarItem tabBarItem2;

tabBarItem1.Construct(L"1", ID_TABBAR_ITEM1);
tabBarItem2.Construct(L"2", ID_TABBAR_ITEM2);

// Adds items to the tab bar
__pTabBar->AddItem(tabBarItem1);
__pTabBar->AddItem(tabBarItem2);
```

Through the IActionEventListener interface, you are notified which item has been pressed.

ColorPicker

The `ColorPicker` provides an interface to select a color, which consists of a hue, luminance, and saturation combination, as shown in Figure 12-20. In the `OnColorChanged()` event handler of the `Tizen::Ui::IColorChangeEventListener` interface, you can get details about the color selected by the user.

FIGURE 12-20

Header and Footer

The Tizen native application framework provides `Header` and `Footer` controls for navigation of an application. `Header` and `Footer` have many predefined styles; they are placed at the top and bottom of the application layout, respectively. For example, `Header` can show the title of an application screen and contain tabs and buttons.

Depending on their format and function, headers can be one of the styles shown in Table 12-1. The basic header appears as a bar containing text. When necessary, you add other UI elements, such as description text, icons, buttons, and animations of content-loading status. Usually, the header's text string appears on the left and any other elements appear on the right.

TABLE 12-1: Header Styles

Style	Screenshot
`HEADER_STYLE_TITLE`	**Title**
`HEADER_STYLE_TITLE` with left and right buttons	**Title** ❘ ⊘ ❘ ✉

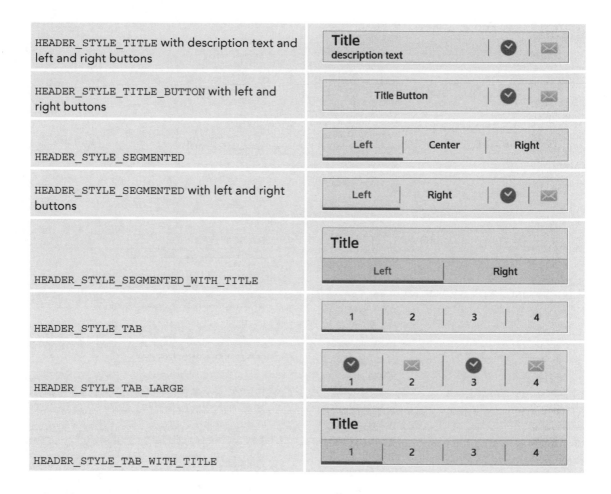

HEADER_STYLE_TITLE with description text and left and right buttons	**Title** description text
HEADER_STYLE_TITLE_BUTTON with left and right buttons	Title Button
HEADER_STYLE_SEGMENTED	Left / Center / Right
HEADER_STYLE_SEGMENTED with left and right buttons	Left / Right
HEADER_STYLE_SEGMENTED_WITH_TITLE	Title / Left / Right
HEADER_STYLE_TAB	1 / 2 / 3 / 4
HEADER_STYLE_TAB_LARGE	1 / 2 / 3 / 4
HEADER_STYLE_TAB_WITH_TITLE	Title / 1 / 2 / 3 / 4

You can place any function as a button in the header. The most common functions are search and refresh, but other functionalities can be added.

Tabs help categorize content, and you should place them at the top of the screen (refer to Table 12-1). Up to four tabs can be shown at one time, and users can scroll horizontally on the tab to see more. The tab with a title style functions in the same way as the basic tab, meaning you cannot use buttons within the tab. If you require an additional title for all tab items, you can combine a row of tabs with a title above it.

The footer is located at the bottom of the screen. Like the header, it can display a multi-purpose area, although it does not contain a title. Table 12-2 lists available footer styles.

TABLE 12-2: Footer Styles

Style	Screenshot
FOOTER_STYLE_BUTTON_ICON	
FOOTER_STYLE_BUTTON_ICON_TEXT	Button 1 Button 2
FOOTER_STYLE_BUTTON_TEXT	Button 1 Button 2
FOOTER_STYLE_SEGMENTED_ICON	
FOOTER_STYLE_SEGMENTED_ICON_TEXT	1 2
FOOTER_STYLE_SEGMENTED_TEXT	1 2
FOOTER_STYLE_TAB	1 2 3 4
FOOTER_STYLE_TAB_LARGE	1 2 3 4

The Header and Footer are created when you construct a Form:

```
Form::Construct(FORM_STYLE_NORMAL | FORM_STYLE_INDICATOR
        | FORM_STYLE_HEADER | FORM_STYLE_FOOTER);
```

To get instances of the header and footer you call GetHeader() and GetFooter() and set up their styles:

```
Header* pHeader = GetHeader();
Footer* pFooter = GetFooter();


pHeader->SetStyle(HEADER_STYLE_TITLE);
pFooter->SetStyle(FOOTER_STYLE_SEGMENTED_TEXT);
```

Header and Footer have ButtonItem and FooterItem instances, respectively, for their items:

```
ButtonItem  buttonLeftItem;
buttonLeftItem.Construct(BUTTON_ITEM_STYLE_ICON, ID_HEADER_LEFTBUTTON);
buttonLeftItem.SetIcon(BUTTON_ITEM_STATUS_NORMAL, __pLeftItemBitmap);
```

```
ButtonItem  buttonRightItem;
buttonRightItem.Construct(BUTTON_ITEM_STYLE_ICON, ID_HEADER_RIGHTBUTTON);
buttonRightItem.SetIcon(BUTTON_ITEM_STATUS_NORMAL, __pRightItemBitmap);

pHeader->SetTitleText(L"Header text");
pHeader->SetButton(BUTTON_POSITION_LEFT, buttonLeftItem);
pHeader->SetButton(BUTTON_POSITION_RIGHT, buttonRightItem);

FooterItem  footerItem1;
footerItem1.Construct(ID_FOOTER_ITEM1);
footerItem1.SetText(L"1");

FooterItem  footerItem2;
footerItem2.Construct(ID_FOOTER_ITEM2);
footerItem2.SetText(L"2");

pFooter->AddItem(footerItem1);
pFooter->AddItem(footerItem2);
```

Remember that both `Header` and `Footer` affect the size of the form's client area: If a form contains either one, the height of the form's client area will be reduced.

ListViews

The `ListView`, `GroupedListView`, and `IconListView` controls are used to create different kinds of lists.

The `ListView` displays both simple and user-configured items. The `SimpleItem` class represents a basic list item such as a bitmap, text, and annex. The `CustomItem` class represents a user-configured item, which can have a different layout and height than other items in the list.

The `GroupedListView` displays a list of grouped items, while the `IconListView` represents a two-dimensional list of bitmap images and icons. Figure 12-21 shows each type of list.

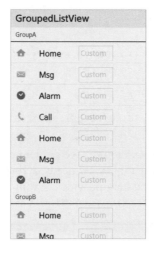

FIGURE 12-21

> **NOTE** *The UiControls sample from the SDK, which we discuss at the end of this chapter, includes code showing how to use a* `ListView`.

TableViews

A `TableView` displays a table that contains simple and interactive items. Unlike the `ListView`, the `TableView` container will contain the `TableViewItems`. `TableViewItem` is a container, which can contain other controls or containers.

Figure 12-22 shows two types of table views, `GroupedTableView` and `SectionTableView`. The `GroupedTableView` can manage items as groups. These groups are displayed in divided areas. The `SectionTableView` divides the table into a number of sections, using a different style than the `GroupedTableView`.

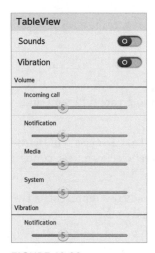 

FIGURE 12-22

To create a `TableView`, call the `Construct()` function, specifying the size of the `TableView`, whether to display an item divider, and the scroll bar style:

```
// Creates an instance of TableView
__pTableView = new TableView();
__pTableView->Construct(Rectangle(0, 0, GetClientAreaBounds().width,
GetClientAreaBounds().height), true, TABLE_VIEW_SCROLL_BAR_STYLE_FADE_OUT);
```

To manage items in the table, all table views should have an item provider. The item provider will create, delete, and update an item when the table view needs to display an item on the screen. Each type of table view has a corresponding item provider — that is, `ITableViewItemProvider`, `IGroupedListViewItemProvider`, and `ISectionTableViewItemProvider`.

For example, you can implement `ITableViewItemProvider` with the following code:

```
TableViewItem*
TableViewItemProvider::CreateItem(int itemIndex, int itemWidth)
{
    // create an item instance
    TableViewAnnexStyle style;
    TableViewItem* pItem = new TableViewItem();

    // change item style based on the item index
    switch (itemIndex % 3)
    {
    case 0:
      style = TABLE_VIEW_ANNEX_STYLE_NORMAL;
      break;
    case 1:
      style = TABLE_VIEW_ANNEX_STYLE_MARK;
      break;
    case 2:
      style = TABLE_VIEW_ANNEX_STYLE_ONOFF_SLIDING;
      break;
    default:
      style = TABLE_VIEW_ANNEX_STYLE_NORMAL
      break;
    }

    // initiate the item
    pItem->Construct(Dimension(itemWidth, GetDefaultItemHeight()), style);

    // add a label the item
    Label* pLabel = new Label();
    pLabel->Construct(Rectangle(0, 0, itemWidth,
          GetDefaultItemHeight()),"TableViewItem");
    pItem->AddControl(pLabel);

    return pItem;
}

bool
TableViewItemProvider::DeleteItem(int itemIndex,
                    Tizen::Ui::Controls::TableViewItem* pItem)
{
    pItem->Destroy();

    return true;
}
```

Then, you need to add the following item provider to the `TableView` instance:

```
__pTableView->SetItemProvider(__pTableViewItemProvider);
```

To listen for table view item events, such as the user reordering a list or changing an item's state, implement the interface provided by the `ITableViewItemEventListener`, `IGroupedTableView ItemEventListener`, or `ISectionTableViewItemEventListener`, depending on which type of table view you're using.

In a basic `TableView`, the `OnTableViewItemStateChanged()` event handler is called when the user selects, checks, or unchecks a table view item. You add the listener instance using the following code:

```
__pTableView->AddTableViewItemEventListener(*__pTableViewItemEventListener);
```

Table view items can have a context item, which is displayed when a table view item is swept horizontally (see Figure 12-23). A context item can be used to hide additional functionality related to the list item, to avoid crowding the screen. The context item is a container, which can hold other controls as well, such as `Button`. The following code shows how to add a context item:

```
// Creates an instance of TableViewContextItem
__pContextItem = new TableViewContextItem();
__pContextItem->Construct(Dimension(720, 100));
...
__pContextItem->AddControl(pButton);
__pContextItem->AddControl(pButton2);
...
TableViewItem* pItem = new TableViewItem();
...
pItem->SetContextItem(__pContextItem);
```

FIGURE 12-23

CUSTOM CONTROLS

If you want to create your own custom UI control, your class must inherit from the `Control`, `Container`, or `Window` class. You should then override the `OnDraw()` callback function and implement your custom drawing. Additionally, you need to override `OnBoundsChanging()`, `OnClearBackground()`, `OnEvaluateSize()`, `OnShowStateChanged()`, and `OnShowStateChanging()`, depending on the type of control you're implementing.

The `CustomButton.cpp` file from the UiControls Sample in the Tizen IDE is a good starting point for creating your own custom control.

SUMMARY

Now you're familiar with the many types of UI controls that Tizen offers, including advanced controls such as lists and tables views. You know about the important concepts such as event handlers and listeners and how the layout features make working with complicated form designs a lot easier. If you're feeling inspired, you may even want to create your own custom control.

While the code snippets in this chapter will give you a good start, there's also an excellent code sample in the Tizen SDK that will help you build on what you've learned in this chapter. Go to the Tizen IDE, select New ➪ Tizen Native Project, and in the New Project Wizard window, click Sample and choose the UiControls project. Build and run the project and start working your way around the code.

13

Multimedia and Content

WHAT'S IN THIS CHAPTER?

➤ Managing content

➤ Playing audio and video

➤ Recording audio and video

➤ Capturing an image from the camera

➤ Encoding and decoding media content

➤ Using the media application controls

In this chapter you'll get an in-depth and practical introduction to the multimedia features of the Tizen native framework. Working through code snippets, you'll learn about managing content and implementing functionality such as playlists. Then the focus moves to the features of the `Media` namespace and you'll walk through code which makes use of the `Media::Player` class to play audio and video, and discover the more advanced audio features offered by the `AudioOut` class, which can play uncompressed audio from multiple channels simultaneously. Capturing audio, video, and images from the camera is covered in detailed code snippets that are ready for use in your own code.

Tizen provides features that allow you to encode and decode images, audio, and video in different formats, as you'll discover in this chapter. If you want to make use of multimedia content and don't want to write a lot of code yourself, then you can always use the media application controls to access the device's built-in media players and camera. You'll find code at the end of the chapter to show you how.

CONTENT AND CONTENT INFORMATION

Content is the logical representation of various types of physical files, such as images, audio, and video. *Content information* includes file attributes such as filename, size, creation time, metadata such as the ID3 tag or Exif, and other user-tagged custom fields such as description and keyword.

> **NOTE** *ID3 is a metadata format for MP3 files. It contains information about a music file such as its title, composer, and so on.*
>
> *Exif (Exchangeable image file format) is an image format for digital cameras. It appends metadata into JPEG, TIFF, RIFF, and WAV file formats. Basically it contains information regarding date, time, camera configuration, copyrights, and geolocations.*

The Tizen native framework defines common content information in the `Tizen::Content::ContentInfo` class, including the following: the unique content ID, content path, content file size, content type, media format (such as JPG), creation date and time, whether the content is DRM protected, and the thumbnail image.

`ContentInfo` also defines custom data fields which store user-specified information. Custom fields are content category, author, content description, keywords, content name, provider, age rating, location tag, and coordinates.

Based on this common content information, media-specific content information is derived. `ImageContentInfo`, `AudioContentInfo`, and `VideoContentInfo` inherit from `ContentInfo`, adding image, audio, and video-specific content information, respectively. Each type of content file might also contain its own metadata information, and Tizen provides classes for metadata such as `ImageMetadata`, `AudioMetadata`, and `VideoMetadata`. Table 13-1 shows media-specific attributes and metadata fields.

TABLE 13-1: Media-Specific Attributes and Metadata

CONTENT TYPES (CLASS NAME)	ATTRIBUTE	METADATA
Image (`ImageContentInfo`, `ImageMetadata`)	`Title, Width, Height, Orientation`	`CameraManufacturer, CameraModel, DateTime, Latitude, Longitude, Software, Thumbnail, WhiteBalance, Width, Height, Orientation`
Audio (`AudioContentInfo`, `AudioMetadata`)	`Title, Artist, Genre, Composer, Bitrate, Album, Copyright, Duration, TrackInfo, ReleaseYear`	`Album, AlbumArt, Artist, Bitrate, ChannelCount, Comment, Composer, Copyright, Description, Duration, Frequency, Genre, RecordingDate, Thumbnail, Title, Track, TrackInfo, Year`

| Video (VideoContentInfo, VideoMetadata) | Title, Artist, Genre, Width, Height, AudioBitrate, VideoBitrate, Framerate, Duration, Album | AlbumArt, Genre, Width, Height, AudioBitrate, VideoBitrate, Comment, Description, Framerate, Duration |

The Tizen native framework stores content information in a content database. The content database stores the data shown in Table 13-2, but it does not store metadata such as ImageMetadata, AudioMetadata, and VideoMetadata because this is contained within the file itself.

TABLE 13-2: Content Database Columns

COLUMN NAME	DATA TYPE	DESCRIPTION
ContentType	String	Content type
ContentFileName	String	Content filename
ContentName	String	User-defined content name
Category	String	Name used to group content using logical categorization, such as "Casual games" or "Action games"
Author	String	Content creator
Keyword	String	Tags added by the user
Provider	String	Content provider
Rating	String	Rating information
LocationTag	String	Location tag, such as "Home" or "Starbucks"
ContentSize	LongLong	Content size (in bytes)
DateTime	DateTime	Content creation time
Latitude	Double	Coordinates of latitude
Longitude	Double	Coordinates of longitude
Altitude	Float	Coordinates of altitude
Title	String	Audio or video title (only for audio, video)
Artist	String	Audio or video artist (only for audio, video)
Genre	String	Audio or video genre (only for audio, video)
Composer	String	Audio composer (only for audio)
Album	String	Audio album (only for audio)

Tizen provides two default content directories: `/opt/usr/media` and `/opt/storage/sdcard` and several pre-defined directories. These content directories are used to organize content files, including images, audio, and video in the physical storage of the device. Content files must be located in these directories. You can check the actual path of these directories on your device by using the `GetMediaPath()`, `GetPredefinedPath()`, and `GetExternalStoragePath()` methods of the `Tizen::System::Environment` class.

An application is responsible for managing the content information of files in these directories. If an application copies a file into or creates a file in these directories, that application should also create the corresponding content information in the content database. If the file is removed by the application, the application should also remove the content information.

The content directories will be synchronized automatically when:

➤ A content file is created or copied by the Tizen framework — e.g., USB MTP copy

➤ A content file is copied by the Connection Explorer in the Tizen IDE

➤ The device is rebooted

➤ An SD card is mounted (only for `/opt/storage/sdcard`)

➤ `Tizen::Content::ContentManager::ScanDirectory()` is called

The `Tizen::Content::ContentManager::ScanDirectory()` method scans the contents of the specified directory and creates, updates, and removes data in the content database based on the directory's contents.

If you want to manage content information manually, use the `Tizen::Content::ContentManager` class to create, update, and remove information from the content database and to register to be notified when the database is updated. To directly extract content type and metadata information from a file, use the `Tizen::Content::ContentManagerUtil` class.

Searching for Content

The `Tizen::Content::ContentSearch` class is used to search the content database. You can search for content using the column names listed in Table 13-2 or build a custom search query.

The `ContentSearch` class provides two search methods: `GetValueListN()` and `SearchN()`. `GetValueListN()` takes a column name as one of its parameters and returns a list of all the values of this column. For example, you can retrieve all artist names for your music files with the following line of code:

```
contentSearch.GetValueListN(pageNo, countPerPage, totalPage,
                            totalCount, L"Artist", SORT_ORDER_NONE);
```

You can search for content based on a custom query using the `SearchN()` method. The syntax of a query is similar to the SQL WHERE statement:

```
[ColumnName] [operator] [value] { [AND|OR] [ColumnName] [operator] [value], …}
```

For example, if you want to retrieve music files from Michael Jackson's *Thriller* album, you would specify the following:

```
Artist='Michael Jackson' AND Album='Thriller'
```

If you want to find images from the "travel" category and with the keyword "New York," then you would specify the following query:

```
Category='travel' and Keyword='New York'
```

To query the DateTime column, use the `ToString()` method of `Tizen::Base::DateTime` to build the query string. An example is shown in the following code:

```
Tizen::Base::DateTime tm;
result r = tm.SetValue(2009, 5, 1);
String whereExpr = L"DateTime >";
whereExpr.Append(L"'");
whereExpr.Append(tm.ToString());
whereExpr.Append(L"'");
```

The supported search operators are described in Table 13-3.

TABLE 13-3: Content Search Query Operators

OPERATOR	DESCRIPTION
=	Equals
>	Greater than
>=	Greater than or equal to
<	Less than
<=	Less than or equal to
!=	Not equal to
LIKE	A specified string pattern: In LIKE conditions, the underscore (_) represents any single character, while the percentage (%) character represents any string with a length of zero or more. For example, to select six-letter-long records that begin with "tizen", use `'tizen_'`; and to select records that begin with "tizen_", use `'tizen\_%'`. Notice that the \ character is used before the _ character to enable using the underscore character as a literal in the search query.
BETWEEN value AND value	A data range between two values

Before calling these search methods, you need to create an instance of `ContentSearch` and specify the type of content for which you want to search. To construct a `ContentSearch` instance to search for audio content, you'd use the following code:

```
ContentSearch search;
search.Construct(CONTENT_TYPE_AUDIO);
```

The content type should be one of `CONTENT_TYPE_OTHER`, `CONTENT_TYPE_IMAGE`, `CONTENT_TYPE_AUDIO`, or `CONTENT_TYPE_VIDEO`.

When using either search method, you must specify a starting page number and the number of items per page for the returned results. You can also specify the sort order, ascending or descending. These parameters enable you to achieve optimal performance in your searches.

Managing Playlists

The `Tizen::Content::PlayListManager` class provides methods to manage playlists — lists of audio, video, and image content — which can be created and managed from within the application. Playlists are represented by the `Tizen::Content::PlayList` class, which includes methods to add and delete items and get information about the playlist, such as its name and the number of items it contains.

The following code snippet shows how to create a playlist, add an item to it, change the name, and use the `PlayListManager` to delete the playlist:

```
PlayList playList;
// Names a playlist
String playListName = L"My Playlist";
result r = playList.Construct(playListName);

// Creates media items to be added to the playlist
ContentManager manager;
r = manager.Construct();

String contentPath = Tizen::System::Environment::GetPredefinedPath
    (PREDEFINED_DIRECTORY_IMAGES) + L"image.jpg";
ImageContentInfo info;
r = info.Construct(&contentPath);

ContentId contentId = manager.CreateContent(info);

// Adds an item to the playlist
r = playList.AddItem(contentId);

// Retrieves the playlist
PlayList* pPlayList = PlayListManager::GetInstance()->GetPlayListN(playListName);

// Updates the playlist name
String newPlayListName = L"New Playlist";
result r = pPlayList->SetPlayListName(newPlayListName);

// Deletes the playlist with the RemovePlayList() method
r = PlayListManager::GetInstance()->RemovePlayList(newPlayListName);
```

PLAYING MEDIA CONTENT

There are two ways to play audio and video content in Tizen, by launching the built-in media player application controls or using the `Tizen::Media::Player` class. This section explains how to use the `Player` class, while the use of application controls is covered later in the chapter.

The `Player` class contains methods to play files on the device or to stream remote content via the Real Time Streaming Protocol (RTSP) and HTTP. It provides basic media player operations such as time-based seeking, repeat, volume control, and so on. The `Player` class can handle the following file formats:

➤ **Audio types** — MP3, AAC, M4A, WAV, AMR

➤ **Video types** — MP4, 3GP, AVI

Table 13-4 shows the status of a player instance, together with the methods that will cause the player to enter that state. You can find out the state of the player by calling the `GetState()` method.

TABLE 13-4: Player Status

STATE	DESCRIPTION	METHOD FOR ENTERING THE STATE
PLAYER_STATE_INITIALIZED	The player is initialised.	Construct()
PLAYER_STATE_OPENING	The player opening behaviour is processed.	OpenFile(), OpenUrl(), OpenBuffer()
PLAYER_STATE_OPENED	The source is opened.	OpenFile(), OpenUrl(), OpenBuffer()
PLAYER_STATE_ENDOFCLIP	The player has reached the end of the clip.	
PLAYER_STATE_STOPPED	The player has stopped and has no current play time, but the media content is still opened and initialized.	Stop()
PLAYER_STATE_PAUSED	The player's playback is paused.	Pause()
PLAYER_STATE_PLAYING	The player is playing the media content.	Play()
PLAYER_STATE_CLOSED	The source is closed.	Close()
PLAYER_STATE_ERROR	An error has occurred.	

Playing Audio

To play audio files, include `FMedia.h` and use namespace `Tizen::Media`:

```
#include <FMedia.h>
using namespace Tizen::Media;
```

You need to implement `Tizen::Media::IPlayerEventListener` to receive player events:

```
class PlayerExample
    : public Tizen::Media::IPlayerEventListener
```

To handle these events you need to implement the callbacks. Using {} means that you are not going to perform an action for the callback and will leave it as an empty inline function:

```
protected:
    // IPlayerEventListener
    // Called when a content is opened asynchronously.
    virtual void OnPlayerOpened(result r) {}
    // Called when the end of the clip is reached.
    virtual void OnPlayerEndOfClip(void) {}
    // Called when the streaming data is being buffered.
    virtual void OnPlayerBuffering(int percent) {}
    // Called when an error has occurred.
    virtual void OnPlayerErrorOccurred(PlayerErrorReason r) {}
    // Called when interrupted by a higher priority task.
    virtual void OnPlayerInterrupted(void) {}
    // Called when released from interruption.
    virtual void OnPlayerReleased(void) {}
    // Called when the position of the content moved.
    virtual void OnPlayerSeekCompleted(result r) {}
    // Called when an audio playback focus is lost.
    virtual void OnPlayerAudioFocusChanged (void) {}
```

Declare a member variable to hold your `Player` instance:

```
private:
    Player __player;
```

Now you need to create an instance of the `Player` class and open an audio file:

```
result r = E_SUCCESS;
String filePath = Tizen::System::Environment::GetMediaPath() + L"example.mp3";

// Consturct() gets a concrete class instance of IPlayerEventListener.
r = __player.Construct(*this);
TryReturn(r == E_SUCCESS, r, "Player Construct Error.");

// Open file synchronously
r = __player.OpenFile(filePath, false);
TryReturn(r == E_SUCCESS, r, "Player Open File Error.");

__player.SetVolume(80);

r = __player.Play();
TryReturn(r == E_SUCCESS, r, "Player Play Error.");
```

The preceding example shows how to open the file in synchronous mode. If you want to open a file asynchronously, the value of the last parameter should be `true` and the `OnPlayerOpened()` callback should be implemented as follows:

```
void
PlayerExample::OnPlayerOpened(result r)
{
    TryReturnVoid(r == E_SUCCESS, "Player Open Error.");

    __player.SetVolume(80);

    __player.Play();
}
```

To stop playing the audio and close the file, call the `Stop()` and `Close()` methods:

```
__player.Stop();
__player.Close();
```

You can also play streaming content by using the `OpenUrl()` and `OpenUrlAsync()` methods, or play content loaded into a buffer in memory using `OpenBuffer()`.

Seeking in the Audio Player

Most media players show the current playing position and enable users to seek — that is, move to a new position in the audio. In this section you'll learn how to add a slider control and the associated code to implement seeking in the audio player.

To show a current playing position, you also need to add a timer control. First you need to add the following headers and namespaces:

```
#include <FUi.h>
#include <FMedia.h>

using namespace Tizen::Base::Runtime;
using namespace Tizen::Media;
using namespace Tizen::Ui;
using namespace Tizen::Ui::Controls;
```

Add more listeners for a timer control and slider control:

```
class PlayerExample
    : public Tizen::Media::IPlayerEventListener
    , public Tizen::Ui::IAdjustmentEventListener
    , public ITimerEventListener
```

Declare callbacks for the new controls:

```
void OnTimerExpired(Timer& timer);
void OnAdjustmentValueChanged(const Tizen::Ui::Control& source, int
adjustment);
```

Add member variables for the timer and slider controls:

```
Timer __timer;
Slider* __pSlider
```

On initialisation, the slider and timer need to be initialised too:

```
// Creates a slider that has 0~100 range.
__pSlider = new Slider();
__pSlider->Construct(Rectangle(0, 200, GetClientAreaBounds().width, 200),
BACKGROUND_STYLE_DEFAULT, false, 0, 100);
__pSlider->SetValue(0);
__pSlider->AddAdjustmentEventListener(*this);

// Adds the slider to the form
AddControl(__pSlider);

// Creates a timer
__timer.Construct(*this);
```

When the audio starts playing, the timer should also start:

```
__player.Play();
__timer.Start(500);
```

To show the current playing position, implement the `OnTimerExpired()` callback. The relative playing position is calculated as the current position divided by the total length of the content for every 0.5 seconds:

```
void
PlayerExample::OnTimerExpired(Timer& timer)
{
    long duration = __player.GetDuration();
    long position = __player.GetPosition();
    long progress = (int)(((float)position / (float) duration) * 100.0);
    __pSlider->SetValue(progress);
    __timer.Start(500);
}
```

The timer needs to be canceled when audio has finished playing. Call `__timer.Cancel()` in the `OnPlayerEndOfClip()` callback or together with the call to `__player.Stop()`.

To change the current playing position, implement the `OnAdjustmentValueChanged()` callback:

```
void
SliderSample::OnAdjustmentValueChanged(const Control& source, int adjustment)
{
    long position = (int)(__player.GetDuration() * adjustment / 100);
    __player.SeekTo(position);
}
```

When you change the slider, the position of the audio will also be changed.

Playing Video

The `Player` class can also play video files. The implementation is similar to playing audio files, but the `Tizen::Ui::Controls::OverlayRegion` instance is needed to display video on the device screen.

Here's the code you need to add to support video playback:

Add a member variable to contain the `OverlayRegion`:

```
OverlayRegion *__pOverlay;
```

To project the video on the overlay, you should retrieve the `BufferInfo` instance from the overlay and set it as the rendering buffer for the `Player` instance by using `SetRenderingBuffer()`:

```
// Construct() gets a concrete class instance of IPlayerEventListener.
r = __player.Construct(*this);
if (IsFailed(r))
TryReturn(r == E_SUCCESS, r, "Player Construct Error.");
Rectangle rect(0, 0, 320, 240);
BufferInfo bufferInfo;

bool isValid = false;
bool modified = false;
isValid = OverlayRegion::EvaluateBounds (OVERLAY_REGION_EVALUATION_OPTION_LESS_THAN,
    rect, modified);
TryReturn(!isValid, E_OUT_OF_RANGE, "Overlay Region's range is not valid.");

// Gets OverlayRegion from this Form
__pOverlay = GetOverlayRegionN(rect, OVERLAY_REGION_TYPE_NORMAL);
TryReturn(__pOverlay != null, GetLastResult(), "Overlay Region Getting Error.");


__pOverlay->GetBackgroundBufferInfo(bufferInfo);

// Adds the overlay region buffer into the player.
r = SetRenderingBuffer(bufferInfo);
if (IsFailed(r))
{
   delete __pOverlay;
   __pOverlay = null;
}
```

Opening and playing a video file are exactly the same as the audio file example in the previous section, except that the `OverlayRegion` instance needs to be deleted when an error occurs or playing is complete:

```
String filePath = Tizen::System::Environment::GetMediaPath() + L"example.mp4";

// Opens file synchronously
r = __player.OpenFile(filePath, false);
if (IsFailed(r))
{
   delete __pOverlay;
   __pOverlay = null;
}

__player.SetVolume(80);

r = __player.Play();
if (IsFailed(r))
{
   delete __pOverlay;
   __pOverlay = null;
}
```

Other features, including pause, stop, and repeat, are the same as shown in the audio player example and you could even use a slider for adjusting the playing position.

Capturing Video in the Player

The `CaptureVideo()` method of the `Player` class enables you to capture a single frame of the video content being played.

To capture a video frame, add the `Tizen::Media::IPlayerVideoEventListener` to the `PlayerExample` class:

```
class PlayerExample
    : public Tizen::Media::IPlayerEventListener
    , public Tizen::Media::IPlayerVideoEventListener
```

To capture a video frame, call `CaptureVideo()` and `Play()` consecutively. The player state should be `PLAYER_STATE_OPENED` before calling `CaptureVideo()`, otherwise an exception will occur:

```
// Makes sure the player state is OPENED
__player.CaptureVideo();
__player.Play();
```

To capture video from a specified position in the video rather than the beginning, call `SeekTo()`. In this case, you don't have to call `CaptureVideo()`, because `SeekTo()` calls `CaptureVideo()` implicitly:

```
// Changes the position from where you want to start capturing
__player.SeekTo(20000);
__player.Play();
```

The video frame will be decoded and the `OnVideoFrameDecode()` callback of the `IPlayerVideo EventListener` will be called. The following code snippet shows how to render the frame or save it to a file:

```
void
PlayerSample::OnVideoFrameDecoded(Player &src,
                        BitmapPixelFormat bitmapPixelFormat,
                        const Dimension &dim,
                        const byte *pBuffer, int sizeOfBuffer, result r)
{
    ByteBuffer buf;
    OverlayRegionBufferPixelFormat overlayPixelFormat;

    if (bitmapPixelFormat == BITMAP_PIXEL_FORMAT_ARGB8888)
    {
        overlayPixelFormat = OVERLAY_REGION_BUFFER_PIXEL_FORMAT_ARGB8888;
    }
    else if (bitmapPixelFormat == BITMAP_PIXEL_FORMAT_RGB565)
    {
        overlayPixelFormat = OVERLAY_REGION_BUFFER_PIXEL_FORMAT_RGB565;
    }
    else // Unsupported pixel format
    {
        return;
    }

    buf.Construct(pBuffer, 0, sizeOfBuffer, sizeOfBuffer);

    // Shows to the overlay region.
```

```
        if (__pOverlay != null)
        {
            __pOverlay->SetInputBuffer(buf, dim, overlayPixelFormat);

        }
        // Or you can save it as a file.
    }
```

Rendering frames in the capture callback will be slower than just rendering it to `BufferInfo`. Note that `SetRenderingBuffer()` cannot be called if an `IPlayerVideoEventListener` instance is set; and if the media file is DRM protected, you cannot capture it.

Playing Multiple Audio Sources

To play several audio sources simultaneously, for games or entertainment applications, you need to use the `Tizen::Media::AudioOut` class instead of `Player`. `AudioOut` can play Pulse-code modulation (PCM) data that contains noncompressed audio. In this section you'll learn how to add support for playing PCM audio.

First, you need to include `FIo.h` and `FMedia.h`:

```
#include <FIo.h>
#include <FApp.h>
#include <FMedia.h>

using namespace Tizen::Base;
using namespace Tizen::Io;
using namespace Tizen::Media;
```

You also need to implement a listener, because `AudioOut` sends events via the `Tizen::Media::IAudioOutEventListener`:

```
class AudioOutExample
    : public Tizen::Media::IAudioOutEventListener
```

`IAudioOutEventListener` has four callback functions. You will implement only `OnAudioOutBufferEndReached()` in this example:

```
protected:
// Called when the device has written a buffer completely.
virtual void OnAudioOutBufferEndReached(Tizen::Media::AudioOut& src);
// Called when interrupted by a higher priority task.
virtual void OnAudioOutInterrupted(Tizen::Media::AudioOut& src) {}
// Called when released from interruption.
virtual void OnAudioOutReleased(Tizen::Media::AudioOut& src) {}
// Called when an audio playback focus is lost.
virtual void OnAudioOutAudioFocusChanged(Tizen::Media::AudioOut& src) {}
```

Declare a member variable for `AudioOut` and a `ByteBuffer` for the PCM file:

```
private:
    AudioOut __audioOut;
    File __file;
    ByteBuffer __buffer;
```

To play PCM, load it from a file into a `ByteBuffer`. Calling `WriteBuffer()` with `ByteBuffer` as a parameter plays the PCM file. You must know the PCM source's channel, sample type, and sample rate, passing these values as parameters to the `Prepare()` method to prepare the audio to be played:

```
FileAttributes attr;
String filePath = Tizen::System::Environment::GetMediaPath() + L"example.pcm ";


// Opens the PCM file
__file.Construct(filePath, L"rb");

// Constructs the AudioOut instance with a listener
result r = __audioOut.Construct(*this);
TryReturn(r == E_SUCCESS, r, "AudioOut Construct Error.");

// Prepares the AudioOut instance
// Considers the input data as signed 16-bit, stereo, 44100 Hz PCM data
__audioOut.Prepare(AUDIO_TYPE_PCM_S16_LE, AUDIO_CHANNEL_TYPE_STEREO, 44100);
int minBufferSize = __audioOut.GetMinBufferSize();

// Constructs the pcm buffer and enqueue the buffer to the __audioOut
__buffer.Construct(minBufferSize);
__file.Read(__buffer);
__audioOut.WriteBuffer(__buffer);

// Starts playing
r = __audioOut.Start();
TryReturn(r == E_SUCCESS, r, "AudioOut Start Error.");
```

When playing reaches the end of the buffer, the rest of the file should be loaded. You need to implement the `OnAudioBufferEndReached()` callback, which is called when the end of the buffer is reached:

```
void
AudioOutExample::OnAudioOutBufferEndReached(Tizen::Media::AudioOut& src)
{
    result r = E_SUCCESS;

    r = __file.Read(__buffer);
    if (IsFailed(r))
    {
        // if there is no more to read
        __audioOut.Stop();
        __audioOut.Unprepare();
        return;
    }

    // keep continuing to load the file.
    src.WriteBuffer(__buffer);
}
```

Depending on the device, audio playback may not be smooth while the rest of the buffer is loaded. You can add more buffers to avoid this situation. For example, while one buffer is being played, another buffer loads data.

To play multiple sources simultaneously, create another `AudioOut` instance and call `Start()` on both instances at the same time.

RECORDING MEDIA CONTENT

In this section you learn how you to capture audio, video, and images within your application. You'll walk through code that shows the different techniques that can be used to record audio and use the device's camera to capture video and still images. You'll also become familiar with the different settings used to control the quality and format of the content being recorded.

Recording Audio

There are two ways to record audio: using `AudioIn` and `AudioRecorder`. `AudioIn` records audio only in PCM format, whereas `AudioRecorder` can record audio in three formats, including AMR, AAC, and WAV. Recording with `AudioIn` is almost the reverse of using `AudioOut`. Here's how you would record audio with the `AudioIn` class:

```
// Create and initialise the required class instances.
AudioIn __audioIn;
AudioInEventListener __audioInEventListener;

// Construct a Tizen::Media::AudioIn instance.
__audioIn.Construct(__audioInEventListener);

// Prepare an AudioIn instance.
__audioIn.Prepare(AUDIO_TYPE_PCM_U8, AUDIO_CHANNEL_TYPE_STEREO, 8000);

// Prepare a buffer to store PCM data.
pByteBuffer = new ByteBuffer();
pByteBuffer->Construct(MAX_BUFFER_SIZE);


// Add buffer
__audioIn->AddBuffer(pByteBuffer);

// Start recording:
__audioIn->Start();
```

In the `OnAudioInBufferIsFilled()` function, you need to clean up the buffer and add it again:

```
void
AudioInExample::OnAudioInBufferIsFilled( Tizen::Base::ByteBuffer* pData)
{
    // Clears the buffer
    pData->Clear();

    // Adds the byte buffer to the __audioIn to fill data again
    __audioIn.AddBuffer(pData);
}
```

Now let's take a look at the `AudioRecorder` class. `AudioRecorder` is more convenient than `AudioIn` because you can record, stop, pause, and mute the audio, and set the audio recording format, the maximum recording time, and the maximum recording size.

First, you need to add a privilege, `http://tizen.org/privilege/audiorecorder`, in your application manifest file, `manifest.xml`:

```
<Apps>
    …
    <Privileges>
    <Privilege>http://tizen.org/privilege/audiorecorder</Privilege>
        …
```

To use `AudioRecorder`, include `FMedia.h` and use the namespace `Tizen::Media`:

```
#include <FMedia.h>
using namespace Tizen::Media;
```

Then you need to implement the `IAudioRecorderEventListener` to receive audio recording events:

```
class AudioRecorderExample
    : public Tizen::Media::IAudioRecorderEventListener
```

Of course, you also need to implement the callbacks. In this example, you do nothing for each event:

```
protected:
    // IAudioRecorderEventListener
    // Called when the AudioRecorder::Stop() method is completed.
    virtual void OnAudioRecorderStopped(result r) {}
    // Called when the AudioRecorder::Cancel() method is completed.
    virtual void OnAudioRecorderCanceled(result r) {}
    // Called when the AudioRecorder::Pause() method is completed.
    virtual void OnAudioRecorderPaused(result r) {}
    // Called when the AudioRecorder::Record() method is completed.
    virtual void OnAudioRecorderStarted(result r) {}
    // Called when AudioRecorder reaches the end of the pre-defined time.
    virtual void OnAudioRecorderEndReached(RecordingEndCondition endCondition) {}
    // Called when the AudioRecorder::Close() method is completed.
    virtual void OnAudioRecorderClosed(result r) {}
    // Called when an error has occurred in AudioRecorder.
    virtual void OnAudioRecorderErrorOccurred(RecorderErrorReason r) {}
```

Declare a member variable at the end of the example class:

```
AudioRecorder __recorder;
```

The following code snippet records audio. `CreateAudioFile()` creates a file to save the recorded audio and `Record()` starts the recording:

```
result r = E_SUCCESS;
String destFilePath =
  Tizen::App::App::GetInstance()->GetAppRootPath()+ L"recorded.amr";
r = __recorder.Construct(*this);
TryReturn(r == E_SUCCESS, r, "Recorder Construct Error.");

r = __recorder.CreateAudioFile(destFilePath, true);
TryReturn(r == E_SUCCESS, r, "Recorder Create Audio File Error.");

r = __recorder.Record();
TryReturn(r == E_SUCCESS, r, "Recorder Record Error.");
```

Using the default `AudioRecorder` settings, this recording works fine, but you can also control settings such as the maximum recording time and the audio file format.

SetmaxRecordingTime() sets the maximum recording time, specified in milliseconds. SetQuality() sets the quality of recording: RECORDING_QUALITY_LOW, RECORDING_QUALITY_MEDIUM, or RECORDING_QUALITY_HIGH. SetFormat() sets the audio file format and its codec. The following example sets it to MP4 and AAC:

```
r = __recorder.SetMaxRecordingTime(60000); // 60 sec

__recorder.SetQuality(RECORDING_QUALITY_HIGH);
pAudioCodecList = __recorder.GetSupportedCodecListN();
pMediaContainerList = __recorder.GetSupportedContainerListN();

if (pAudioCodecList->Contains(CODEC_AAC) &&
    pMediaContainerList->Contains(MEDIA_CONTAINER_MP4))
{
    r = __recorder.SetFormat(CODEC_AAC, MEDIA_CONTAINER_MP4);
    TryReturn(r == E_SUCCESS, r, "Recorder Set Format Error.");
}
r = __recorder.Record();
TryReturn(r == E_SUCCESS, r, "Recorder Record Error.");
```

While recording, you can pause the recording with the Pause() method. If you want to stop recording, call Stop() and close the recorder by calling Close():

```
__recorder.Stop();
__recorder.Close();
```

Recording Video

You can record video with the device's internal camera using the Tizen::Media::VideoRecorder class. If you are using the Emulator to test, you can use a PC with a webcam to simulate the device's internal camera.

To use video recording, you need to add the privileges — http://tizen.org/privilege/videorecorder and http://tizen.org/privilege/camera — to your application manifest file, manifest.xml:

```
<Apps>
    ...
    <Privileges>
    <Privilege>http://tizen.org/privilege/videorecorder</Privilege>
    <Privilege>http://tizen.org/privilege/camera</Privilege>
        ...
```

To use VideoRecorder, include FMedia.h, and use the namespace Tizen::Media:

```
#include <FMedia.h>
using namespace Tizen::Media;
```

Then you need to implement both ICameraEventListener and IVideoRecorderEventListener to receive events for video recording events:

```
class VideoRecorderExample
    : public Tizen::Media::ICameraEventListener
    , public Tizen::Media::IVideoRecorderEventListener
```

Next, implement the callbacks. In this example, you do nothing for each event:

```
protected:
    // ICameraEventListener
    // Called when the Camera::SetAutoFocus() method is completed.
    virtual void OnCameraAutoFocused(bool completeCondition) {}
    // Called when the Camera::Capture() method is completed.
    virtual void OnCameraCaptured(Tizen::Base::ByteBuffer &capturedData, result r) {}
    // Called when an error occurs in Camera.
    virtual void OnCameraErrorOccurred(CameraErrorReason err) {}
    // Called after the Camera::StartPreview() method is called with previewedData true.
    virtual void OnCameraPreviewed(Tizen::Base::ByteBuffer &previewedData, result r) {}


    // IVideoRecorderEventListener
    // Called when the VideoRecorder::Cancel() method is completed.
    virtual void OnVideoRecorderCanceled(result r) {}
    // Called when the VideoRecorder::Close() method is completed.
    virtual void OnVideoRecorderClosed(result r) {}
    // Called when VideoRecorder reaches the end of the pre-defined time.
    virtual void OnVideoRecorderEndReached(RecordingEndCondition endCondition) {}
    // Called when an error occurred in VideoRecorder.
    virtual void OnVideoRecorderErrorOccurred( RecorderErrorReason r) {}
    // Called when the VideoRecorder::Pause() method is completed.
    virtual void OnVideoRecorderPaused(result r) {}
    // Called when the VideoRecorder::Record() method is completed.
    virtual void OnVideoRecorderStarted(result r) {}
    // Called when the VideoRecorder::Stop() method is completed.
    virtual void OnVideoRecorderStopped(result r) {}
```

Declare a member variable at the end of the example class. An `OverlayRegion` is used to show a preview of the video recording on the device screen:

```
Camera __camera;
VideoRecorder __recorder;
OverlayRegion *__pOverlay;
```

The following code snippet shows how to record video:

```
result r = E_SUCCESS;
Tizen::Graphics::Rectangle rect(0, 0, 320, 240);
BufferInfo bufferInfo;
String filePath = Tizen::App::App::GetInstance()->GetAppRootPath() + L"data/test.mp4";

bool isValid = false;
bool modified = false;
isValid = OverlayRegion::EvaluateBounds(OVERLAY_REGION_EVALUATION_OPTION_LESS_THAN,
    rect, modified);
TryCatch(!isValid, r=E_OUT_OF_RANGE, "Overlay Region's range is not valid.");

__pOverlay = GetOverlayRegionN(rect, OVERLAY_REGION_TYPE_PRIMARY_CAMERA);
if (__pOverlay == null)
{
return GetLastResult();
}


__pOverlay->GetBackgroundBufferInfo(bufferInfo);
```

(1)

```
r = __camera.Construct(*this, CAMERA_PRIMARY);
TryCatch(r == E_SUCCESS, ,"Camera Construct Error.");

r = __camera.PowerOn();
TryCatch(r == E_SUCCESS, ,"Camera Power On Error.");

r = __camera.StartPreview(&bufferInfo, false);
TryCatch(r == E_SUCCESS, ,"Camera Start Preview Error.");


(2)
r = __recorder.Construct(*this, __camera);
TryCatch(r == E_SUCCESS, ,"Recorder Construct Error.");

r = __recorder.CreateVideoFile(filePath, true);
TryCatch(r == E_SUCCESS, ,"Recorder Create Video File Error.");

r = __recorder.Record();
TryCatch(r == E_SUCCESS, ,"Recoder Record Error.");

return E_SUCCESS;

CATCH:
if (__pOverlay)
{
delete __pOverlay;
__pOverlay = null;
}
return r;
```

(1) `Camera::Construct()` initializes the camera. The first parameter of `Construct()` is an event listener, and the second parameter is either `CAMERA_PRIMARY` or `CAMERA_SECONDARY`, depending on whether the back-facing or front-facing camera will be used for capturing video. To project the camera preview on the overlay, retrieve `BufferInfo` from the overlay and put it into a `Camera` instance by calling `Camera::StartPreview()`.

`Camera::PowerOn()` must be called to turn on the device's camera.

(2) The camera instance should be passed to `VideoRecorder::Construct()`.

The `VideoRecorder::CreateVideoFile()` method is called to create a file to which the recorded video can be saved, and `Record()` starts the recording.

To stop video recording, call `VideoRecorder::Stop()`, stop the camera preview by calling `Camera::StopPreview()`, and power off the camera using `Camera::PowerOff()`. You also need to delete the overlay region handle:

```
__recorder.Stop();
__camera.StopPreview();
__camera.PowerOff();
if (__pOverlay)
{
  delete __pOverlay;
  __pOverlay = null;
}
```

Capturing Images from the Camera

Capturing still images from the camera is simpler than capturing video because the `Camera` class provides the functionality. Much of the code for capturing a still image is the same as the `VideoRecorderExample` in the previous section, except you need to call `Camera::Capture()` to capture the image.

The `Camera` class provides many settings you can use to control the way your image is captured, including contrast, exposure, brightness, effects, white balance, zoom, flash, focus, metering, and resolution.

The `Camera::GetSupportedCaptureResolutionListN()` method returns a list of `Dimension` types representing the supported capture resolutions, with the first element being the highest resolution, and `Camera::SetCaptureResolution()` method sets the resolution used for taking a picture:

```
IList* pCaptureResolutionList = pCamera->GetSupportedCaptureResolutionListN();
Dimension* pCaptureResolution = (Dimension*)pCaptureResolutionList->
                               GetAt(pCaptureResolutionList->GetCount()-1);
r = pCamera->SetCaptureResolution(*pCaptureResolution);
```

Similarly, you can get and set preview resolutions:

```
IList* pPreviewResolutionList = pCamera->GetSupportedPreviewResolutionListN();
Dimension* pPreviewResolution = (Dimension*)pPreviewResolutionList->
                               GetAt(pPreviewResolutionList->GetCount()-1);
r = pCamera->SetPreviewResolution(*pPreviewResolution);
```

`Camera::GetSupportedCaptureFormatListN()` returns a list of capture formats supported by the camera as a `Tizen::Graphics::PixelFormat` type, which is actually an enum. Among the list of supported formats, `PIXEL_FORMAT_JPEG` is a JPEG format and `PIXEL_FORMAT_RGB565` is an uncompressed format. The following code sets the camera capture format to JPEG if it's available:

```
IListT<PixelFormat>* pCaptureFormatList = pCamera->GetSupportedCaptureFormatListN();
if (pCaptureFormatList->Contains(PIXEL_FORMAT_JPEG))
{
    r = pCamera->SetCaptureFormat(PIXEL_FORMAT_JPEG);
```

The following code sets autofocus if it is supported and captures the image from within the `OnCameraAutoFocused()` handler:

```
// check whether the device camera supports auto-focus
    bool supportAutoFocus = false;
    result r = MediaCapability::GetValue(CAMERA_PRIMARY_SUPPORT_FOCUS
                            , supportAutoFocus);

    // Auto-focus is supported
    if (supportAutoFocus)
    {
        r = SetAutoFocus(true);
    }
...
void
CameraCapturePreviewForm::OnCameraAutoFocused(bool completeCondition)
```

```
{
    result r = E_SUCCESS;

    r = pCamera->Capture();
}
```

To set other camera options, use the following methods of the `Camera` class:

➤ **Contrast** — `SetContrast()`

➤ **Exposure** — `SetExposure()`

➤ **Brightness** — `SetBrightness()`

➤ **Effects** — `SetEffects()`: none, color, black & white, sepia, solarize, negative, and night

➤ **ISO** — `IsoLevel()`: default, min, auto, max, 50, 100, 200, 400, 800, and 1600

➤ **White balance** — `SetWhiteBalance()`: auto, sunny, cloudy, fluorescent, and tungsten

➤ **Zoom** — `ZoomIn()`, `ZoomOut()`

➤ **Metering** — `SetMeteringMode()`: none, average, center-weighted, and spot

➤ **Flash** — `SetFlashMode()`: off, on, auto, red-eye reduction, and continuous

➤ **Focus** — `SetFocusMode()`: none, normal, macro, continuous auto, and infinite

---

MEDIA CAPABILITIES

Because you don't know which media capabilities each Tizen-compatible device supports, it's a good idea to check the device before using media features. The `Tizen::Media::MediaCapability` class provides information about the supported capabilities of the device, such as audio sample rate and types, camera count, camera preview formats, and supported codecs for playing and recording audio and video. See the Media: Handling Audio, Video, Camera, and Images section in the SDK for more details about device capabilities that the `MediaCapability` class can retrieve.

WORKING WITH IMAGES

The `ImageBuffer` class is used to encode and decode different image formats. The class also includes methods to support image-editing features, such as resizing, flipping, rotating, and converting the color-space of an image. In this section you learn how to decode, edit, and encode images.

Decoding Images

The `ImageBuffer` class is constructed with either encoded or raw data. If the buffer is constructed with encoded data, the data will be decoded and the `ImageBuffer` will be initialised.

To construct an `ImageBuffer` with encoded data, provide a data buffer or the file path containing the encoded data:

```
ImageBuffer imgBuff;
result r = imgBuff.Construct(L"filepath");
```

`ImageBuffer` can be used to decode images in the following formats:

➤ **JPEG** — `IMG_FORMAT_JPG`

➤ **PNG** — `IMG_FORMAT_PNG`

➤ **TIFF** — `IMG_FORMAT_TIFF`

➤ **BMP** — `IMG_FORMAT_BMP`

➤ **WBMP** — `IMG_FORMAT_WBMP`

To construct the buffer with raw data, provide the dimensions of the image, its color-space, the raw data buffer, and the length of the data in bytes:

```
ImageBuffer imgBuff;
byte* pImgData;
int width, height, dataLength;
MediaPixelFormat pixFmt;
/* Get raw data in pImgData */
/* Get the dimensions of the raw data in width and height variables. */
/* Get pixelformat of the data. */

/* Construct image buffer with the raw data*/
result r = imgBuff.Construct(width, height, pixFmt, pImgData, dataLength);
```

Not all color-spaces enumerated in `MediaPixelFormat` are supported by `ImageBuffer`. To find which color-spaces are supported, use the `ImageBuffer::GetSupportedPixelFormatListN()` function:

```
IListT<MediaPixelFormat>* pPixFmtList = imgBuff.GetSupportedPixelFormatListN();
```

To obtain the decoded data to display, call `ImageBuffer::GetBitmapN()`, while to get the raw data/decoded buffer, call `ImageBuffer::GetByteBufferN()`. In both functions, you must specify the color-space in which the data is required:

```
// Gets the raw data in bgra format.
ByteBuffer* pBuff = imgBuff.GetByteBufferN(MEDIA_PIXEL_FORMAT_BGRA);
r = GetLastResult();

Bitmap* pBmp = imgBuff.GetBitmapN(BITMAP_PIXEL_FORMAT_ARGB8888);
r = GetLastResult();
```

You can get information about an image using the following functions:

➤ **Dimensions** — `ImageBuffer::GetWidth()`, `ImageBuffer::GetHeight()`

➤ **Color-space** — `ImageBuffer::GetPixelFormat()`

➤ **Exif information** — `ImageBuffer::GetExifOrientation()`

Editing Images

The `ImageBuffer` class provides basic image manipulation, including the following features:

➤ Resize to any non-zero dimension (this does not preserve the aspect ratio)

➤ Rotate in integral angles (90, 180, and 270 degrees)

➤ Flip (horizontally and vertically)

To perform any of these operations, first construct an `ImageBuffer` instance and then call any of the APIs shown in the following code to return a new instance with the edited properties:

```
ImageBuffer imgBuff;
result r = imgBuff.Construct(L"filepath");

// Resizing the image to 50 x 50;
ImageBuffer* pResized = imgBuff.ResizeN(50, 50);
r = GetlastResult();

// Rotating image by 90degrees clockwise;
ImageBuffer* pRotated = imgBuff.RotateN(IMAGE_ROTATION_90);
r = GetlastResult();

// Flipping image horizontally;
ImageBuffer* pFlipped = imgBuff.FlipN(IMAGE_FLIP_HORIZONTAL);
r = GetlastResult();
```

Encoding Images

The `ImageBuffer` class is used to encode raw data in a variety of formats. This is useful if the user has raw data, received from the camera, for example, or has performed operations on an existing `ImageBuffer`, such as resizing and flipping an image. The `ImageBuffer` class can be used to encode data in the following formats:

➤ **JPEG** — `IMG_FORMAT_JPG`

➤ **PNG** — `IMG_FORMAT_PNG`

➤ **BMP** — `IMG_FORMAT_BMP`

For example, if you want to resize an image, flip it, and save it to a file in JPEG format, use the following code:

```
ImageBuffer imgBuff;
result r = imgBuff.Construct(L"filepath");

// Resizes the image to 50 x 50;
ImageBuffer* pResized = imgBuff.ResizeN(50, 50);
r = GetlastResult();

// Flips image horizontally;
ImageBuffer* pEdited = pResized->FlipN(IMAGE_FLIP_HORIZONTAL);
r = GetlastResult();

r = pEdited->EncodeToFile(L"new filepath", IMG_FORMAT_JPG);
```

DECODING AUDIO AND VIDEO

Compressed audio and video content can be decoded using the `Tizen::Media::AudioDecoder` and `Tizen::Media::VideoDecoder` classes respectively.

To decode a compressed audio stream to raw audio data, use the `Tizen::Media::AudioDecoder` class. This class supports audio-decoding formats, including `CODEC_MP3`, `CODEC_AAC`, `CODEC_AMR`, `CODEC_VORBIS`, `CODEC_ALAW`, and `CODEC_MULAW`.

To decode a compressed video stream to raw video data, use the `Tizen::Media::VideoDecoder` class. This class supports video-decoding formats, including `CODEC_H263`, `CODEC_MPEG4`, and `CODEC_H264`.

Decoding Audio Content

To decode a compressed audio stream, create an instance of the `Tizen::Media::AudioDecoder` class:

```
AudioDecoder dec;
result r = E_SUCCESS;
```

Construct `AudioDecoder` specifying the `CodecType`:

```
r = dec.Construct(CODEC_MP3);
```

Call the `Probe()` method of the `AudioDecoder` to check whether the audio data can be decoded successfully, and specify the `sampleType`, `channelType`, and `sampleRate` settings:

```
r = dec.Probe(srcBuf, sampleType, channelType, sampleRate);
if (IsFailed(r))
{
        return r;
}
```

Decode the encoded data using the `Decode()` method:

```
r = dec.Decode(srcBuf, dstBuf);
```

The Audio Decoder reads the audio data from the source buffer and stores the decoded data in the destination buffer.

Continue the decoding operation until all the input data is consumed completely.

Decoding Video Content

The process for decoding video content is similar to that used to decode audio. To decode a compressed video stream, create an instance of the `Tizen::Media::VideoDecoder` class:

```
VideoDecoder dec;
result r = E_SUCCESS;
```

Construct a `VideoDecoder` instance, specifying the `CodecType`:

```
r = dec.Construct(CODEC_H264);
```

Call the `Probe()` method of the `VideoDecoder` class to check whether the video data can be successfully decoded, and specify the `width`, `height`, and `pixelFormat` of the video data:

```
r = dec.Probe(srcBuf, width, height, pixelFormat);
```

To decode the video data, call `Decode()`:

```
r = dec.Decode(srcBuf, dstBuf);
```

The Video Decoder reads the video data from the source buffer and stores the decoded data in the destination buffer.

Continue the decoding operation until all the input data is consumed completely.

ENCODING AUDIO AND VIDEO

Raw audio and video content can be encoded using the `Tizen::Media::AudioEncoder` and `Tizen::Media::VideoEncoder` classes, respectively.

To encode raw audio data to a compressed audio stream, use the `Tizen::Media::AudioEncoder` class. This class supports the `CODEC_AAC` and `CODEC_AMR` audio encoding formats.

To encode raw video data to a compressed video stream, use the `Tizen::Media::VideoEncoder` class. This class supports the `CODEC_H263` and `CODEC_MPEG4` video encoding formats.

Encoding Audio Content

To encode raw audio data, create an instance of the `Tizen::Media::AudioEncoder` class:

```
AudioEncoder enc;
result r = E_SUCCESS;
HashMap option;
```

Then construct the `AudioEncoder`, specifying the `CodecType` and a `HashMap` containing the audio options `channelType`, `sampleType`, and `bitRate`:

```
option.Construct();
option.Add(*(new Integer(MEDIA_PROPERTY_AUDIO_CHANNEL_TYPE)),
           *(new Integer(channelType)));
option.Add(*(new Integer(MEDIA_PROPERTY_AUDIO_SAMPLE_RATE)),
           *(new Integer(sampleRate)));
option.Add(*(new Integer(MEDIA_PROPERTY_AUDIO_BIT_RATE)), *(new Integer(bitRate)))
enc.Construct(CODEC_AAC, &option);
```

Call the `Encode()` method of `AudioEncoder` to encode the raw data:

```
r = enc.Encode(srcBuf, dstBuf);
```

The Audio Encoder reads the audio data from the source buffer and stores the encoded data in the destination buffer.

Continue the encoding operation until all the input data is consumed completely.

Encoding Video Content

To encode raw video YUV data, create an instance of the `Tizen::Media::VideoEncoder` class:

```
    __pEnc = new (std::nothrow) VideoEncoder();
    result r = E_SUCCESS;
```

Then construct the Video Encoder, specifying the CodecType and a `HashMap` that contains the encoding options:

```
    r =__pEnc->Construct(CODEC_H263, &option);
```

Call the `Encode()` method of `VideoEncoder` to encode the raw video YUV data:

```
    r =__pEnc->Encode(*__pSrcBuf, *__pDstBuf);
```

The Video Encoder reads and encodes the video data in the source buffer and stores the encoded data in the destination buffer.

Continue the encoding operation until all the input data is consumed completely.

Extracting Frames from Video

To get an I-frame (a single frame of digital content) from a video file, create an instance of the `Tizen::Media::VideoFrameExtractor` class.

```
    VideoFrameExtractor pFrameExtractor = new (std::nothrow) VideoFrameExtractor();
    result r = E_SUCCESS;
```

Then, construct the `VideoFrameExtractor`, specifying the path of the video file and the pixel format:

```
    String path = Tizen::App::App::GetInstance()->GetAppRootPath() + L"data/test.mp4";
    r = pFrameExtractor->Construct(path, MEDIA_PIXEL_FORMAT_BGRA8888);
```

To get the duration of the Video file, use the `GetDuration` method:

```
    long duration = pFrameExtractor->GetDuration();
```

Extract individual frames from the specified positions in the video:

```
    for (int i = 0; i < 10; i++)
    {
        ImageBuffer* pImage = extractor.GetFrameN(duration*i/10);
        // Add some code that handles extracted video frame
        delete pImage;
    }
```

MEDIA APPLICATION CONTROLS

The Tizen native framework enables applications to access the built-in music player, video player, and camera through the `Tizen::App::AppControl` class. Earlier in this chapter you saw how to play audio and video content using the classes in the `Tizen::Media` namespace; and while using `AppControl` does provide similar functionality, there are some important differences. Application controls have a fixed user interface, which cannot be customized by the application launching the control. The built-in application controls also provide fully featured audio and video players and access to all the device's camera functions, so while they're not as flexible, you won't have to write

as much code to access multimedia features. To use the application controls, the `http://tizen`
`.org/privilege/application.launch` privilege should be specified.

Music Player Application Control

The Music Player application control enables you to play audio files using the device's preloaded
Media Player application. The Music Player application control supports the following two
operations:

➤ **View operation:**

 ➤ Accessed by App ID `tizen.musicplayer` and operation ID `http://tizen.org/`
  `appcontrol/operation/view`

 ➤ Launches the Media Player and plays a specified audio file

➤ **Pick operation:**

 ➤ Accessed by App ID `tizen.musicplayer` and operation ID `http://tizen.org/`
  `appcontrol/operation/pick`

 ➤ Displays and browses audio files from the Media folder

 ➤ Returns user-selected files

The input data of the view operation is the URI of the media file to play. The following code shows
how to get the Music Player application control and start the view operation to play the specified
audio file:

```
String uri = String(L"file://") + Environment::GetMediaPath()
            + L"Sounds/sample_audio.mp3";
AppControl* pAc = AppManager::FindAppControlN(L"tizen.musicplayer",
            L"http://tizen.org/appcontrol/operation/view");

if (pAc)
{
    pAc->Start(&uri, null, null, null);
    delete pAc;
}
```

`AppManager::FindAppControlN()` returns an `AppControl` instance based
on the application ID and operation ID. The `AppControl::Start()` method
starts the retrieved application control with the specified operation. In this
Music Player view operation, the first parameter is a filename to play and
other parameters are null. When the operation starts, the Music Player
shows up in the caller application as shown in Figure 13-1.

Calling the pick operation is similar:

```
String mime = L"audio/*";
    HashMap extraData;
    extraData.Construct();
```

FIGURE 13-1

```
String selectKey = L"http://tizen.org/appcontrol/data/selection_mode";
String selectVal = L"multiple";
extraData.Add(&selectKey, &selectVal);

AppControl* pAc = AppManager::FindAppControlN(L"tizen.musicplayer",
                            L"http://tizen.org/appcontrol/operation/pick");
if (pAc)
{
   pAc->Start(null, &mime, &extraData, this);
   delete pAc;
}
```

The pick operation returns the files selected by the user, so your application needs to implement the `OnAppControlCompleteResponseReceived()` callback of the `IAppControlResponseListener` interface. The following example retrieves the selected files:

```
void
MyAppClass::OnAppControlCompleteResponseReceived(const Tizen::App::AppId& appId,
                     const Tizen::Base::String& operationId,
                     const Tizen::App::AppCtrlResult appControlResult,
                     const Tizen::Base::Collection::IMap* pExtraData)
{
   if (appId.Equals(String(L"tizen.musicplayer")) &&
       operationId.Equals(String(L"http://tizen.org/appcontrol/operation/pick")))
   {
      if (appControlResult  == APP_CTRL_RESULT_SUCCEEDED)
      {
         AppLog("Music list retrieving succeeded.");
         // Use the selected audio paths
         if (pExtraData)
         {
            IList* pValueList = const_cast< IList* >
                (dynamic_cast< const IList* >
                (pExtraData->
                GetValue(String(L"http://tizen.org/appcontrol/data/selected"))));

            if (pValueList)
            {
               for (int i = 0; i < pValueList->GetCount(); i++)
               {
                  String* pValue = dynamic_cast< String* >(pValueList->GetAt(i));
                  // TODO: Use the file path
               }
            }
         }
      }
      else if (appControlResult  == APP_CTRL_RESULT_FAILED)
      {
         AppLog("Music list retrieving failed.");
      }
      else if (appControlResult  == APP_CTRL_RESULT_CANCELED)
      {
         AppLog("Music list retrieving was canceled.");
      }
      else if (appControlResult == APP_CTRL_RESULT_TERMINATED)
      {
```

```
        AppLog("Music list retrieving was terminated.");
    }
    else if (appControlResult == APP_CTRL_RESULT_ABORTED)
    {
        AppLog("Music list retrieving was aborted.");
    }
  }
}
```

Video Player Application Control

The Video Player application control enables an application to play video files using the device's preloaded Video Player application. The Video Player application control supports the view operation. The view operation is accessed by App ID `tizen.videoplayer` and operation ID `http://tizen.org/appcontrol/operation/view`, and it launches the Media Player and plays a specified video file.

The input data of the view operation is the URI of the media file to play. The following code shows how to get the Video Player application control and start the view operation to play the video (see Figure 13-2):

FIGURE 13-2

```
String uri = String(L"file://") + Environment::GetMediaPath()
        + L"Videos/sample_video.mp4";
AppControl* pAc = AppManager::FindAppControlN(L"tizen.videoplayer",
        L"http://tizen.org/appcontrol/operation/view");

if (pAc)
{
    pAc->Start(&uri, null, null, null);
    delete pAc;
}
```

Camera Application Control

The Camera application control (see Figure 13-3) enables an application to use the features of the device's preloaded camera application to capture images and record video. The create content operation is accessed by App ID `tizen.camera` and operation ID `http://tizen.org/appcontrol/operation/create_content`, and it launches the device's predefined camera application to capture images and videos.

When you call the operation, you need to send extra data that indicates whether the camera can be switched between still image and video capture modes. The extra data can be set up as a `HashMap` with a specified key and value. Setting `true` for `allow_switch` means that the camera can be switched between capture and video recording modes:

FIGURE 13-3

```
HashMap extraData;
extraData.Construct();
String typeKey = L"http://tizen.org/appcontrol/data/camera/allow_switch";
String typeVal = L"true";
extraData.Add(&typeKey, &typeVal);
```

Then start the create content operation with the extra data and a MIME type specifying the format of the captured content, in this case a JPEG:

```
String mime = L"image/jpg";
AppControl* pAc = AppManager::FindAppControlN(L"tizen.camera",
        L"http://tizen.org/appcontrol/operation/create_content");
if (pAc)
{
  pAc->Start(null, &mime, &extraData, this);
  delete pAc;
}
```

The create content operation returns the file path of the captured file, so your application needs to implement the OnAppControlCompleteResponseReceived() callback of the IAppControlResponseListener interface. The following example traverses the selected files:

```
void
MyAppClass::OnAppControlCompleteResponseReceived(const Tizen::App::AppId& appId,
            const Tizen::Base::String& operationId,
            const Tizen::App::AppCtrlResult appControlResult,
            const Tizen::Base::Collection::IMap* pExtraData)
{
    if (appId.Equals(String(L"tizen.camera")) &&
    operationId.Equals(String(L"http://tizen.org/appcontrol/operation/create_content")))
    {
        if (appControlResult == APP_CTRL_RESULT_SUCCEEDED)
        {
            AppLog("Camera capture succeeded.");
            // Uses the captured image
            if (pExtraData)
            {
            IList* pValueList = const_cast< IList* >
            (dynamic_cast< const IList* >
            (pExtraData->
            GetValue(String(L"http://tizen.org/appcontrol/data/selected"))));
                if (pValueList)
                {
                    for (int i = 0; i < pValueList->GetCount(); i++)
                    {
                        String* pValue = dynamic_cast< String* >(pValueList->GetAt(i));
                        // TODO: Use the file path
                    }
                }
            }
        }
        else if (appControlResult == APP_CTRL_RESULT_FAILED)
        {
            AppLog("Camera capture failed.");
        }
        else if (appControlResult == APP_CTRL_RESULT_CANCELED)
        {
            AppLog("Camera capture was canceled.");
        }
        else if (appControlResult == APP_CTRL_RESULT_TERMINATED)
        {
```

```
        AppLog("Camera capture was terminated.");
    }
    else if (appControlResult == APP_CTRL_RESULT_ABORTED)
    {
        AppLog("Camera capture was aborted.");
    }
    else if (appControlResult == APP_CTRL_RESULT_FAILED)
    {
        AppLog("Camera capture failed.");
    }
}
}
```

Image Viewer Application Control

The Image Viewer application control allows you to display image files in your application and is accessed using the App ID `tizen.imageviewer`. The application control supports image display, as shown in Figure 13-4, and image cropping, the user interface for which is shown in Figure 13-5.

FIGURE 13-4   **FIGURE 13-5**

To display an image file stored on the device, use the operation ID `http://tizen.org/appcontrol/operation/view`. To crop an image file and retrieve the trimmed image, use the operation ID `http://tizen.org/appcontrol/operation/image/crop`.

The following input MIME types can be used:

➤ image/bmp

➤ image/gif

➤ image/jpeg

➤ image/png

To display an image, you can use the following code:

```
String uri = String(L"file://") + Environment::GetMediaPath()
                        + L"Images/sample_image.jpg";
AppControl* pAc = AppManager::FindAppControlN(L"tizen.imageviewer",
                            L"http://tizen.org/appcontrol/operation/view");
if (pAc)
{
    pAc->Start(&uri, null, null, null);
    delete pAc;
}
```

If you use the crop operation, you need to implement the
OnAppControlCompleteResponseReceived() event handler to receive the trimmed data. The
following code shows how to crop an image:

```
HashMap extraData;
extraData.Construct();
String typeKey = L"http://tizen.org/appcontrol/data/image/crop_mode";
String typeVal = L"fit_to_screen";
extraData.Add(&typeKey, &typeVal);

String uri = String(L"file://") + Environment::GetMediaPath()
                        + L"Images/sample_image.jpg";
AppControl* pAc = AppManager::FindAppControlN(L"tizen.imageviewer",
                        L"http://tizen.org/appcontrol/operation/image/crop");
if (pAc)
{
    pAc->Start(&uri, null, &extraData, this);
    delete pAc;
}
```

Here's how you retrieve the cropped image data in OnAppControlCompleteResponseReceived():

```
void
MyAppClass::OnAppControlCompleteResponseReceived(const Tizen::App::AppId& appId,
                                const Tizen::Base::String& operationId,
                            const Tizen::App::AppCtrlResult appControlResult,
                            const Tizen::Base::Collection::IMap* pExtraData)
{
    if (appId.Equals(String(L"tizen.imageviewer")) &&
        operationId.Equals(String(L"http://tizen.org/appcontrol/operation/image/crop")))
    {
        if (appControlResult == APP_CTRL_RESULT_SUCCEEDED)
        {
            AppLog("Image crop succeeded.");
            // Uses the cropped image
            if (pExtraData)
            {
                IList* pValueList = const_cast< IList* >(dynamic_cast< const IList* >
                    (pExtraData->GetValue
                    (String(L"http://tizen.org/appcontrol/data/selected"))));
                if (pValueList)
                {
                    for (int i = 0; i < pValueList->GetCount(); i++)
                    {
```

```
                    String* pValue = dynamic_cast< String* >(pValueList->GetAt(i));
                    // Use the file path
                }
            }
        }
    }
    else if (appControlResult == APP_CTRL_RESULT_FAILED)
    {
        AppLog("Image crop failed.");
    }
    else if (appControlResult == APP_CTRL_RESULT_CANCELED)
    {
        AppLog("Image crop was canceled.");
    }
    else if (appControlResult == APP_CTRL_RESULT_TERMINATED)
    {
        AppLog("Image crop was terminated.");
    }
    else if (appControlResult == APP_CTRL_RESULT_ABORTED)
    {
        AppLog("Image crop was aborted.");
    }
}
```

SUMMARY

This chapter provided you with a practical introduction to Tizen's multimedia features. You learned about creating and manipulating content, which is vital if you're writing any kind of application that works with audio, video, or images. While playing audio and video is relatively straightforward, using the code in this chapter should save you time when adding these features to your own code, as should the code snippets in the media-capturing sections. You also know how to access the built-in application controls, especially useful if you want quick access to the device's camera without having to write a lot of your own code. Of course, if you want to add your own video recording capabilities, then the code in this chapter should provide you with some inspiration.

In the next few chapters you'll find out more about some of the Tizen features vital to connected smart devices, including location services, networking, and telephony.

14

Telephony and Networking

WHAT'S IN THIS CHAPTER?

- ➤ Making calls
- ➤ Managing the network environment
- ➤ Sending and receiving messages
- ➤ Discovering Wi-Fi Direct
- ➤ Getting to grips with near field communication (NFC)

WROX.COM CODE DOWNLOADS FOR THIS CHAPTER

The wrox.com code downloads for this chapter are found at www.wrox.com/go/professionaltizen on the Download Code tab. The code is in the Chapter 14 download and named according to the names throughout the chapter. After decompressing the downloaded Zip file, you will have a ch14-samplecode directory thjjat contains three folders: CallSample, MessageSample, and NetworkSample. In each folder you'll find the all code explained in this chapter, ready for you to use in your own applications.

In this chapter you learn about some of the most important features of any smart device, from the most basic of all, making a phone call, to advanced networking features such as Wi-Fi Direct and near field communication (NFC). You'll also learn the different ways to make a call from within your application and how to get call information. Then you discover how to detect changes in the network state, such as when the data service becomes unavailable or there is a problem with the SIM card.

Most people generally use their devices more for messaging than they do for making phone calls, and Tizen offers support for SMS, MMS, e-mail, and push messages. Through a series of code snippets, this chapter will show you how to send and receive SMS messages and how to search SMS messages in your inbox. You'll discover hints and tips for sending MMS and e-mail messages and learn how to use the Tizen service for building push messaging features into your applications.

The final part of the chapter deals with networking and covers some of the technologies that you can use to create connected applications. You'll find out how to join devices together in a Wi-Fi network without an access point using Wi-Fi Direct and walk through code that demonstrates Bluetooth and NFC. Numerous technologies are packed into a smart device, and you will find many of them described in this chapter.

TELEPHONY

The telephony service can be used in an application to show the dialing screen or to make a call. When you're searching for a store, restaurant, or other place of interest from within a mobile application, it's great to be able to dial the number provided from within the application. Using the Tizen telephony service and the Phone or Call application control, it's easy to provide such features in your application.

The Tizen telephony service provides the following:

➤ Application controls for making calls

➤ Telephony network and current call information

➤ SIM information

Phone and Call Application Controls

Tizen application controls are a standard way to use specific features provided by the platform or other applications. There are several platform application controls, which provide features such as a music player, a gallery, access to the device's camera, and, of course, making a call. The Phone and Call application controls enable you to implement a call feature within your application with very little code.

There are two ways to make a call from within a Tizen application, the first of which is to use the Phone application control, which shows the dial screen with the specified number selected, waiting for the user to place the call.

The Phone application control can be implemented with just few code lines (see Listing 14-1).

LISTING 14-1: The Phone application control (CallSample.cpp)

```cpp
#include "CallSample.h"

using namespace Tizen::App;
using namespace Tizen::Base;
using namespace Tizen::Base::Collection;
```

```
using namespace Tizen::Telephony;

result
CallSample::ShowPhoneAppControl(const String& uri)
{
        result r = E_SUCCESS;
        String telUri = L"tel: 123456789012";

        AppControl* pAc = AppManager::FindAppControlN(L"tizen.phone",
          L"http://tizen.org/appcontrol/operation/dial");
        if (pAc)
        {
            telUri.Append(uri);
          r = pAc->Start(&telUri, null, null, null);
          delete pAc;
        }
        return r;
}
```

The Phone application control is provided by the Tizen platform. To use the control, you need to supply the application and operation IDs and the input data, which in this case is the number to be dialed. Table 14-1 describes the Phone application control interface and shows values which need to be passed to `AppManager::FindAppControlN()` and `ApplicationControl::Start()` in order to launch the phone control and dial a number.

TABLE 14-1: Phone Application Control Interface

APPLICATION CONTROL INTERFACE	VALUE
Application ID	`tizen.phone`
Operation ID	`http://tizen.org/appcontrol/operation/dial`
Input Data	The phone number as a URI, including "tel:" (e.g., `tel:123456789012`)

If `uri` is "123456789012," you will see the screen shown in Figure 14-1 when you run the application. The number is set up, enabling the user to dial.

If you want to make a call without waiting for confirmation from the user, then you can use the Call application control. Its implementation is similar to the Phone application control (see Listing 14-2).

FIGURE 14-1

LISTING 14-2: The Call application control (CallSample.cpp)

```
CallSample::ShowCallAppControl(const String& uri)
{
        result r = E_SUCCESS;

        String uri = L"tel:123456789012";
        HashMap extraData;
        extraData.Construct();
        String key = L"http://tizen.org/appcontrol/data/call/type";
        String val = L"voice";
        extraData.Add(&key, &val);

        AppControl* pAc = AppManager::FindAppControlN(L"tizen.call",
           L"http://tizen.org/appcontrol/operation/call");
        if (pAc)
        {
                pAc->Start(&uri, null, &extraData, null);
                delete pAc;
        }
        return r;
}
```

The values for the Call application control are shown in Table 14-2.

TABLE 14-2: Call Application Control Interface

APPLICATION CONTROL INTERFACE	VALUE	
Application ID	`tizen.call`	
Operation ID	`http://tizen.org/appcontrol/operation/call`	
Input Data	URI	The phone number as a URI, including "tel:" (e.g., `tel:123456789012`)
	Extra Data	Key: `http://tizen.org/appcontrol/data/call/type` Value: `video` or `voice`

Whereas the Phone application control uses the application ID `tizen.phone` and just shows the display to make a call (the call is not started), the Call application control uses the application ID `tizen.call` and the call will be started without a user action as soon as the interface is called. When the application runs, the user interface shows the call being made with the number taken from the `uri` value (see Figure 14-2).

Getting the Current Call Information

If you want to make an application that handles information about the current call, the `Telephony::CallManager` class provides the functionality you need. To capture information about the current call, implement the `Telephony::ITelephonyCallEventListener`. The event handler for this listener will

FIGURE 14-2

be invoked on an incoming or outgoing call and whenever the call status has changed. The information passed includes the incoming number and whether it's a voice or video call.

Listing 14-3 shows the definition of the `CallSample` class which inherits from the `ITelephonyCallEventListener` and must implement the methods that the listener defines.

LISTING 14-3: The declaration for the call status change (CallSample.h)

```cpp
#include <FTelephony.h>

class CallSample
        : public Tizen::Telephony::ITelephonyCallEventListener
{
public:
        result UseCallManager(void);

private:
        virtual void OnTelephonyCallStatusChangedN(Tizen::Telephony::CallStatus
            callStatus, Tizen::Telephony::CallInfo* pCallInfo);

 private:
        Tizen::Telephony::CallManager* __pCallManager;
        Tizen::Telephony::CallType __callType;
        Tizen::Telephony::CallStatus __callStatus;
};
```

After inheriting the `Telephony::ITelephonyCallEventListener`, it can be added through the input parameter of `CallManager::Construct()`, as shown in Listing 14-4.

LISTING 14-4: The listener registration for the call status change (CallSample.cpp)

```cpp
result
CallSample:: UseCallManager(void)
{

        result r = E_SUCCESS;

        __pCallManager = new (std::nothrow) CallManager();
        r = __pCallManager->Construct(*this);

        return r;

}
```

Using the Event Injector in the Tizen IDE (see Figure 14-3), you can change the call status. To open the Event Injector, select Window ⇨ Show View ⇨ Event Injector. The Event Injector is available when the Emulator is launched.

In the Telephony tab of the Event Injector, the MT Call section enables you to make a call to the Emulator. If you enter a number and click the Connect button, you can confirm that the Emulator shows an incoming call. Even if the Emulator is in sleep mode, it's activated automatically when an incoming call is received.

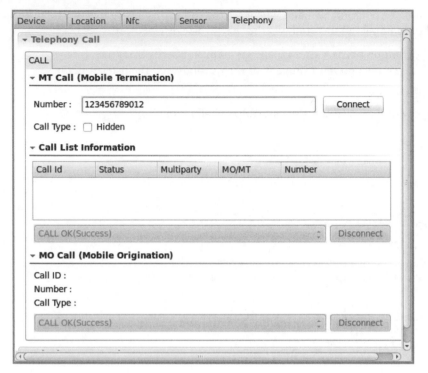

FIGURE 14-3

Information about the incoming call can be accessed in the event handler shown in Listing 14-5. The call status is CALL_STATUS_RINGING and the number is 123456789012 (or whatever number you entered).

LISTING 14-5: The event handling for the call status change (CallSample.cpp)

```
void
CallSample::OnTelephonyCallStatusChangedN(CallStatus callStatus, CallInfo* pCallInfo)
{
        CallType callType;
        String number;

        if (callStatus == CALL_STATUS_RINGING)
        {
                callType = pCallInfo->GetCallType();
                number = pCallInfo->GetNumber();
        }
}
```

You can also check current call information instantly by using the static API of the call manager (see Listing 14-6). You can get the call type as well as the current call status.

LISTING 14-6: Current call information (CallSample.cpp)

```
void
CallSample::CheckCurrentCallInfo(void)
{
        __callStatus = __pCallManager->GetCurrentCallStatus();
        __callType = __pCallManager->GetCurrentCallType();
}
```

Checking the Telephony Network and SIM State

Your application may need to handle changes in the network environment, which could include the following:

➤ The telephony network or data service is not available.

➤ The roaming service is activated.

➤ The SIM is not ready.

To prevent unexpected errors in your application when such a change occurs, you can implement the event handlers for SIM status and network status events so that you can respond if the user can no longer make calls or use data, or if there's a problem with the device's SIM.

Listings 14-7 and 14-8 show how to set up your code to receive these events.

LISTING 14-7: The declaration for telephony network and SIM state (CallSample.h)

```
#include <FTelephony.h>

class CallSample
        : …
        , public Tizen::Telephony::ITelephonyNetworkSettingListener
        , public Tizen::Telephony::ITelephonySimEventListener
{
public:
        result UseNetworkManager(void);

private:
        virtual void OnTelephonyNetworkStatusChanged (
          const Tizen::Telephony::NetworkStatus& networkStatus);
        virtual void OnTelephonySimStateChanged(Tizen::Telephony::SimState state);

private:
        Tizen::Telephony::NetworkManager* __pNetworkManager;
        Tizen::Telephony::SimStateManager* __pSimStateManager;
};
```

LISTING 14-8: The listener registration for telephony network and SIM state (CallSample.cpp)

```cpp
result
CallSample::UseNetworkManager(void)
{
        result r = E_SUCCESS;

        __pNetworkManager = new (std::nothrow) NetworkManager();
        r = __pNetworkManager->Construct(this);

        __pSimStateManager = new (std::nothrow) SimStateManager();
        r = __pSimStateManager->Construct();
        r = __pSimStateManager->SetSimEventListener(this)

        return r;
}
```

After setting a listener for the telephony network status, the event handler is invoked to provide network status information. You add your own code to handle each type of event (see Listing 14-9).

LISTING 14-9: The event handling for telephony network status change (CallSample.cpp)

```cpp
void
CallSample::OnTelephonyNetworkStatusChanged (const NetworkStatus& networkStatus)
{
        result r = E_SUCCESS;

        if(!networkStatus.IsCallServiceAvailable())
        {
                AppLogException("The call service is unavailable!");
                //Handle a case
        }

        if(!networkStatus.IsDataServiceAvailable())
        {
                AppLogException("The data service is unavailable!");
                //Handle a case
        }
        if(networkStatus.IsRoaming())
        {
                AppLog("You're using a roaming service.");
                //Handle a case
        }
}
```

If the SIM state changes, an event is received in the event handler shown in Listing 14-10.

LISTING 14-10: The event handling for SIM status change (CallSample.cpp)

```cpp
void
CallSample::OnTelephonySimStateChanged(SimState state)
{
```

```
            if (state != SIM_STATE_READY)
            {
                    AppLogException("The SIM is not ready!");
            }
    }
```

MESSAGES

The message service is a useful feature that can be used in many different types of applications. The message service that Tizen provides includes the following:

➤ Short Message Service (SMS) messages

➤ Multimedia Messaging Service (MMS) messages

➤ E-mail

➤ Push messages

SMS Messages

SMS messages are the most popular type of mobile messaging, with trillions of messages sent each year. It's not just individuals who send SMS messages; companies send messages to contact their customers, and government agencies send messages to provide information in an emergency. While SMS faces competition from other types of messaging, it is still the most important type of messaging for a mobile platform.

The Tizen SMS provides features to enable the following:

➤ Sending an SMS

➤ Checking for an incoming SMS

➤ Searching SMS content in your inbox

Sending SMS Messages

To send an SMS, use the code shown in Listings 14-11 and 14-12. The text of an SMS should not exceed the 80-character limit and the sent result can be checked in the event handler provided by the SMS listener.

LISTING 14-11: The declaration for SMS (SmsSample.h)

```
    #include <FMessaging.h>

    class SmsSample
            : public Tizen::Messaging::ISmsListener
    {
    public:
            result Initialize(void);
            result SendSms(const Tizen::Base::String& text,
```

continues

LISTING 14-11 *(continued)*

```
                const Tizen::Messaging::RecipientList& receipientList);

private:
        virtual void OnSmsMessageSent(result r);

private:
        Tizen::Messaging::SmsManager* __pSmsManager;
};
```

LISTING 14-12: Sending SMS (SmsSample.cpp)

```cpp
#include "SmsSample.h"

using namespace Tizen::Base;
using namespace Tizen::Base::Collection;
using namespace Tizen::Messaging;

SmsSample::Initialize(void)
{
        result r = E_SUCCESS;

        __pSmsManager = new (std::nothrow) SmsManager;
        r = __pSmsManager->Construct(*this);

        return r;
}

result
SmsSample::SendSms(const String& text, const RecipientList& recipientList)
{
        result r = E_SUCCESS;

        SmsMessage sms;
        sms.SetText(text);
        __pSmsManager->Send(sms, recipientList, true);

        return r;
}

void
SmsSample::OnSmsMessageSent(result r)
{
        if(!IsFailed(r))
        {
                AppLogException("Exception[%s]", GetErrorMessage(r));
                //Do something
        }
}
```

Figure 14-4 shows messaging in the Event Injector. After the SMS is sent, the sent number and message is shown in the Receive SMS Message tab of the Telephony Messaging section.

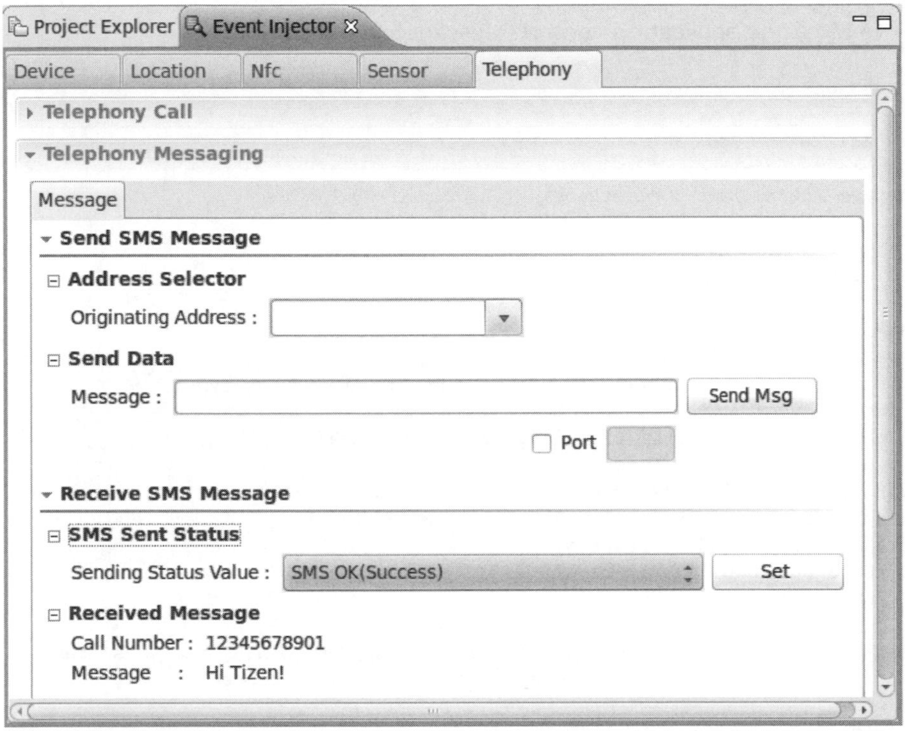

FIGURE 14-4

If you need to display a user interface when sending an SMS, use the Message application control. This enables the user to send both SMS and MMS messages. Listings 14-13 and 14-14 show how to use this application control.

LISTING 14-13: The declaration for the Message application control (MessageSample.h)

```
#include <FMessaging.h>

class MessageSample
        : public Tizen::App::IAppControlResponseListener
{
public:
            void UseMessageAppControl(void);

private:
            virtual void OnAppControlCompleteResponseReceived(
                        const Tizen::App::AppId& appId,
                        const Tizen::Base::String& operationId,
                        Tizen::App::AppCtrlResult appControlResult,
                        const Tizen::Base::Collection::IMap* pExtraData);
};
```

LISTING 14-14: The Message application control (MessageSample.cpp)

```cpp
#include "MessageSample.h"

using namespace Tizen::App;
using namespace Tizen::Base;
using namespace Tizen::Base::Collection;

void
MessageSample::UseMessageAppControl(void)
{
        HashMap extraData;
        extraData.Construct();
        String typeKey = L"http://tizen.org/appcontrol/data/messagetype";
        String typetVal = L"sms";
        String textKey = L"http://tizen.org/appcontrol/data/text";
        String textVal = L"Hi, Tizen!";
        String toKey = L"http://tizen.org/appcontrol/data/to";
        String toVal = L"12345678901,12345678902,12345678903";
        extraData.Add(&typeKey, &typeVal);
        extraData.Add(&textKey, &textVal);
        extraData.Add(&toKey, &toVal);

        Tizen::App::AppControl* pAc = AppManager::FindAppControlN(L"tizen.messages",
                    L"http://tizen.org/appcontrol/operation/compose");

        if (pAc)
        {
                pAc->Start(null, null, &extraData, null);
                delete pAc;
        }
}

void
MessageSample::OnAppControlCompleteResponseReceived(const AppId& appId,
        const String& operationId,
        AppCtrlResult appControlResult,
        const IMap* pExtraData)
{
if ((appId == L"tizen.messages") &&
    (operationId == L"http://tizen.org/appcontrol/operation/compose"))
        {
                if (appControlResult == APP_CTRL_RESULT_SUCCEEDED)
                {
                        //Do something
                }
        }
}
```

If you run the preceding code, the Message application control will be displayed, as shown in Figure 14-5.

Receiving SMS Messages

Specific information about an incoming SMS can be captured and used in various applications, such as an account book or a scheduler. Applications can catch an incoming short message in the SMS event listener and check the text of the message — for example, to see if certain predefined words are included. To receive information about incoming SMS messages, implement the `OnSmsReceived()` event handler provided by the `Messaging::ISmsMessageEventListener` interface. From within this function you will be able to access the date and time when the message was received and the message content. Listings 14-15 and 14-16 show how to receive and process information about incoming SMS messages.

FIGURE 14-5

LISTING 14-15: The declaration to receive SMS (SmsSample.h)

```cpp
#include <FMessaging.h>

class SmsSample
        :
public Tizen::Messaging::ISmsMessageEventListener
{
public:
        result Initialize(void);

private:
        virtual void OnSmsMessageReceived(const Tizen::Messaging::SmsMessage& message);

private:
        Tizen::Messaging::SmsManager* __pSmsManager;
        Tizen::Base::Collection::IList* __pKeywordList;
};
```

LISTING 14-16: The event handling for received SMS (SmsSample.cpp)

```cpp
result
SmsSample::Initialize(void)
{
        result r = E_SUCCESS;

        __pSmsManager = new (std::nothrow) SmsManager;
        r = __pSmsManager->Construct(*this);
        r = __pSmsManager->AddSmsMessageEventListener(*this);

        return r;
```

continues

LISTING 14-16 *(continued)*

```
        }

        void
        SmsSample::OnSmsMessageReceived(const SmsMessage& message)
        {
                String text = message.GetText();
                IEnumerator* pEnum = __pKeywordList->GetEnumeratorN();
                while (pEnum->MoveNext() == E_SUCCESS)
                {
                        String* pKeyword = static_cast<String*>(pEnum->GetCurrent());
                        if (text.Contains(*pKeyword))
                        {
                                AppLog("The keyword is included (%ls)", pKeyword->GetPointer());
                                //Do something
                        }
                }
                delete pEnum;
        }
```

As shown in Figure 14-6, you can test incoming message functionality with the Emulator by using the Event Injector in the IDE. Launch the Event Injector by selecting Window ⇨ Show View ⇨ Event Injector and select the Telephony tab. Expand the Send SMS Message tab in the Telephony Messaging section, fill in the originating address and your message, and click the Send Msg button.

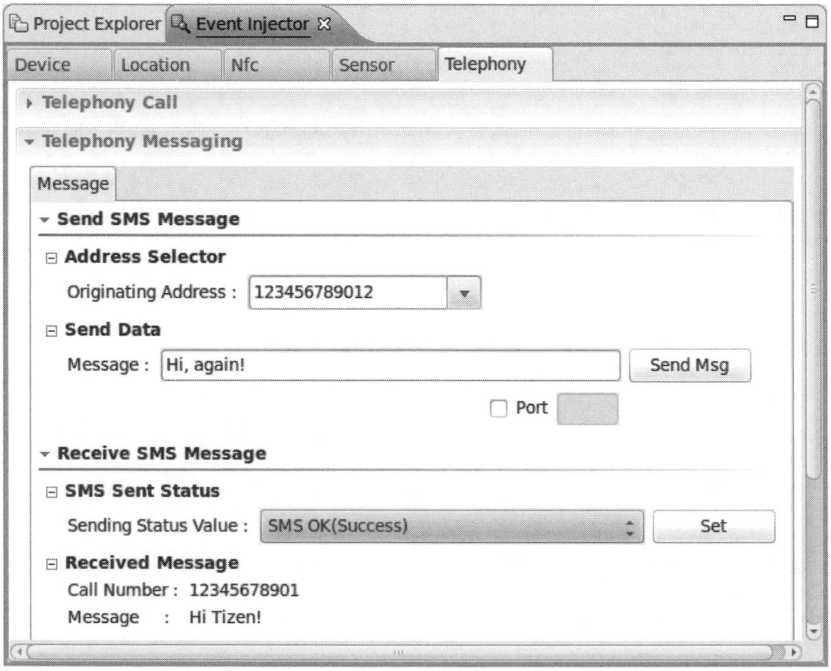

FIGURE 14-6

As soon as you send the SMS from the Event Injector, the message should be received in the Emulator as shown in Figure 14-7. The indicator informs you that an incoming message has been received and you can see a summary with the text and originating number you entered in the notification panel.

FIGURE 14-7

Searching SMS Messages

It's useful to be able to search the content of SMS messages in your inbox, and the SmsManager class provides message searching functionality, so you can search for SMS messages containing a certain keyword or from a specific sender, for example.

Listing 14-17 shows how to search the inbox for a specified keyword — in this case, the string "Sat". The SearchInboxN() function returns a list of SmsMessage objects, which contain this string in their message text.

LISTING 14-17: The SMS search in the inbox (SmsSample.cpp)

```
result
SmsSample::SearchSmsInInbox(void)
{
        result r = E_SUCCESS;

        //Suppose __pSmsManager is constructed. Refer to Listing 14-15.

        String* pKeyword = new String (L"Sat");
        IList* pInboxResult = null;
        int totalResultCount = 0;
        pInboxResult = __pSmsManager->SearchInboxN(pKeyword, null, 0, 100,
           totalResultCount);

        IEnumerator* pEnum = pInboxResult->GetEnumeratorN();
```

continues

LISTING 14-17 *(continued)*

```
        while (pEnum->MoveNext() == E_SUCCESS)
        {
                SmsMessage* pSmsMessage =
                    static_cast<SmsMessage*>(pEnum->GetCurrent());
                //Check the message
        }
        delete pEnum;
        delete pInboxResult;

        return r;
}
```

You are not limited to searching the inbox; you can search SMS content in all message boxes, as shown in Listing 14-18.

LISTING 14-18: The SMS search in all message boxes (SmsSample.cpp)

```
result
SmsSample::SearchSmsInbox(void)
{
        result r = E_SUCCESS;

        //Suppose __pSmsManager is constructed. Refer Listing 14-15.

        String* pKeyword = new String (L"meet");
        IList* pResult = null;
        int totalResultCount = 0;
        pResult = __pSmsManager->SearchMessageBoxN(SMS_MESSAGE_BOX_TYPE_ALL, pKeyword, 0,
            100, totalResultCount);

        IEnumerator* pEnum = pResult->GetEnumeratorN();
        while (pEnum->MoveNext() == E_SUCCESS)
        {
                SmsMessage* pSmsMessage = static_cast<SmsMessage*>(pEnum->GetCurrent());
                //Check the message
        }
        delete pEnum;
        delete pResult;

        return r;
}
```

MMS Messages

A multimedia messaging service (MMS) provides a useful way to share content such as video, images, and audio files. Tizen supports sending MMS messages to multiple recipients and checking the sent message state.

Listings 14-19 and 14-20 show how to send an MMS message — in this case, containing an image and some audio — to multiple recipients and monitor whether the message was sent.

LISTING 14-19: The declaration to send MMS (MmsSample.h)

```cpp
#include <FMessaging.h>

class MmsSample
      : public Tizen::Messaging::IMmsListener
{
public:
            result SendMms(void);

private:
            virtual void OnMmsMessageSent(result r);

private:
            Tizen::Messaging::MmsManager* __pMmsManager;
};
```

LISTING 14-20: Sending MMS (MmsSample.cpp)

```cpp
#include "MmsSample.h"

using namespace Tizen::Base;
using namespace Tizen::Messaging;

result
MmsSample::SendMms(void)
{
      result r - E_SUCCESS;

      __pMmsManager = new (std::nothrow) MmsManager();
      r = __pMmsManager->Construct(*this);

      MmsMessage mmsMessage;
      r = mmsMessage.SetSubject(L"MMS Subject");
      r = mmsMessage.SetText(L"Please refer to the attached file.");
      r = mmsMessage.AddAttachment(MMS_IMAGE, L"res/image.jpg");
      r = mmsMessage.AddAttachment(MMS_AUDIO, L"res/audio.wav");

      RecipientList recipient;
      r = recipient.Add (RECIPIENT_TYPE_TO, L"1012345678901");
      r = recipient.Add (RECIPIENT_TYPE_TO, L"1012345678902");
      r = recipient.Add (RECIPIENT_TYPE_TO, L"1012345678903");

      r = __pMmsManager->Send(mmsMessage, recipient, true);

      return r;
}

void
MmsSample::OnMmsMessageSent(result r)
{
      AppLog("result(%s)", GetErrorMessage(r));
}
```

The image, audio, video, vCard, or vCalendar file can be attached and sent to the recipients. However, an image or audio file cannot be combined with a video attachment.

E-mail

The E-mail application control provides a unified user interface for sending e-mail. You can specify the recipients as to, cc, or bcc, add other content, and send the e-mail message. Because this is a platform-provided application control, the user interface is provided by Tizen, not the individual application.

Listings 14-21 and 14-22 show how to use the E-mail application control.

LISTING 14-21: The declaration for the E-mail application control (EmailSample.h)

```
#include <FMessaging.h>

class EmailSample
        : public Tizen::App::IAppControlResponseListener
{
public:
            void UseEmailAppControl(void);

private:
            virtual void OnAppControlCompleteResponseReceived(
                    const Tizen::App::AppId& appId,
                    const Tizen::Base::String& operationId,
                    Tizen::App::AppCtrlResult appControlResult,
                    const Tizen::Base::Collection::IMap* pExtraData);
};
```

LISTING 14-22: The E-mail application control (EmailSample.cpp)

```
#include "EmailSample.h"

using namespace Tizen::App;
using namespace Tizen::Base;
using namespace Tizen::Base::Collection;
using namespace Tizen::Messaging;

void
EmailSample::UseEmailAppControl(void)
{
        HashMap extraData;
        extraData.Construct();
        String subjectKey = L"http://tizen.org/appcontrol/data/subject";
        String subjectVal = L"Email Subject!!!";
        String textKey = L"http://tizen.org/appcontrol/data/text";
        String textVal = L"Hello, refer to the attached file.";
```

```
            String toKey = L"http://tizen.org/appcontrol/data/to";
            String toVal = L"recipient1@company.com";
            String ccKey = L"http://tizen.org/appcontrol/data/cc";
            String ccVal = L"recipient2@company.com";
            String bccKey = L"http://tizen.org/appcontrol/data/bcc";
            String bccVal = L"recipient3@company.com";
            String attachKey = L"http://tizen.org/appcontrol/data/path";
            String attachVal = App::GetInstance()->GetAppRootPath() + L"res/image.jpg";
            attachList.Construct();
            attachList.Add(attachVal);
            extraData.Add(&subjectKey, &subjectVal);
            extraData.Add(&textKey, &textVal);
            extraData.Add(&toKey, &toVal);
            extraData.Add(&ccKey, &ccVal);
            extraData.Add(&bccKey, &bccVal);
            extraData.Add(&attachKey, &attachList);

            AppControl* pAc = AppManager::FindAppControlN(L"tizen.email",
                        L"http://tizen.org/appcontrol/operation/compose");
            if (pAc)
            {
                  pAc->Start(null, null, &extraData, null);
                  delete pAc;
            }
      }

      void
      EmailSample::OnAppControlCompleteResponseReceived(const AppId& appId,
                              const String& operationId,
                              AppCtrlResult appControlResult,
                              const IMap* pExtraData)
      {
            if ((appId == L"tizen.email") &&
                (operationId == L"http://tizen.org/appcontrol/operation/compose"))
            {
                if (appControlResult == APP_CTRL_RESULT_SUCCEEDED)
                {
                    //Do something
                    return;
                }
            }
      }
```

To use the e-mail feature, a user's e-mail account must be set up. If the account is not predefined, the e-mail account setting menu will be displayed before the E-mail application control. Figure 14-8 shows the Add accounts dialog.

FIGURE 14-8

If you want to provide your own user interface for sending e-mail, use the `EmailManager` class, as shown in Listings 14-23 and 14-24. You can check the sent status of an e-mail in the `OnEmailMessageSent()` event handler.

LISTING 14-23: The declaration to send e-mail (EmailSample.h)

```
#include <FMessaging.h>

class EmailSample
        : public Tizen::Messaging::IEmailListener
{
public:
            result SendEmail(void);
private:
            virtual void OnEmailMessageSent(result r);
private:
            Tizen::Messaging::EmailManager* __pEmailManager;
};
```

LISTING 14-24: Sending e-mail (EmailSample.cpp)

```
#include "EmailSample.h"

using namespace Tizen::App;
using namespace Tizen::Base;
using namespace Tizen::Messaging;

result
EmailSample::SendEmail(void)
{
        result r = E_SUCCESS;

        __pEmailManager = new (std::nothrow) EmailManager();
        __pEmailManager->Construct(*this);

        EmailMessage emailMessage;
        r = emailMessage.SetSubject(L"Email Subject!!!");
        r = emailMessage.SetText(L"Hello, refer to the attached file.");
        r = emailMessage.AddAttachment(L"res/file.dat");

        RecipientList recipient;
        r = recipient.Add (RECIPIENT_TYPE_TO, L"recipient1@company.org");
        r = recipient.Add (RECIPIENT_TYPE_CC, L"recipient2@company.org");
        r = recipient.Add (RECIPIENT_TYPE_BCC, L"recipient3@compony.org");

        r = __pEmailManager->Send(emailMessage, recipient, true);

        return r;
}
```

Push Messages

The push service is a feature in Tizen that enables an application to send or receive messages that are pushed to a Tizen device from a messaging server. This feature could be used for all kinds of innovative applications, from instant messaging to advertising and any kind of application that needs a messaging component.

To use the push service, the following is required:

➤ **Application server** — Operates the application service

➤ **Tizen devices** — Register to use the push service with a push application

➤ **Tizen Server** — Receives the push message from the application server and sends it to Tizen devices

Figure 14-9 shows the Tizen push message flow.

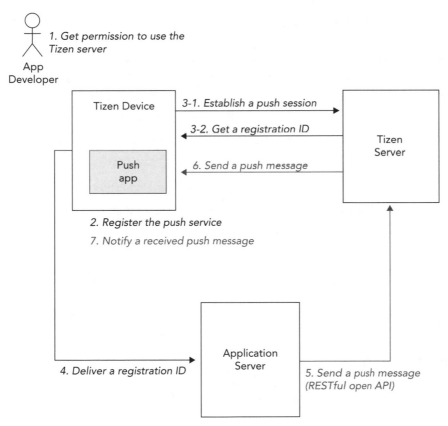

FIGURE 14-9

To use the Tizen push service, the following steps are required:

1. A push application developer gets permission to use the Tizen Server.

2. The Tizen application on the Tizen device calls the API for push service registration. To use the Tizen push service, all push applications must register with the Tizen Server.

3. The Tizen Server handles the request and returns the registration ID as a unique key to the push application.

4. The push application sends the ID to the Application Server. If the push message is sent from the Application Server, it is sent as explained in the following steps.

5. The Application Server sends a push message to the Tizen Server using the RESTful open API. A text message is limited to 1,024 bytes. If large-size data must be shared, include a link in the push message.

6. The Tizen Server sends a push message to the Tizen device with the registration ID.

7. The push application gets the push message and notifies the user.

Getting Permission to Use the Tizen Server

Applications that use the Tizen push interface should first get permission to use the Tizen Server. You can request permission by e-mailing the Tizen Server administrator at push.tizen@samsung .com. In addition to your full name, e-mail address, and country, include the following information about your application:

➤ **Application ID** — The 10-byte, alphanumeric value in the manifest file.

➤ **Application name** — The name of your application — for example, "My Push Messenger."

➤ **Testing purpose** — If yes, the duration limit is 3 weeks.

➤ **Purpose of the push message usage** — To send a push message between registered users.

➤ **App launch date** — The launch date of your application, in the format *YYYY/MM/DD*.

➤ **Service area/country** — Such as Asia, Africa, America, or Europe.

➤ **Daily push requests** — The total number of daily requests.

➤ **Transactions per second** — The peak number per second (fewer than 100 as possible).

You will receive an acknowledgment e-mail if the request is approved. You can then use the Tizen Server for the push service.

Registering the Push Service

To register to use the push server, you must implement the IPushManagerListener and IPushEventListener listeners, as shown in Listing 14-25.

LISTING 14-25: The declaration for push messages (PushSample.h)

```
#include <FMessaging.h>

class PushSample
      : public Tizen::Messaging::IPushManagerListener
      , public Tizen::Messaging::IPushEventListener
{
public:
      void Initialize(void);
      result Register(void);

private:
      void OnPushMessageSent(RequestId reqId,
         const Tizen::Base::String& registrationId,
         result r, const Tizen::Base::String& errorCode,
         const Tizen::Base::String& errorMsg);
      void OnPushServiceRegistered(RequestId reqId,
         const Tizen::Base::String &registrationId,
         result r,
         const Tizen::Base::String& errorCode,
         const Tizen::Base::String& errorMsg);
      void OnPushServiceUnregistered(RequestId reqId,
         result r,
         const Tizen::Base::String& errorCode,
         const Tizen::Base::String& errorMsg);
      void OnPushMessageReceived(const Tizen::Messaging::PushMessage& message);

private:
      Tizen::Messaging::PushManager* __pPushManager;
};
```

Send a registration request as shown in Listing 14-26.

LISTING 14-26: The push service registration (PushSample.cpp)

```
#include "PushSample.h"

using namespace Tizen::Base;
using namespace Tizen::Messaging;

void
PushSample::Initialize(void)
{
      if(__pPushManager == null)
      {
            __pPushManager = new (std::nothrow) PushManager();
            __pPushManager->Construct(*this, *this);
      }
}

result
```

continues

LISTING 14-26 *(continued)*

```
PushSample::Register(void)
{
        result r = E_SUCCESS;

        Initialize();
        RequestId reqId;
        r = __pPushManager->RegisterPushService(reqId);

        return r;
}
```

The registration result can be checked in following handler shown in Listing 14-27. If it succeeds, you will get the registration ID. The application must share this registration ID with the Application Server.

LISTING 14-27: The event handling for the push service registration (PushSample.cpp)

```
void
PushSample::OnPushServiceRegistered(RequestId reqId,
                                    const String &registrationId,
                                    result r,
                                    const String& errorCode,
                                    const String& errorMsg)
{
        //Check an error
        //Send 'registrationId' to the Application Server
}
```

Handling Incoming Push Messages

If a push message is received, the event handler will be called. You can find out the time the message was received and the message contents, as shown in Listing 14-28.

LISTING 14-28: The event handling for the received push message (PushSample.cpp)

```
void
PushSample::OnPushMessageReceived(const PushMessage& message)
{
        DateTime receivedTime;
        receivedTime = message.GetReceivedTime();

        LocalManager localManager;
        localeManager.Construct();
        TimeZone timezone = localeManager.GetSystemTimeZone();
        DateTime wallTime = timezone.UtcTimeToWallTime(receivedTime);

        String text = message.GetNotification().GetAppMessage();
}
```

You can also check for unread messages using Listing 14-29.

LISTING 14-29: Checking unread push messages (PushSample.cpp)

```cpp
#include "FLocales.h"

using namespace Tizen::Base::Collection;

result
PushSample::CheckUnreadMessage(void)
{
        result r = E_SUCCESS;

        IList* pUnreadMessageList = __pPushManager->GetUnreadMessagesN();
        IEnumerator* pEnum = pUnreadMessageList->GetEnumeratorN();
        while(pEnum->MoveNext() == E_SUCCESS)
        {
                PushMessage* pPushMessage =
                    static_cast<PushMessage*>(pEnum->GetCurrent());
                //Handle the message
        }

        delete pUnreadMessageList;

        return r;
}
```

NETWORKING

Networking has always been an important feature of smart devices, but technologies such as Wi-Fi Direct, Bluetooth, and NFC are opening up huge possibilities in terms of how devices connect and share data. The `Tizen::Net` namespace provides support for the following networking features:

➤ Network connection management

➤ HTTP

➤ Socket handling

➤ Wi-Fi

➤ Wi-Fi Direct

➤ Bluetooth

➤ NFC

While the HTTP and Socket classes are the essential building blocks for sending and receiving data using the Internet, it's the other classes that show how much Tizen has to offer in terms of innovative networking features.

The Wi-Fi and Wi-Fi Direct classes include functions for creating and managing wireless connections and linking devices together for multi-player games, for example.

Bluetooth supports peer-to-peer connection over a short-range connection and is useful for exchanging files between devices and supporting hands-free devices such as phone handsets.

NFC is one of the most exciting networking technologies. It's designed for very short range wireless communication and has found uses in mobile payments, exchanging small amounts of data such as URLs between devices by just touching them together.

This section looks at Tizen's networking features in detail. Figure 14-10 shows an overview.

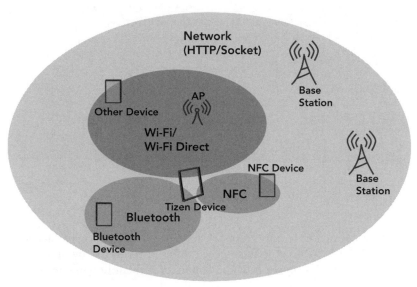

FIGURE 14-10

Network Connection Management

Being charged for data is a big issue for users of smart devices. Application developers are required to consider that users should be allowed to set a preference to specify the data connection that an application uses. For example, users may want to ensure that a data-hungry application uses only a Wi-Fi connection and not cellular data. The Net::NetConnectionManager class enables an application to set the preferred network connection.

Listings 14-30 and 14-31 show how to set up Wi-Fi as the preferred network connection. The code specifies NET_WIFI_FIRST, but you could also specify NET_WIFI_ONLY if an alternative data connection should not be used.

LISTING 14-30: The declaration for the network connection preference (NetworkSample.h)

```
#include <FNet.h>

class NetworkSample
{
public:
        result SetNetworkPreference(void);

private:
        Tizen::Net::NetConnectionManager* __pNetConnectionManager;
};
```

LISTING 14-31: Setting the network connection preference (NetworkSample.cpp)

```
#include "NetworkSample.h"

using namespace Tizen::Net;

result
NetworkSample::SetNetworkPreference(void)
{
        result r = E_SUCCESS;

                __pNetConnectionManager = new (std::nothrow) NetConnectionManager();
        r = __pNetConnectionManager->Construct();
        r = __pNetConnectionManager->SetNetPreference(NET_WIFI_FIRST);

        return r;
}
```

The default network connection that the Tizen platform manages can be used with the ManagedNetConnection connection, as shown in Listings 14-32 and 14-33. After setting a managed network event listener, you can receive the default network connection event whenever it is changed.

LISTING 14-32: The declaration for the default network connection (NetworkSample.h)

```
#include <FNet.h>
class NetworkSample
        : public Tizen::Net::IManagedNetConnectionEventListener
{
public:
        result UseDefaultNetConnection(void);

private:
        void OnManagedNetConnectionBearerChanged(
            Tizen::Net::ManagedNetConnection& managedNetConnection);
        void OnManagedNetConnectionResumed(
            Tizen::Net::ManagedNetConnection& managedNetConnection);
        void OnManagedNetConnectionStarted(
```

continues

LISTING 14-32 *(continued)*

```
            Tizen::Net::ManagedNetConnection& managedNetConnection);
        void OnManagedNetConnectionStopped(
            Tizen::Net::ManagedNetConnection& managedNetConnection,
            Tizen::Net::NetConnectionStoppedReason reason);
        void OnManagedNetConnectionSuspended(
            Tizen::Net::ManagedNetConnection& managedNetConnection);

private:
        Tizen::Net::NetConnectionManager*  __pNetConnectionManager;
        Tizen::Net::ManagedNetConnection*  __pDefaultNetConnection;
};
```

LISTING 14-33: The event handling for the default network connection (NetworkSample.cpp)

```
#include "NetworkSample.h"

using namespace Tizen::Net;

result
NetworkSample::UseDefaultNetConnection(void)
{
        result r = E_SUCCESS;

        __pDefaultNetConnection = __pNetConnectionManager->GetManagedNetConnectionN();
        r = __pDefaultNetConnection->SetManagedNetConnectionEventListener(this);

        return r;
}

void
NetworkSample::OnManagedNetConnectionBearerChanged(
    ManagedNetConnection& managedNetConnection)
{
        NetConnectionInfo* pNetConnectionInfo =
            managedNetConnection.GetNetConnectionInfo();
        NetBearerType bearerType = pNetConnectionInfo->GetBearerType();
}

void
NetworkSample::OnManagedNetConnectionStopped(
    ManagedNetConnection& managedNetConnection,
    NetConnectionStoppedReason reason)
{
        NetConnectionState state = managedNetConnection.GetConnectionState();
        //Handle the default network connection

        switch(reason)
        {
        case NET_CONNECTION_STOPPED_REASON_RESOURCE_RELEASED:
                //Handle the reason
                return;
```

```
            case NET_CONNECTION_STOPPED_REASON_NETWORK_FAILED:
                    //Handle the reason
                    return;
            //For other cases
            default:
                    return;
            }
    }
```

Application developers can use the default network connection and custom network connection. The default network connection event is received by the platform automatically, but the custom network connection event should be defined by applications. Applications which use the custom network service can set events for starting or stopping the connection by themselves, as demonstrated in Listings 14-34 and 14-35.

LISTING 14-34: The declaration for the custom network connection (NetworkSample.h)

```
#include <FNet.h>

class NetworkSample
        : public Tizen::Net::INetConnectionEventListener
{
public:
        result UseCustomNetConnection(void);
private:
        void OnNetConnectionResumed(Tizen::Net::NetConnection& netConnection);
        void OnNetConnectionStarted(Tizen::Net::NetConnection& netConnection, result r);
        void OnNetConnectionStopped(Tizen::Net::NetConnection& netConnection, result r);
        void OnNetConnectionSuspended(Tizen::Net::NetConnection& netConnection);

private:
        Tizen::Net::NetAccountManager* __pNetAccountManager;
        Tizen::Net::NetConnection* __pCustomNetConnection;
};
```

LISTING 14-35: The event handling for the custom network connection (NetworkSample.cpp)

```
#include "NetworkSample.h"

using namespace Tizen::Net;

result
NetworkSample::UseCustomNetConnection(void)
{
        result r = E_SUCCESS;

        __pNetAccountManager = new (std::nothrow) NetAccountManager();
        r = __pNetAccountManager->Construct();

        NetAccountInfo* pNetAccountInfo = new (std::nothrow) NetAccountInfo();
        r = pNetAccountInfo->Construct();
```

continues

LISTING 14-35 *(continued)*

```
        //Set the network account info
        __pNetAccountManager->CreateNetAccount(*pNetAccountInfo);
        NetAccountId accountId = __pNetAccountManager->GetNetAccountId(NET_BEARER_PS);

        __pCustomNetConnection = new (std::nothrow) NetConnection();
        r = __pCustomNetConnection->Construct(accountId);

        r = __pCustomNetConnection->AddNetConnectionListener(*this);
        r = __pCustomNetConnection->Start();

        return r;
}
```

You can start or stop the custom network by calling `Start()` or `Stop()` of the `NetConnection`
class, respectively. If `Start()` is called, the event is received in `OnNetConnectionStarted()`;
if `Stop()` is called, you can get the event in `OnNetConnectionStopped()`.

HTTP

Tizen supports the HTTP 1.1 specification and enables your application to communicate with
HTTP servers on the Internet, make HTTP requests, and receive HTTP responses. In this section
you learn how to use Tizen's HTTP classes to create an HTTP session, make an HTTP request, and
handle the response.

Making HTTP Requests

Listings 14-36 and 14-37 show you how to send an HTTP request. This code first sets up an HTTP
session and then you use this session to create a transaction that will be used to handle the HTTP
request and response. In the non-pipeline mode, do not send a request before the response to the
previous request is received.

LISTING 14-36: The declaration for HTTP requests (HttpSample.h)

```
#include <FBase.h>
#include <FNet.h>

class HttpSample
        : public Tizen::Net::Http::IHttpTransactionEventListener
{
public:
        result SendHttpRequest();

private:
        void OnTransactionAborted(
            Tizen::Net::Http::HttpSession& httpSession,
            Tizen::Net::Http::HttpTransaction& httpTransaction,
            result r);
        bool OnTransactionCertVerificationRequestedN(
            Tizen::Net::Http::HttpSession& httpSession,
```

```
        Tizen::Net::Http::HttpTransaction& httpTransaction,
        Tizen::Base::Collection::IList* pCertList);
    void OnTransactionCertVerificationRequiredN(
        Tizen::Net::Http::HttpSession& httpSession,
        Tizen::Net::Http::HttpTransaction& httpTransaction,
        Tizen::Base::String* pCert);
    void OnTransactionCompleted(
        Tizen::Net::Http::HttpSession& httpSession,
        Tizen::Net::Http::HttpTransaction& httpTransaction);
    void OnTransactionHeaderCompleleted(
        Tizen::Net::Http::HttpSession& httpSession,
        Tizen::Net::Http::HttpTransaction& httpTransaction,
        int headerLen, bool bAuthRequired);
    void OnTransactionReadyToRead(
        Tizen::Net::Http::HttpSession& httpSession,
        Tizen::Net::Http::HttpTransaction& httpTransaction,
        int availableBodyLen);
    void OnTransactionReadyToWrite(
        Tizen::Net::Http::HttpSession& httpSession,
        Tizen::Net::Http::HttpTransaction& httpTransaction,
        int recommendedChunkSize);

private:
    Tizen::Net::Http::HttpTransaction* __pHttpTransaction;
    Tizen::Net::Http::HttpSession* __pHttpSession;
};
```

LISTING 14-37: Making HTTP requests (HttpSample.cpp)

```
#include "HttpSample.h"

using namespace Tizen::Base;
using namespace Tizen::Base::Collection;
using namespace Tizen::Net::Http;

result
HttpSample::SendHttpRequest()
{
    result r = E_SUCCESS;
    String hostAddr = L"http://www.tizen.org";

    __pHttpSession = new (std::nothrow) HttpSession();
    r = __pHttpSession->Construct(NET_HTTP_SESSION_MODE_NORMAL, null, hostAddr,
            null);

    __pHttpTransaction = __pHttpSession->OpenTransactionN();
    r = __pHttpTransaction->AddHttpTransactionListener(*this);

    HttpRequest* pHttpRequest = __pHttpTransaction->GetRequest();
    r = pHttpRequest->SetMethod(NET_HTTP_METHOD_POST);
    r = pHttpRequest->SetUri(L"http://www.tizen.org/sample");

    HttpHeader* pHttpHeader = pHttpRequest->GetHeader();
```

continues

LISTING 14-37 *(continued)*

```
        r = pHttpHeader->AddField(L"Content-Length", L"1024");
        //Set other fields

        r = __pHttpTransaction->Submit();

        return r;
    }
```

When sending an HTTP request in non-chunked mode, you must add the `Content-Length: body-length` field in the request header.

To send the request in chunked mode, add the `Transfer-encoding: checked` field to the request header and call the `HttpTransaction::EnableTransactionReadyToWrite ()` method. The chunks can be sent in the implementation of `IHttpTransactionEventListener::OnTransactionReadyToWrite()`. An empty chunk is considered as the last chunk.

Receiving HTTP Responses

To get an HTTP response, implement the `IHttpTransactionEventListener::OnTransactionReadyToRead()` event handler and check the received header, as shown in Listing 14-38.

LISTING 14-38: Receiving HTTP responses (HttpSample.cpp)

```
    //For its declaration, refer to Listing 14-36
    void
    HttpSample::OnTransactionReadyToRead(HttpSession& httpSession,
                                  HttpTransaction& httpTransaction,
                                  int availableBodyLen)
    {
        HttpResponse* pHttpResponse = httpTransaction.GetResponse();
        if(pHttpResponse->GetHttpStatusCode() == HTTP_STATUS_OK)
        {
            HttpHeader* pHttpHeader = pHttpResponse->GetHeader();
            String* pRawHeader = pHttpHeader->GetRawHeaderN();
            ByteBuffer* pBody = pHttpResponse->ReadBodyN();
            //Handle the body
            delete pBody;
            delete pRawHeader;
        }
    }
```

Wi-Fi and Wi-Fi Direct

Wi-Fi can transfer data over the network by connecting to a wireless local area network (WLAN). Wi-Fi Direct connects to nearby Wi-Fi Direct devices. Connected Wi-Fi devices can transfer data to each other. See the API Reference documentation of the `Tizen::Net::Wifi` namespace for related classes for each use.

Wi-Fi

To be notified of different kinds of Wi-Fi-related events, such as when the device is connected to a Wi-Fi access point or the device's Wi-Fi connection is activated, you need to implement the `Net::Wifi::IWifiManagerEventListener`, as shown in Listing 14-39.

LISTING 14-39: The declaration for Wi-Fi (WifiSample.h)

```cpp
#include <FBase.h>
#include <FNet.h>

class WifiSample
        : public Tizen::Net::Wifi::IWifiManagerEventListener
{
public:
        result UseWifi(void);

private:
        void OnWifiActivated(result r);
        void OnWifiConnected(const Tizen::Base::String& ssid, result r);
        void OnWifiDeactivated(result r);
        void OnWifiDisconnected(void);
        void OnWifiRssiChanged(long rssi);
        void OnWifiScanCompletedN(
            const Tizen::Base::Collection::IList* pWifiBssInfoList,
            result r);

private:
        Tizen::Net::Wifi::WifiManager* __pWifiManager;
};
```

Listing 14-40 checks whether the Wi-Fi connection is activated and activates it if it is not.

LISTING 14-40: Activating Wi-Fi (WifiSample.cpp)

```cpp
#include "WifiSample.h"

result
WifiSample::UseWifi(void)
{
        result r = E_SUCCESS;
        __pWifiManager = new (std::nothrow) WifiManager();
        r = __pWifiManager->Construct(*this);

        if(!__pWifiManager->IsActivated())
        {
                r = __pWifiManager->Activate();
        }

        return r;
}
```

If Wi-Fi is activated successfully, you scan the available access points (see Listing 14-41).

LISTING 14-41: The event handling for Wi-Fi activation (WifiSample.cpp)

```
//For its declaration, refer to Listing 14-39
void
WifiSample::OnWifiActivated(result r)
{
        result rr = E_SUCCESS;
        if(!IsFailed(r))
        {
                rr = __pWifiManager->Scan();
        }
}
```

The scanned list of access points is returned as a list of basic service set (BSS) information in the event handler `IWifiManagerEventListener::OnWifiScanCompletedN()`. In Listing 14-42, you choose an access point from the list and attempt to connect to it using a network key.

LISTING 14-42: The event handling for scanned Wi-Fi (WifiSample.cpp)

```
//For its declaration, refer to Listing 14-39
void
WifiSample::OnWifiScanCompletedN(const IList* pWifiBssInfoList, result r)
{
        result rr = E_SUCCESS;
        if(!IsFailed(r))
        {
                IEnumerator* pEnum = pWifiBssInfoList->GetEnumeratorN();
                while(pEnum->MoveNext() == E_SUCCESS)
                {
                    WifiBssInfo* pBssInfo =
                        static_cast<WifiBssInfo*>(pEnum->GetCurrent());
                    WifiSecurityInfo* pSecurityInfo =
                        const_cast<WifiSecurityInfo*>(pBssInfo->GetSecurityInfo());
                    if(pSecurityInfo->GetEncryptionType() != WIFI_ENCRYPTION_NONE)
                    {
                            pSecurityInfo->SetNetworkKey(L"01234");
                    }
                    rr = __pWifiManager->Connect(*pBssInfo);
                }
        }
}
```

When the connection is established, the `IWifiManagerEventListener::OnWifiConnected` handler is called, as shown in Listing 14-43.

LISTING 14-43: The event handling for Wi-Fi connection (WifiSample.cpp)

```
//For its declaration, refer to Listing 14-39
void
WifiSample::OnWifiConnected(const String& ssid, result r)
{
        if (!IsFailed(r))
        {
                WifiBssInfo* pBssInfo = __pWifiManager->GetConnectionTargetInfoN();
                //Check BSS info
        }
}
```

Wi-Fi Direct

Wi-Fi Direct enables you to join a group of wireless devices together in a peer-to-peer network without using a wireless access point. Listing 14-44 shows how to search for and create a group of connected Wi-Fi Direct devices. To use Wi-Fi Direct, implement its listener as shown.

LISTING 14-44: The declaration for Wi-Fi Direct (WifiSample.h)

```
#include <FBase.h>
#include <FNet.h>

class WifiSample
        : public Tizen::Net::Wifi::IWifiDirectDeviceListener
{
public:

        result UseWifiDirect(void);

private:
        void OnWifiDirectAutonomousGroupCreated(
           Tizen::Net::Wifi::WifiDirectDeviceId localDeviceId,
           result r);
        void OnWifiDirectConnected(
           Tizen::Net::Wifi::WifiDirectDeviceId localDeviceId,
           const Tizen::Net::Wifi::WifiDirectDeviceInfo& remoteDeviceInfo,
           result r);
        void OnWifiDirectDeviceActivated(
           Tizen::Net::Wifi::WifiDirectDeviceId localDeviceId,
           result r);
        void OnWifiDirectDeviceDeactivated(
           Tizen::Net::Wifi::WifiDirectDeviceId localDeviceId,
           result r);
        void OnWifiDirectDisconnected(
           Tizen::Net::Wifi::WifiDirectDeviceId localDeviceId,
           const Tizen::Base::String& peerMacAddress,
           result r);
        void OnWifiDirectGroupLeft(
           Tizen::Net::Wifi::WifiDirectDeviceId localDeviceId,
```

continues

LISTING 14-44 *(continued)*

```
            result r);
        void OnWifiDirectRemoteDeviceFound(
            Tizen::Net::Wifi::WifiDirectDeviceId localDeviceId,
            const Tizen::Net::Wifi::WifiDirectDeviceInfo& remoteDeviceInfo);
        void OnWifiDirectScanCompletedN(
            Tizen::Net::Wifi::WifiDirectDeviceId localDeviceId,
            Tizen::Base::Collection::IList* pWifiDirectDeviceInfoList,
            result r);

    private:
        Tizen::Net::Wifi::WifiManager* __pWifiManager;
}
```

Before scanning for nearby Wi-Fi Direct devices, you need to check if Wi-Fi Direct is activated on the local device, activating it if it's not (see Listing 14-45).

LISTING 14-45: Activating Wi-Fi Direct (WifiSample.cpp)

```
#include "WifiSample.h"

using namespace Tizen::Base;
using namespace Tizen::Base::Collection;
using namespace Tizen::Net::Wifi;

result
WifiSample::UseWifiDirect(void)
{
    result r = E_SUCCESS;

    __pWifiDirectDevice = WifiDirectDeviceManager::GetWifiDirectDeviceN();
    if(!__pWifiDirectDevice->IsActivated())
    {
        r = __pWifiDirectDevice->Activate();
    }

    return r;
}
```

When Wi-Fi Direct is activated on the local device, the OnWifiDirectDeviceActivated() event handler is called as shown in Listing 14-46. In this method, you scan for nearby Wi-Fi Direct devices.

LISTING 14-46: The event handling for activated Wi-Fi Direct (WifiSample.cpp)

```
//For its declaration, refer to Listing 14-44
void
WifiSample::OnWifiDirectDeviceActivated(WifiDirectDeviceId localDeviceId, result r)
{
```

```
result rr = E_SUCCESS;

if(!IsFailed(r))
{
        rr = __pWifiDirectDevice->Scan();
}
}
```

Once the scan has completed, you try to connect with the first Wi-Fi Direct device that has been found, as shown in Listing 14-47.

LISTING 14-47: The event handling for the scanned Wi-Fi Direct device (WifiSample.cpp)

```
//For its declaration, refer to Listing 14-44
void
WifiSample::OnWifiDirectScanCompletedN(WifiDirectDeviceId localDeviceId,
    IList* pWifiDirectDeviceInfoList, result r)
{
        result rr = E_SUCCESS;

        if(!IsFailed(r))
        {
                WifiDirectDeviceInfo* pTargetDeviceInfo =
                    static_cast<WifiDirectDeviceInfo*>(pWifiDirectDeviceInfoList->GetAt(0));
                rr = __pWifiDirectDevice->Connect(*pTargetDeviceInfo);
        }
}
```

To create a Wi-Fi Direct group, you need to disconnect the Wi-Fi Direct connection from the remote device (see Listing 14-48).

LISTING 14-48: The event handling for Wi-Fi Direct connection (WifiSample.cpp)

```
//For its declaration, refer to Listing 14-44
void
WifiSample::OnWifiDirectConnected(WifiDirectDeviceId localDeviceId,
    const WifiDirectDeviceInfo& remoteDeviceInfo, result r)
{
        result rr = E_SUCCESS;

        if(!IsFailed(r))
        {
                //Handle the connected Wi-Fi Direct device
                WifiDirectDeviceId remoteDeviceId = remoteDeviceInfo.GetDeviceId();
                //...
                rr = __pWifiDirectDevice->Disconnect(remoteDeviceInfo);
        }
}
```

After checking the disconnected result, you create a Wi-Fi Direct group (see Listing 14-49).

LISTING 14-49 The event handling for Wi-Fi Direct disconnection (WifiSample.cpp)

```
//For its declaration, refer Listing 14-44
void
WifiSample::OnWifiDirectDisconnected(WifiDirectDeviceId localDeviceId,
    const String& peerMacAddress, result r)
{
    result rr = E_SUCCESS;

    if(!IsFailed(r))
    {
        rr = __pWifiDirectDevice->CreateAutonomousGroup();
    }
}
```

The result for creating a Wi-Fi Direct group successfully is received in `OnWifiDirectAutonomousGroupCreated()`, as shown in Listing 14-50.

LISTING 14-50: The event handling for the created Wi-Fi Direct group (WifiSample.cpp)

```
//For its declaration, refer to Listing 14-44
void
WifiSample::OnWifiDirectAutonomousGroupCreated(WifiDirectDeviceId localDeviceId,
    result r)
{
    result rr = E_SUCCESS;

    if(!IsFailed(r))
    {
        WifiDirectGroupInfo* pWifiDirectGroupInfo =
            __pWifiDirectDevice->GetGroupSettingInfoN();
        if(pWifiDirectGroupInfo != null)
        {
            rr = pWifiDirectGroupInfo->SetMaxNumberOfClients(
                MAX_WIFI_DIRECT_CONNECTED_CLIENTS);
            //Set more information
        }
    }
}
```

After creating the Wi-Fi Direct group, you can set up group information, such as the maximum number of clients that can be connected.

Bluetooth

Tizen provides another method to share data between paired devices: the Bluetooth feature. Tizen supports several different Bluetooth profiles, each of which has a different usage:

➤ **Generic Access Profile (GAP)** — A basic profile, it defines the generic procedure, which includes discovering available devices and establishing a connection for the paired device.

➤ **Object Push Profile (OPP)** — This covers sending objects such as images or vCards. The *client* is the sender that pushes objects to the *server*, which is the receiver.

➤ **Serial Port Profile (SPP)** — This profile emulates an RS-232 serial port.

➤ **Health Device Profile (HDP)** — This is a profile designed for transmitting and receiving healthcare and fitness device data.

To use Bluetooth, you need to implement various listeners to activate Bluetooth and discover other devices. Listings 14-51 and 14-52 show how to activate Bluetooth and set up your code to implement some of the Bluetooth event handlers.

LISTING 14-51: The declaration for Bluetooth (BluetoothSample.h)

```
#include <FBase.h>
#include <FNet.h>

class BluetoothSample
        : public Tizen::Net::Bluetooth::IBluetoothManagerEventListener,
          public Tizen::Net::Bluetooth::IBluetoothDeviceEventListener
{
public:
        result UseBluetooth(void);

private:
        void OnBluetoothActivated(result r);
        void OnBluetoothDeactivated(result r);
        void OnBluetoothDiscoverableModeChanged(
           Tizen::Net::Bluetooth::BluetoothDiscoverableMode mode);

        void OnBluetoothDiscoveryDone(bool isCompleted);
        void OnBluetoothDiscoveryStarted(result r);
        void OnBluetoothPaired(
           const Tizen::Net::Bluetooth::BluetoothDevice& pairedDevice);
        void OnBluetoothPairingFailed(result r);
        void OnBluetoothRemoteDeviceFoundN(
           Tizen::Net::Bluetooth::BluetoothDevice* pFoundDevice);
        void OnBluetoothServiceListReceived(
           const Tizen::Net::Bluetooth::BluetoothDevice& targetDevice,
           unsigned long serviceList,
           result r);
        void OnBluetoothUnpaired(
           const Tizen::Net::Bluetooth::BluetoothDevice& unpairedDevice);
private:
        Tizen::Net::Bluetooth::BluetoothManager* __pBluetoothManager;
        Tizen::Base::Collection::ArrayList* __pBluetoothDeviceList;
};
```

LISTING 14-52: Activating Bluetooth (BluetoothSample.cpp)

```
#include <FSystem.h>
#include "BluetoothSample.h"

using namespace Tizen::Base;
```

continues

LISTING 14-52 *(continued)*

```
using namespace Tizen::Base::Collection;
using namespace Tizen::Net::Bluetooth;
using namespace Tizen::System;

result
BluetoothSample::UseBluetooth(void)
{
        result r = E_SUCCESS;

        r = SystemInfo::GetValue(L"http://tizen.org/feature/network.bluetooth",
                isBluetooth);
        if(!isBluetooth)
        {
                AppLog("The Bluetooth is not supported.");
                return r;
        }

        __pBluetoothManager = new (std::nothrow) BluetoothManager();
        r = __pBluetoothManager->Construct(*this);

        r = __pBluetoothManager->Activate();

        return r;
}
```

In Listing 14-53 you can check whether Bluetooth activation is successful in the
`OnBluetoothActivated()` event handler.

LISTING 14-53: The event handling for Bluetooth activation (BluetoothSample.cpp)

```
//For its declaration, refer to Listing 14-51
void
BluetoothSample::OnBluetoothActivated(result r)
{
        result rr = E_SUCCESS;

        if(!IsFailed(r))
        {
                rr = __pBluetoothManager->SetBluetoothDeviceListener(this);
                rr = __pBluetoothManager->StartDiscovery();
        }
}
```

You can set up a Bluetooth device listener and begin searching for other Bluetooth devices
(see Listing 14-54). When a device is found, but before the process is completed, the
`OnBluetoothRemoteDeviceFoundN()` handler is called.

LISTING 14-54: The event handling for the found Bluetooth device (BluetoothSample.cpp)

```cpp
//For its declaration, refer to Listing 14-51
void
BluetoothSample::OnBluetoothRemoteDeviceFoundN(BluetoothDevice* pFoundDevice)
{
        result r = E_SUCCESS;

        if(__pBluetoothDeviceList == null)
        {
                __pBluetoothDeviceList = new (std::nothrow) ArrayList();
                r = __pBluetoothDeviceList->Construct();
        }
        if(pFoundDevice != null)
        {
                r = __pBluetoothDeviceList->Add(pFoundDevice);
        }
}
```

As shown in Listing 14-55, once discovery is completed, you can pair with one of the devices that were found.

LISTING 14-55: The event handling if Bluetooth device discovery is done (BluetoothSample.cpp)

```cpp
//For its declaration, refer to Listing 14-52
void
BluetoothSample::OnBluetoothDiscoveryDone(bool isCompleted)
{
        result r = E_SUCCESS;

        if(isCompleted)
        {
                BluetoothDevice* pTargetDevice =
                    static_cast<BluetoothDevice*>(__pBluetoothDeviceList->GetAt(0));
                if(pTargetDevice != null)
                {
                        r = __pBluetoothManager->Pair(*pTargetDevice);
                }
        }
}

void
BluetoothSample::OnBluetoothPaired(const BluetoothDevice& pairedDevice)
{
        //Check the paired device
}
```

If you use the basic functions of Bluetooth and don't want to create your own user interface, the Bluetooth application control provided by the Tizen platform provides a standard way to enable users to discover a list of available devices to pair with.

Listings 14-56 and 14-57 shows how to use the Bluetooth application control.

LISTING 14-56: The declaration for the Bluetooth application control (BluetoothSample.h)

```
#include <FApp.h>
#include <FBase.h>
#include <FNet.h>

class BluetoothSample
        : public Tizen::App::IAppControlResponseListener
{
public:
        result UseBluetoothAppControl(void);

private:
        void OnAppControlCompleteResponseReceived(const Tizen::App::AppId& appId,
                    const Tizen::Base::String& operationId,
                    Tizen::App::AppCtrlResult appControlResult,
                    const Tizen::Base::Collection::IMap* pExtraData);
};
```

LISTING 14-57: The Bluetooth application control (BluetoothSample.cpp)

```
#include "BluetoothSample.h"
result
BluetoothSample::UseBluetoothAppControl(void)
{
        result r = E_SUCCESS;
        AppControl* pAc = AppManager::FindAppControlN(L"tizen.bluetooth",
           L"http://tizen.org/appcontrol/operation/bluetooth/pick");
        if (pAc != null)
        {
                r = pAc->Start(null, null, null, this);
                delete pAc;
        }

        return r;
}

void
BluetoothSample::OnAppControlCompleteResponseReceived(
    const AppId& appId,
    const String& operationId,
    AppCtrlResult appControlResult,
    const IMap* pExtraData)
{
        if ((appId == L"tizen.bluetooth") &&
            (operationId == L"http://tizen.org/appcontrol/operation/bluetooth/pick"))
        {
                if (appControlResult == APP_CTRL_RESULT_SUCCEEDED)
                {
                        BluetoothDevice* pDevice =
                            BluetoothDevice::GetInstanceFromAppControlResultN(*pExtraData);
```

```
                                    //Handle the received bluetooth device
                    }
                }
        }
```

The Bluetooth application control shows two parts in one display. A controller to activate or deactivate the Bluetooth function is located on the top. If the Bluetooth control is activated, a list of available Bluetooth devices appears (see Figure 14-11). When the device user selects one, the pairing progresses.

FIGURE 14-11

NFC

NFC is one of the most exciting technologies on mobile devices, and Tizen has extensive support for it. The `Net::Nfc` namespace includes classes to support all the core NFC functionalities:

➤ Detecting NFC tags

➤ Detecting NDEF (NFC data exchange format) messages

➤ Pushing NDEF messages

In this section you will learn how to add support for these features in your own code.

By implementing the `INfcManagerEventListener` event listener, you can check if NFC is supported and activated on a device. Listings 14-58 and 14-59 show how to set up your code to receive NFC activation and deactivation events and determine if a device supports NFC.

LISTING 14-58: The declaration to enable NFC (NfcSample.h)

```cpp
#include <FNet.h>

class NfcSample
        : public Tizen::Net::Nfc::INfcManagerEventListener
{
public:
        result UseNfc(void);
private:
        void OnNfcActivated (result r);
        void OnNfcDeactivated (result r);
private:
        Tizen::Net::Nfc::NfcManager*  __pNfcManager;
};
```

LISTING 14-59: Activating NFC (NfcSample.cpp)

```cpp
#include <FSystem.h>
#include "NfcSample.h"

using namespace Tizen::Net::Nfc;
```

continues

LISTING 14-59 *(continued)*

```
using namespace Tizen::System;

result
NfcSample::UseNfc(void)
{
        result r = E_SUCCESS;
        bool isNfc = false;

        r = SystemInfo::GetValue(L"http://tizen.org/feature/network.nfc", isNfc);
        if(!isNfc)
        {
                AppLog("The NFC is not supported.");
                return r;
        }

        __pNfcManager = new (std::nothrow)NfcManager();
        r = __pNfcManager->Construct(*this);

        if(!(__pNfcManager->IsActivated()))      {
                r = __pNfcManager->Activate();

        }

        return r;
}
```

The event handlers in Listing 14-60 receive NFC activation and deactivation events.

LISTING 14-60: The event handling for NFC activation (NfcSample.cpp)

```
//For its declaration, refer to Listing 14-58
void
NfcSample::OnNfcActivated (result r)
{
        AppLogIf(!IsFailed(r), "Activate() is failed.");
}

void
NfcSample::OnNfcDeactivated (result r)
{
        AppLogIf(!IsFailed(r), "Deactivate() is failed.");
}
```

Detecting NFC Tags

If NFC is activated, an NFC tag can be detected in the INfcTagDiscoveryEventListener, as shown in Listings 14-61 and 14-62.

LISTING 14-61: The declaration for NFC tag discovery (NfcSample.h)

```cpp
class NfcSample
        : public Tizen::Net::Nfc::INfcTagDiscoveryEventListener
{
public:
        result CheckTagConnection(void);
private:
        void OnNfcTagDetectedN(Tizen::Net::Nfc::TagConnection* pConnection);
        void OnNfcTagLost(void);
private:
        Tizen::Net::Nfc::TagConnection* __pTagConnection;
};
```

LISTING 14-62: Adding a listener to detect an NFC tag (NfcSample.cpp)

```cpp
#include "NfcSample.h"

result
NfcSample::CheckTagConnection(void)
{
        result r = E_SUCCESS;

        if(__pNfcManager->IsTagConnected())
        {
                __pTagConnection = __pNfcManager->GetCurrentTagConnectionN();
        }
        else
        {
                r = __pNfcManager->AddTagDiscoveryEventListener(*this, NFC_TAG_TYPE_ALL);
        }

        return r;
}
```

When an NFC tag is detected, the OnNfcTagDetectedN() method is invoked with TagConnection passed as a parameter, as shown in Listing 14-63. You can use TagConnection to get more information about the detected tag, such as the tag ID and tag type. Most tags have an ID, which is generated every time they are detected, but some tags don't have an ID. The tag type can be a single tag or multiple tags.

LISTING 14-63: The event handling for the detected NFC tag (NfcSample.cpp)

```cpp
//For its declaration, refer Listing 14-61
void
NfcSample::OnNfcTagDetectedN(TagConnection* pConnection)
{
        NfcTag* pNfcTag = null;

        __pTagConnection = pConnection;
        //Handle tag information
}
```

You can send a command to the detected tag by calling the `SendCommand()` method of the `TagConnection` class.

Detecting NDEF Messages

You can detect an NDEF message by implementing the `INdefMessageDiscoveryEventListener`, using the code shown in Listings 14-64 and 14-65 to set up your application to handle these events.

LISTING 14-64: The declaration for NDEF messages (NfcSample.h)

```
class NfcSample
      : public Tizen::Net::Nfc::INfcManagerEventListener,
        public Tizen::Net::Nfc::INfcTagDiscoveryEventListener,
        public Tizen::Net::Nfc::INdefMessageDiscoveryEventListener,
{
public:
      result UseNdefMessage(void);
};
```

LISTING 14-65: Adding a listener for NDEF message detection (NfcSample.cpp)

```
#include <FBase.h>
#include "NfcSample.h"

using namespace Tizen::Base;

result
NfcSample::UseNdefMessage(void)
{
      result r = E_SUCCESS;

      r = __pNfcManager->AddNdefMessageDiscoveryEventListener(*this,
         NdefRecordType(NDEF_TNF_ALL));

      return r;
}
```

As shown in Listing 14-66, the detected NDEF message will be passed as a parameter to `OnNdefMessageDetectedN()`.

LISTING 14-66: The event handling for detected NDEF message (NfcSample.cpp)

```
void
NfcSample::OnNdefMessageDetectedN (NdefMessage *pMessage)
{
      NdefRecord* pRecord = pMessage->GetRecordAt(0);
      String id = pRecord->GetPayloadId();
      ByteBuffer* pPayload = pRecord->GetPayload();
      NdefRecordType type = pRecord->GetRecordType();
      NdefRecordTypeNameFormat typeNameFormat = type.GetNameFormat();
      String typeName = type.GetName();
}
```

As shown in Figure 14-12, the NDEF message includes multiple NDEF records, which contain payload ID, payload, and record type, which specifies the type format and its name.

Pushing NDEF Messages

Tizen supports NFC peer-to-peer mode, which enables two NFC-enabled devices to exchange information. Information is exchanged in the form of NDEF messages, using the Push() method of the Nfc::NdefPushManager class.

Before pushing an NDEF message, you need to discover a target device using the INfcDeviceDiscoveryEventListener. Listings 14-67 and 14-68 show the code you need to add to be ready to discover a target device.

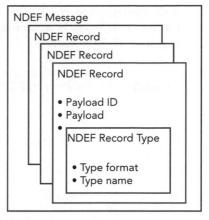

FIGURE 14-12

LISTING 14-67: The declaration for push of NDEF messages (NfcSample.h)

```
class NfcSample
        : public Tizen::Net::Nfc::INfcManagerEventListener,
          public Tizen::Net::Nfc::INdefPushManagerListener,
          public Tizen::Net::Nfc::INfcDeviceDiscoveryEventListener
{
public:
        result PushNdefMessage(void);

private:
        void OnNfcDeviceDetected(void);
        void OnNfcDeviceLost(void);
        void OnNdefPushMessageSent(result r);

private:
        Tizen::Net::Nfc::NdefPushManager* __pNdefPushManager;
};
```

LISTING 14-68: Adding a listener for NDEF message detection (NfcSample.cpp)

```
#include "NfcSample.h"

result
NfcSample::UseNdefMessage(void)
{
        result r = E_SUCCESS;

        r = __pNfcManager->AddNdefMessageDiscoveryEventListener(*this,
            NdefRecordType(NDEF_TNF_ALL));

        return r;
}
```

After adding a listener for INdefPushManagerListener, you can push an NDEF to the detected device. Listing 14-69 shows how to push a message, while the implementation of OnNdefPushMessageSent() in Listing 14-70 is where you will check to see if the push message was sent.

LISTING 14-69: Pushing an NDEF message (NfcSample.cpp)

```
//For its declaration, refer Listing to 14-67
void
NfcSample::OnNfcDeviceDetected (void)
{
        result r = E_SUCCESS;

        __pNdefPushManager->SetNdefPushManagerListener(this);

        NdefMessage ndefMessage;
        //Set NDEF message
        r = __pNdefPushManager->Push(ndefMessage);
}
```

LISTING 14-70: Checking if the NDEF message is pushed (NfcSample.cpp)

```
//For its declaration, refer to Listing 14-67
void
NfcSample::OnNdefPushMessageSent (result r)
{
        AppLogIf(!IsFailed(r), "Push() is failed.");
}
```

Launching NFC Applications Conditionallly

Tizen provides a conditional application launch feature that enables an application to register itself with the platform to launch automatically when a certain NFC event occurs, such as receiving an NDEF message of a certain type.

To use this functionality, perform the following steps:

1. Register a launch condition with the Tizen::App::AppManager::RegisterAppLaunch() method.

2. Set the Tizen::App::IAppLaunchConditionEventListener in OnAppInitializing().

3. When the event is received the IAppLaunchConditionEventListener::OnAppLaunchCondi tionMetN() method will be called.

4. Check the NdefMessage with the NfcManager::GetCachedNdefMessageN() method.

You can test out your NFC code in the Emulator by using the Event Injector, as shown in Figure 14-13.

FIGURE 14-13

SUMMARY

In this chapter you learned how to implement a wide range of features, from making a phone call to detecting an NFC tag. You should now have a good understanding of how to use Tizen's application controls to make a call, send an e-mail or SMS, or choose a device to pair with over Bluetooth. You also know about the different types of messages that Tizen supports and how to add messaging to your application.

If you want to start creating applications using features such as Wi-Fi Direct or NFC, you can find some good examples in the Tizen SDK, so dive in and begin developing smart, connected applications.

15

Location and Social Services

WHAT'S IN THIS CHAPTER?

➤ Monitoring locations

➤ Creating accounts

➤ Managing contacts

➤ Calendars, events, and tasks

WROX.COM CODE DOWNLOADS FOR THIS CHAPTER

The wrox.com code downloads for this chapter are found at www.wrox.com/go/
professionaltizen on the Download Code tab. The code is in the Chapter 15 download folder.

In this chapter you'll be introduced to two features at the heart of any smart device: location
and social services. Tizen's location service enables you to track the location of the device and
be notified if the user moves into or out of a particular region, or travels a certain distance. Of
course, some users may not want you to access their location information, and users have full
control over location privacy.

The second key feature is social services. The Social namespace is responsible for managing
the address book and calendar on a device. You'll write code to manage contacts and
construct complex contact searches and then find out how to create calendars and add events
and tasks. Throughout the chapter there are practical examples to help you master features
such as recurring events and reminders, all designed to help you create your own applications.

THE LOCATION SERVICE

Positioning is a key function of a location-based service. The Tizen::Locations namespace
provides the following services when used in conjunction with a location provider:

➤ Retrieving the device location

➤ Registering a region for location-based monitoring

Before using these features, you must check that the user has allowed your application to access location-based services on the device.

Location Settings

To use the location feature, the device's location-related settings must be enabled. If the settings are not enabled, then trying to use certain location APIs will result in an E_USER_NOT_CONSENTED exception, which indicates the user has blocked the application from accessing location information. This error will be returned in the following cases:

➤   Any option in Settings ➪ Locations is not enabled.

➤   The privacy setting in Settings ➪ Privacy ➪ [Application name] is not enabled.

Location Positioning

To use the location feature, a positioning method setting is needed. The SystemInfo::GetValue() function lets you know whether the device can provide positioning information and whether this feature is enabled. If the GPS (Global Positioning System) and WPS (Wi-Fi-based Positioning System) features are supported but neither is enabled, show users a pop-up requesting that they change the settings.

Listing 15-1 shows how to check whether the location positioning features are enabled.

LISTING 15-1: Checking the location positioning setting (LocationSample.cpp)

```cpp
#include <FSystem.h>
#include "LocationSample.h"

using namespace Tizen::System;

void
LocationSample::CheckLocationSetting(void)
{
    bool gpsAvailable;
    bool wpsAvailable;

    //Check GPS and WPS features are supported
    result gpsResult = SystemInfo::GetValue(L"http://tizen.org/feature/location.gps",
      gpsAvailable);
    result wpsResult = SystemInfo::GetValue(L"http://tizen.org/feature/location.wps",
      wpsAvailable);
    if (!gpsAvailable)
    {
        AppLog("Your device doesn't support the GPS positioning");
    }
    if (!wpsAvailable)
    {
        AppLog("Your device doesn't support the WPS positioning");
    }

    //Check GPS and WPS settings are enabled
    result gpsResult = SystemInfo::GetValue(L"http://tizen.org/setting/location.gps",
```

```
        gpsAvailable);
    result wpsResult = SystemInfo::GetValue(L"http://tizen.org/setting/location.wps",
    wpsAvailable);
    if (!gpsResult && !wpsResult)
    {
        AppLog("Your device doesn't support the location positioning");
    }
}
```

In the Settings ⇨ Locations menu, the user can choose the settings for GPS and network position separately, as shown in Figure 15-1. At least one of these settings must be enabled to obtain the device's current position.

The GPS setting enables the use of GPS satellite signals to obtain the position of the device. While it generally works better in an outdoor environment, GPS does provide more accurate positioning information than network-based positioning, which combines Wi-Fi and cell tower location information to provide an accurate position even in situations where the GPS signal is weak, such as indoors.

Location Privacy Setting

Some location APIs require the http://tizen.org/privilege/location privacy-related privilege, which should be added to the application manifest file. Including this privilege will ensure that location APIs operate properly when the user has allowed the application to use location-based features. The application installer checks the privacy-related privileges of the downloaded application package and registers them in the Settings ⇨ Privacy ⇨ [Application name] menu, as shown in Figure 15-2.

FIGURE 15-1

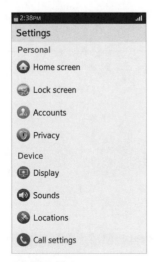

FIGURE 15-2

If an item in the privacy settings menu is checked, it means the user consents to the application using the feature. These privacy settings are provided on a per-application basis, not for all applications on the device. More information about privileges can be found in Chapter 2.

Location Criteria

To create an instance of the location provider, the location criteria needs to be defined. This specifies the service quality that your application wants from the location provider, including location accuracy. The possible values of the `Tizen::Locations::LocationAccuracy` enum used to specify location accuracy are as follows:

➤ `LOC_ACCURACY_FINEST` — This means your application wants to use the finest possible level of accuracy from the location provider.

➤ `LOC_ACCURACY_TEN_METERS` — This value indicates that location accuracy should be within 10 metres.

➤ `LOC_ACCURACY_HUNDRED_METERS` — This value indicates that location accuracy should be within 100 metres.

➤ `LOC_ACCURACY_ONE_KILOMETER` — This value indicates that location accuracy should be within 1 kilometre.

➤ `LOC_ACCURACY_ANY` — This setting means that any level of location accuracy is acceptable to the application.

Getting the Location

From within your application, you can retrieve the last known and current location of the device. The last known location retrieves the last location present in the system and may not match the precise current position of the device. However, it is useful to figure out the device location without having to make a new request to the positioning system.

Listing 15-2 shows how to get the last known location of the device.

LISTING 15-2: Getting the last known location (LocationSample.cpp)

```cpp
#include <FBase.h>
#include "LocationSample.h"

using namespace Tizen::Base;
using namespace Tizen::Locations;

result
LocationSample::GetLastKnownLocation(void)
{
        result r = E_SUCCESS;

        Location location = LocationProvider::GetLastKnownLocation();
        r = GetLastResult();
```

```
        if (!IsFailed(r) && location.IsValid())
        {
                Coordinates coords = location.GetCoordinates();
                DateTime timeStamp = location.GetTimestamp();
                String locationMethod = location.GetExtraInfo(L"location_method");
        }
        return r;
}
```

In Listing 15-2 the coordinates and timestamp are retrieved after checking that no errors occurred and a valid location was returned.

To get the current location, use the `LocationProvider::GetLocation()` method and specify the location criteria. Listing 15-3 requests the current location with an accuracy of within 10 metres.

LISTING 15-3: Getting the current location (LocationSample.cpp)

```cpp
#include <FBase.h>
#include "LocationSample.h"

using namespace Tizen::Base;
using namespace Tizen::Locations;

result
LocationSample::GetCurrentLocation(void)
{
        result r = E_SUCCESS;

        LocationCriteria criteria;
        criteria.SetAccuracy(LOC_ACCURACY_TEN_METERS);
        Location location = LocationProvider::GetLocation(criteria);
        r = GetLastResult();

        if (!IsFailed(r) && location.IsValid())
        {
                Coordinates coords = location.GetCoordinates();
                DateTime timeStamp = location.GetTimestamp();
                String locationMethod = location.GetExtraInfo(L"location_method");
        }

        return r;
}
```

Monitoring Locations

In addition to getting the device's location, it's also useful for an application to register for location events when the user is on the move. You can receive location events at set intervals, when the device has moved a certain distance, or when the device location moves into or out of a specified region. These features make possible a wide range of location-aware applications, from fitness apps to shopping apps. In this section you'll work through the code to monitor the device location by distance, interval, and region.

Monitoring by Distance or Interval

Applications can receive location update events for a specific distance or interval with the `ILocationProviderListener`. Listing 15-4 shows you how.

LISTING 15-4: Declaring the location monitoring listener (LocationSample.h)

```cpp
#include <FLocations.h>

class LocationSample
      : public Tizen::Locations::ILocationProviderListener
{
public:
      result InitializeLocationProvider(void);
      result UpdateLocationByDistance(double distance);
      result UpdateLocationByInterval(int interval);
private:
      void OnAccuracyChanged (Tizen::Locations::LocationAccuracy accuracy);
      void OnLocationUpdated (const Tizen::Locations::Location &location);
      void OnLocationUpdateStatusChanged (Tizen::Locations::LocationServiceStatus
          status);
private:
      Tizen::Locations::LocationProvider* __pLocationProvider;
};
```

After setting the location accuracy, construct an instance of `LocationProvider` and specify the `ILocationProviderListener`, as shown in Listing 15-5. The LocationSample class inherits `ILocationProviderListener` and implements the event handlers it defines.

LISTING 15-5: Setting the location monitoring listener (LocationSample.cpp)

```cpp
result
LocationSample::InitializeLocationProvider(void)
{
      result r = E_SUCCESS;

      if (__pLocationProvider == null)
      {
            LocationCriteria criteria;
            criteria.SetAccuracy(LOC_ACCURACY_FINEST);

            __pLocationProvider = new (std::nothrow)LocationProvider();
            r = __pLocationProvider->Construct(criteria, *this);
      }

      return r;
}
```

If you want to get events when the location changes by a specified distance, use `StartLocation UpdatesByDistance()`, where the distance parameter is specified in metres (see Listing 15-6).

LISTING 15-6: Starting the location monitoring with the specific distance (LocationSample.cpp)

```cpp
result
LocationSample::UpdateLocationByDistance(double distance)
{
        result r = E_SUCCESS;

        r = InitializeLocationProvider();
        r = __pLocationProvider->StartLocationUpdatesByDistance(distance);

        return r;
}
```

StartLocationUpdateByInterval() requests updated location events at an interval specified in seconds (see Listing 15-7). You can't receive location update events for distance and interval at the same time, only the last request is valid.

LISTING 15-7: Starting the location monitoring with the specific interval (LocationSample.cpp)

```cpp
result
LocationSample::UpdateLocationByInterval(int interval)
{
        result r = E_SUCCESS;

        r = InitializeLocationProvider();
        r = __pLocationProvider->StartLocationUpdatesByInterval(interval);

        return r;
}
```

The location update event is received in the appropriate event, which for periodic and distance updates is OnLocationUpdated(). In this method you can check the updated location, including the coordinates (see Listing 15-8).

LISTING 15-8: Checking an event for the changed location (LocationSample.cpp)

```cpp
void
LocationSample::OnLocationUpdated (const Tizen::Locations::Location &location)
{
        //Check the updated location
        Coordinates coords = location.GetCoordinates();
}
```

Testing location applications in a real environment is a challenge, since you're moving with the test device, so it may be easier in the early stages of your development to test your application in the Emulator and use the Event Injector. The Event Injector provides a Location tab that is used to inject location information into the application, as shown in Figure 15-3. The Location tab includes a Map viewer, a Coordinate section for injecting latitude and longitude, and supports the loading of a GPS data log file (in NMEA 183 format) to inject location data.

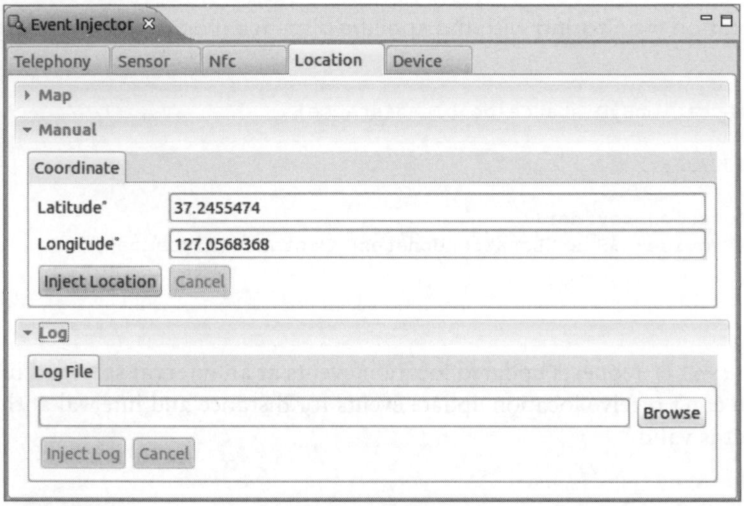

FIGURE 15-3

If you're registered to receive location events when the location has been updated by a certain distance, then you can use the Event Injector to inject an updated location and check that the `OnLocationUpdated()` handler is called when the registered distance is passed.

The location service status can change depending on the device state — for example, if the screen is locked or the application is running in the background. When you first register for location updates, and the location service provider is successfully running the requested service, the `OnLocationUpdateStatusChanged()` method will be called with a `LocationServiceStatus` of `LOC_SVC_STATUS_RUNNING`. `OnLocationUpdateStatusChanged()` will be called again whenever the service status changes. A status of `LOC_SVC_STATUS_PAUSED` occurs when the application is not running in the foreground or the screen is off. To prevent this from happening and to continue to receive location updates, call `KeepLocationUpdateAwake(true)` before `StartLocationUpdatesByDistance()` or `StartLocationUpdatesByInterval()`.

Listing 15-9 shows how to respond to location service status events when you're notified that the service has been paused.

LISTING 15-9: Getting location service status events (LocationSample.cpp)

```
void
LocationSample::OnLocationUpdateStatusChanged (
    Tizen::Locations::LocationServiceStatus status)
{
        result r = E_SUCCESS;

        switch (status)
        {
        case LOC_SVC_STATUS_RUNNING:
            break;
```

```
            case LOC_SVC_STATUS_PAUSED:
                r = __pLocationProvider->KeepLocationUpdateAwake(true);
                break;
            default:
                AppLog("Location Service Status is changed: %d", status);
                break;
        }
    }
```

When the accuracy level that the location provider is able to provide changes, the `OnAccuracyChanged()` event handler is called (see Listing 15-10). If the new accuracy is set to `LOC_ACCURACY_INVALID`, this means that the location provider is not running the requested services.

LISTING 15-10: Checking the changed location accuracy level (LocationSample.cpp)

```
void
LocationSample::OnAccuracyChanged (Tizen::Locations::LocationAccuracy accuracy)
{
        //Check the accuracy
}
```

Location-Based Monitoring of Regions

The location monitoring service enables an application to register to be notified whenever the device enters or leaves a specified region. A region is defined using coordinates for its centre point and a radius, which can range from 50 metres to 100 kilometres. If the monitored region is successfully added, a region ID is returned which will be used to identify the particular region among the multiple regions that may be monitored. During region monitoring, the accuracy changed-event may be received, in addition to the `OnRegionEntered()` and `OnRegionLeft()` events, which we discuss next.

Listings 15-11 and 15-12 show how to register to receive location update events for the specified region.

LISTING 15-11: Declaration for region monitoring (LocationSample.h)

```
class LocationSample
        : public Tizen::Locations::ILocationProviderListener
{
public:
        result InitializeLocationProvider(void);
        result AddRegion(double longitude, double latitude, double radius, const
        Tizen::Base::String& regionName);
        Tizen::Base::String CheckRegionName(Tizen::Locations::RegionId regionId);
private:
        Tizen::Locations::LocationProvider* __pLocationProvider;
        Tizen::Base::Collection::HashMap* __pRegions;
};
```

LISTING 15-12: Adding a region-monitoring event (LocationSample.cpp)

```
result
LocationSample::AddRegion(double longitude, double latitude, double radius,
    const String& regionName)
{
        result r = E_SUCCESS;

        r = InitializeLocationProvider();

        Coordinates interestedRegion;
        interestedRegion.Set(longitude, latitude, 0.0);
        double radious = radius;
        RegionId regionId = 0;

        r = __pLocationProvider->AddMonitoringRegion(interestedRegion, radious,
            regionId);

        if (!IsFailed(r))
        {
                __pRegions = new (std::nothrow) HashMap();
                r = __pRegions->Construct();
                r = __pRegions->Add(new Integer(regionId), new String(regionName));
        }

        return r;
}
```

When the device enters the region, `OnRegionEntered()` is called with the specific region ID. `OnRegionLeft()` is called when the device leaves the region. Both of these are shown in Listing 15-13.

LISTING 15-13: Checking if the device entered the region (LocationSample.cpp)

```
void
LocationSample::OnRegionEntered (Tizen::Locations::RegionId regionId)
{
        String regionName = CheckRegionName(regionId);
        AppLog("You're entered in %ls.", regionName.GetPointer());
}
void
LocationSample::OnRegionLeft (Tizen::Locations::RegionId regionId)
{
        String regionName = CheckRegionName(regionId);
        AppLog("You're left from %ls.", regionName.GetPointer());
}
```

By using a `HashMap` to store key-value pairs for the `region ID` and a region name, you can return the region name based on its region ID and vice versa. Listing 15-14 shows you how.

LISTING 15-14: Checking the region name (LocationSample.cpp)

```cpp
String
LocationSample::CheckRegionName(RegionId regionId)
{
        String* pRegionName = null;
        IMapEnumerator* pMapEnum = __pRegions->GetMapEnumeratorN();
        while (pMapEnum->MoveNext() == E_SUCCESS)
        {
                Integer* pTempRegionId = static_cast<Integer*>(pMapEnum->GetKey());
                if (pTempRegionId->ToInt() == regionId)
                {
                        pRegionName = static_cast<String*>(pMapEnum->GetValue());
                        return *pRegionName;
                }
        }

        return null;
}
```

If the service status for region monitoring changes, OnRegionMonitoringStatusChanged() will be called, as shown in Listing 15-15.

LISTING 15-15: Checking the region-monitoring status (LocationSample.cpp)

```cpp
void
LocationSample::OnRegionMonitoringStatusChanged (
    Tizen::Locations::LocationServiceStatus status)
{
        result r = E_SUCCESS;

        if (status != LOC_SVC_STATUS_RUNNING)
        {
                r = __pLocationProvider->RemoveAllMonitoringRegions();
        }
}
```

Using a Map

The Tizen::Locations namespace provides the positioning features, but mapping solutions are left to third parties. If you're writing an application that displays maps, then the Maps Powered by HERE SDK add-on is a good solution. Before using it in your application, check its license and authentication credentials. You can download the SDK from the Tizen developer site (https://developer.tizen.org/downloads/add-on-sdks).

THE SOCIAL SERVICE

With the rise of social media and other cloud-based services, users often have many accounts, address books, and calendars on their devices, all of which need to be managed. The Tizen::Social namespace provides the features necessary to help keep track of this information, from managing contacts to creating calendar events and tasks. The rest of this chapter focuses on these features.

Social Privacy Setting

Making use of the features of the social service involves accessing the user's private data, such as their contacts and calendars. As with the location feature, users can choose to allow access to such private information on a per-application basis. The Settings ⇨ Privacy ⇨ [Application name] menu is where the Calendar and Contact privacy settings can be enabled or disabled by the user. If the user doesn't allow the application permission to access these features, then the privileged APIs will return an error.

Account Management

In Tizen, user accounts (for account providers such as Google) are accessed from the Settings ⇨ Accounts menu on a device. An application that manages accounts for a particular service will register an account provider in its manifest file. This account provider will be shown in the Settings ⇨ Accounts menu, and the application that registered it will be responsible for adding, editing, and deleting user accounts with the service. The application will interact with the Settings ⇨ Accounts menu using the account provider application control.

The following section shows how to register an account provider in your application and implement the application control to manage user account information.

Registering an Account Provider

If you want to manage accounts with a particular service, the account provider should be defined. To register the account provider, first open the manifest editor by double-clicking your application's manifest.xml file in the Project Explorer. Then select the Account tab in the manifest editor.

1. Click the Add button in the Account section, select Account, and click OK.

2. Set Multiple account if multiple accounts are allowed with this provider.

3. Set Icon.

   ➤ Its size is 72 × 72 for Xhigh (HD) or 48 × 48 for High (WVGA).

   ➤ The icon should be stored in a shared directory because it is shown in the Settings ⇨ Accounts menu in the device.

4. Set Icon small.

   ➤ Its size is 45 × 45 for Xhigh (HD) or 30 × 30 for High (WVGA).

   ➤ This icon should also be located in a shared directory because it is used by other applications.

5. Add a display name for the account provider. This will be displayed in Settings ⇨ Accounts (see Figure 15-4).

6. Add the following capabilities if the account needs to access the address book or calendars.

   ➤ http://tizen.org/account/capability/contact

   ➤ http://tizen.org/account/capability/calendar

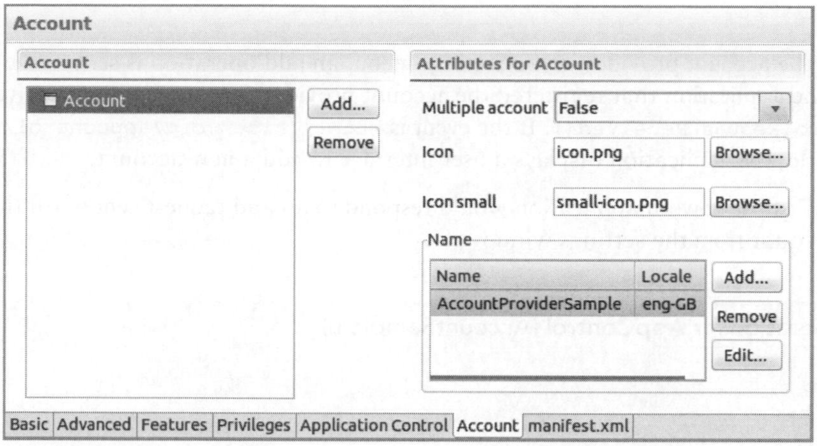

FIGURE 15-4

Once you've edited your `manifest.xml` file as explained above, the `<Accounts>` section should look something like this:

```
<Accounts>
    <AccountProvider MultipleAccountsSupport="False">
        <Icons>
            <Icon Section="Account">icon.png</Icon>
            <Icon Section="AccountSmall">small-icon.png</Icon>
        </Icons>
        <DisplayNames>
            <DisplayName Locale="eng-GB">AccountProviderSample</DisplayName>
        </DisplayNames>
        <Capabilities>
            <Capability>http://tizen.org/account/capability/contact</Capability>
            <Capability>http://tizen.org/account/capability/calendar</Capability>
        </Capabilities>
    </AccountProvider>
</Accounts>
```

Application Control for Account Provider

If an application that registers an account provider is installed on a device, the account provider it registered is shown under the Settings ➪ Accounts menu automatically. However, every application that registers an account provider needs to implement the UI to add and configure user account information. To do this they use the Account Provider application control. This application control does not need to be defined in your `manifest.xml` and supports the following operations:

➤   `http://tizen.org/appcontrol/operation/account/add`

➤   `http://tizen.org/appcontrol/operation/account/configure`

The following sections describe how to implement the application control for the account provider to add and configure user accounts in your application.

Add Operation

When the user chooses the account provider in the Settings menu, an add operation is sent to the application control of the application that registered the account provider. The application receives an event in OnAppControlRequestReceived(). If the event is http://tizen.org/appcontrol/operation/account/add, the application displays a user interface to add a new account.

Listings 15-16 and 15-17 show how an application would respond to an add request sent when the user chose to add an account from the settings window.

LISTING 15-16: Add operation for AppControl (AccountSample.h)

```cpp
#include <FApp.h>
#include <FBase.h>

class AccountSample
        : Tizen::App::IAppControlProviderEventListener
{
private:
        void OnAppControlRequestReceived(RequestId reqId,
                        const Tizen::Base::String& operationId,
                        const Tizen::Base::String* pUriData,
                        const Tizen::Base::String* pMimeType,
                        const Tizen::Base::Collection::IMap* pExtraData);
};
```

LISTING 15-17: Add operation for AppControl (AccountSample.cpp)

```cpp
#include "AccountSample.h"

using namespace Tizen::Base;
using namespace Tizen::Base::Collection;

void
AccountSample::OnAppControlRequestReceived(RequestId reqId, const String& operationId,
                const String* pUriData, const String* pMimeType, const IMap* pExtraData)
{
        if (operationId == L"http://tizen.org/appcontrol/operation/account/add")
        {
                AppLog("Connect to the menu to add an account in your application.");
                //Implement the user interface to add an account
        }
}
```

The application has to implement the user interface to handle the add operation. The application's user interface will be shown if the user selects the account provider in the settings window.

Configure Operation

When a user selects an account in the Settings ⇨ Account menu, the configure operation of the application control is launched. If the application handles the configure operation, it then needs to display the UI to update the user account. The application retrieves the account ID for the account to be updated from the information passed to OnAppControlRequestReceived(), as shown in Listing 15-18.

LISTING 15-18: Configure operation for AppControl (AccountSample.cpp)

```
void
AccountSample::OnAppControlRequestReceived(RequestId reqId, const String& operationId,
          const String* pUriData, const String* pMimeType, const IMap* pExtraData)
{
      __requestId = reqId;
      if (operationId == L"http://tizen.org/appcontrol/operation/account/configure")
      {
            const String* pAccountId = static_cast<const String*>(
               pExtraData->GetValue(String(
                  "http://tizen.org/appcontrol/data/account/id")));
            AppLog(
               "Connect to the menu to update the account in your application.");
            //Implement the user interface to configure for the account ID
      }
}
```

Monitoring Accounts

The previous two cases show what happens when users change account information in Settings ⇨ Accounts, but the application can also update account information using the AccountManager API. To ensure that any changes made within the application code, such as adding or removing an account, are reflected in Settings ⇨ Accounts, the application doesn't actually need to do anything. Settings ⇨ Accounts implements the IAccountEventListener and receives account update events generated by the actions of other applications.

If an application manages account information, it needs to implement the IAccountEventListener to be notified of any account changes caused by other applications. Listings 15-19 and 15-20 show the code for an application called AnotherAccountSample that registers an event listener to receive account events.

LISTING 15-19: Adding a listener to check the account change (AnotherAccountSample.h)

```
#include <FSocial.h>

class AnotherAccountSample
      : Tizen::Social::IAccountEventListener
{

public:
```

continues

LISTING 15-19 *(continued)*

```
        result Initialize(void);

private:
        void OnAccountAdded(Tizen::Social::AccountId accountId);
        void OnAccountRemoved(Tizen::Social::AccountId accountId);
        void OnAccountUpdated(Tizen::Social::AccountId accountId);

private:
        Tizen::Social::AccountAccessor* __pAccountAccessor;
};
```

LISTING 15-20: Adding a listener to check the account change (AnotherAccountSample.cpp)

```
result
AnotherAccountSample::Initialize(void)
{
        result r = E_SUCCESS;

        __pAccountAccessor = AccountAccessor::GetInstance();
        r = __pAccountAccessor->SetEventListener(this);

        return r;
}
```

If the AccountSample application adds an account after the other application has registered its account event listener, then the `OnAccountAdded()` handler will be called in AnotherAccountSample.

Listing 15-21 shows how the account is added in AccountSample and as a result the account-added event handler is invoked in AnotherAccountSample.

LISTING 15-21: Adding an account (AccountSample.cpp)

```
result
AccountSample::AddAccount(Account& account)
{
        result r = E_SUCCESS;

        AccountManager* pAccountManager = AccountManager::GetInstance();
        r = pAccountManager->AddAccount(account);

        return r;
}
```

As shown in Listing 15-22, the `accountId` of the newly added account is passed as a parameter to `OnAccountAdded()`.

```
void
AnotherAccountSample::OnAccountAdded(AccountId accountId)
{
    // Check the account information for the account ID
    Account account = __pAccountAccessor->GetAccount(accountId);
}
```

> **NOTE** *For more information about adding accounts for an account service provider, see the AccountApp sample in the Tizen SDK.*

The Address Book

In this section you'll learn how to manage the address book on a Tizen device and the key classes in the `Tizen::Social` namespace that provide this functionality. You'll walk through sample code which shows you how to create an address book, manage contacts, and find contacts using a variety of search conditions.

Address Book Class Relationships

Before using the address book feature of `Tizen::Social`, it's helpful to understand the relationship between the various classes with which the address book interacts. Figure 15-5 shows the relationships between the address book, user profile, contact, category, and person.

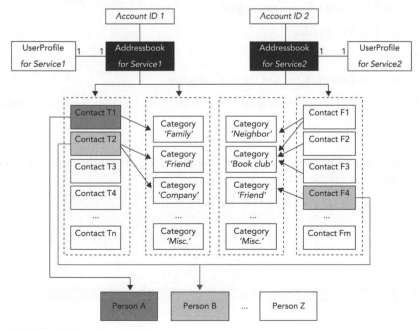

FIGURE 15-5

User Profile

The user profile contains the contact information for the owner of the address book. One address book will have one user profile. You can set the following user profile information and export the profile in vCard format:

- ➤ Name
- ➤ Thumbnail
- ➤ Nicknames
- ➤ E-mail addresses
- ➤ Instant message addresses
- ➤ Phone numbers
- ➤ Organisations
- ➤ Addresses
- ➤ URLs
- ➤ Events
- ➤ Relationships
- ➤ Notes

Address Book

The address book is a collection of contacts, and multiple address books can be created to contain contact information from service providers such as Google.

The address book enables the following tasks:

- ➤ Contact management
- ➤ Category management and assigning a contact to a category
- ➤ Contact searching with a specific condition such as the name, e-mail address, or phone number

Contact

The contact contains a collection of a person's contact information. Contacts can be imported from and exported to vCard format.

The following contact information is supported by the `Contact` class:

- ➤ Name
- ➤ Thumbnail
- ➤ Nicknames

➤ E-mail addresses

➤ Instant message addresses

➤ Phone numbers

➤ Organisations

➤ Addresses

➤ URLs

➤ Events

➤ Relationships

➤ Notes

Category

A category is a group of contacts, and users can supply the category name, a thumbnail, and a ringtone. Each category name must be unique within the address book that contains it, and contacts can belong to more than one category. Therefore, if you have a friend who also works in your company, he or she could be in both the Friend and Company categories.

Person

A person object is created at the same time as a contact is created and is an aggregation of one or more contacts associated with the same person. There is no way to add a person; it is created automatically. If you have many address books (from services, for example), then you may have contacts that exist in one or more address books, each containing slightly different information but all relating to the same person.

Figure 15-5 illustrates this concept. 'Contact T2' and 'ContactF4' are saved in different address books but are actually the same person. The Tizen platform handles this case by linking Person B to both 'Contact T2' and 'ContactF4'. Merging two or more contacts to one person is done automatically by the platform, but it can also be performed manually using `AddressbookManager::MergePersons()`.

Person information can be exported to vCard format and the following `Person` attributes can be set:

➤ Whether the person is a favourite

➤ Primary e-mail address

➤ Primary phone number

Creating an Address Book

An address book is created by passing the account ID and name to `AddressbookManager::CreateAddressbookN()`. If the address book is created successfully, an address book instance is returned with the address book ID set. The address book name must be unique and an address book can be used by multiple applications.

Listing 15-23 shows how to create an address book.

LISTING 15-23: Creating an address book (AddressbookSample.cpp)

```cpp
using namespace Tizen::Base;
using namespace Tizen::Social;

result
AddressbookSample::Initialize(void)
{
        result r = E_SUCCESS;

        if (__pAddressbookManager == null)
        {
                __pAddressbookManager = AddressbookManager::GetInstance();
                TryReturn(__pAddressbookManager != null, r = GetLastResult(), "[%s]",
                    GetErrorMessage(r));
        }
        return r;
}

void
AddressbookSample::CreateAddressbook(AccountId accountId)
{
        result r = E_SUCCESS;

        r = Initialize();

        String strAccountId(accountId);
        String accountName = strAccountId + L"address book";
        Addressbook* pAddressbook = __pAddressbookManager->CreateAddressbookN(accountId,
            accountName);
        r = GetLastResult();
        if (!IsFailed(r))
        {
            AppLog("The ID of the created address book is %d", pAddressbook->GetId());
        }
        else
        {
            AppLog("Addressbook is not created - [%s] exception", GetErrorMessage(r));
        }
}
```

Managing Contacts

Contacts are managed by the Addressbook and AddressbookManager. When the Address
bookManager is used to add a contact, the address book ID must be specified. After the contact is
added it will be assigned a unique record ID, which is then used to uniquely identify the contact. One
contact can be added to one or more categories, as illustrated by Listing 15-24.

LISTING 15-24: Adding and updating contacts (AddressbookSample.cpp)

```
result
AddressbookSample::AddContact(void)
{
        result r = E_SUCCESS;

        r = Initialize();
        Addressbook* pAddressbook = __pAddressbookManager->GetAddressbookN();

        Contact contact;
        r = contact.SetValue(CONTACT_PROPERTY_ID_FIRST_NAME, L"Emile");
        r = contact.SetValue(CONTACT_PROPERTY_ID_LAST_NAME, L"Johnson");
        PhoneNumber phoneNumber(PHONENUMBER_TYPE_MOBILE, L"0123456789");
        r = contact.AddPhoneNumber(phoneNumber);

        r = pAddressbook->AddContact(contact);

        Category category1;
        Category1.SetName(L"Friend");
        r = pAddressbook->AddCategory(category1);
        r = pAddressbook->AddMemberToCategory(category1.GetRecordId(),
           contact.GetRecordId());

        Category category2;
        Category2.SetName(L"Company");
        r = pAddressbook->AddCategory(category2);
        r = pAddressbook->AddMemberToCategory(category2.GetRecordId(),
           contact.GetRecordId());
        delete pAddressbook;

        return r;
}
```

Managing Categories

Managing categories is similar to managing contacts. The category can be added to a specific
address book, and a unique record ID is assigned. Both `Addressbook` and `AddressbookManager`
provide APIs to manage categories.

Merging Multiple Persons into One

If you find that two `Person` objects actually refer to the same person, you can merge them together.
The `AddressbookManager` provides the `MergePersons()` method, which takes a source person ID
and target person ID as parameters. If `MergePersons()` is successful, the person link for the contact
linked to the source person will be eliminated and a new link will be added from this contact to
the target person. At the same time, the source person will be removed because it no longer has a
contact linked to it. Listing 15-25 shows the use of `MergePersons()`.

LISTING 15-25: Merging Persons (AddressbookSample.cpp)

```
result
AddressbookSample::MergeContacts(Contact& sourceContact, Contact& targetContact)
{
        result r = E_SUCCESS;

        r = Initialize();
        r = __pAddressbookManager->MergePersons(sourceContact.GetPersonId(),
           targetContact.GetPersonId());

        return r;
}
```

Searching with Conditions

You can search for contacts in one address book by name, e-mail address, phone number, and category, as demonstrated by Listing 15-26.

LISTING 15-26: Searching contacts (AddressbookSample.cpp)

```
using namespace Tizen::Base;
using namespace Tizen::Base::Collection;
using namespace Tizen::Social;

result
AddressbookSample::SearchContacsInAddressbook(void)
{
        result r = E_SUCCESS;

        r = Initialize();
        Addressbook* pAddressbook = __pAddressbookManager->GetAddressbookN();
        IList* pContactList = pAddressbook->SearchContactsByNameN(L"Cooper");

        Contact* pContact = null;
        IEnumerator* pEnumerator = pContactList->GetEnumeratorN();
        while (pEnumerator->MoveNext())
        {
                pContact = static_cast<Contact*>(pEnumerator->GetCurrent());
                // Check values in the contact
        }
        delete pEnumerator;
        delete pContactList;
        delete pAddressbook;
        return r;
}

result
AddressbookSample::SearchContacsWithCategoryInAddressbook(void)
{
        result r = E_SUCCESS;

        r = Initialize();
```

```
        Addressbook* pAddressbook = __pAddressbookManager->GetAddressbookN();

        IList* pCategoryList = pAddressbook->GetAllCategoriesN();

        Category *pCategory = static_cast<Category*>(pCategoryList->GetAt(0));
        IList* pContactList = pAddressbook->GetContactsByCategoryN(
           pCategory->GetRecordId());

        Contact* pContact = null;
        IEnumerator* pEnumerator = pContactList->GetEnumeratorN();
        while (pEnumerator->MoveNext())
        {
              pContact = static_cast<Contact*>(pEnumerator->GetCurrent());
              // Check values in the contact
        }

        delete pEnumerator;
        delete pContactList;
        delete pCategoryList;
        delete pAddressbook;
        return r;
}
```

As shown in Listing 15-27, you can also search for all categories containing a specified contact.

LISTING 15-27: Searching categories (AddressbookSample.cpp)

```
result
AddressbookSample::SearchCategoriesWithContactInAddress(void)
{
        result r = E_SUCCESS;

        r = Initialize();
        Addressbook* pAddressbook = __pAddressbookManager->GetAddressbookN();
        IList* pContactList = pAddressbook->SearchContactsByNameN(L"Emile");

        Contact* pContact = static_cast<Contact*>(pContactList->GetAt(0));
        IList* pCategoryList = pAddressbook->GetCategoriesByContactN(
           pContact->GetRecordId());
        Category* pCategory = null;
        IEnumerator* pEnumerator = pContactList->GetEnumeratorN();
        while (pEnumerator->MoveNext())
        {
              pCategory = static_cast<Category*>(pEnumerator->GetCurrent());
              // Check the category
        }

        delete pEnumerator;
        delete pContactList;
        delete pCategoryList;
        delete pAddressbook;
        return r;
}
```

If you want to search for contacts in multiple address books, you can use the search methods provided by the AddressbookManager class. In addition to the search conditions demonstrated in the preceding code, the AddressBookManager class supports searching with an address book filter.

The address book filter enables complex searches to be made on the address book, contact, category, and person, as well as phone number contact and e-mail contact, which are data types designed to improve the search efficiency. The PhoneNumberContact and EmailContact classes provide summarized contact information.

Searching with the address book filter is performed using a combination of the following conditions:

➤ Conjunction operator — none, and, or. This is the operator used for the entire search filter. If the filter condition is appended first, the conjunction operator will be none.

➤ Value to search for and the value comparison operator to apply to this search. The available value comparison operators are listed in Table 15-2.

TABLE 15-2: Value Comparison Operators

FOR BOOL, INT, DOUBLE, OR DATETIME VALUE	FOR STRING VALUE
FI_CMP_OP_EQUAL	FI_STR_OP_EQUAL
FI_CMP_OP_LESS_THAN	FI_STR_OP_FULL_STRING
FI_CMP_OP_LESS_THAN_OR_EQUAL	FI_STR_OP_START_WITH
FI_CMP_OP_GREATER_THAN	FI_STR_OP_END_WITH
FI_CMP_OP_GREATER_THAN	FI_STR_OP_CONTAIN

Listing 15-28 shows how to search contacts with filters for the name and the category.

LISTING 15-28: Search with the address book filter (AddressbookSample.cpp)

```
result
AddressbookSample::SearchWithAddressbookFilter(void)
{
    result r = E_SUCCESS;

    r = Initialize();

    AddressbookFilter filter(AB_FI_TYPE_CONTACT);
    filter.AppendString(FI_CONJ_OP_NONE, CONTACT_FI_PR_DISPLAY_NAME,
        FI_STR_OP_CONTAIN, L"Emil");

    IList* pContactList = __pAddressbookManager->SearchN(filter,
        CONTACT_FI_PR_DISPLAY_NAME, SORT_ORDER_ASCENDING);
    // Check contacts

    return r;
}
```

> **NOTE** *The* AddressbookManager *class provides the* SearchPersonsN() *method to search for persons containing a specified keyword. The result is a list of Persons ordered by display name.*

Handling Changes to Contacts and Categories

If you share an address book with other applications and need to be notified of any changes, then you need to implement the IAddressbookChangeEventListener to receive an event when contacts or categories are changed by another application.

Listings 15-29 and 15-30 show how to set up the listener to be notified of changes to contacts and categories in the default address book.

LISTING 15-29: Declaration of a listener for the address book change (AnotherAddressbookSample.h)

```cpp
#include <FBase.h>
#include <FSocial.h>

class AnotherAddressbookSample
        : Tizen::Social::IAddressbookChangeEventListener
{
public:
        result Initialze(void);
        void CheckAddressbookVersion(void);

private:
        void OnCategoriesChanged(
            const Tizen::Base::Collection::IList &categoryChangeInfoList);
        void OnContactsChanged(
            const Tizen::Base::Collection::IList &contactChangeInfoList);

private:
        int __addressbookVersion;
        Tizen::Social::Addressbook* __pDefaultAddressbook;
};
```

LISTING 15-30: Setting a listener for the address book change (AnotherAddressbookSample.cpp)

```cpp
result
AnotherAddressbookSample::Initialze(void)
{
        result r = E_SUCCESS;

        __pDefaultAddressbook = AddressbookManager::GetInstance()->GetAddressbookN();
        __addressbookVersion = __pDefaultAddressbook->GetLatestVersion();
        r = __pDefaultAddressbook->SetAddressbookChangeEventListener(this);

        return r;
}
```

When the `OnCategoriesChanged()` or `OnContactsChanged()` event handlers are called, check the address book version and process the list of changed categories or contacts as appropriate (see Listing 15-31).

LISTING 15-31: Checking the address book change (AnotherAddressbookSample.cpp)

```cpp
void
AnotherAddressbookSample::OnCategoriesChanged(const IList &categoryChangeInfoList)
{
    CheckAddressbookVersion();
    IEnumerator* pEnum = categoryChangeInfoList.GetEnumeratorN();
    Category* pCategory = null;
    while (pEnum->MoveNext())
    {
        pCategoryChangeInfo = static_cast<CategoryChangeInfo*>(pEnum->GetCurrent());
        Category* pCategory = __pDefaultAddresbook->GetCategoryN(
            pCategoryChangeInfo ->GetCategoryId());
        //Do something
    }
    delete pEnum;
}

void
AnotherAddressbookSample::OnContactsChanged(const IList &contactChangeInfoList)
{
    CheckAddressbookVersion();
    IEnumerator* pEnum = contactChangeInfoList.GetEnumeratorN();
    Contact* pContact = null;
    while (pEnum->MoveNext())
    {
        pContactChangeInfo = static_cast<ContactChangeInfo*>(pEnum->GetCurrent());
        Contact* pContact = __pDefaultAddresbook->GetContactN(
            pContactChangeInfo ->GetContactId());
        //Do something
    }
    delete pEnum;
}
```

The Calendar Book

The `Calendarbook` class manages calendar data, including events, tasks, and one or more calendars. `Tizen` provides default calendars for events and tasks, but developers can create their own calendars to provide support for services such as Google, or for their own applications. The last part of this chapter provides you with the code to create calendars and manage events and tasks, as well as build complex searches for calendar events.

Calendar Book Class Relationships

To use the calendar book feature, it is important to understand the relationships between the important calendar book-related classes. Figure 15-6 shows their relationships.

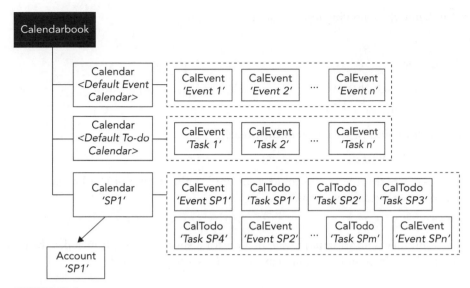

FIGURE 15-6

Calendar Book

The `Calendarbook` is a collection of one or more calendars. When a calendar is successfully created, it is assigned a calendar ID which is used to uniquely identify the calendar and to update or remove the calendar and to add events and tasks (also referred to as to-dos).

Searching with the calendar book filter enables you to build a complex search for all kinds of data for calendars, events, and tasks.

`Calendarbook` can import and export `CalEvents` or `CalTodos` in vCalendar 2.0 format.

Calendar

Application developers can use the default event or task calendars but usually a separate calendar is required for specific service providers and this will be linked to the account ID.

As it inherits Record, the calendar ID is actually the record ID which is assigned when it is added to the calendar book.

The calendar can be typed as event only, to-do only, or a mixed type, which contains both events and to-dos. The calendar type is set in the default constructor and cannot be changed after the calendar has been created.

Calendar Event

The calendar event is information which defines a specific appointment or meeting at a specific time for a specified duration. You can also set up recurring events.

Calendar events can define the following information:

➤ Subject

➤ Start and end time

➤ Priority (low, normal, high)

➤ Recurrence information

  ➤ Frequency — Daily, weekly, monthly, yearly.

  ➤ Count — Number of times the event should recur.

  ➤ Until — Date that the event should recur until. Either Count or Until must be specified for a recurring event.

➤ Reminders

  The reminder is information to set an alert for a specified time. It includes the time and path to the sound file to be played when the time is reached.

➤ Attendees

  The calendar event can also include attendees. The attendee must include the e-mail address. You can also define the name, phone number, role, or attendee status (not postponed, accepted, declined, tentative).

➤ Description

➤ All-day flag

➤ Location name and coordinates

➤ Event status (none, confirmed, cancelled, tentative)

➤ Busy status (free, busy, unavailable, tentative)

➤ Sensitive (public, private, confidential)

➤ Global unique ID for vCalendar

Calendar To-Do

The calendar to-do is designed to encapsulate tasks and can include the following information.

➤ Subject

➤ Start and due date

➤ Priority (low, normal, high)

➤ Reminders

➤ Description

➤ Status (none, needs action, completed, in progress, cancelled)

➤ Location name and coordinates

➤ Sensitivity (public, private, confidential)

Adding Calendars

To create a calendar, set the calendar item type to event, to-do, or both, as shown in Listings 15-32 and 15-33.

LISTING 15-32: Declaration for the calendar book (CalendarbookSample.h)

```cpp
#include <FBase.h>
#include <FSocial.h>

class CalendarbookSample
{
public:
        CalendarbookSample();
        result Initialize(void);
        result AddCalendar(void);

private:
        Tizen::Social::Calendarbook* __pCalendarbook;
        Tizen::Social::Calendar __myCalendar;
};
```

LISTING 15-33: Creating the Calendarbook instance (CalendarbookSample.cpp)

```cpp
#include "CalendarbookSample.h"

using namespace Tizen::Base;
using namespace Tizen::Base::Collection;
using namespace Tizen::Social;

CalendarbookSample::CalendarbookSample()
        : __pCalendarbook(null), __myCalendar(CALENDAR_ITEM_TYPE_EVENT_AND_TODO)
{
}
result
CalendarbookSample::Initialize(void)
{
        result r = E_SUCCESS;

        if (__pCalendarbook == null)
        {
                __pCalendarbook = new (std::nothrow) Calendarbook();
                r = __pCalendarbook->Construct();
        }

        return r;
}
```

After constructing the calendar book, add the calendar and specify the account ID of the account to which it is linked (see Listing 15-34).

LISTING 15-34: Adding a calendar book (CalendarbookSample.cpp)

```
result
CalendarbookSample::AddCalendar(void)
{
        result r = E_SUCCESS;

        r = Initialize();

        IList* pAccountList = AccountAccessor::GetInstance()->GetAllAccountsN();
        IEnumerator* pIEnum = pAccountList->GetEnumeratorN();
        AccountId accountId;
        while (pIEnum->MoveNext() == E_SUCCESS)
        {
                Account* pAccount = static_cast<Account*>(pIEnum->GetCurrent());
                String providerName = pAccount->GetAccountProvider().GetDisplayName();
                if (providerName == L"My Service")
                {
                        accountId = pAccount->GetId();
                }
        }

        __myCalendar.SetName(L"My Calendar");
        r = __pCalendarbook->AddCalendar(__myCalendar, accountId);

        return r;
}
```

Once the calendar has been added successfully, its ID is assigned and can be retrieved with `Calendar::GetRecordId()`. All calendars in the calendar book can be retrieved by calling `Calendarbook::GetAllCalendarsN()`.

Handling Calendar Events

Many types of events can be added to the calendar, such as business meetings, appointments, monthly meetings with a friend, and family birthdays. A simple event can be added with just a subject and a start and end date, but you can also create more complex events with recurrence and reminder options.

To create an all-day event, set the difference between the start and end times to be one day. Listing 15-35 shows how to add a birthday event to My Calendar. The start time and end time is set in UTC time and the event is set to recur once a year for 100 years.

LISTING 15-35: Adding a birthday event (CalendarbookSample.cpp)

```cpp
#include <FLocales.h>
#include "CalendarbookSample.h"

using namespace Tizen::Locales;
using namespace Tizen::Social;

result
CalendarbookSample::AddCalendarEvent(void)
{
        result r = E_SUCCESS;

        r = AddCalendar();

        CalEvent birthdayEvent;
        r = birthdayEvent.SetSubject(L"Eric's Birthday");

        LocaleManager localeManager;
        r = localeManager.Construct();
        TimeZone timeZone = localeManager.GetSystemTimeZone();

        DateTime startWallDateTime, startUtcDateTime;
        DateTime endWallDateTime, endUtcDateTime;
        r = startWallDateTime.SetValue(1977, 2, 7);
        r = endWallDateTime.SetValue(1977, 2, 8);
        startUtcDateTime = timeZone.WallTimeToUtcTime(startWallDateTime);
        endUtcDateTime = timeZone.WallTimeToUtcTime(endWallDateTime);
        r = birthdayEvent.SetStartAndEndTime(startUtcDateTime, endUtcDateTime);

        birthdayEvent.SetAllDayEvent(true);

        Recurrence recur1;
        recur1.SetFrequency(FREQ_YEARLY);
        r = recur1.SetCounts(100);
        r = birthdayEvent.SetRecurrence(&recur1);

        r = __pCalendarbook->AddEvent(birthdayEvent, __myCalendar.GetRecordId());
```

Listing 15-36 adds a meeting event which occurs once a week, on a Wednesday, for five weeks.

LISTING 15-36: Adding a recursive meeting event (CalendarbookSample.cpp)

```cpp
        CalEvent meetingEvent;
        r = startWallDateTime.SetValue(2014, 3, 5, 9);
        r = endWallDateTime.SetValue(2014, 3, 5, 11);
        startUtcDateTime = timeZone.WallTimeToUtcTime(startWallDateTime);
        endUtcDateTime = timeZone.WallTimeToUtcTime(endWallDateTime);

        r = meetingEvent.SetStartAndEndTime(startUtcDateTime, endUtcDateTime);

        Recurrence recur2;
```

continues

LISTING 15-36 *(continued)*

```
        recur2.SetFrequency(FREQ_WEEKLY);
        recur2.SetDayOfWeek(CAL_WEDNESDAY);
        r = recur2.SetCounts(5);
        r = meetingEvent.SetRecurrence(&recur2);

        r = __pCalendarbook->AddEvent(meetingEvent, __myCalendar.GetRecordId());
        return r;
}
```

Events can be easily updated and removed. If a recurring event is set up, then each recurrence of the event will be a separate event instance. In the meeting event example, the event recurs five times, so there are five event instances. This means you can update a single event instance among all instances without updating the meeting event itself when the meeting schedule is changed. `CalEventInstance` is designed for this usage and you can update a single event instance with `CalendarBook::UpdateEventInstance()`.

Handling Calendar To-Dos

Whether you have to finish a marketing report, do your laundry, or buy groceries, these are all tasks which can be added to the to-do calendar managed by the `Calendarbook`.

Listing 15-37 shows how to set a reminder option for a `CalTodo` item.

LISTING 15-37: Adding a task (CalenderbookSample.cpp)

```
result
CalendarbookSample::AddCalendarTodo(void)
{
        result r = E_SUCCESS;

        r = AddCalendar();

        CalTodo calTodo;
        r = calTodo.SetSubject("Marketing report!");

        LocaleManager localeManager;
        r = localeManager.Construct();
        TimeZone timeZone = localeManager.GetSystemTimeZone();

        DateTime startWallDateTime, startUtcDateTime;
        DateTime dueWallDateTime, dueUtcDateTime;
        r = startWallDateTime.SetValue(2014, 3, 5, 9);
        r = dueWallDateTime.SetValue(2014, 3, 7, 9);
        startUtcDateTime = timeZone.WallTimeToUtcTime(startWallDateTime);
        dueUtcDateTime = timeZone.WallTimeToUtcTime(dueWallDateTime);

        calTodo.SetStartDate(startUtcDateTime);
        calTodo.SetDueDate(dueUtcDateTime);

        calTodo.SetPriority(TODO_PRIORITY_HIGH);
```

```
calTodo.SetStatus(TODO_STATUS_IN_PROCESS);

Reminder reminder;
DateTime absoluteWallDateTime, absoluteUtcDateTime;
r = absoluteWallDateTime.SetValue(2014, 3, 6, 11);
absoluteUtcDateTime = timeZone.WallTimeToUtcTime(absoluteWallDateTime);
r = reminder.SetAbsoluteTime(absoluteUtcDateTime);

r = calTodo.AddReminder(reminder);

r = __pCalendarbook->AddTodo(calTodo, __myCalendar.GetRecordId());

return r;
}
```

Calendar Book Search

As with the address book search, the calendar book can be searched using a calendar book filter. The following filter types are available:

➤ Event

➤ To-do

➤ Calendar

➤ All-day event instance

➤ Non all-day event instance

Multiple search conditions can be appended with the conjunctive operator, filter property for each filter type, comparison operator, and the value to search for. The search result list returns objects of the same type as the filter type. If you set the filter type as CB_FI_TYPE_EVENT, the search result will be a list of CalEvent objects.

Listing 15-38 shows how to put that all together into a search for events in all calendars whose subject contains "meeting".

LISTING 15-38: Searching the meeting event with the filter (CalendarbookSample.cpp)

```
result
CalendarbookSample::SearchCalendarbook(void)
{
    result r = E_SUCCESS;

    r = AddCalendar();

    CalendarbookFilter filter1(CB_FI_TYPE_EVENT);
    filter1.AppendInt(FI_CONJ_OP_NONE, EVENT_FI_PR_CALENDAR_ID, FI_CMP_OP_EQUAL,
        __myCalendar.GetRecordId());

    CalendarbookFilter filter2(CB_FI_TYPE_EVENT);
```

continues

LISTING 15-38 *(continued)*

```
        filter2.AppendString(FI_CONJ_OP_AND, EVENT_FI_PR_SUBJECT, FI_STR_OP_CONTAIN,
            L"meeting");
        filter1.AppendFilter(FI_CONJ_OP_NONE, filter2);

        IList* pEventList = __pCalendarbook->SearchN(filter1, EVENT_FI_PR_PRIORITY,
            SORT_ORDER_ASCENDING);

        return r;
}
```

SUMMARY

This chapter covered a lot of ground, but working through the code should provide you with a lot of inspiration for creating your own applications that use Tizen's location and social features. You can now write code to find and monitor the user's location, be notified if they move in or out of a particular region, or travel a certain distance. If you're writing any kind of location-aware application, the information presented here should give you a good start.

Most of the examples in the chapter focused on the `Social` namespace and contacts and calendars. The `Social` namespace provides you with all the tools you need to work with multiple address books, set up accounts with service providers, and handle multiple calendars. If you're writing a more traditional personal information management (PIM) application, the `Social` namespace contains everything you need to manage contacts, events, and tasks.

16

Advanced UI and Graphics

WHAT'S IN THIS CHAPTER?

➤ Animating UI controls

➤ Managing application screens

➤ Drawing shapes on the screen

➤ Recognising faces and speech

➤ Using sensors

This chapter describes advanced UI features which can enhance the way your application interacts with users. You'll learn about animations, see how the Tizen scene manager makes it easy to keep track of transitions between screens, and learn how to get the most out of 2D drawing on a canvas. Everything is demonstrated with sample code, ready for you to use in your own applications.

The Uix namespace contains the features which will make your application stand out from the rest. You can create augmented reality applications with the image recognition feature, take advantage of face recognition, and find new ways to work with the many sensors Tizen supports, including the accelerometer and the gyroscope. You'll find code demonstrating all of these features in this chapter, together with speech recognition and text-to-speech.

ADVANCED UIs

In this section you discover how to add animation effects to UI controls and learn about visual elements, the scene manager, and 2D graphics.

Animations

Animation is an effect that shows sequential frames in quick succession to give the illusion of movement. In the Tizen native framework, animations can contain key frames, which have a time, position, and alpha value setting. Interpolator frames are generated between these key frames to create a smooth animation of a target object. You'll be familiar with key frames if you've used animation or video editing applications. The important animation terms that are used in this chapter are shown in Figure 16-1.

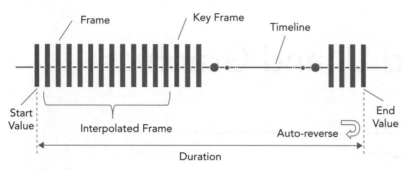

FIGURE 16-1

The `Tizen::Ui::Animations` namespace provides animation effects for objects such as images and UI controls. Its animation functions calculate the position of a target object based on interpolation to generate interpolator frames.

Figure 16-2 shows an animation containing three key frames with position and time information, between which interpolator frames have been generated. Notice how the position of the target object has been calculated in each frame, based on the position setting and time of each key frame.

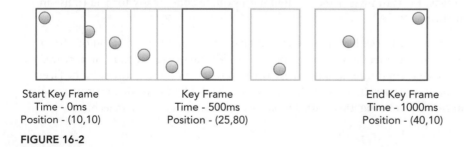

FIGURE 16-2

Animating Images

The `Tizen::Ui::Controls::Animation` class displays a sequence of still images one by one, for a predefined time in a specified area. The `Constructor()` of the class takes an `ArrayList` of `Tizen::Ui::Controls::AnimationFrame` objects. Each `AnimationFrame` contains an instance of a `Tizen::Graphics::Bitmap` and a duration — the time, in milliseconds, for which it will be displayed.

First you need to implement `IAnimationEventListener` and define an `ArrayList` to contain `AnimationFrame` instances:

```
class AnimationExample
: public Tizen::Ui::Controls::Form
    , public Tizen::Ui::IAnimationEventListener
{
    …

    // IAnimationEventListener
    virtual void OnAnimationStopped(const Tizen::Ui::Control& source) {}
    …
private :
    Tizen::Base::Collection::ArrayList __animationFrameList;
};
```

Load each image into an instance of `Bitmap`. This example loads four images from the application's resource directory (`res`):

```
AppResource *pAppResource = Application::GetInstance()->GetAppResource();
Bitmap* pBitmap1 = pAppResource->GetBitmapN(L"still1.png");
Bitmap* pBitmap2 = pAppResource->GetBitmapN(L"still2.png");
Bitmap* pBitmap3 = pAppResource->GetBitmapN(L"still3.png");
Bitmap* pBitmap4 = pAppResource->GetBitmapN(L"still4.png");
```

Assign each image to an `AnimationFrame` together with a duration; in this case each frame will be displayed for one second. If you want to use the same image multiple times, create a separate frame:

```
AnimationFrame* pAniFrame1 = new AnimationFrame(*pBitmap1, 1000);
AnimationFrame* pAniFrame2 = new AnimationFrame(*pBitmap2, 1000);
AnimationFrame* pAniFrame3 = new AnimationFrame(*pBitmap3, 1000);
AnimationFrame* pAniFrame4 = new AnimationFrame(*pBitmap4, 1000);
// pBitmap2 is reused for the 5th frame.
AnimationFrame* pAniFrame5 = new AnimationFrame(*pBitmap2, 1000);
```

Create an `ArrayList` and add frames to it. Frames will be displayed in the order in which they appear in the list. Don't forget to deallocate the bitmap images when you have finished with the animation:

```
__animationFrameList.Construct(SingleObjectDeleter);
__animationFrameList.Add(*pAniFrame1);
__animationFrameList.Add(*pAniFrame2);
__animationFrameList.Add(*pAniFrame3);
__animationFrameList.Add(*pAniFrame4);
__animationFrameList.Add(*pAniFrame5);

delete pBitmap1;
delete pBitmap2;
delete pBitmap3;
delete pBitmap4;
```

Create an instance of `Animation`. In `Construct()`, define the animation area:

```
// Creates an instance of Animation
Animation* pAnimation = new Animation();
```

```
Rectangle rect = Rectangle((GetClientAreaBounds().width - pBitmap1->GetWidth()) / 2,
                    100, pBitmap1->GetWidth(), pBitmap1->GetHeight());
pAnimation->Construct(rect, __animationFrameList);
```

Set the repeat count for the animation, add the `Tizen::Ui::IAnimationEventListener` interface to listen for animation stop events, and add the instance of `Animation` to the form:

```
pAnimation->SetRepeatCount(100);
pAnimation->AddAnimationEventListener(*this);

// Adds the animation to the form
AddControl(pAnimation);
```

To play the animation, call `Play()`. Pause and stop the animation by calling `Pause()` and `Stop()`, respectively:

```
// Plays the animation
pAnimation->Play();
```

Animating UI Controls

You can animate the size, position, rotation, and alpha properties of UI controls. A developer should manage the size of child controls when the parent's size is changed by an animation effect. However, child controls and their contents will be changed along with the parent when an animation changes the parent's rotation, position, or alpha properties.

The `Tizen::Ui::Animations::ControlAnimator` class provides methods to apply animations to UI controls. All UI controls are derived from the `UI::Controls` class, which includes the `GetControlAnimator()` method that returns an instance of a `ControlAnimator`:

```
ControlAnimator* pControlAnimator = pMyControl->GetControlAnimator();
```

To use the retrieved `ControlAnimator` instance, you need to create the appropriate animation class to generate values of `Integer`, `Float`, `Point`, `Dimension`, or `Rectangle` for the animation:

➤   `Tizen::Ui::Animations::IntegerAnimation`

➤   `Tizen::Ui::Animations::FloatAnimation`

➤   `Tizen::Ui::Animations::PointAnimation`

➤   `Tizen::Ui::Animations::DimensionAnimation`

➤   `Tizen::Ui::Animations::RectangleAnimation`

➤   `Tizen::Ui::Animations::RotateAnimation`

Each of these classes animates an object between start and end values, based on the specified interpolator type. The `RotateAnimation` class also generates `Float`-type values to represent angles:

```
// Creates animation for Point data type
PointAnimation pointAnimation(pMyControl->GetPosition(),
                              Point(100,100),
                              2000,
                              ANIMATION_INTERPOLATOR_LINEAR);

// Creates animation for Float data type
FloatAnimation floatAnimation(0.2, 1.0, 0.25, ANIMATION_INTERPOLATOR_EASE_IN);
```

```
// Creates animation for Dimension data type
DimensionAnimation dimensionAnimation(Dimension(100, 100), Dimension(600, 600), 3000,
                    ANIMATION_INTERPOLATOR_EASE_OUT);
```

The animation can be started by the `Tizen::Ui::Animations::ControlAnimator::StartUser Animation()` method:

```
// Start animation with position property
pControlAnimator->StartUserAnimation(ANIMATION_TARGET_POSITION, pointAnimation);
// Start animation with alpha property
pControlAnimator->StartUserAnimation(ANIMATION_TARGET_ALPHA, floatAnimation);
// Start animation with size property
pControlAnimator->StartUserAnimation(ANIMATION_TARGET_SIZE, dimensionAnimation);
```

Or you can apply multiple animations, which are added to the `Tizen::Ui::Animations::AnimationGroup` before the control animator is started. To apply multiple animations simultaneously, add them to a `ParallelAnimationGroup`; or to apply the animations consecutively, use a `SequentialAnimationGroup`.

In the following example the animations are applied simultaneously:

```
ParallelAnimationGroup aniGroup;
aniGroup.AddAnimation(ANIMATION_TARGET_POSITION, pointAnimation);
aniGroup.AddAnimation(ANIMATION_TARGET_ALPHA, floatAnimation);
aniGroup.AddAnimation(ANIMATION_TARGET_SIZE, dimensionAnimation);
```

You can start the animation with the animation group using the following code:

```
pControlAnimator->StartUserAnimation(aniGroup);
```

Figure 16-3 shows the resulting animation.

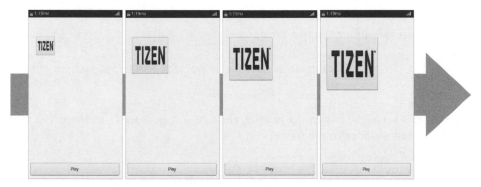

FIGURE 16-3

What we just did is termed *explicit animation triggering*. Explicit triggering starts an animation by calling `ControlAnimator::StartUserAnimation()`. To trigger an animation implicitly, a trigger point must be set. For UI controls, the trigger point is changing the control's size, location, or state. For example, the following code snippet triggers the animation when the control's show state property is changed:

```
pControlAnimator->SetAnimation(ANIMATION_TRIGGER_SHOW_STATE_CHANGE, &aniGroup);
```

Animating a Form Transition

The `Tizen::Ui::Animations::FrameAnimator` class provides methods to apply animations to form transitions, and it works in a similar way to the `ControlAnimator` for UI control animation.

An instance of `FrameAnimator` can be obtained by calling `Frame::GetFrameAnimator()`:

```
FrameAnimator* pFrameAnimator = pMyForm->GetFrameAnimator();
```

`FrameAnimator::SetFormTransitionAnimation()` sets the transition animation effect by specifying the animation type. The `FrameAnimator` provides seven types of form transition animation types which are set using the `FrameAnimatorFormTransitionAnimation` enum. The available animation types include left/right translation, fade in/fade out, zoom in/zoom out, and depth in/depth out. A form transition animation is shown in Figure 16-4.

FIGURE 16-4

Here's how to set a fade-in transition type to a form:

```
pFrameAnimator->SetFormTransitionAnimation(
                    FRAME_ANIMATOR_FORM_TRANSITION_ANIMATION_FADE_IN_OUT,
                    500,
                    ANIMATION_INTERPOLATOR_LINEAR);
```

A transition target form is set as the current form using the `SetCurrentForm()` method. The target form must be constructed and added to the frame.

```
pFrameAnimator->SetCurrentForm(targetForm);
```

When we called `SetFormTransitionAnimation()` earlier, one of the parameters was an interpolator. An interpolator defines the rate at which an animation changes in the given environment. Interpolators can generate various acceleration effects in an animation, and applications can use any of these interpolators to control the speed at which the key values change.

Tizen supports the following interpolators, each of which is listed together with the corresponding rate at which the key value changes:

➤ `ANIMATION_INTERPOLATOR_LINEAR` — Consistent throughout the animation

➤ `ANIMATION_INTERPOLATOR_DISCRETE` — Changes from one value to the next without interpolation

➤ `ANIMATION_INTERPOLATOR_EASE_IN` — Slow at the beginning and increases dramatically

➤ `ANIMATION_INTERPOLATOR_EASE_OUT` — Normal at the beginning and decreases until the end

➤ `ANIMATION_INTERPOLATOR_EASE_IN_OUT` — Like the ease-in interpolator until halfway through the animation and then changes to the ease-out interpolator until the end

➤ `ANIMATION_INTERPOLATOR_BEZIER` — Follows a Bézier curve based on custom points specified using `SetBezierControlPoints()`

Figure 16-5 shows the supported interpolators and the rate at which the key values change.

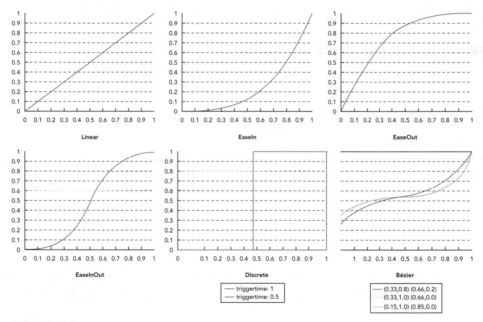

FIGURE 16-5

Animation with Visual Elements

A visual element is a conceptual 2D rectangular model for animation and composition. The `Tizen::Ui::Animations::VisualElement` class is the foundation of all displayable UI objects, such as UI controls, in the Tizen native framework. As shown in Figure 16-6, each UI control is built upon a `VisualElement`, which has properties such as bounds, transform, and opacity. The `VisualElement` is used for the control's animations and content, and a new `VisualElement` instance is created for each control.

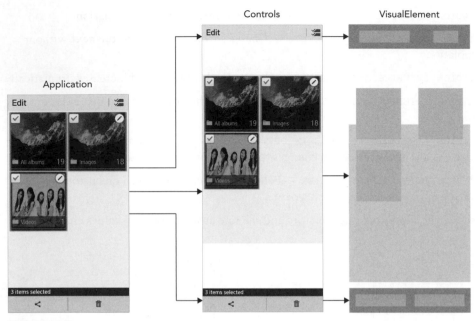

FIGURE 16-6

Visual elements provide the following features:

➤ Clipping

➤ Z-order (the display order)

➤ Hit-testing

➤ Surface

➤ Configurable display properties

➤ Animation

Clipping restricts drawing to the areas of a child element that are overlapped by its parent area, as shown in Figure 16-7. You can enable clipping by calling the SetClipChildrenEnabled() method of the VisualElement class.

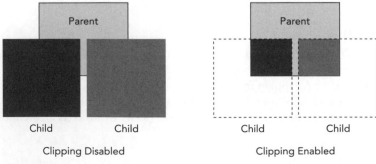

FIGURE 16-7

The Z-order, or display order, of overlapping visual elements can be specified by using SetZOrderGroup():

```
pPopup->SetZOrderGroup(WINDOW_Z_ORDER_GROUP_HIGHEST);
```

As shown in Figure 16-8, the visual element Z-order has three groups, Z_ORDER_GROUP_LOWEST, Z_ORDER_GROUP_NORMAL, and Z_ORDER_GROUP_HIGHEST, corresponding to the values of -1,000, 0, and 1,000, respectively. You can also set an integer value of between -1,000 and 1,000 to set the Z-order:

```
// between the normal and highest
pPopup->SetZOrderGroup(200);
```

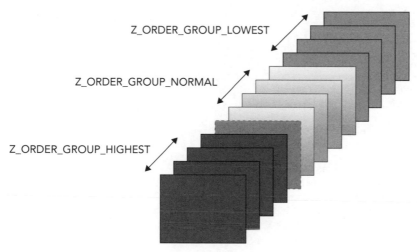

FIGURE 16-8

The Hit-testing feature finds and returns a VisualElement instance at a specific point. To identify which visual element on the screen is hit when a touch or a key event occurs, use the GetChildAt() method:

```
VisualElement* pTarget = __pVisualElement->GetChildAt(
                           FloatPoint(currentPosition.x, currentPosition.y));
```

The visual element surface is similar to a canvas that has bitmap data to be displayed directly on screen. A surface object can be shared between several visual elements, as shown in the following code:

```
VisualElement original;
VisualElement shared;

VisualElementSurface* pSurface = original.GetSurfaceN();
shared.SetSurface(pSurface);
```

The properties of a visual element include the following:

➤ Coordinates — Bounds, transform matrix, children transform matrix.

➤ Contents — Content bounds, clipping, opacity, show state.

➤ Custom properties — You can define font color, font size, and so on, by inheriting the `VisualElement` class.

You can manipulate these properties to display a visual element and apply animations to it using `AddAnimation()` and `RemoveAnimation()`. The following example creates a rectangular visual element and adds an animation that changes its opacity:

```
Tizen::Ui::Animations::VisualElement* pRectVe = new VisualElement;
float  startOpacity, endOpacity;
startOpacity = 1.0f;
endOpacity = 0.0f;

pRectVe->.Construct();
pRectVe->.SetName(L"Opacity");
pRectVe->.SetBounds(FloatRectangle(100.f, 100.f, 200.f, 200.f));
pRectVe->.SetShowState(true);
pRectVe->.SetImplicitAnimationEnabled(false);

// attaches this visual element to the current form
pForm->GetVisualElement()->AttachChild(pRectVe);

// gets a canvas from the visual element
pCanvas = rectVe.GetCanvasN();
pCanvas->FillRectangle(Color::GetColor(COLOR_ID_GREY),
                    FloatRectangle(100.f, 100.f, 200.f, 100.f));
delete pCanvas;

// creates animation for opacity
pAnimation = new (std::nothrow) VisualElementPropertyAnimation();
pAnimation->SetPropertyName(L"opacity");
pAnimation->SetStartValue(Variant(startOpacity));
pAnimation->SetEndValue(Variant(endOpacity));
pAnimation->SetDuration(2000);


// adds animation to the visual element.
rectVe.AddAnimation(L"opacity", *pAnimation);
delete pAnimation;
pAnimation = null;
```

Instead of explicitly creating a `VisualElementPropertyAnimation`, you can just change properties with a prepared animation effect called *implicit animation*. It even sets the animation duration automatically:

```
rectVe.SetImplicitAnimationEnabled(true);
rectVe.SetOpacity(0.5f);
rectVe.SetBounds(FloatRectangle(400.f, 400.f, 200.f, 200.f));
```

An animation transaction is used to create and manage a group of animations. If you want to set up an animation transaction and be notified of transaction events, use the `AnimationTransaction` class, as shown in the following code:

```
rectVe.SetImplicitAnimationEnabled(true);
// creates a transaction
AnimationTransaction::Begin();
AnimationTransaction::SetVisualElementAnimationDuration(2000);
rectVe.SetOpacity(0.5f);
rectVe.SetBounds(FloatRectangle(400.f, 400.f, 200.f, 200.f));
AnimationTransaction::SetTransactionEventListener(this);
AnimationTransaction::Commit();
```

To set an event listener, use the `SetTransactionEventListener()` method and implement the `IAnimationTransactionEventListener()` interface. The appropriate event handler will be called when the animation starts, stops, or finishes:

```
void
ListenerExample::OnAnimationTransactionFinished(int transactionId)
{
    // called when animation is finished.
}
```

Scene Management

You should manage the transitions between all the forms and panels in your application's UI screens. Managing UI switching is not trivial because most applications have many screens and it can be difficult to keep track of the path of screen transitions, as Figure 16-9 shows. The backward screen transition is one of the most common transitions that you'll have to manage.

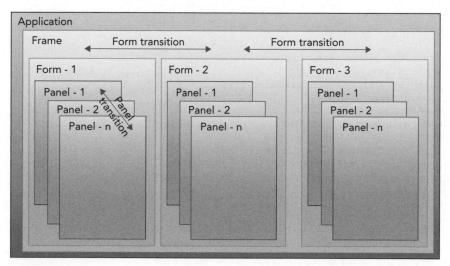

FIGURE 16-9

Tizen defines a UI screen that consists of a form or panels as a *scene* and provides scene management and navigation features to make UI switching easy.

Tizen scene management provides the following features:

➤ Jumping directly to a specific scene

➤ Going back to the previous scene

➤ Going forward to the next designated scene

Because a scene is a combination of a form and a panel, it contains a form ID and a panel ID. All scenes are registered and managed by a class called `Tizen::Ui::Scenes::SceneManager`. Before scene registration, you need to implement the `Tizen::Ui::Scenes::IFormFactory` and `Tizen::Ui::Scenes::IPanelFactory` interfaces to create appropriate forms and panels with a specified form ID and panel ID, respectively:

```
class FormFactory
    : public Tizen::Ui::Scenes::IFormFactory
…

Tizen::Ui::Controls::Form*
FormFactory::CreateFormN(const Tizen::Base::String& formId, const
                         Tizen::Ui::Scenes::SceneId& sceneId)
{
    Tizen::Ui::Controls::Form* pNewForm = null;
    SceneManager* pSceneManager = SceneManager::GetInstance();
    AppAssert(pSceneManager);

    if (formId == "InitialForm")
    {
        InitialForm* pForm = new (std::nothrow) InitialForm ();
        pForm->Initialize();
        pNewForm = pForm;
    }
    else if (formId == "MainForm")
    {
        MainForm* pForm = new (std::nothrow) MainForm();
        pForm->Initialize();
        pSceneManager->AddSceneEventListener(sceneId, *pForm);
        pNewForm = pForm;
    }
    else if (formId == "DetailForm")
    {
        DetailForm * pForm = new (std::nothrow) DetailForm();
        pForm->Initialize();
        pSceneManager->AddSceneEventListener(sceneId, *pForm);
        pNewForm = pForm;
    }

    return pNewForm;
}
```

If required, implement the `Tizen::Ui::Scenes::IPanelFactory` interface and create a panel with the specified panel ID parameter using the `CreatePanelN()` method:

```
class PanelFactory
   : public Tizen::Ui::Scenes::IPanelFactory

…

Tizen::Ui::Controls::Panel*
PanelFactory::CreatePanelN(const Tizen::Base::String& panelId, const
                           Tizen::Ui::Scenes::SceneId& sceneId)
{
   Panel* pNewPanel = null;
   SceneManager* pSceneManager = SceneManager::GetInstance();
   AppAssert(pSceneManager);

   if (panelId == GroupsPanel)
   {
      ClockPanel* pPanel = new (std::nothrow) ClockPanel();
      pNewPanel = pPanel;
   }
   else if (panelId == ContactsListPanel)
   {
      StopwatchPanel* pPanel = new (std::nothrow) StopwatchPanel();
      pNewPanel = pPanel;
   }
   else if (panelId == FavouritesListPanel)
   {
      TimerPanel* pPanel = new (std::nothrow) TimerPanel();
      pNewPanel = pPanel;
   }
   pNewPanel->Initialize();
   pSceneManager->AddSceneEventListener(sceneId, *pNewPanel);
   return pNewPanel;
}
```

The created form factory or panel factory object should be registered with the `SceneManager` instance:

```
SceneManager* pSceneManager = SceneManager::GetInstance();

static FormFactory myFormFactory;
static PanelFactory myPanelFactory;

pSceneManager->RegisterFormFactory(myFormFactory);
pSceneManager->RegisterPanelFactory(myPanelFactory);
```

Register all the scenes of your application with the scene manager using the `RegisterScene()` method. If the scene consists only of a form and no panel, pass an empty string as a parameter:

```
pSceneManager->RegisterScene(L"InitialScene", L"InitialForm", L"");
pSceneManager->RegisterScene(L"MainContactsListScene",
                             L"MainForm", L"ContactsListPanel");
pSceneManager->RegisterScene(L"MainGroupsListScene", L"MainForm", L"GroupsPanel");
pSceneManager->RegisterScene(L"MainFavouritesListScene",
                             L"MainForm", L"FavouritesListPanel");
pSceneManager->RegisterScene(L"DetailScene", L"DetailForm", L"");
```

Use the `GoForward()` method to set the default scene to `"InitialScene"`:

```
pSceneManager->GoForward(ForwardSceneTransition(L"InitialScene"));
```

Call `GoBack()` to navigate to the previous scene:

```
pSceneManager->GoBackward(
            BackwardSceneTransition(SCENE_TRANSITION_ANIMATION_TYPE_RIGHT));
```

You can set a transition animation type and history option by passing an additional parameter:

```
pSceneManager->GoForward(ForwardSceneTransition(L"InitialScene",
                        SCENE_TRANSITION_ANIMATION_TYPE_LEFT,
                        SCENE_HISTORY_OPTION_NO_HISTORY));
```

Graphics

The Tizen `Graphics` namespace provides 2D and 3D graphics features. For 3D graphics, it includes OpenGL ES 1.1/2.0 (www.khronos.org/opengles) and EGL (www.khronos.org/registry/egl) features, which are industry standard APIs for embedded graphics. Because OpenGL ES and EGL are well-known cross-platform libraries, their features are not described in detail in this chapter, but you can find out more in the help documentation at Tizen Native App Programming ➪ Programming Guide ➪ Graphics: Rendering Primitives and Using OpenGL ➪ OpenGL.

Tizen 2D Graphics supports the following features:

- ➤ 32-bit color
    - ➤ ARGB 32-bit color manipulation
- ➤ Vector font
    - ➤ System font
    - ➤ Dynamic font loading
- ➤ Bitmap
    - ➤ 16-bit bitmap (masking color)
    - ➤ 32-bit bitmap (alpha channel)
- ➤ Drawing primitives
    - ➤ Point, line, rectangle, ellipse, polygon, text, bitmap
    - ➤ Canvas for rendering drawing primitives
- ➤ Direct buffer read/write

Drawing Shapes

2D graphics are drawn to a `Tizen::Graphics::Canvas`, an example of which is shown in Figure 16-10. The `Tizen::Ui::Control` class includes a `GetCanvasN()` method, which is used to retrieve a canvas for drawing, corresponding to the bounds of the control or a specified area within it.

FIGURE 16-10

The following code shows how to get a canvas instance from a control (e.g., a form or a frame) and draw shapes and text on it:

```
// gets a instance of Canvas
Tizen::Graphics::Canvas pCanvas = pControl->GetCanvasN();

// clears the canvas with white color
pCanvas->Clear(Tizen::Graphics::Color(255, 255, 255));

// sets foreground color
pCanvas->SetForegroundColor(Color::GetColor(COLOR_ID_GREEN));

// draws shapes
pCanvas->DrawEllipse(Tizen::Graphics::Rectangle(50, 50, 50, 80));
pCanvas->DrawLine(Tizen::Graphics::Point(100, 100), Tizen::Graphics::Point(150, 150));
pCanvas->DrawArc(Tizen::Graphics::Rectangle(10, 200, 50, 50), 30, 60, ARC_STYLE_PIE);
pCanvas->DrawRectangle(Tizen::Graphics::Rectangle(50, 50, 100, 100));

// creates and sets a font
Tizen::Graphics::Font font;
font.Construct(FONT_STYLE_PLAIN, 32);
pCanvas->SetFont(font);

// draws a text
pCanvas->DrawText(Tizen::Graphics::Point(50, 50), String(L"Hello World"));

// shows changes on screen
pControl->Invalidate(true);

// deletes canvas
delete pCanvas;
```

Accessing the Canvas Buffer

Instead of using the basic drawing functions of Tizen::Graphics, you can directly access the bitmap buffer of a canvas using Tizen::Graphics::BufferInfo. The Canvas::Lock(BufferInfo&) method locks the canvas for direct pixel access, and while the canvas is locked the data can be written. Canvas::Unlock() must be called when the operation is complete.

After getting a BufferInfo instance from the canvas, you know the width, height, pitch, bits per pixel, and color format of the canvas buffer. You access the buffer using BufferInfo::pPixels, which contains a pointer to the pixel bits.

First get a canvas and its buffer:

```
Canvas* pCanvas = GetCanvasN();
if (!pCanvas)
{
    return;
}

BufferInfo* pBuffer = new BufferInfo();
if (pBuffer == null)
```

```
    {
        delete pCanvas;
        pCanvas = null;
        return;
    }

    result r = pCanvas->Lock(*pBuffer);
    if (IsFailed(r))
    {
        return;
    }
```

Check the properties of the extracted `BufferInfo` instance:

```
AppLog("width %d, height %d, pitch %d, bits per pixel %d\n",
        pBuffer->width, pBuffer->height,
        pBuffer->pitch, pBuffer->bitsPerPixel);

PixelFormat format = pBuffer->pixelFormat;
if (format != PIXEL_FORMAT_ARGB8888)
{
    AppLog("Pixel Format is not ARGB8888\n");
    return;
}
```

Retrieve the `pPixels` pointer and draw a blue line on it:

```
byte* pPixels = (byte*) pBuffer->pPixels;

int bytesPerPixel = pBuffer->bitsPerPixel / 8;
pPixels = pPixels + 100 * pBuffer->pitch + 100 * bytesPerPixel;

// draw a line blue line
for (int i = 0; i < 200; i = i + bytesPerPixel)
{
    *pPixels++ = 255; // blue
    *pPixels++ = 0;   // green
    *pPixels++ = 0;   // red
    *pPixels++ = 255; // alpha
}
```

Clean everything up when you're done:

```
pCanvas->Unlock();
delete pCanvas;
pCanvas = null;

delete pBuffer;
pBuffer = null;
```

UI EXTENSIONS

The Tizen native framework includes vision, sensor, and speech-related features as UI extensions available to application developers in the `Tizen::Uix` namespace. `Tizen::Uix::Vision` provides access to vision recognition, tracking, and augmented reality features; `Tizen::Uix::Sensor` supports various physical/virtual sensors for user interaction; and `Tizen::Uix::Speech` provides text-to-speech and speech-to-text functionalities. This section shows you how to use all of these features, which offer a range of ways to interact with the user.

Vision

The `Tizen::Uix::Vision` namespace provides face, optical character, image, and QR code recognition. The following sections explain how to use these features.

Face Recognition

`Tizen::Uix::Vision::FaceDetector` detects multiple faces from a camera preview or video. `DetectFacesFromStillImageN()` detects faces from an image, while `DetectFacesFrom VideoStreamN()` detects faces from a video stream. Both of these methods take a `ByteBuffer` as input, containing either image or video data. The only difference between the two methods is the pixel format type of the byte buffer data:

```
// face detection from image data
const IList* pImageFaceDetectList = faceDetect.DetectFacesFromStillImageN(
                                      *pByteBuffer,
                                      Dimension(width,height),
                                      BITMAP_PIXEL_FORMAT_RGB565);

// face detection from video data
const IList* pImageFaceDetectList = faceDetect. DetectFacesFromVideoStreamN(
                                      *pByteBuffer,
                                      Dimension(width,height),
                                      PIXEL_FORMAT_ARGB8888);
```

The returned list contains pointers of `Tizen::Graphics::Rectangle` instances that identify the areas of the detected faces in the input area. You can limit the maximum number of faces to detect by calling the `FaceDetector::SetProperty()` method and passing `FACEDETECTOR_MAXNUMBER_FACES` as the property to set.

`Tizen::Uix::Vision::FaceRecognizer` extracts faces from an image or video and compares two faces to determine whether they are the same person. For example, the following code extracts one person from `pByteBuffer1` and compares it with the people in `pByteBuffer2`:

```
// extracts FaceRecognitionInfo list from the first image.
IList* pList1 = pFRecog->ExtractFaceInfoFromStillImageN(
                      *pByteBuffer1,
                      Dimension(width1, height1),
                      BITMAP_PIXEL_FORMAT_RGB565);

if (null != pList1)
{
    // suppose we have only one person in the image
    pFindThisGuy = (FaceRecognitionInfo*)pList1->GetAt(0);
}

// extracts FaceRecognitionInfo list from the second image
IList* pList2 = pFRecog->ExtractFaceInfoFromStillImageN(
```

```
                            *pByteBuffer2,
                            Dimension(width2, height2),
                            BITMAP_PIXEL_FORMAT_RGB565);

    for (int i = 0; i < pList2->GetCount(); i++)
    {
        FaceRecognitionInfo* pOneOfPeople = (FaceRecognitionInfo*) pList2->GetAt(i);

        if (pFRecog->IsMatching(*pOneOfPeople, *pFindThisGuy))
        {
            AppLog("I found the guy!\n");
        }
    }
}
```

Image Recognition

The image recognition functionality in Tizen works by extracting feature data from one or more images and using this data to detect objects and features in a still image or video.

In the following example, image1, image2, and image3 are files containing the objects that you want to recognise, and pByteBuffer contains an image captured from the camera. You'll use the image recognition feature to see if the objects contained in the three images files can be detected in the camera image.

To use the image recognition feature, you first need to create an image feature set from one or more images by using the Tizen::Uix::Vision::ImageFeatureManager class. This class generates feature data from each image and manages a set of the data:

```
ImageFeatureManager imageFeatureManager;
r = imageFeatureManager.Construct();

// generates feature data and adds to manager
String contentPath = Environment::GetPredefinedPath(PREDEFINED_DIRECTORY_IMAGES);
imageFeatureManager.AddFeature(contentPath + L"image1.jpg");
imageFeatureManager.AddFeature(contentPath + L"image2.jpg");
imageFeatureManager.AddFeature(contentPath + L"image3.jpg");

// saves the feature set as a file
r = imageFeatureManager.Flush(new String(contentPath + L"FeatureSet.xdb"));
// load the feature set
r = imageFeatureManager.Load(new String(contentPath + L"FeatureSet.xdb"));
```

To recognise images based on the generated feature data, construct an ImageRecognizer object and set the instance of FeatureManager to it:

```
// creates an image recognizer
ImageRecognizer imageRecognizer;
r = imageRecognizer.Construct();

// sets the feature manager
r imageRecognizer.SetFeatureManager(featureManager);

// sets image size
imageRecognizer.SetImageSize(imgWidth, imgHeight);
```

The `ProcessImage()` method processes a target image based on the feature data set and generates a list of recognized objects. Note that the target image should be in `PIXEL_FORMAT_YCbCr420_PLANAR` format. You can check the number of recognized objects by calling `GetRecognizedObjectCount()` and retrieve an `ImageObject` using `GetRecognizedObject()`, as shown in the following code:

```
// Processes the camera image
imageRecognizer.ProcessImage(*pByteBuffer);

// Loops through all recognized images
for (int i = 0; i < imageRecognizer.GetRecognizedObjectCount(); i++)
{
    const ImageObject *o = imageRecognizer.GetRecognizedObject(i);
    int featId = o->GetFeatureId();
}
```

QR Code Recognition

A Quick Response (QR) code is a type of two-dimensional barcode. QR codes can contain numeric, alphanumeric, byte, and binary information. Tizen recognises QR codes from image data and supports QR code versions from 1 to 10.

To use the QR code recognition feature, create a `QrCodeRecognizer` object and call `ProcessImage()`, passing the QR code image byte buffer as a parameter:

```
// creates an QR code recogniser
Tizen::Uix::Vision::QrCodeRecognizer qrRecognizer;
qrRecognizer.Construct();

// sets image size
qrRecognizer.SetImageSize(imgWidth, imgHeight);

// processes input images to recognize the QR code image
qrRecognizer.ProcessImage(*pByteBuffer);
```

The recognised objects in the target image are retrieved using `GetRecognizedObject()`, as the following code demonstrates:

```
// gets and reads the QR code
for (int i = 0; i < qrRecognizer.GetRecognizedObjectCount(); i++)
{
    const Tizen::Uix::Vision::QrCodeObject *qrObj = qrRecognizer.GetRecognizedObject(i);
    AppLog("ID %d, Version %d, %s\n", qrObj->GetId(),
                                      qrObj->GetVersion(),
                                      qrObj->GetText());

    QrCodeErrorCorrectionLevel qrCodeEcLevel = qrObj->GetErrorCorrectionLevel();

    switch(qrCodeEcLevel)
    {
    case QR_CODE_ERROR_CORRECTION_LEVEL_L:
        AppLog("Low\n");
        break;
    case QR_CODE_ERROR_CORRECTION_LEVEL_M:
```

```
            AppLog("Medium\n");
            break;
        case QR_CODE_ERROR_CORRECTION_LEVEL_Q:
            AppLog("Quartile\n");
            break;
        case QR_CODE_ERROR_CORRECTION_LEVEL_H:
            AppLog("High\n");
            break;
        default:
            break;

    }

}
```

You can also generate a QR code by using the `QrCodeGenerator` class:

```
QrCodeGenerator qrGen;
qrGen.Construct();

int width = -1;
int height = -1;
String contentPath = Environment::GetPredefinedPath(PREDEFINED_DIRECTORY_IMAGES);
r = qrGen.EncodeToFile("QR Code Example",        // Text
        QR_CODE_MODE_UTF8,                       // Code Mode
        QR_CODE_ERROR_CORRECTION_LEVEL_Q,        // Error Correction Level
        true,                                    // Compatibile Mode
        ContentPath + L"genQR.png",              // File name
        Tizen::Media::IMG_FORMAT_PNG,            // File Type
        width,                                   // Out param for width
        height);                                 // Out param for height
```

Sensors

Tizen supports several types of sensors to detect device position, movement, surroundings, and motion patterns:

➤ **Acceleration sensor** — Measures the device's acceleration vectors from the three-axis accelerometer

➤ **Magnetic sensor** — Measures magnetic field strength and fluctuations from the three-axis electronic compass

➤ **Proximity sensor** — Detects the presence of nearby objects

➤ **Tilt sensor** — Gets roll, pitch, and azimuth values from the three-axis accelerometer and electronic compass

➤ **Gyro sensor** — Calculates angular velocity from the three-axis gyroscope

➤ **Light sensor** — Gets the brightness level from the ambient light sensor

➤ **Gravity sensor** — Measures gravity using the three-axis accelerometer

➤ **Device Orientation sensor** — Measures yaw, pitch, and roll from the three-axis accelerometer

➤ **User Acceleration sensor** — Detects user-defined motion

All these sensors are managed by the `Tizen::Uix::Sensor::SensorManager` class, which can wake up, connect, and disconnect a sensor and retrieve data from it. The `SensorManager` is also used to add and remove sensor listeners. Listeners retrieve sensor data periodically and deliver it to an application.

To use the sensor manager, first create an instance and check that the type of sensor you want to access is available:

```
SensorManager* pSensorManager = new SensorManager;
pSensorManager->Construct();

// check a sensor is available.
pSensorManager->IsAvailable(SENSOR_TYPE_ACCELERATION);
```

Add a listener for the chosen type of sensor and specify the interval, in milliseconds, at which the sensor data will be received:

```
long interval = 0L;
__sensorMgr.GetMinInterval(SENSOR_TYPE_ACCELERATION, interval);
r = pSensorManager->AddSensorListener(*pListener,
                                      SENSOR_TYPE_ACCELERATION,
                                      interval,
                                      false);
```

If the last parameter of `AddSensorListener()` is `true`, then the listener will be called only when the sensor data has changed; otherwise, the listener will be called at the specified interval.

You can get the sensor data in the listener's `OnDataReceived()`:

```
void SensorExample::OnDataReceived(SensorType sensorType,
                                   SensorData& sensorData, result r)
{
    AccelerationSensorData& data = static_cast< AccelerationSensorData& >
                                   (sensorData);
    AppLog("AccelerationSensorData x = %5.4f, y = %5.4f, z = %5.4f",
              data.x, data.y, data.z);
}
```

There are predefined motions in Tizen such as double-tap, shake, snap, and move-to-ear. The `Tizen::Uix::Sensor::Motion` class manages and provides notification of motion events. When a movement is observed, the `IMotionEventListener` will be called:

```
class MotionListener: public Tizen::Uix::IMotionEventListener
 {
…
    // IMotionEventListener
    void OnDoubleTapDetected(void);
    void OnShakeDetected(Tizen::Uix::Sensor::MotionState motionState);
    void OnSnapDetected(Tizen::Uix::Sensor::MotionSnapType snapType);
};
```

When you create an instance of `Motion`, set a listener and specify which motion event types the listener will capture:

```
Tizen::Uix::Sensor::Motion motion;

// register IMotionEventListener
motion->Construct(*pMotionListener);
// set motion types
motion->SetEnabled(MOTION_TYPE_DOUBLETAP | MOTION_TYPE_SHAKE);
```

Speech

The `Uix::Speech` namespace provides support for speech-to-text (STT), which translates spoken words to text, and text-to-speech (TTS), a feature that enables you to convert normal text language into synthesised speech. In this section, you'll walk through code which shows how to implement both of these features.

Speech-to-Text

The `Tizen::Uix::Speech::SpeechToText` class recognises speech and converts it to text. You can set properties for the speech recognition, including locale, grammar, and silence detection.

To use this feature, first implement the `Tizen::Uix::Speech::ISpeechToTextEventListener` :

```
class SpeechToTextExample
    : public Tizen::Uix::Speech::ISpeechToTextEventListener
    ...
{
...
    virtual void OnSpeechToTextInitialized(void);
    virtual void OnSpeechToTextCompleted (const Tizen::Base::String &result);
...
};
```

Create and initialise the `SpeechToText` class. When the `Construct()` method is called, the listener should be registered. Then call the `Initialize()` method:

```
__pStt = new SpeechToText();
r = __pStt->Construct(*this);
r = __pStt->Initialize();
```

The `OnSpeechToTextInitialized()` method will be invoked when the service has been initialised. You can set the locale and other properties here:

```
void
SpeechToTextExample::OnSpeechToTextInitialized(void)
{
    __pStt->SetLocale(Locale(LANGUAGE_ENG, COUNTRY_US));
    __pStt->SetSilenceDetectionEnabled(true);
}
```

Start the TTS service to record the user's speech and convert it to text:

```
if (__pStt->GetCurrentStatus() == SPEECH_TO_TEXT_STATUS_READY)
```

```
    {
        __pStt->Start()
    }
```

Get the converted text in the `ISpeechToTextEventListener::OnSpeechToTextCompleted()`
method:

```
    void
    SpeechToTextExample::OnSpeechToTextCompleted(Tizen::Base::String& result)
    {
        AppLog("Recognized Test %ls\n", result.GetPointer());
    }
```

Any errors that occur during speech recognition are handled in the
`ISpeechToTextEventListener::OnSpeechToTextErrorOccurred()` event handler.

> **NOTE** *The Tizen Emulator does not support STT. You can check
> whether the target device supports the feature by using the feature key. For more
> information, select Tizen Native App Programming ⇨ Programming Guide ⇨
> System: Getting System Information and Using Alarms, in the help documenta-
> tion* http://tizen.org/feature/speech.recognition.

Text-to-Speech

The `Tizen::Uix::Speech::TextToSpeech` class synthesises speech from a given piece of text and
plays it. It also enables you to set various properties, such as the locale and speech rate.

To add code to support this feature, first implement the `Tizen::Uix::Speech::`
`ITextToSpeechEventListener`:

```
    class TextToSpeechExample
      : public Tizen::Uix::Speech::ITextToSpeechEventListener
      ...
    {
      ...
      virtual void OnTextToSpeechInitialized(void);
      virtual void OnTextToSpeechStatusChanged
                (Tizen::Uix::Speech::TextToSpeechStatus status);
      virtual void OnTextToSpeechErrorOccurred
                (Tizen::Uix::Speech::TextToSpeechError error);
      virtual void OnTextToSpeechCompleted();
      ...
    };
```

Create and initialise the `TextToSpeech` class. When the `Construct()` method is called, the listener
should be registered. Then you should call the `Initialize()` method:

```
    __pTts = new TextToSpeech();
    r = __pTts->Construct(*this);
    r = __pTts->Initialize();
```

The `OnTextToSpeechInitialized()` method is invoked when the service has been initialised. You can set the locale and other properties here:

```
void
TextToSpeechExample::OnTextToSpeechInitialized(void)
{
    if (status == TTS_STATUS_INITIALIZED)
    {
        __pTts->SetLocale(Locale(LANGUAGE_ENG, COUNTRY_US));
        __pTts->SetSpeechRate(TEXT_TO_SPEECH_SPEECH_RATE_NORMAL);
    }
}
```

Start the TTS service to say the specified text:

```
if (__pTts->GetCurrentStatus() == TEXT_TO_SPEECH_STATUS_READY)
{
    __pTts->Speak(L"Hello World. Hello Tizen.", TEXT_TO_SPEECH_REQUEST_MODE_APPEND);
}
```

The last parameter, `TEXT_TO_SPEECH_REQUEST_MODE_APPEND`, means that the new request is played after any request currently playing. If you want to play the current request immediately, use `TEXT_TO_SPEECH_REQUEST_MODE_REPLACE`.

SUMMARY

After working through the many code samples in this chapter, you will be familiar with Tizen's advanced UI features and have the practical foundation to start implementing these features in your own applications. In the first part of the chapter, you learned how to apply animation effects to images, UI controls, and form transitions, and use the scene manager to simplify the complicated task of transitioning between screens in your application's UI. You also walked through code that demonstrated 2D drawing on a canvas. To learn more about these features, take a look at the AnimationApp and UiVisualElement samples from the Tizen SDK.

The rest of the chapter focused on the `Uix` namespace, which provides developers with a range of advanced UI interactions, including face and image recognition, whose uses include augmented reality, games, and much more. Tizen also has comprehensive sensor support, providing easy access to everything from the accelerometer to motion events and gravity sensors. Together with speech-to-text and text-to-speech, these features give you the tools to create applications that interact with users in ways far beyond just simple touch.

17

I/O and Internationalisation

WHAT'S IN THIS CHAPTER?

➤ Working with files

➤ Mastering database features

➤ Supporting text encoding

➤ Locales, dates, and numbers

WROX.COM CODE DOWNLOADS FOR THIS CHAPTER

The wrox.com code downloads for this chapter are found at www.wrox.com/go/professionaltizen on the Download Code tab. The code is in the Chapter 17 download and named according to the names throughout the chapter. After decompressing the downloaded Zip file you will have a tizen-io-i18n directory that contains the finished application.

This chapter focuses on two very important subjects: how to store your data, whether it's in a simple file or a database, and how your application can use Tizen's internalisation features to adapt to different languages, text encodings, and number and date formats. With a little work, you can make sure that your application is accessible to as many potential markets as possible by ensuring that it works worldwide — no matter the country, language, or character set.

With the popularity of cloud computing, the importance of storing files on a local device can sometimes be forgotten. Even web applications should support working offline and saving data locally. That's why the features of Tizen's Io namespace are so important. In this chapter, you'll learn about some basic features, such as creating files and reading from and writing to files using the Io::File class; and some more complex features, such as using file locking to control access to files shared between processes. You'll also discover how to create a database using Tizen's database classes.

Once you understand how to safely store your data, the rest of the chapter looks at internationalisation. Using a series of code snippets, you'll find out how to list the available text encodings, convert between one encoding and another, and support different currency, date, and number formats.

PREDEFINED DIRECTORIES

For security reasons, Tizen restricts the parts of the file system that an application can access to the application's own private directory, shared directories used to exchange data with other applications, and predefined system directories containing images, videos, music, and other types of media.

When an application is installed on a device or the Emulator, the application's directories are organised as shown in Table 17-1. Each directory name is relative to the application's root directory, which is returned by the `GetAppRootPath()` method of the `Tizen::App::App` class. In the Access Control column, Y stands for your application, T for trusted applications, and O for Other applications.

TABLE 17-1: Application's Predefined Directories

DIRECTORY NAME	DESCRIPTION	ACCESS CONTROL
`data/`	You can store your application's private data in this directory. Get this directory path by calling the `GetAppDataPath()` method of the `Tizen::App::App` class. Use this method rather than combining the path `GetAppRootPath() + L"data/"` because the directory name may be changed later.	Y: RW O: Denied
`res/`	The resources stored in the "res" directory during application development will be stored in this directory after installation. See Figure 17-1 for the folder layout of an application project in the IDE. You can get this directory path by calling the `GetAppResourcePath()` method of the `Tizen::App::App` class. Use this method instead of combining the path `GetAppRootPath() + L"res/"` because the directory name may be changed later.	Y: R O: Denied

`shared/`	This directory is the parent directory of the `data`, `res`, and `trusted` subdirectories. You can get this directory path by calling the `GetAppSharedPath()` method of the `Tizen::App::App` class. Use this method instead of combining the path `GetAppRootPath() + L"shared/"` because the directory name may be changed later. If you know another application's ID and want to access that application's shared directory path, use the `GetAppSharedPath(otherAppId)` static method of the `Tizen::App::AppManager` class.	Y: R O: R
`shared/data/`	Here you can store your application's public data, which can be accessed by any other application. You can get your application's shared data directory by calling `GetAppSharedPath() + L"data/"` and another application's shared data directory by calling `AppManager::GetAppSharedPath(otherAppId) + L"data/"`.	Y: RW O: R
`shared/res/`	You store read-only resources which can be shared with any other application in this directory. The resources stored in the `"shared/res"` directory during application development will be stored here after installation. You can get your application's shared data directory by calling `GetAppSharedPath() + L"res/"` and another application's shared data directory by calling `GetAppSharedPath(otherAppId) + L"res/"`.	Y: R O: R
`shared/trusted/`	You can also share files with trusted applications signed with the same certificate as your application. This is useful for sharing data between a family of applications. You can get your application's trusted data directory by calling `GetAppSharedPath() + L"trusted/"` and another application's trusted data directory by calling `GetAppSharedPath(otherAppId) + L"trusted/"`.	Y: RW T: RW O: Denied

There are also various predefined system directories, as shown in Table 17-2. You can get the path of these directories by calling the `GetPredefinedPath (PredefinedDirectoryType)` static method of the `Tizen::System::Environment` class. Note that the macro names in the PredefinedDirectoryType and Description columns should be prefixed by `PREDEFINED_DIRECTORY`. The A in the Access Control column stands for all applications.

FIGURE 17-1

TABLE 17-2: System Predefined Directories

PREDEFINEDDIRECTORYTYPE	DESCRIPTION	ACCESS CONTROL
IMAGES	The internal storage directory for images. Currently `GetPredefinedPath(IMAGES)` returns "`/opt/usr/media/Images/`" on the Emulator. Note that the real path may be changed later.	A: RW
SOUNDS	The internal storage directory for sounds. Currently `GetPredefinedPath(SOUNDS)` returns "`/opt/usr/media/Sounds/`" on the Emulator. Note that the real path may be changed later.	A: RW
VIDEOS	The internal storage directory for videos. Currently `GetPredefinedPath(VIDEOS)` returns "`/opt/usr/media/Videos/`" on the Emulator. Note that the real path may be changed later.	A: RW
CAMERA	The internal storage directory for files captured by the camera application. Currently `GetPredefinedPath(CAMERA)` returns "`/opt/usr/media/Camera/`" on the Emulator. Note that the real path may be changed later.	A: RW
DOWNLOADS	The internal storage directory for downloaded files. Currently `GetPredefinedPath(DOWNLOADS)` returns "`/opt/usr/media/Downloads/`" on the Emulator. Note that the real path may be changed later.	A: RW
OTHERS	The internal storage directory for other files. Currently `GetPredefinedPath(OTHERS)` returns "`/opt/usr/media/Others/`" on the Emulator. Note that the real path may be changed later.	A: RW
SYSTEM_RINGTONES	The read-only internal storage directory for system ringtones. Currently `GetPredefinedPath(SYSTEM_RINGTONES)` returns "`/opt/share/settings/Ringtones`" on the Emulator. Note that the real path does not contain the trailing "`/`" character (only for this macro name), and this bug has been fixed with the Tizen SDK 2.2.1 release.	A: R
APPLICATIONS	The internal storage directory into which applications are installed.	

APPLICATIONS	Currently `GetPredefinedPath(APPLICATIONS)` returns "`/opt/usr/apps/`" on the Emulator. Note that the real path may be changed later.	A: R
EXTERNAL_IMAGES	The external MMC (MultiMediaCard) storage directory for images. Currently `GetPredefinedPath(EXTERNAL_IMAGES)` returns "`/opt/storage/sdcard/Images/`" on the Emulator. Note that the real path may be changed later.	A: RW
EXTERNAL_SOUNDS	The external MMC storage directory for sounds. Currently `GetPredefinedPath(EXTERNAL_SOUNDS)` returns "`/opt/storage/sdcard/Sounds/`" on the Emulator. Note that the real path may be changed later.	A: RW
EXTERNAL_VIDEOS	The external MMC storage directory for videos. Currently `GetPredefinedPath(EXTERNAL_VIDEOS)` returns "`/opt/storage/sdcard/Videos/`" on the Emulator. Note that the real path may be changed later.	A: RW
EXTERNAL_CAMERA	The external MMC directory for files captured by the camera application. Currently `GetPredefinedPath(EXTERNAL_CAMERA)` returns "`/opt/storage/sdcard/Camera/`" on the Emulator. Note that the real path may be changed later.	A: RW
EXTERNAL_DOWNLOADS	The external MMC storage directory for downloaded files. Currently `GetPredefinedPath(EXTERNAL_DOWNLOADS)` returns "`/opt/usr/media/Images/`" on the Emulator. Note that the real path may be changed later.	A: RW
EXTERNAL_OTHERS	The external MMC storage directory for other files. Currently `GetPredefinedPath(EXTERNAL_OTHERS)` returns "`/opt/storage/sdcard/Others/`" on the Emulator. Note that the real path may be changed later.	A: RW
EXTERNAL_APPLICATIONS	The external MMC storage directory into which applications are installed. Currently `GetPredefinedPath(EXTERNAL_APPLICATIONS)` returns "`/opt/storage/sdcard/app2sd/`" on the Emulator. Note that the real path may be changed later.	A: R

HANDLING FILE I/O

This section describes basic file operations, including reading, writing, copying, moving, deleting, and getting the attributes of files and directories. You'll also learn about file locking to share files between applications in a safe way. Finally, a comprehensive example will show how to monitor directory and file changes.

Basic File Operations

The most basic file operations are open, read, write, and close. Listing 17-1 shows how to perform these operations on files in a Tizen application.

LISTING 17-1: Basic file operations

```
#include <FApp.h>
#include <FBase.h>
#include <FIo.h>

using namespace Tizen::App;
using namespace Tizen::Base;
using namespace Tizen::Io;
using namespace Tizen::System;

void CreateFile(const String& filePath);
void ReadAndPrintFile(const String& filePath);

void
BasicFileOpExample()
{
    // (1)
    String filePath(App::GetInstance()->GetAppDataPath()
                    + L"sample.txt");
    CreateFile(filePath);
    AppLogTag("PTAP", "%ls has been successfully created",
             filePath.GetPointer());
    ReadAndPrintFile(filePath);

    // (2)
    filePath = Environment::GetPredefinedPath(
                   PREDEFINED_DIRECTORY_OTHERS)
               + L"sample.txt";
    CreateFile(filePath);
    AppLogTag("PTAP", "%ls has been successfully created",
        filePath.GetPointer());
    ReadAndPrintFile(filePath);
}

void
CreateFile(const String& filePath)
{
    File file;
```

```
    // (3)
    file.Construct(filePath, "w+");
    // (4)
    file.Write(L"Created a new file\n");
    file.Write(L"And wrote two lines\n");
} // (5)
void
ReadAndPrintFile(const String& filePath)
{
    File file;
    // (6)
    file.Construct(filePath, "r");
    String line;
    // (7)
    while (file.Read(line) != E_END_OF_FILE)
    {
        AppLogTag("PTAP", "%ls", line.GetPointer());
    }
} // (8)
```

(1) Creates a file in your application's private data directory.

(2) Creates a file in the system's predefined other data directory.

(3) `File` is a kind of resource and thus designed according to the Resource Acquisition Is Initialization (RAII) idiom, which is discussed in Chapter 11.

The `filePath` `String` is first converted to a UTF-8 encoded string inside the `Construct()` method because Tizen assumes UTF-8 encoding is used for the file system.

The `Construct()` method initialises the `File` object, opens the file if it exists, or creates a new one. The file-opening mode is the same as that used in the C function `fopen()` and the mode used in this case is `w+`, which means open the file with read/write access and create it if it doesn't exist.

(4) Writes data to a file using the `File::Write()` method. The `File::Write(const String&)` method converts the `String` into a UTF-8 C string first and writes the string. You are writing two lines in UTF-8 encoding with the preceding code.

(5) When the `File` instance goes out of scope, its destructor is called and the file is closed.

(6) The actual file is opened in `r` mode, which means read-only. This is enough for the `ReadAndPrintFile()` function.

(7) Data is read from a file using the `File::Read()` method. There are three overloaded `Read()` methods, and the `Read()` method which takes a `String` instance will read data until a newline character is read or end of file is reached. This method assumes that the file is in UTF-8 format.

(8) The actual file resource is released when the `File` object goes out of scope.

To write or read binary data to or from a file, use the overloaded `Write()` and `Read()` methods, which take a `ByteBuffer` argument. Listing 17-2 shows how to read and write binary data.

LISTING 17-2: Binary file I/O

```
void
CreateBinaryFile(const String& filePath)
{
    static const int BUFFER_SIZE = 10;

    File file;
    file.Construct(filePath, "w+");

    // (1)
    ByteBuffer buf;
    buf.Construct(BUFFER_SIZE);
    for (byte i = 0; i < BUFFER_SIZE; ++i)
    {
        buf.SetByte('A' + i);
    }

    // (2)
    buf.SetPosition(0);

    // (3)
    file.Write(buf);
}

void
ReadAndPrintBinaryFile(const String& filePath)
{
    File file;
    file.Construct(filePath, "r");

    // (4)
FileAttributes attrs;
    File::GetAttributes(filePath, attrs);
    int fileSize = static_cast< int >(attrs.GetFileSize());
    ByteBuffer buf;
    buf.Construct(fileSize);

    // (5)
    file.Read(buf);
    buf.SetPosition(0);

    // (6)
    for (int i = 0; i < fileSize; ++i)
    {
        AppLogTag("PTAP", "%c", buf[i]);
    }
}

void
BinaryFileOpExample()
{
    String filePath(App::GetInstance()->GetAppDataPath()
                    + L"sample.bin");
```

```
        CreateBinaryFile(filePath);
        AppLogTag("PTAP", "%ls has been successfully created",
                    filePath.GetPointer());
        ReadAndPrintBinaryFile(filePath);
    }
```

(1) Constructs a `ByteBuffer` instance with `"ABCDEFGHIJ"`. After construction, the `buf` instance's internal position will be `BUFFER_SIZE`.

(2) Resets the `buf` instance's internal position to 0 so that the `File::Write()` method writes data from the start position. The data length will be `buf`'s length.

(3) Writes all of `buf`'s data.

(4) Constructs a `ByteBuffer` with a capacity matching the file's size. You can get the file size using the `FileAttributes::GetFileSize()` method, which is explained in detail in the "Getting File Attributes" section.

(5) Reads data from the file until `buf` is full.

(6) Prints the buffer read from the file, which contains the characters from `'A'` to `'J'`.

Getting File Attributes

In many cases you may need to get information about the properties of files and directories. One example is a file manager application which displays information about items such as file size, file type, creation and modification dates, and whether an item is a file or a directory.

All this information is available using the `File::GetAttributes()` static method, with the exception of the file extension, which can be obtained using the `File::GetFileExtension()` static method.

The Listing 17-3 shows these methods in use.

LISTING 17-3: Getting file attributes

```
    void FileAttrExample()
    {
        String filePath(
                    App::GetInstance()->GetAppDataPath()
                    + L"sample.txt"
                    );
        CreateFile(filePath);
        AppLogTag(
            "PTAP", "%ls has been successfully created",
            filePath.GetPointer()
            );

        // (1)
        FileAttributes attrs;
        File::GetAttributes(filePath, attrs);
        AppLogTag(
```

continues

LISTING 17-3 *(continued)*

```
                "PTAP", "%ls: size = %lld, last modified at %ls, "
                "ext = %ls"
                  filePath.GetPointer(), attrs.GetFileSize(),
                attrs.GetLastModifiedTime().ToString().GetPointer(),
                File::GetFileExtension(filePath).GetPointer()
        );

        // (2)
        filePath = App::GetInstance()->GetAppResourcePath();
        File::GetAttributes(filePath, attrs);
        if (attrs.IsDirectory())
        {
                AppLogTag(
                  "PTAP", "%ls is a directory", filePath.GetPointer()
                  );
        }
        else
        {
                AppLogTag(
                  "PTAP", "%ls is not a directory", filePath.GetPointer()
                  );
        }
        if (attrs.IsReadOnly())
        {
            AppLogTag(
                "PTAP", "%ls is read-only", filePath.GetPointer()
            );
        }
        else
        {
                AppLogTag(
                  "PTAP", "%ls is not read-only", filePath.GetPointer()
                  );
        }
        if (attrs.IsHidden())
        {
                AppLogTag("PTAP", "%ls is hidden", filePath.GetPointer());
        }
        else
        {
                AppLogTag(
                  "PTAP", "%ls is not hidden", filePath.GetPointer()
            );
        }

        // (3)
        File::Remove(filePath);
}
```

(1) The `File::GetAttributes()` method is used to retrieve the file's attributes, and the size and modification time are printed, together with the file extension obtained from the `File::GetFileExtension()` method.

(2) `GetAttributes()` is used to get the attributes of a file, but this time the file is actually a directory.

The following will be written to the IDE's log view:

```
... : INFO / PTAP ... > /opt/apps/yWWzhKznCJ/res/ is a directory
... : INFO / PTAP ... > /opt/apps/yWWzhKznCJ/res/ is read-only
... : INFO / PTAP ... > /opt/apps/yWWzhKznCJ/res/ is not hidden
```

The log shows that the item is a read-only directory which is not hidden.

(3) The `File::Remove()` method deletes the file whose path is specified in `filePath`. The following section explains `File::Remove()` in greater detail.

Copying, Moving, and Deleting Files

Copying, moving, and deleting files is easy using the `File::Copy()`, `Move()`, and `Remove()` methods, respectively, although there are some subtleties that you need to bear in mind.

Listing 17-4 shows how to copy, move, and delete files.

LISTING 17-4: File management

```
void FileManagementExample()
{
    // (1)
    String srcFilePath(App::GetInstance()->GetAppDataPath() + L"tmp.txt");
    CreateFile(srcFilePath);
    AppLogTag("PTAP", "%ls has been successfully created",
            srcFilePath.GetPointer());

    // (2)
    String destFilePath(
        Environment::GetPredefinedPath(PREDEFINED_DIRECTORY_EXTERNAL_OTHERS)
        + L"sample.txt"
        );
    result r = File::Copy(srcFilePath, destFilePath, true);
    if (r == E_FILE_ALREADY_EXIST)
    {
        AppLogTag("PTAP", "%ls already exists in the destination directory",
                destFilePath.GetPointer());
        return;
    }

    // (3)
    File::Remove(srcFilePath);

    // (4)
```

continues

LISTING 17-4 *(continued)*

```
    String renamedFilePath(
        Environment::GetPredefinedPath(PREDEFINED_DIRECTORY_EXTERNAL_OTHERS)
        + L"README.txt"
        );
    File::Move(destFilePath, renamedFilePath);
}
```

(1) Creates a temporary text file for this example.

(2) Copies the temporary text file into the "other" directory on external storage. The third argument means "fail if already exists". You pass true for this argument and if `Copy()` returns `E_FILE_ALREADY_EXIST`, an error message is printed and the function immediately returns. Note that the filename part is extracted from `srcFilePath` using the `File::GetFileName()` static method.

(3) Removes the temporary text file. If you combine (2) and (3), it's effectively a move operation, the same functionality as provided by `File::Move()`.

(4) Renames the copied file to `README.txt` and does not change its location, as in this case both the source and destination paths are in the same directory on the external storage.

> **NOTE** `File::Move()` *will work differently depending on the location of the source and destination files.*
>
> ➤ *If both files are in the same storage, then this just results in one move operation.*
>
> ➤ *If the files are in different storage then this results in a copy and remove operation, which will be slower.*

Handling Directories

If you're developing a file manager application, the main view might display a list of files and directories as shown in Figure 17-2.

To display such a view, you need to be able to read each item in a directory, determine whether an item is a file or directory, and display the type of file — whether it's an image, video, or audio file, for example.

The Listing 17-5 shows how to read a directory and identify the type of each directory entry.

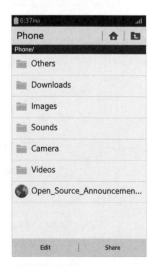

FIGURE 17-2

LISTING 17-5: Reading directories

```
// (1)
IList*
ReadDirectory(const String& dirPath)
{
    Directory dir;
    dir.Construct(dirPath);
    std::unique_ptr< DirEnumerator > pDirEnum(dir.ReadN());
    std::unique_ptr< ArrayList > pArrayList(new ArrayList(SingleObjectDeleter));
    while (pDirEnum->MoveNext() == E_SUCCESS)
    {
        pArrayList->Add(new DirEntry(pDirEnum->GetCurrentDirEntry()));
    }

    return pArrayList.release();
}

// (2)
void
DisplayDirEntry(const DirEntry* pDirEntry)
{
    if (pDirEntry->IsDirectory())
    {
        AppLogTag("PTAP", "%ls: a directory",
                  pDirEntry->GetName().GetPointer());
    }
    else
    {
        AppLogTag("PTAP", "%ls: a plain file",
                  pDirEntry->GetName().GetPointer());
    }
}

// (3)
void
DisplayDirRecursively(const String& dirPath)
{
    // (4)
    Directory dir;
    result r = dir.Construct(dirPath);
    TryReturnVoidTag(
        "PTAP", r == E_SUCCESS,
        "%ls may not be a directory", dirPath.GetPointer()
        );

    AppLogTag("PTAP", "Entering %ls", dirPath.GetPointer());
    // (5)
    std::unique_ptr< IList > pList(ReadDirectory(dirPath));
    std::unique_ptr< IEnumerator > pEnumerator(pList->GetEnumeratorN());
    while (pEnumerator->MoveNext() == E_SUCCESS)
    {
```

continues

LISTING 17-5 *(continued)*

```
        // (6)
        DirEntry* pDirEntry =
            static_cast< DirEntry* >(pEnumerator->GetCurrent());
        // (7)
        DisplayDirEntry(pDirEntry);
        String entryName = pDirEntry->GetName();
        // (8)
        if (pDirEntry->IsDirectory() && entryName != L"." &&
            entryName != L"..")
        {
            String newDirPath = dirPath + entryName + L"/";
            DisplayDirRecursively(newDirPath);
        }
    }
}

void
ReadDirExample()
{
    // (9)
    DisplayDirRecursively(Environment::GetMediaPath());
    // (10)
    DisplayDirRecursively(
        Environment::GetMediaPath() + L"Open_Source_Announcement.html"
        );
}
```

(1) Reads the given directory and returns directory entries as a list. You can loop over directory entries using `DirEnumerator`, which you can obtain using the `Directory::ReadN()` method.

(2) Displays the given directory entry with its name and type: either a directory or a file. The `DirEntry` class provides `GetName()` and `IsDirectory()` methods.

(3) Displays the given directory recursively.

(4) `DisplayDirRecursively()` first checks whether the given path is referring to a directory. If it's not, it returns immediately.

(5) Gets the list of `DirEntry` objects using the `ReadDirectory()` function.

(6) You must cast the return value of `pEnumerator->GetCurrent()` because it's an `Object*`.

(7) `DisplayDirRecursively()` displays the current directory entry using the `DisplayDirEntry()` function.

(8) Calls recursively `DisplayDirRecursively()` for each directory except "." and "..".

(9) Tries to display the `Environment::GetMediaPath()` directory recursively.

(10) Tries to display the `Environment::GetMediaPath() + L"Open_Source_Announcement.html"` file, for which `DisplayDirRecursively()` will fail.

If you execute the preceding code, the following log file appears in the IDE:

```
... : INFO / PTAP ... > Entering /opt/usr/media/
... : INFO / PTAP ... > Downloads: a directory
... : INFO / PTAP ... > Entering /opt/usr/media/Downloads/
... : ERROR / Tizen::Io ... > [E_END_OF_FILE] End of directory entries
... : INFO / PTAP ... > ..: a directory
... : INFO / PTAP ... > .: a directory
... : INFO / PTAP ... > Exiting /opt/usr/media/Downloads/
... : INFO / PTAP ... > ..: a directory
... : INFO / PTAP ... > Images: a directory
... : INFO / PTAP ... > Entering /opt/usr/media/Images/
... : ERROR / Tizen::Io ... > [E_END_OF_FILE] End of directory entries
... : INFO / PTAP ... > ..: a directory
... : INFO / PTAP ... > image13.jpg: a plain file
... : INFO / PTAP ... > Default.jpg: a plain file
... : INFO / PTAP ... > image15.jpg: a plain file
...
... : INFO / PTAP ... > Exiting /opt/usr/media/Images/
...
... : INFO / PTAP ... > Exiting /opt/usr/media/Sounds/Voice recorder/
... : INFO / PTAP ... > Exiting /opt/usr/media/Sounds/
... : INFO / PTAP ... > Exiting /opt/usr/media/
... : ERROR / Tizen::Io ... > [SECURE_LOG] [E_INVALID_ARG] \
                             Failed to open directory \
                             (/opt/usr/media/Open_Source_Announcement.html).
... : ERROR / Tizen::Io ... > [E_INVALID_ARG] Propagated.
... : ERROR / PTAP ... > /opt/usr/media/Open_Source_Announcement.html \
                         may not be a directory
```

Locking Files

The `File` class provides the capability to lock an entire file or a section of a file using the `LockN()` and `TryToLockN()` methods. The locking feature enables processes to manage access to a shared file so that only one process is updating the file at a time. File locking in Tizen follows the advisory locking model, in which processes use locks to collaborate with each other to control access to a file, but other processes may ignore locking.

The locking feature supports both exclusive and shared locking of whole files or regions within files. Exclusive locks, also referred to as writer locks, can only be acquired by one process at a time, whereas shared locks, or reader locks, can be acquired by several processes.

`LockN()` and `TryToLockN()` return a `FileLock` instance. `FileLock` is designed according to the RAII idiom and the lock is released when the object is destroyed.

You can use file locking in the following example. Assume you have a file which is shared temporarily between several processes and when this file is no longer needed, the last reader should delete the file. Another file is used to store the number of readers, and this file should be locked before the reader count is updated.

Listing 17-6 updates the reader count safely by 1 or -1.

LISTING 17-6: Updating reader count

```
int UpdateReaderCount(File& file, int diff)
{
    File countFile;
    countFile.Construct(file.GetName() + L".cnt", "rw");
    ByteBuffer buf;
    buf.Construct(sizeof(int));
    countFile.Read(buf);
    unique_ptr<IntBuffer> pIntBuf(buf.AsIntBufferN());
    (*pIntBuf)[0] += diff;
    countFile.Seek(FILESEEKPOSITION_BEGIN, 0);

    // (1)
    std::unique_ptr<FileLock>
        pCountFileLock(countFile.LockN(FILE_LOCK_EXCLUSIVE));

    pCountFileLock.reset(file.LockN(FILE_LOCK_EXCLUSIVE));
    countFile.Write(buf);

    return (*pIntBuff)[0];
} // (2)
```

(1) `LockN(FILE_LOCK_EXCLUSIVE)` requests an exclusive lock on the file, but if the file lock is already acquired by another process, then the current process will be blocked until the other process releases the lock. To request a lock without blocking, use the `TryToLockN()` function instead, which returns an error if the lock cannot be acquired but will not block the current process.

If the lock can be acquired, `LockN()` returns a newly created `FileLock` instance pointer. Otherwise, it returns null. It is the application's responsibility to release the returned `FileLock` instance. If you want to lock the file in shared mode, call `LockN(FILE_LOCK_SHARED)`.

In this code, the function will write back the updated reader count, so it will lock the file in exclusive mode. To lock a portion of a file, use `LockN()` and `TryToLockN()` with two additional arguments for offset and length.

(2) The `FileLock` instance returned in step (1) is released by `unique_ptr`, and in turn the file lock will be released.

Observing File and Directory Changes

The `Tizen::Io` namespace provides a feature for monitoring files and directories, notifying the application when an event occurs to update the directory or file being monitored. Events include a monitored file being opened or modified or files added or removed from the monitored directory. The supported event types are defined in the `Tizen::Io::FileEventType` enum.

In the following example, assume you're developing an image browser and want to update content from directories specified by the user. To implement this functionality, you'll need to monitor a given directory. Listing 17-7 shows how a directory can be monitored.

LISTING 17-7: Monitoring directories

```cpp
class DirectoryMonitor
    : public IFileEventListener // (1)
{
public:
    DirectoryMonitor(const vector<String>& monitoredFileExtList)
        : __monitoredFileExtList(monitoredFileExtList)
    {
        // (2)
        __mgr.Construct(*this);
    }

    // (1)
    virtual void OnFileEventOccurred(
        const unsigned long events,
        const String& path,
        const unsigned int eventId
    )
    {
        if (!IsMonitoredFileType(path))
        {
            return;
        }

        if (events & FILE_EVENT_TYPE_CREATE)
        {
            AppLogTag("PTAP", "%ls is created", path.GetPointer());
            // (3)
            AddFile(path);
            // (5) Add the file to some database
        }
        else if (events & FILE_EVENT_TYPE_DELETE)
        {
            AppLogTag("PTAP", "%ls is deleted", path.GetPointer());
            // (4)
            RemoveFile(path);
            // (5) Remove the file from some database
        }
        else if (events & FILE_EVENT_TYPE_MODIFY)
        {
            // (5) Update the database for the file
        }
    }

    void AddDirectory(const String& dirPath)
    {
        // (2)
        __mgr.AddPath(dirPath, MONITORED_EVENTS_ON_DIR);
    }

    // (3)
    void AddFile(const String& filePath)
```

continues

LISTING 17-7 *(continued)*

```
        {
            __mgr.AddPath(filePath, MONITORED_EVENTS_ON_FILE);
        }

        // (4)
        void RemoveFile(const String& filePath)
        {
            __mgr.RemovePath(filePath);
        }

        bool IsMonitoredFileType(const String& filePath)
        {
            return true;
        }

private:
    static const unsigned long MONITORED_EVENTS_ON_DIR =
        FILE_EVENT_TYPE_CREATE | FILE_EVENT_TYPE_DELETE;
    // (3)
    static const unsigned long MONITORED_EVENTS_ON_FILE =
        FILE_EVENT_TYPE_MODIFY;
    FileEventManager __mgr; // (2)
    vector<String> __monitoredFileExtList;
};
```

(1) To handle file and directory monitoring events, create a class which implements the `IFileEventListener` interface.

The `IFileEventListener` interface defines only one callback method, `OnFileEventOccurred()`, which is given three arguments. The first argument is the type of event, the `Tizen::Io::FileEventType` that has occurred. In the preceding code, the `DirectoryMonitor` class handles the `FILE_EVENT_TYPE_CREATE` and `FILE_EVENT_TYPE_DELETE` events, generated when files are created or deleted in the monitored directory.

The second argument `path` specifies the file or directory that has been changed, while the last argument `eventId` is used only when a file or directory is moved or renamed.

(2) You can monitor directories using the `FileEventManager` class. Construct an instance of `FileEventManager`, passing the object which implements the `IFileEventListener` as a parameter. In this case it will be the current instance of the `DirectoryMonitor` class (`*this`).

(3) The `DirectoryMonitor` class adds the newly added file to the set of monitored files so that an event will be generated if the file is modified. This is useful for keeping track of any changes to the newly added image, which might include an updated thumbnail image, for example.

(4) When a file is deleted, remove it from the list of monitored files.

(5) If you are maintaining a database of image files, you may want to update the database in response to events in a monitored directory. For example, you could add an entry to the database when a file is created, delete an entry when a file is deleted, and update the entry when a file is modified.

BUILDING A DATABASE

Tizen includes a database engine which enables you to create, store, and manipulate your data using SQL-compatible syntax. The classes used to implement database functionality are `Io::Database`, which includes the methods for creating a database and executing SQL statements; `Io::DbStatement`, the class that contains methods for building complex statements; and `Io::DbEnumerator`, which is used to evaluate the results of a SELECT query.

This section demonstrates how to use these classes to build on the code from the previous section to create an image database. The database will be created in the application data directory and have the following table structure:

➤ **Path** — Path to the image file

➤ **Title** — Title of the image (The initial value is the same as the filename.)

➤ **Width** — Image width

➤ **Height** — Image height

The following code shows how to create the image database, add and manipulate data, and process the results of SQL queries.

Creating a Table

The first time the application is launched, the database file is created, together with the "imagedb" table (see Listing 17-8).

LISTING 17-8: ImageDatabaseManager

```
class ImageDatabaseManager
{
public:
    // (1)
    static ImageDatabaseManager& GetInstance()
    {
        static ImageDatabaseManager inst;
        return inst;
    }
    ...

private:
    ImageDatabaseManager()
    {
        // (2)
        const static String dbPath =
            App::GetInstance()->GetAppDataPath() + L"image.db";
        // (3)
        __db.Construct(dbPath, "a+");

        // (4)
```

continues

LISTING 17-8 *(continued)*

```
        String crStmt = L"CREATE TABLE IF NOT EXISTS imagedb "
            "(Path TEXT PRIMARY KEY "
            "Title TEXT, Width INTEGER, Height INTEGER)";
        __db.ExecuteSql(crStmt, true);
    }

    ~ImageDatabaseManager()
    {
    }

    Database __db;
};
```

(1) The database manager is implemented according to the Meyer's Singleton pattern and needs to be created only once.

> **NOTE** *The Meyer's Singleton pattern is a Singleton implementation in C++. It uses the C++ language feature that ensures a function-local static object is initialised once and only once when the code is executed for the first time, to guarantee creation of only one instance.*

(2) The database file will be created in the application's private data directory because it doesn't need to be shared with any other process.

(3) The open mode for the database file is specified as "a+", which indicates that the file should be opened for reading and writing, and created if it does not already exist.

(4) Use the ExecuteSql() method with the CREATE TABLE SQL statement to create a table. IF NOT EXISTS ensures that the database engine only attempts to create the table if it doesn't already exist in the database. Path is the primary key for the table.

Creating a Row

The DirectoryMonitor introduced in the previous section needs to insert a row in the database whenever a new file is created in the directory being monitored. To provide this functionality, an AddImage(const String& imagePath) method is added to the ImageDatabaseManager class and the DirectoryMonitor::OnFileEventOccurred() event handler is modified as follows:

```
class DirectoryMonitor
    : public IFileEventListener
{
public:
    ...
    virtual void OnFileEventOccurred(
        const unsigned long events,
        const String& path,
        const unsigned int eventId
```

```
        )
        {
            ...

            if (events & FILE_EVENT_TYPE_CREATE)
            {
                AppLogTag("PTAP", "%ls is created", path.GetPointer());
                AddFile(path);
                ImageDatabaseManager::GetInstance().AddImage(path);
            }
            ...
        }
```

The ImageDatabaseManager::AddImage() method in the following code inserts a row in the database to store data from the newly created image file. Assume that ImageDatabaseManager::GetImageMetadata() returns proper metadata, as extracting image metadata is out of the scope of this section.

ADDING AN IMAGE

```
class ImageDatabaseManager
{
public:
    ...
    void AddImage(const String& imagePath)
    {
        ImageMetadata data = GetImageMetadata(imagePath);
        // (5)
        String insertStmt = L"INSERT INTO imagedb "
            "(Path, Title, Width, Height) VALUES (?, ?, ?, ?)";
        // (6)
        std::unique_ptr<DbStatement> pStmt(
            __db.CreateStatementN(insertStmt)
            );
        // (7)
        pStmt->BindString(0, data.path);
        pStmt->BindString(1, data.title);
        pStmt->BindInt(2, data.width);
        pStmt->BindInt(3, data.height);

        // (8)
        __db.ExecuteStatementN(*pStmt);
    }

private:
    struct ImageMetadata
    {
        String path;
        String title;
        int width;
        int height;
    };

    ImageMetadata GetImageMetadata(const String& imagePath)
```

```
        {
            . . .
        }
        . . .
};
```

(5) To insert a row, first composes a SQL statement string with placeholders for values.

(6) Creates a `DbStatement` instance to bind each placeholder to a real value.

(7) Binds each placeholder to a real value using the appropriate bind method for each type of data, including `BindString()`, `BindInt()`, and `BindDatetime()`.

(8) Executes the `DbStatement` instance using the `ExecuteStatementN()` method. You do not need to free the returned `DbEnumerator` instance from `ExecuteStatementN()` because it returns null for the INSERT SQL command.

Updating a Row

Whenever the `DirectoryMonitor` class is notified that a file in the monitored directory has been modified, it needs to update the row in the database that contains the information for the file. To implement this functionality, the `ImageDatabaseManager` class provides an `UpdateImage(const String& imagePath)` method, which is invoked from the `DirectoryMonitor::OnFileEventOccurred()` event handler as follows:

```cpp
class DirectoryMonitor
    : public IFileEventListener
{
public:
    . . .
    virtual void OnFileEventOccurred(
        const unsigned long events,
        const String& path,
        const unsigned int eventId
    )
    {
    . . .
        else if (events & FILE_EVENT_TYPE_MODIFY)
        {
            ImageDatabaseManager::GetInstance().UpdateImage(path);
        }
    }
    . . .
};
```

`ImageDatabaseManager::UpdateImage()` finds the row to update by searching on the `Path` and updates the record with the new metadata:

UPDATING AN IMAGE

```cpp
class ImageDatabaseManager
{
public:
```

```
    ...
    void UpdateImage(const String& imagePath)
    {
        ImageMetadata data = GetImageMetadata(imagePath);
        // (9)
        String updateStmt = L"UPDATE imagedb SET Title = ?, "
            "Width = ?, Height = ? WHERE Path = ?";
        std::unique_ptr<DbStatement> pStmt(
            __db.CreateStatementN(updateStmt)
            );
        pStmt->BindString(0, data.title);
        pStmt->BindInt(1, data.width);
        pStmt->BindInt(2, data.height);
        pStmt->BindString(3, data.path);
        __db.ExecuteStatementN(*pStmt);
    }
    ...
};
```

(9) To update a row, first composes an UPDATE SQL statement string with placeholders for values, and then executes the update by calling `CreateStatementN()`.

Deleting a Row

When a file is deleted, `DirectoryMonitor` also needs to delete the appropriate row from the image database. To implement this functionality, the `ImageDatabaseManager` provides a `RemoveImage(const String& imagePath)` method and the `DirectoryMonitor::OnFileEventOccurred()` event handler is modified as follows:

```
class DirectoryMonitor
    : public IFileEventListener
{
public:
    ...
    virtual void OnFileEventOccurred(
        const unsigned long events,
        const String& path,
        const unsigned int eventId
    )
    {
        ...
        else if (events & FILE_EVENT_TYPE_DELETE)
        {
            AppLogTag("PTAP", "%ls is deleted", path.GetPointer());
            RemoveFile(path);
            ImageDatabaseManager::GetInstance().RemoveImage(path);
        }
        ...
    }
}
```

`ImageDatabaseManager::RemoveImage()` deletes the row specified by its `path`:

REMOVING AN IMAGE

```
class ImageDatabaseManager
{
public:
    ...
    void RemoveImage(const String& imagePath)
    {
        // (10)
        String updateStmt = L"DELETE FROM imagedb WHERE Path = ?";
        std::unique_ptr<DbStatement> pStmt(
            __db.CreateStatementN(updateStmt)
        );
        pStmt->BindString(0, imagePath);
        __db.ExecuteStatementN(*pStmt);
    }
    ...
};
```

(10) To delete a row, composes a DELETE SQL statement string with a placeholder for the unique key, which in this case is the `path`. Then bind the value of the `path` string and execute the DELETE statement.

Querying a Table

You're now familiar with adding, updating, and deleting database rows, but you have one more feature to implement, a gallery. For this example, assume that there's a `GalleryView` class in your image browser that displays all the images in the database.

To return a list of all entries in the database, `ImageDatabaseManager` provides the following method:

GETTING IMAGE METADATA

```
class ImageDatabaseManager
{
public:
    ...
    std::unique_ptr< IList > GetAllImagesN()
    {
        std::unique_ptr< IList > pList(new ArrayList(SingleObjectDeleter));
        // (11)
        String selectStmt = L"SELECT Path, Title, Width, Height "
            "FROM imagedb";
        // (12)
        std::unique_ptr<DbEnumerator> pEnum(
            __db.QueryN(selectStmt)
        );
        // (13)
        while (pEnum->MoveNext() == E_SUCCESS)
        {
            ImageMetadata* pData = new ImageMetadata();
            pEnum->GetStringAt(0, pData->path);
```

```
            pEnum->GetStringAt(1, pData->title);
            pEnum->GetIntAt(2, pData->width);
            pEnum->GetIntAt(3, pData->height);
            pList->Add(pData);
        }
        return std::move(pList);
    }
    ...

public: // (14)
    struct ImageMetadata
        : public Object // (14)
    {
        String path;
        String title;
        int width;
        int height;
    };
    ...
};
```

(11) Composes a SELECT SQL command to read all rows.

(12) The QueryN() method returns a DbEnumerator instance which enables you to loop over all returned entries.

(13) Retrieves a value for each field using GetStringAt(), GetIntAt(), GetDoubleAt(), and other related methods for each data type.

(14) Creates an ImageMetadata public datatype member which inherits from Object so that the GalleryView class can use it from outside the ImageDatabaseManager class.

MONITORING STORAGE EVENTS

In this section you will learn how to add a very useful feature to the image browser example: the capability to manage removable storage. The images stored and displayed by the image browser could be stored on removable media such as an MMC card, so the application needs to detect when a storage card is mounted or unmounted and update the user interface in response. By monitoring storage-related events, the image browser can provide a better user experience by updating the list of images when an MMC card, potentially full of images, is inserted or removed.

Handling the events generated when an external storage card is mounted or unmounted is part of the functionality provided by the DeviceManager class and IDeviceEventListener interface in the Tizen::System namespace.

The IDeviceEventListener interface enables you to monitor various external devices such as Bluetooth headsets, storage cards, and keyboards.

Supported external devices are defined in the Tizen::System::DeviceType enum and you can use the DEVICE_TYPE_STORAGE_CARD value to monitor the state of an external storage card.

IDeviceEventListener defines one callback method, OnDeviceStateChanged(DeviceType deviceType, const String& state), which is called with deviceType equal to

DEVICE_TYPE_STORAGE_CARD and state equal to L"Mounted" when the platform detects that an external storage card has been inserted, and called with deviceType equal to DEVICE_TYPE_STORAGE_CARD and state equal to L"Unmounted" when the user removes an external storage card — i.e., it's no longer available.

> **NOTE** *The Tizen platform is based on an open-source operating system, Linux, and mount and unmount are Linux terminologies for storage management. The mount operation makes storage available, and the unmount operation makes it unavailable.*

The GalleryView class monitors the storage events and provides the Scan() and Refresh() methods, which will update the in-memory image list and refresh the current view. Listing 17-9 shows how to monitor and respond to storage-related events.

LISTING 17-9: Monitoring storage events

```
class GalleryView
    : public IDeviceEventListener        // (1)
{
public:
    result Construct()
    {
        // ... other initialisation
        // (2)
        return DeviceManager::AddDeviceEventListener(
            DEVICE_TYPE_STORAGE_CARD, *this);
    }

    void Scan(const String& dirPath)
    {
        AppLogTag(
            "PTAP", "Started to scan %ls",
            dirPath.GetPointer()
            );
        // ... Do some useful things.
        // For example, update in-memory image list
        AppLogTag(
            "PTAP", "Scanning %ls is done",
            dirPath.GetPointer()
            );
    }

    void Refresh()
    {
        AppLogTag("PTAP", "Refreshing the view");
    }

    // ... Assume that there are other methods for GalleryView

    // (3)
```

```
        virtual void OnDeviceStateChanged(
            DeviceType deviceType,
            const String& state
            )
    {
        if (deviceType == DEVICE_TYPE_STORAGE_CARD)
        {
            if (state == L"Mounted")
            {
                AppLogTag("PTAP", "An external MMC inserted");
                Scan(Environment::GetExternalStoragePath());
                Refresh();
            }
            else if (state == L"Unmounted")
            {
                AppLogTag("PTAP", "An external MMC removed");
                Scan(Environment::GetExternalStoragePath());
                Refresh();
            }
        }
    }
};
```

(1) Implements the `IDeviceEventListener` interface to monitor storage events. It's better to register the callback in the `Construct()` method, not in the constructor because it's dangerous to use the `this` pointer in the constructor.

(2) Uses the `DeviceManager::AddDeviceEventListener()` method to set the instance of `GalleryView` as the device event listener. `GalleryView` implements the interface defined by `IDeviceEventListener`, which consists of the `OnDeviceStateChanged()` event handler.

(3) When you implement the `OnDeviceStateChanged()` callback method, check that `deviceType` is `DEVICE_TYPE_STORAGE_CARD`, as the callback is called for all external devices, not just for storage events. Note that `Environment::GetExternalStoragePath()` returns the path to the external storage, which is then passed to the `Scan()` method to scan the path for images.

INTERNATIONALISING YOUR APPLICATIONS

In this section, you learn how to internationalise your applications, including handling character sets and character encodings, and formatting dates, time, and currency, depending on a geographical region. This basic information will be helpful to make your applications accessible to as many potential markets as possible by ensuring that it works on any region.

Handling Different Text Encodings

Supporting multiple languages, text encodings, and character sets is becoming increasingly important, especially for mobile developers who want to make their applications available to as many markets as possible.

A set of all characters in which every character is mapped to a number in one language is called a *character set*. Each character in a character set should be encoded to a sequence of bytes to transfer and/or store it — a process called *character encoding*. There are many languages and multiple encodings even for one language. So, it is crucial that your application be capable of handling multiple character sets and character encodings to support multiple languages.

In this section you'll learn about the various text encodings that Tizen supports and the methods used to convert text from one encoding format to another.

The following code snippet shows how to get available character encoding types:

GETTING AVAILABLE CHARACTER ENCODINGS

```
// (1)
#include <FText.h>

// (2)
using namespace Tizen::Text;

// (3)
void PrintTextEncodingList()
{
    unique_ptr< IList > pEncodingList(
        Encoding::GetAvailableEncodingsN()
        );
    IteratorT< String* > iter =
        StlConverter::GetBeginIterator< String* >(
            pEncodingList.get()
            );
    IteratorT< String* > end =
        StlConverter::GetEndIterator< String* >(
            pEncodingList.get()
        );
    for (;iter != end; ++iter)
    {
        AppLogTag("PTAP", "%ls", (*iter)->GetPointer());
    }
}
```

(1) The classes defined in the Tizen::Text namespace are used to handle various character encodings. Include the FText.h header file to make use of these features.

(2) The using declaration for Tizen::Text is a convenience to cut down on typing.

(3) The Encoding::GetAvailableEncodingsN() method will return a list of strings representing all available encodings.

The following log file is generated if you run the preceding code in the Emulator:

```
... : INFO / PTAP ... > ASCII
... : INFO / PTAP ... > GSM
... : INFO / PTAP ... > KSC5601
... : INFO / PTAP ... > Big5
```

```
... : INFO / PTAP ... > GB2312
... : INFO / PTAP ... > UTF-8
... : INFO / PTAP ... > UTF-16
... : INFO / PTAP ... > UTF-16BE
... : INFO / PTAP ... > UTF-16LE
... : INFO / PTAP ... > UTF-32
... : INFO / PTAP ... > UTF-32BE
... : INFO / PTAP ... > UTF-32LE
... : INFO / PTAP ... > UCS-2
... : INFO / PTAP ... > UCS-2BE
... : INFO / PTAP ... > UCS-2LE
... : INFO / PTAP ... > UCS-4
... : INFO / PTAP ... > UCS-4BE
... : INFO / PTAP ... > UCS-4LE
... : INFO / PTAP ... > ISO-8859-1
... : INFO / PTAP ... > ISO-8859-2
... : INFO / PTAP ... > ISO-8859-3
... : INFO / PTAP ... > ISO-8859-4
... : INFO / PTAP ... > ISO-8859-5
... : INFO / PTAP ... > ISO-8859-6
... : INFO / PTAP ... > ISO-8859-7
... : INFO / PTAP ... > ISO-8859-8
... : INFO / PTAP ... > ISO-8859-9
... : INFO / PTAP ... > ISO-8859-10
... : INFO / PTAP ... > ISO-8859-11
... : INFO / PTAP ... > ISO-8859-13
... : INFO / PTAP ... > ISO-8859-14
... : INFO / PTAP ... > ISO-8859-15
... : INFO / PTAP ... > ISO-8859-16
... : INFO / PTAP ... > Windows-874
... : INFO / PTAP ... > Windows-1250
... : INFO / PTAP ... > Windows-1251
... : INFO / PTAP ... > Windows-1252
... : INFO / PTAP ... > Windows-1253
... : INFO / PTAP ... > Windows-1254
... : INFO / PTAP ... > Windows-1255
... : INFO / PTAP ... > Windows-1256
... : INFO / PTAP ... > Windows-1257
... : INFO / PTAP ... > Windows-1258
... : INFO / PTAP ... > Shift-JIS
... : INFO / PTAP ... > ISO-2022-JP
```

This list represents all character encodings supported by Tizen.

The Encoding::GetEncodingN() static method returns an instance of the Encoding class for a specified encoding type. For example, if you call Encoding::GetEncodingN() with L"Shift-JIS", you'll get an instance which can encode Unicode characters into characters encoded with the Shift-JIS encoding type, and decode Shift-JIS characters back into Unicode.

The encoding type name is case sensitive, so if you specify "shift_jis", "SHIFT_JIS", "shift-jis", or "Shift_JIS" for Shift-JIS encoding, GetEncodingN() will return null.

> **NOTE** *You can get more information on each character encoding in the Tizen developer's guide (*`https://developer.tizen.org/help/index.jsp?`
> `topic=%2Forg.tizen.native.appprogramming%2Fhtml%2Fguide%2Ftext%2`
> `Funicode.htm`*).*

The following code snippet shows how to get an encoding instance corresponding to an encoding name:

GETTING A TEXT ENCODING INSTANCE

```
void TextEncodingExample()
{
    unique_ptr< IList > pEncodingList(
        Encoding::GetAvailableEncodingsN()
        );
    IteratorT< String* > iter =
        StlConverter::GetBeginIterator< String* >(
            pEncodingList.get()
            );
    IteratorT< String* > end =
        StlConverter::GetEndIterator< String* >(
            pEncodingList.get()
        );
    for (;iter != end; ++iter)
    {
        AppLogTag("PTAP", "available: %ls", (*iter)->GetPointer());
        // (1)
        unique_ptr< Encoding > pEnc(
            Encoding::GetEncodingN(*(*iter))
            );
        AppLogTag(
            "PTAP", "returned: %ls",
            pEnc->GetEncodingType().GetPointer()
            );
        AppAssert(*(*iter) == pEnc->GetEncodingType());
    }
}
```

(1) Use the `Encoding::GetEncodingN()` static method to return an encoding instance corresponding to an encoding name.

The preceding code creates an instance for each available encoding and prints the encoding type obtained through the `Encoding::GetEncodingType()` virtual method. The encoding type returned by `Encoding::GetEncodingType()` must be the same as the encoding name given to `Encoding::GetEncodingN()`, so the assertion will never happen in the preceding code.

The following log shows what happens when you run the preceding code in the Emulator:

```
... : INFO / PTAP ... > available: ASCII
... : INFO / PTAP ... > returned: ASCII
... : INFO / PTAP ... > available: GSM
... : INFO / PTAP ... > returned: GSM
```

```
... : INFO / PTAP ... > available: KSC5601
... : INFO / PTAP ... > returned: KSC5601
...
... : INFO / PTAP ... > available: Windows-1258
... : INFO / PTAP ... > returned: Windows-1258
... : INFO / PTAP ... > available: Shift-JIS
... : INFO / PTAP ... > returned: Shift-JIS
... : INFO / PTAP ... > available: ISO-2022-JP
... : INFO / PTAP ... > returned: ISO-2022-JP
```

Figure 17-3 shows the operations possible with the features provided by the `Encoding` class.

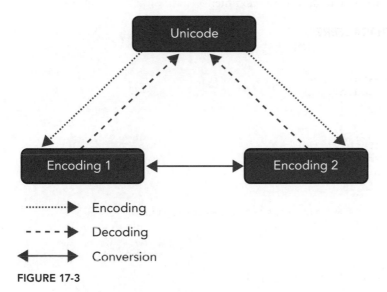

FIGURE 17-3

The virtual methods defined by the `Encoding` class can be divided into two categories:

➤ **Encoding** — These are methods which have "Byte" in their name. The term "Byte" is used because characters are encoded as a sequence of bytes. `Tizen::Base::ByteBuffer* GetBytesN(const Tizen::Base::String& str)` is an example of an encoding method.

➤ **Decoding** — These are methods which have "Char" or "String" in their name. In this context, `Char` is a Unicode character and `String` is a sequence of Unicode characters. `result GetString(const Tizen::Base::ByteBuffer& bytes, Tizen::Base::String& str)` is an example of a decoding method.

The `Encoding` class also defines static conversion methods to convert a sequence of bytes directly from one encoding format to another. The `Tizen::Base::ByteBuffer* ConvertN(const Encoding& src, const Encoding& dst, const Tizen::Base::ByteBuffer& srcBytes)` method is an example of a conversion method.

To see how text encoding and decoding work in a real application, consider the example of a text viewer which is used by an e-mail application to display message content. A user has received a text file in Korean script as an attachment, written on MS Windows and encoded in KSC5601 Korean script format.

The text file has the following content:

테스트
테스트
테스트

The e-mail application places the encoded text file into the text viewer's shared directory and requests the services of the text viewer to decode and display the file. The application should read the text file into a byte buffer and then convert this buffer into a Unicode string for display.

The following code snippet shows how to decode the text file:

DECODING ENCODED CHARACTERS

```
String
ReadFileByEncoding(
    const String& filePath,
    const Encoding* pEncoding
    )
{
    File file;
    file.Construct(filePath, "r");
    FileAttributes attrs;
    File::GetAttributes(filePath, attrs);
    // (1)
    ByteBuffer buf;
    buf.Construct(static_cast< int >(attrs.GetFileSize()));
    file.Read(buf);

    // (2)
    String decodedStr;
    pEncoding->GetString(buf, decodedStr);
    return decodedStr;
}

void FileDecodeExample()
{
    // (3)
    ReadAndPrintFile(
        App::GetInstance()->GetAppSharedPath()
            + L"data/windows-korean-text.txt"
        );
    String str =
        ReadFileByEncoding(
            App::GetInstance()->GetAppSharedPath()
                + L"data/windows-korean-text.txt",
            unique_ptr< Encoding >(
                Encoding::GetEncodingN(L"KSC5601")  // (4)
                ).get()
            );
    AppLogTag("PTAP", "decoded: %ls", str.GetPointer());
}
```

(1) The `Encoding::GetString()` virtual method takes a `ByteBuffer` as its first argument, which in this case will be the buffer containing the contents of the text file.

(2) `Encoding::GetString()` will decode encoded characters into the given Unicode `String`.

(3) `ReadAndPrintFile()` is same function used in the "Basic File Operations" section. In this example, the file is placed in the application's shared directory by the e-mail application.

(4) The encoding instance for `"KSC5601"` encoding is passed to the `ReadFileByEncoding()` function. For the purposes of this example, assume that the correct encoding name is exchanged between the e-mail application and text viewer.

Running the preceding code produces the following log file:

```
... : INFO / PTAP ... : void ReadAndPrintFile(...) > □┌□┐
... : INFO / PTAP ... : void ReadAndPrintFile(...) > □┌□┐
... : INFO / PTAP ... : void ReadAndPrintFile(...) > □┌□┐
... : INFO / PTAP ... : void FileDecodeExample() > decoded: 테스트
... : INFO / PTAP ... : 테스트
... : INFO / PTAP ... : 테스트
```

As you can see, the text is not shown properly inside `ReadAndPrintFile()` but is shown properly after decoding.

You can apply a similar mechanism when you want to convert a buffer received from a website into a Unicode `String`. For example, currently `www.ntt.co.jp` returns content in `Shift-JIS` encoding as follows:

```
<html lang="ja">
<head>
<meta http-equiv="content-language" content="ja">
<meta http-equiv="content-type"
      content="text/html; charset=shift_jis">
…
</head>
…
</html>
```

The meta tag in the preceding example has the same effect as `"content-type: text/html; charset=shift_jis"` in an HTTP response header. To manipulate the returned buffer as a `String`, you need to convert the buffer into a Unicode `String` as follows:

DECODING SHIFT-JIS ENCODED CHARACTERS

```
ByteBuffer buf = …;
// (1)
unique_ptr< Encoding > pEncoding(Encoding::GetEncodingN(L"Shift-JIS"));
String decodedStr;
pEncoding->GetString(buf, decodedStr);
```

(1) `"shift_jis"` is not a standard encoding name on Tizen. Use `"Shift-JIS"` instead.

An internationalised e-mail application should be able to handle multiple encoding formats. For example, an e-mail application may support ISO-2022-JP encoding for Japanese because it is well-established text encoding for Japanese e-mail.

To encode text in ISO-2022-JP format, you need to convert a Tizen Unicode String into an encoded buffer as follows:

ENCODING TEXT IN ISO-2022-JP ENCODING

```
void
StringEncodeExample()
{
    // (1)
    String jaText(
L"<html>\n"
L"<head>\n"
L"<meta http-equiv=\"content-language\" content=\"ja\">\n"
L"<meta http-equiv=\"content-type\" content=\"text/html; \
charset=ISO-2022-JP\">\n"
L"</head>\n"
L"<body>\n"
L"ABCDE あいうえお\n"
L"</body>\n"
L"</html>\n"
        );
    AppLogTag("PTAP", "jaText = %ls", jaText.GetPointer());

    // (2)
    unique_ptr< Encoding > pEnc(
        Encoding::GetEncodingN(L"ISO-2022-JP")
        );
    unique_ptr< ByteBuffer > pBuf(pEnc->GetBytesN(jaText));

    // (3)
    String jaTextFilePath(
        App::GetInstance()->GetAppSharedPath()
            + L"data/iso-2022-jp.html"
        );
    File jaTextFile;
    jaTextFile.Construct(jaTextFilePath, "w");
    jaTextFile.Write(*pBuf);
}
```

(1) Composes an HTML buffer with ISO-2022-JP encoding. Here all characters are treated as Unicode characters by the compiler and Tizen native APIs.

(2) Uses Encoding::GetBytesN() to encode the HTML buffer stored in a Unicode String into a ByteBuffer using ISO-2022-JP encoding.

(3) Writes the encoded buffer to a file.

You can check whether encoding is done correctly by using your browser to load the HTML file as follows:

```
C:\tizen-sdk\tools> sdb pull /opt/apps/YourAppId/shared/data/iso-2022-jp.html
C:\tizen-sdk\tools> chrome iso-2022-jp.html
```

The browser displays the HTML file with ISO-2022-JP encoding correctly as shown in Figure 17-4.

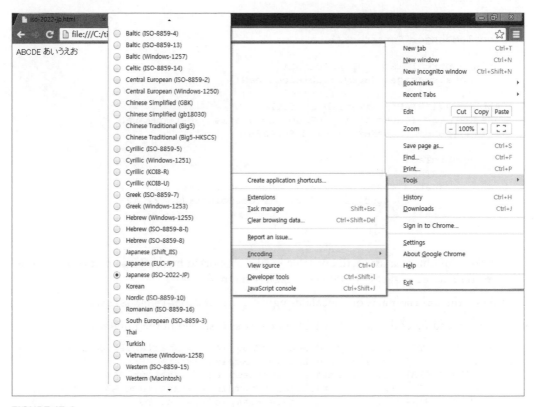

FIGURE 17-4

Handling Locale-Sensitive Information

Specific geographical and cultural regions have their own rules for displaying information such as numbers, dates and times, currency, and time zones. For example, France uses a space and a comma (,) as the thousands separator and the decimal separator, but the United States uses a comma (,) and a period (.), as shown in the following example:

➤ **France** — 123 456,789

➤ **United States** — 123,456.789

As you can see, the decimal separator is used to separate the integer part from the fractional part of a number written in decimal form. The thousands separator is used in digit grouping. The thousands separator groups 2–3 digits, dependent on a region.

The set of information and rules specific to a region is collectively called a *locale*. This locale affects the way such region-specific information is displayed. The following code snippet shows how to get available locales on the Tizen platform:

GETTING AVAILABLE LOCALES

```
void
LocalesExample()
{
    LocaleManager localeManager;
    localeManager.Construct();
    // (1)
    unique_ptr< IList > pLocaleList(
        localeManager.GetAvailableLocalesN()
        );
    AppLogTag("PTAP", "Available locales: ");
    unique_ptr< IEnumerator > pEnum(pLocaleList->GetEnumeratorN());
    while (pEnum->MoveNext() == E_SUCCESS)
    {
        AppLogTag(
            "PTAP", "%ls",
            static_cast< Locale* >(pEnum->GetCurrent())
                ->GetLocaleCodeString().GetPointer()  // (2)
            );
    }
}
```

(1) You can obtain a list of all available locales supported by the Tizen platform by using the `LocaleManager::GetAvailableLocalesN()` method.

(2) Get the `String` name of a locale using `Locale::GetLocaleCodeString()`.

If you run the preceding code, the following list of locales is shown in the Emulator:

```
... : INFO / PTAP (...) : void LocalesExample() > Available locales:
... : INFO / PTAP (...) : void LocalesExample() > ara_AE
... : INFO / PTAP (...) : void LocalesExample() > aze-cyrl_AZ
... : INFO / PTAP (...) : void LocalesExample() > aze-latn_AZ
... : INFO / PTAP (...) : void LocalesExample() > bul_BG
... : INFO / PTAP (...) : void LocalesExample() > cat_ES
... : INFO / PTAP (...) : void LocalesExample() > ces_CZ
... : INFO / PTAP (...) : void LocalesExample() > dan_DK
... : INFO / PTAP (...) : void LocalesExample() > deu_DE
... : INFO / PTAP (...) : void LocalesExample() > ell_GR
... : INFO / PTAP (...) : void LocalesExample() > eng_GB
... : INFO / PTAP (...) : void LocalesExample() > eng_PH
... : INFO / PTAP (...) : void LocalesExample() > eng_US
... : INFO / PTAP (...) : void LocalesExample() > eng_US_POSIX
... : INFO / PTAP (...) : void LocalesExample() > spa_ES
... : INFO / PTAP (...) : void LocalesExample() > spa_MX
... : INFO / PTAP (...) : void LocalesExample() > est_EE
... : INFO / PTAP (...) : void LocalesExample() > eus_ES
... : INFO / PTAP (...) : void LocalesExample() > fin_FI
```

```
... : INFO / PTAP (...) : void LocalesExample() > fra_CA
... : INFO / PTAP (...) : void LocalesExample() > fra_FR
... : INFO / PTAP (...) : void LocalesExample() > gle_IE
... : INFO / PTAP (...) : void LocalesExample() > glg_ES
... : INFO / PTAP (...) : void LocalesExample() > hin_IN
... : INFO / PTAP (...) : void LocalesExample() > hrv_HR
... : INFO / PTAP (...) : void LocalesExample() > hun_HU
... : INFO / PTAP (...) : void LocalesExample() > hye_AM
... : INFO / PTAP (...) : void LocalesExample() > isl_IS
... : INFO / PTAP (...) : void LocalesExample() > ita_IT
... : INFO / PTAP (...) : void LocalesExample() > jpn_JP
... : INFO / PTAP (...) : void LocalesExample() > kat_GE
... : INFO / PTAP (...) : void LocalesExample() > kaz-cyrl_KZ
... : INFO / PTAP (...) : void LocalesExample() > kor_KR
... : INFO / PTAP (...) : void LocalesExample() > lit_LT
... : INFO / PTAP (...) : void LocalesExample() > lav_LV
... : INFO / PTAP (...) : void LocalesExample() > mkd_MK
... : INFO / PTAP (...) : void LocalesExample() > nob_NO
... : INFO / PTAP (...) : void LocalesExample() > nld_NL
... : INFO / PTAP (...) : void LocalesExample() > pol_PL
... : INFO / PTAP (...) : void LocalesExample() > por_BR
... : INFO / PTAP (...) : void LocalesExample() > por_PT
... : INFO / PTAP (...) : void LocalesExample() > ron_RO
... : INFO / PTAP (...) : void LocalesExample() > rus_RU
... : INFO / PTAP (...) : void LocalesExample() > slk_SK
... : INFO / PTAP (...) : void LocalesExample() > slv_SI
... : INFO / PTAP (...) : void LocalesExample() > srp-cyrl_RS
... : INFO / PTAP (...) : void LocalesExample() > srp-latn_RS
... : INFO / PTAP (...) : void LocalesExample() > swe_SE
... : INFO / PTAP (...) : void LocalesExample() > tur_TR
... : INFO / PTAP (...) : void LocalesExample() > ukr_UA
... : INFO / PTAP (...) : void LocalesExample() > uzb-cyrl_UZ
... : INFO / PTAP (...) : void LocalesExample() > uzb-latn_UZ
... : INFO / PTAP (...) : void LocalesExample() > zho-hans_CN
... : INFO / PTAP (...) : void LocalesExample() > zho-hans_HK
... : INFO / PTAP (...) : void LocalesExample() > zho-hans_SG
... : INFO / PTAP (...) : void LocalesExample() > zho-hant_HK
... : INFO / PTAP (...) : void LocalesExample() > zho-hant_TW
```

As you can see, the locale name is composed of two parts. The first part is a three-letter language code defined by ISO 639-2 and the second part is a two-letter country code defined by ISO 3166-1 alpha-2. Each part is separated by an underscore (_), not by a hyphen (-). The lowercase, three-letter language code and the ISO-15924 abbreviation script code are separated by a hyphen (-). For example, if the language code is aze and the script code is latn, then the language code string is aze-latn. The supported ISO-15924 script codes are Arabic, Cyrillic, Latin, Hans, Hant, and Gurmukhi.

> **NOTE** *For more information on locale script codes, see* http://unicode.org/iso15924/iso15924-codes.html.

To retrieve information about the current system locale, use the LocaleManager::GetSystemLocale() method. The following code snippet shows how this method is used:

GETTING SYSTEM LOCALE

```
void
GetSystemLocaleExample()
{
    LocaleManager localeManager;
    localeManager.Construct();
    Locale locale = localeManager.GetSystemLocale();
    AppLogTag(
        "PTAP", "system locale = %ls",
        locale.GetLocaleCodeString().GetPointer()
        );
}
```

The default system locale on the Emulator is eng_US. You can change the system locale by selecting Settings ⇨ Language and keyboard, as shown in Figure 17-5.

Figure 17-6 shows the Language and keyboard screen when French is chosen for the language and France is selected for the region.

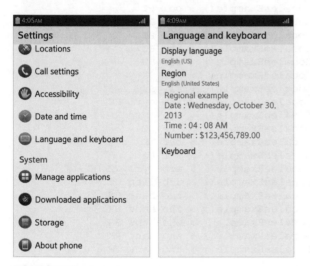

FIGURE 17-5   **FIGURE 17-6**

To look at locale features in more detail, we'll use the example of a currency calculator application. Numbers, of course, have to be displayed according to the currency formatting rules of the current system locale. The following code snippet shows how you can use the features of the Tizen::Locales namespace to format numbers to match the locale setting:

DISPLAYING CURRENCY

```
void
DisplayCurrency()
{
    LocaleManager localeManager;
    localeManager.Construct();
    // (1)
    Locale locale = localeManager.GetSystemLocale();
```

```
    // (2)
    unique_ptr< NumberFormatter > pFormatter(
        NumberFormatter::CreateCurrencyFormatterN(locale)
        );
    String str;
    double d1 = 123456789.543;
    // (3)
    pFormatter->Format(d1, str);
    AppLogTag(
        "PTAP", "%f => %ls in %ls",
        d1, str.GetPointer(),
        locale.GetLocaleCodeString().GetPointer()
        );
}
```

(1) Gets the system locale.

(2) Obtains the currency formatter specific to the system locale. The currency formatter is different from the normal number formatter because it returns a string formatted specifically for displaying currency. The returned string will also have the currency symbol in the correct position as defined for the current locale.

You can retrieve a normal number formatter using `NumberFormatter::CreateNumberFormatterN()`, and a percentage formatter using `NumberFormatter::CreatePercentFormatterN()`.

(3) Formats the number using the `NumberFormatter::Format()` method.

Table 17-3 shows some currency examples formatted for the corresponding locale.

TABLE 17-3: CURRENCY EXAMPLES

LOCALE NAME	CURRENCY EXAMPLE
fra_FR	123 456 789,54 €
jpn_JP	¥123,456,790
kor_KR	₩123,456,790
eng_US	$123,456,789.54

The calculator application may also need to display dates and times in the correct format for the system locale. The following code shows how to do it:

DISPLAYING DATE AND TIME

```
void
DisplayCurrentDateTime()
{
    LocaleManager localeManager;
    localeManager.Construct();
    // (1)
    Locale locale = localeManager.GetSystemLocale();
    // (2)
    unique_ptr< DateTimeFormatter > pFormatter(
```

```
            DateTimeFormatter::CreateDateTimeFormatterN(
                locale, DATE_TIME_STYLE_FULL
                )
            );
        DateTime today;
        // (3)
        SystemTime::GetCurrentTime(TIME_MODE_UTC, today);
        String str;
        // (4)
        pFormatter->Format(today, str);
        AppLogTag(
            "PTAP", "%ls => %ls in %ls",
            today.ToString().GetPointer(), str.GetPointer(),
            locale.GetLocaleCodeString().GetPointer()
            );
    }
```

(1) Gets the system locale.

(2) Gets the date and time formatter specific to the system locale. Use the DATE_TIME_ STYLE_FULL option to make the formatter display the date and time in the longest format.

(3) Gets the current system time.

(4) Formats the number using the DateTimeFormatter::Format() method.

Table 17-4 shows some data and time examples in the corresponding locale.

TABLE 17-4: DATE AND TIME EXAMPLES

LOCALE NAME	DATE AND TIME EXAMPLES
fra_FR	vendredi 30 août 2013 08:20:24
jpn_JP	2013年8月30日金曜日8:20:53
kor_KR	2013. 8. 30. 오전 8:14:58
eng_US	Friday, August 30, 2013 8:20:57 AM

SUMMARY

In the first half of this chapter, you became familiar with manipulating files and directories, on both internal and external storage. You learned about file locking and the safest way to share access to files between applications. Storing and retrieving data was covered in detail, from saving data to a file to creating and managing your own database. You also learned about how to monitor directory, file, and storage changes to make your application smarter and more sophisticated. You should now be well equipped to build these features into your own application.

The second half of the chapter explained some of Tizen's internationalisation features and how to make your application adapt to locale settings, including number formats, date and time, and currency. Text encoding was explained in detail, complete with code snippets. You're now armed with enough information to send your application out into the wide world.

PART IV
Advanced Tizen

18

Multithreading

WHAT'S IN THIS CHAPTER?

➤ Worker threads

➤ Using mutexes and monitors

➤ Timers

➤ Event-driven threads

➤ Inter-thread communication

WROX.COM CODE DOWNLOADS FOR THIS CHAPTER

The wrox.com code downloads for this chapter are found at www.wrox.com/go/professionaltizen on the Download Code tab. After decompressing the downloaded zip file you will have a tizen-multithread directory that contains the finished application.

This chapter explains how to write a multithreaded application.

From time to time, an application task requires a lengthy operation. If you try to perform this task in the same thread that handles the user interface, your UI may be blocked and your application may become unresponsive to the user. All readers are likely familiar with the notorious spinning hourglass or circle in Windows or the spinning beach ball in Mac OS X.

To prevent this problem from occurring, you can delegate a lengthy operation to another thread, enabling your complex processing to continue while your application remains responsive. Tizen includes native APIs for multithread programming in the Tizen::Base::Runtime namespace, the main classes of which are Thread, Mutex, and Event. The Thread class represents the concept of a separate thread of control; Mutex is a basic synchronisation primitive between Threads; and Event represents a multicast event channel between Threads.

The chapter includes code that shows you how to make use of these classes, and advanced topics such as inter-thread communication.

WORKER THREADS

`Tizen::Base::Runtime` supports two kinds of threads: worker threads and event-driven threads. A worker thread runs a user-provided method from the start to the end. An event-driven thread executes a loop waiting for and responding to events until it is told to terminate. For simplicity, it's better to start with a worker thread. The following code shows how a worker thread is constructed and run:

WORKER THREAD

```
// file: SimpleWorker.h
#ifndef SIMPLE_WORKER_H_
#define SIMPLE_WORKER_H_

#include <vector>
#include <unique_ptr.h>
#include <FBase.h>

class SimpleWorker
    : public Tizen::Base::Runtime::Thread        // (1)
{
public:
    // (2)
    SimpleWorker(std::unique_ptr< std::vector< int > > pData);
    // (3)
    result Construct();
    virtual ~SimpleWorker();
    // (4)
    int GetSum() const;
    // (4)
    double GetAverage() const;

private:
    // (5)
    virtual Tizen::Base::Object* Run();

    std::unique_ptr< std::vector< int > > __pData;
    int __sum;
    double __avg;
};

#endif /* SIMPLE_WORKER_H_ */

// file: SimpleWorker.cpp
#include <unique_ptr.h>
#include <vector>
#include <numeric>
#include <FBase.h>
#include "SimpleWorker.h"

// (2)
SimpleWorker::SimpleWorker(
    std::unique_ptr< std::vector< int > > pData
```

```
    )
    : __pData(std::move(pData))
{
}

// (3)
result
SimpleWorker::Construct()
{
    return Tizen::Base::Runtime::Thread::Construct();
}

SimpleWorker::~SimpleWorker()
{
}

// (5)
Tizen::Base::Object*
SimpleWorker::Run()
{
    AppLogTag("PTAP", "Entered");
    __sum = std::accumulate(__pData->begin(), __pData->end(), 0);
    __avg = static_cast< double >(__sum) / __pData->size();
    AppLogTag(
        "PTAP", "sum = %d, average = %f", __sum, __avg
        );

    return null;
}

// (4)
int
SimpleWorker::GetSum() const
{
    return __sum;
}

// (4)
double
SimpleWorker::GetAverage() const
{
    return __avg;
}

void
SimpleWorkerExample()
{
    static const int NELEM = 10000000;

    AppLogTag("PTAP", "Creating a simple worker");
    // (6)
    unique_ptr< vector< int > > pData(new vector< int >(NELEM));
    pData3->assign(NELEM, 3);
    // (7)
    unique_ptr< SimpleWorker > pSimpleWorker(
```

```
        new SimpleWorker(std::move(pData))
        );
    pSimpleWorker->Construct();
    // (8)
    pSimpleWorker->Start();
    AppLogTag("PTAP", "Thread successfully created");

    // (9)
    pSimpleWorker->Join();
    // (10)
    AppLogTag(
        "PTAP", "sum = %d, average = %f",
        pSimpleWorker->GetSum(),
        pSimpleWorker->GetAverage()
        );
}
```

(1) You can implement a worker thread by inheriting publicly from the `Tizen::Base::Runtime::Thread` class. The `Thread` class provides basic thread operations such as `Start()` and `Join()`. The `Start()` method starts the thread running and `Join()` makes the caller wait for the thread to terminate.

(2) This simple worker takes a list of integers through its `pData` argument and computes the sum and the average.

(3) `SimpleWorker::Construct()` simply calls `Thread::Construct()` because no special action is required to initialise the instance properly.

(4) `GetSum()` and `GetAverage()` return the calculation result.

(5) `Run()` is the heart of the thread and should be implemented by you. The method will be run in a thread separate from the caller's thread. Even though the return value is `Object*`, it will always be ignored by the native framework and you should always return `null`.

(6) Prepares the data for the simple worker.

(7) Creates the simple worker and passes the prepared data as an argument.

(8) Makes the simple worker run. After this call, the `SimpleWorker::Run()` method runs in a separate thread.

(9) Waits synchronously for the simple worker to terminate.

(10) Prints out the calculation result.

Executing the preceding code will produce the following log:

```
... : INFO / PTAP ( 3524 : 3524 ) : SimpleWorkerExample() > Creating a simple worker
... : INFO / PTAP ( 3524 : 3524 ) : SimpleWorkerExample() > Thread successfully ...
... : INFO / PTAP ( 3524 : 3543 ) : Run() > Entered
... : INFO / PTAP ( 3524 : 3543 ) : Run() > sum = 30000000, average = 3.000000
... : INFO / PTAP ( 3524 : 3524 ) : SimpleWorkerExample() > sum = 30000000, ...
```

The number in bold is the ID of the thread. As shown in the preceding log, `Run()` is executed in a different thread (3543) from the caller thread (3524) of `SimpleWorkerExample()`.

You may have noticed that the preceding code would not be responsive because `Thread::Join()` blocks the caller until the thread exits. In the Tizen native UI framework, the UI rendering task is executed in the main thread, so if your UI handling code invokes a separate thread and calls `Thread::Join()`, then all UI operations will be blocked until the thread terminates, giving users a very bad experience with your app.

MAKING AN ASYNCHRONOUS WORKER

In this section, assume that you're developing a common library for your colleagues to use in their applications. You get complaints that your `SimpleWorker` class is hard to use, so you decide to support an asynchronous operation as follows:

ASYNCHRONOUS WORKER PUBLIC INTERFACE

```
// (1)
struct Result
{
    int sum;
    double avg;
};

class Worker
    : public Tizen::Base::Runtime::IRunnable  // (2)
{
public:
    Worker();
    virtual ~Worker();
    // (3)
    std::unique_ptr< std::vector< int > > CalculateAsync(
        std::unique_ptr< std::vector< int > > pData
        );
    // (4)
    bool IsDone() const;
    // (5)
    Result Get() const;
    // (6)
    void Quit();

private:
    // (7)
    virtual Tizen::Base::Object* Run();
};
```

(1) Represents the calculation result.

(2) The `Thread` class provides a `Construct(IRunnable& target)` method which makes the `target`'s `Run()` method in a separate thread, not the user-provided `Run()` method. If you give a `Worker` instance to `Thread::Construct()` method, `YourWidget::Construct()`, `Worker::Run()` is executed in the context of `Thread`.

(3) `CalculateAsync()` is the heart of the `Worker` class. It operates asynchronously and just signals the thread to calculate and return immediately so that the caller is not blocked.

(4) Checks whether the calculation is done. It is necessary to provide a method which enables checking the availability of the calculation result because `CalculateAsync()` returns immediately.

(5) Gets the calculation result.

(6) Makes the thread terminate. The `Worker` class is an asynchronous worker and always waits for a request during idle time, rather than running straight from the start to the end. Therefore, an explicit call to `Quit()` is required to exit the thread.

(7) The `Run()` method should be called only by the thread. Therefore, it should be defined as private.

In order to support asynchronous operations, `Worker::Run()` should be implemented internally as an event loop, and `CalculateAsync()` and `Quit()` are called to send an event to that event loop. This kind of event loop can be implemented using mutexes and monitors. For simplicity, assume that the `Worker` does not queue calculation requests. You need to mark the running state so that if the event loop is running, no other requests can be made, and store the calculation result that will be returned by `Get()`.

The last thing to mention is that the calculation logic itself should be run in the event loop thread, not the caller's thread. Therefore, you need to define an implementation method to perform the calculation logic — for example, `CalculateImpl()`.

This approach leads to the following class design:

ASYNCHRONOUS WORKER PRIVATE MEMBERS

```
class Worker
    : public Tizen::Base::Runtime::IRunnable
{
public:
    ...

private:
    virtual Tizen::Base::Object* Run();
    // (1)
    void CalculateImpl(
        std::unique_ptr< std::vector< int > > pData
        );

    // (2)
    enum ReqType
    {
        REQ_TYPE_NONE,
        REQ_TYPE_CALC,
        REQ_TYPE_QUIT
    };

    // (3) mutex for __req, __pData, __running, __r
    mutable Tizen::Base::Runtime::Mutex __m;
    // (4)
    Tizen::Base::Runtime::Monitor __mon;
    // (5)
```

```
    ReqType __req;
    std::unique_ptr< std::vector< int > > __pData;
    // (6)
    bool __running;
    // (7)
    Result __r;
};
```

(1) The calculation logic which will run in the event loop thread.

(2) This represents the request type. Only two types of requests are supported: one for `CalculateAsync()`, the other for `Quit()`.

(3) The mutex for requests — that is, the `__req`, `__pData`, `__running`, and `__r` member variables. These member variables are shared between the caller's thread and the separate thread. Therefore, they should be protected from the race condition.

(4) This plays the role of the condition variable for the event loop. The condition variable allows the event loop to wait until a request is received from the caller thread, which calls `CalculateAsync()` and `Quit()` to wake up the event loop.

(5) These are member variables for requests.

(6) This marks the event loop as running so that another request cannot be made. If you add a queue for requests, you can easily support queued operations.

(7) A member variable for the calculation result.

With this design, you can implement the `Worker` class as shown in the following code. This implementation shows how to use synchronisation primitives such as `Mutex`, `Monitor`, and `MutexGuard`. It also shows how to implement the `IRunnable` target.

ASYNCHRONOUS WORKER IMPLEMENTATION

```
#include <vector>
#include <numeric>       // for std::accumulate
#include <unique_ptr.h>
#include <FBase.h>       // for Object, Mutex, Monitor and etc
#include "Worker.h"

using Tizen::Base::Runtime::MutexGuard;
using std::unique_ptr;
using std::vector;
using std::accumulate;

// (1)
Worker::Worker()
    : __m(), __mon(), __req(REQ_TYPE_NONE)
    , __pData(), __running(false), __r()
{
    __m.Create();
    __mon.Construct();
}

Worker::~Worker()
```

```
    {
    }

    unique_ptr< vector< int > >
    Worker::CalculateAsync(unique_ptr< vector< int > > pData)
    {
        // (2)
        MutexGuard lck(__m);
        // (3)
        if (__running)
        {
            AppLogTag(
                "PTAP",
                "Thread is busy. returning the original data intact"
                );
            return move(pData);
        }
        // (4)
        __pData = move(pData);
        __req = REQ_TYPE_CALC;
        __mon.Notify();
        return unique_ptr< vector< int > >();
    }

// (5)
bool
Worker::IsDone() const
{
    MutexGuard lck(__m);
    return !__running;
}

// (6)
Result
Worker::Get() const
{
    MutexGuard lck(__m);
    return __r;
}

// (7)
void
Worker::Quit()
{
    MutexGuard lck(__m);
    __req = REQ_TYPE_QUIT;
    __mon.Notify();
}

Tizen::Base::Object*
Worker::Run()
{
    AppLogTag("PTAP", "Running...");
    // (8)
    while (true)
```

```
    {
        AppLogTag("PTAP", "Waiting a request...");
        // (8)
        __mon.Wait();
        AppLogTag("PTAP", "Received a request: %d", __req);
        // (9)
        {
            MutexGuard lck(__m);
            __running = true;

            if (__req == REQ_TYPE_QUIT)
            {
                // (10)
                lck.Unlock();
                AppLogTag("PTAP", "exiting...");
                break;
            }
            else if (__req == REQ_TYPE_CALC)
            {
                unique_ptr< vector < int > > pData =
                    std::move(__pData);
                // (10)
                lck.Unlock();
                // (11)
                CalculateImpl(std::move(pData));
            }
            else
            {
                // (10)
                lck.Unlock();
                AppAssert(!"unknown command");
            }
        }
    }

    return null;
}

// (11)
void
Worker::CalculateImpl(unique_ptr< vector < int > > pData)
{
    AppLogTag("PTAP", "calculating...");
    int sum = accumulate(pData->begin(), pData->end(), 0);
    double avg = static_cast< double >(sum) / pData->size();
    // (12)
    {
        MutexGuard lck(__m);
        __r.sum = sum;
        __r.avg = avg;
        __req = REQ_TYPE_NONE;
        __running = false;
    }

    AppLogTag(
```

```
                "PTAP", "calculation done: sum = %d, average = %f",
                __r.sum, __r.avg
            );
    }
```

(1) Both `Mutex` and `Monitor` are two-phase construction classes.

(2) The `CalculateAsync()` method will be executed in the caller's thread, so member variables should be protected from concurrent access. `MutexGuard` is a helper class for `Mutex`, following the RAII idiom (see Chapter 11 for a detailed explanation of RAII). The `Mutex` is unlocked when `MutexGuard` goes out of the enclosing scope.

(3) The `Worker` class does not support request queueing. If the event loop thread is busy executing a previous request, it simply returns the data intact.

(4) This takes ownership of the given data. Because the event loop thread is free to execute the request, it stores the request type of the requested operation and wakes up the event loop thread using `Monitor::Notify()`. In this case, it returns null data to indicate that the request will be executed.

(5) `IsDone()` checks whether the calculation is complete. Even though this method is a simple read, the access to __running should be protected because another thread may call `CalculateAsync()` concurrently, in which case the result data may no longer be available even after __running has been read.

(6) For similar reasons to those explained in (5), the calculation result should be protected from concurrent access.

(7) `Quit()` stores the request type and wakes up the event loop thread.

(8) `Run()` runs an infinite loop in a separate thread until the quit operation is requested and waits for incoming requests using `Monitor::Wait()` at each iteration.

(9) This is the main body of the loop. It executes the logic according to the request. For the `Quit()` request, it simply exits the loop. For `CalculateAsync()`, it calls the `CalculateImpl()` method.

(10) This code tries to minimize the duration of the critical section using an explicit `Unlock` call on the `MutexGuard`.

(11) `CalculateImpl()` does the real work and stores the result in the __r member variable.

(12) The `Mutex` is locked before storing the result. The preceding code tries to minimise the duration for which the `Mutex` is locked. However, if you were to write `CalculateImpl()` as follows, the performance would be poor because the mutex would remain locked while the calculation in bold was being processed:

BAD CALCULATEIMPL() IMPLEMENTATION

```
void
Worker::CalculateImpl(unique_ptr< vector < int > > pData)
{
    AppLogTag("PTAP", "calculating...");
    {
```

```
        MutexGuard lck(__m);
        __r.sum = accumulate(pData->begin(), pData->end(), 0);
        __r.avg = static_cast< double >(sum) / pData->size();
        __req = REQ_TYPE_NONE;
        __running = false;
    }

    AppLogTag(
        "PTAP", "calculation done: sum = %d, average = %f",
        __r.sum, __r.avg
        );
}
```

The preceding code saves space only for two local variables at the huge cost of bad performance, so be very careful when writing this type of code.

USING TIMERS

If you look carefully at the interface of the Worker class, you'll find that the caller of the CalculateAsync() method should check whether the calculation is done. If the caller continually checks whether the calculation is done without any delay, it may be blocked.

To avoid a blocking operation, you can choose to check periodically whether the calculation is done. Use the Tizen::Base::Runtime::Timer class to create a periodic task and check the result in the event handling callback of the Tizen::Base::Runtime::ITimerEventListener.

The following code shows how to use Timer. Assume that YourWidget is a client of the Worker class:

CHECKING RESULT USING TIMER
```
class YourWidget
    : public Tizen::Base::Runtime::ITimerEventListener  // (1)
{
public:
    YourWidget();
    void Construct();
    virtual ~YourWidget();
    void Run();
    // (2)
    virtual void OnTimerExpired(
        Tizen::Base::Runtime::Timer& timer
        );

private:
    bool CheckCalcResult();

    std::unique_ptr< Worker > __pWorker;
    std::unique_ptr< Tizen::Base::Runtime::Thread > __pThread;
    // (3)
    Tizen::Base::Runtime::Timer __timer;
};

YourWidget::YourWidget()
```

```
    : __pWorker(new Worker())
    , __pThread(new Thread())
{
}

void
YourWidget::Construct()
{
    __pThread->Construct(*__pWorker);
    // (3)
    __timer.Construct(*this);
    __pThread->Start();
}

YourWidget::~YourWidget()
{
    __pWorker->Quit();
    __pThread->Join();
}

void
YourWidget::Run()
{
    // Prepare worker thread data
    static const int NELEM = 10000000;
    unique_ptr< vector< int > > pData(new vector< int >(NELEM));
    pData->assign(NELEM, 3);

    __pWorker->CalculateAsync(std::move(pData));
    // (4)
    __timer.StartAsRepeatable(100);
}

// (5)
void
YourWidget::OnTimerExpired(Timer& timer)
{
    AppLogTag("PTAP", "Entered");
    if (CheckCalcResult())
    {
        timer.Cancel();
    }
}

bool
YourWidget::CheckCalcResult()
{
    if (__pWorker->IsDone())
    {
        Result r = __pWorker->Get();
        AppLogTag("PTAP", "sum = %d, average = %f", r.sum, r.avg);
        return true;
    }
    else
```

```
        {
            AppLogTag("PTAP", "Calculation not yet done.");
            return false;
        }
    }
```

(1) You should implement the `ITimerEventListener` interface to perform a periodic task. In this example, the task is checking whether the calculation is done.

(2) The `ITimerEventListener` interface defines the `OnTimerExpired()` callback method. You can implement the logic for your periodic task in here.

(3) The `Tizen::Base::Runtime::Timer::Construct()` method takes an instance which implements the `ITimerEventListener` — in this example, it's the `YourWidget` class.

(4) `Tizen::Base::Runtime::Timer` provides both `Start()` and `StartAsRepeatable()` methods. `Start()` makes the timer expire once only, but if you call `StartAsRepeatable()` the timer will expire periodically until `Cancel()` is called. `StartAsRepeatable(100)` will make the timer expire at each 100ms, at which interval the `OnTimerExpired()` method will be called.

(5) `OnTimerExpired()` checks whether the calculation is done and prints the calculation result by calling `CheckCalcResult()`. When the task is done, it cancels the timer.

ASYNCHRONOUS INTER-THREAD COMMUNICATION

You're continuously trying to enhance your library. With the preceding `Worker` class, it is still not convenient for application developers to check periodically whether the requested task is done or not. It would be much more convenient for users of your library to specify a callback that is called once the task is done.

While the `Worker` class implements a custom-made event loop, the `Tizen::Base::Runtime::EventDrivenThread` already provides similar functionality. The `Tizen::Base::Runtime::Event` class provides a generic asynchronous inter-thread communication channel. It enables multiple callbacks to be called in an `EventDrivenThread` when an `Event` is received. If you combine the `EventDrivenThread` and `Event` concepts, you can enhance the `Worker` class so that the callback is invoked only when the task is done.

> **NOTE** *Currently, only an* `EventDrivenThread` *can create an* `Event` *instance due to the way this feature is implemented. A normal* `Thread` *can't create an* `Event` *instance.*

You should create two `Events` for inter-thread communication: one for requesting a task and the other for receiving the result of the task. You also need to create an `EventDrivenThread` which will perform the requested task and send the result to the requester. Users of your library should also be able to specify the callback when they make the request.

Here's a conceptual design for your class, StatisticsCalculator:

DESIGN OF STATISTICSCALCULATOR

```
class StatisticsCalculator
    : private Tizen::Base::Runtime::EventDrivenThread // (1)
{
public:
    // (2)
    struct IResponseListener
    {
        virtual void OnResponseReceived(
            int sum, double average
            ) = 0;
    };

    StatisticsCalculator();
    virtual ~StatisticsCalculator();
    result Construct();
    // (2)
    void CalculateAsync(
        std::unique_ptr< std::vector< int > > pData,
        IResponseListener& listener
        );

private:
    // (3)
    std::unique_ptr< Event > __pRequestEvent;
    std::unique_ptr< Event > __pResponseEvent;
};
```

(1) Inherits from EventDrivenThread privately because the StatisticsCalculator class is not an EventDrivenThread (StatisticsCalculator is not a subtype of EventDrivenThread) but is implemented in terms of an EventDrivenThread. (StatisticsCalculator is using EventDrivenThread to implement its designated functionality.)

StatisticsCalculator encapsulates the whole inter-thread communication process between the caller's thread and the event-driven thread. Therefore, you can't simply call it an event-driven thread.

(2) This is the heart of this class. You should enable users to specify the response listener, which will be called only when the requested task is done.

(3) __pRequestEvent is an Event for receiving requests. __pResponseEvent is an Event for receiving responses. These two Events encapsulate the whole inter-thread communication process.

To make a callback that will be called when an event is received, you need to do three things:

1. Define an argument, which should inherit from IEventArg, for an event.

2. Define your own event listener interface which should inherit from IEventListener and register an instance which implements it.

3. Define your own Event class which should inherit from Event and implement the FireImpl() virtual method of the Event class and call your own event listener inside it.

Here's how you would do each of those steps. The request event argument is defined as follows:

```
struct RequestEventArg
    : public Tizen::Base::Runtime::IEventArg
{
    std::unique_ptr< std::vector< int > > pData;
    Tizen::Base::Runtime::Event* pResponseEvent;
};
```

pResponseEvent is required to send back the calculation result to the caller thread. Next, define the event listener for the request:

```
struct RequestListener
    : public Tizen::Base::Runtime::IEventListener
{
    void OnRequestReceived(const RequestEventArg& arg);
};
```

In your Event class you should implement FireImpl() and call RequestListener::OnRequestReceived() as follows:

```
class RequestEvent
    : public Tizen::Base::Runtime::Event
{
protected:
    virtual void FireImpl(
        Tizen::Base::Runtime::IEventListener& listener,
        const Tizen::Base::Runtime::IEventArg& arg
        )
    {
        RequestListener* pListener =
            dynamic_cast< RequestListener* >(&listener);
        pListener->OnRequestReceived(
            dynamic_cast< const RequestEventArg& >(arg)
            );
    }
};
```

You need to define response-related classes as well. Define the argument for the response event as follows:

```
struct ResponseEventArg
    : public Tizen::Base::Runtime::IEventArg
{
    int sum;
    double avg;
};
```

RequestListener::OnRequestReceived() can be implemented as follows:

```
void
StatisticsCalculator::RequestListener::OnRequestReceived(
    const RequestEventArg& arg
    )
{
    AppLogTag("PTAP", "Entered");
    ResponseEventArg* pSum = new ResponseEventArg();
```

```
            pSum->sum =
                std::accumulate(arg.pData->begin(), arg.pData->end(), 0);
            pSum->avg =
                static_cast< double >(pSum->sum) / arg.pData->size();
            AppLogTag(
                "PTAP", "Returning sum = %d & average = %f",
                pSum->sum, pSum->avg
                );
            arg.pResponseEvent->Fire(*pSum);
        }
```

`Event::Fire()` will deliver the event argument to the owner thread of the `Event`, and the `Event` will call the registered callback.

You can define the response listener as follows:

```
        struct IResponseListener
            : public Tizen::Base::Runtime::IEventListener
        {
            virtual void OnResponseReceived(int sum, double average) = 0;
        };
```

Finally, here's the `Event` class for the response event:

```
        class ResponseEvent
            : public Tizen::Base::Runtime::Event
        {
        protected:
            virtual void FireImpl(
                Tizen::Base::Runtime::IEventListener& listener,
                const Tizen::Base::Runtime::IEventArg& arg
                )
            {
                IResponseListener* pListener =
                    dynamic_cast< IResponseListener* >(&listener);
                const ResponseEventArg* pArg =
                    dynamic_cast< const ResponseEventArg* >(&arg);
                pListener->OnResponseReceived(pArg->sum, pArg->avg);
            }
        };
```

You probably want to hide the implementation details of `StatisticsCalculator` to make the service easier to use. `RequestEventArg`, `RequestListener`, `RequestEvent`, `ResponseEventArg`, and `ResponseEvent` are all implementation details. Only the `IResponseListener` needs to be public.

Add the implementation details to the private section of the `StatisticsCalculator` and add the `IResponseListener` to the public section which inherits from `IEventListener`:

```
        class StatisticsCalculator
            : private Tizen::Base::Runtime::EventDrivenThread
        {
        private:
            struct RequestEventArg ...
```

```
class RequestListener ...
class RequestEvent ...
struct ResponseEventArg ...
class ResponseEvent ...
...

public:
struct IResponseListener
    : public Tizen::Base::Runtime::IEventListener
{
    virtual void OnResponseReceived(
        int sum, double average
        ) = 0;
};
...
};
```

Next, initialise the `StatisticsCalculator`. Add the methods and member variables for proper initialisation as follows:

```
class StatisticsCalculator
    : private Tizen::Base::Runtime::EventDrivenThread
{
private:
    virtual bool OnStart();

public:
    StatisticsCalculator();
    result Construct();
    ...

private:
    ...
    std::unique_ptr< RequestEvent > __pRequestEvent;
    std::unique_ptr< RequestListener > __pRequestListener;
    std::unique_ptr< ResponseEvent > __pResponseEvent;
};
```

`EventDrivenThread::OnStart()` is a virtual method that developers can override to customize a thread's behaviour before the thread starts running.

You should initialise the `Events` for both request and response and create and register a request listener:

```
StatisticsCalculator::StatisticsCalculator()
    : __pRequestEvent()     // (1)
    , __pRequestListener(new RequestListener())
    , __pResponseEvent(new ResponseEvent())     // (2)
{
}

result
StatisticsCalculator::Construct()
{
    AppLogTag("PTAP", "Creating thread...");
```

```
      EventDrivenThread::Construct();
      Start();
      AppLogTag("PTAP", "Thread successfully started");

      return E_SUCCESS;
}

bool
StatisticsCalculator::OnStart()
{
      AppLogTag("PTAP", "Starting...");
      // (1)
      __pRequestEvent.reset(new RequestEvent());
      AppLogTag("PTAP", "Registering request event callback");
      // (3)
      __pRequestEvent->AddListener(*__pRequestListener);
      return true;
}
```

(1) `RequestEvent` should not be created within the context of the caller's thread but the `StatisticsCalculator`'s thread because an `Event` instance is bound to a creating thread internally when created and should be bound to the `StatisticsCalculator`'s thread so that `StatisticsCalculator`'s thread can receive requests from the caller's thread. `StatisticsCalculator::OnStart()` will be called in the context of the `StatisticsCalculator`'s thread.

(2) `ResponseEvent` should be created within the context of the caller's thread and bound to the caller's thread so that the caller's callback is called in the context of the caller's thread.

(3) `AddListener()` should be called in the context of `StatisticsCalculator`'s own thread so that the callback for the request will be called in the context of `StatisticsCalculator`'s thread.

The preceding code deliberately doesn't show error checking in order to focus on the core initialisation code.

Now that you've added the initialisation code, implement `StatisticsCalculator::CalculateAsync()` as follows:

```
void
StatisticsCalculator::CalculateAsync(
      std::unique_ptr< std::vector< int > > pData,
      IResponseListener& listener
      )
{
      AppLogTag("PTAP", "Entered");
      RequestEventArg* pArg = new RequestEventArg();
      pArg->pData = std::move(pData);
      pArg->pResponseEvent = __pResponseEvent.get();
      __pRequestEvent->Fire(*pArg);
      result r = __pResponseEvent->AddListener(listener);
      TryLogTag("PTAP", r == E_SUCCESS, "error occurred");
}
```

Users can now make use of your library.

Assume that a user's `ButtonPanel` is using `StatisticsCalculator` and implementing the callback for the response:

```cpp
#include "StatisticsCalculator.h"

class ButtonPanel
    : public Tizen::Ui::Controls::Panel
    , public Tizen::Ui::IActionEventListener
    , public StatisticsCalculator::IResponseListener
{
public:
    ...
    virtual result OnInitializing(void);
    virtual void OnResponseReceived(int sum, double average);

private:
    std::unique_ptr< StatisticsCalculator >
        __pStatisticsCalculator;
};

result
ButtonPanel::OnInitializing(void)
{
    AppLogTag("PTAP", "Creating a statistics calculator");
    __pStatisticsCalculator.reset(new StatisticsCalculator());
    __pStatisticsCalculator->Construct();
    AppLogTag("PTAP", "Thread successfully created");
    return E_SUCCESS;
}

void
ButtonPanel::OnActionPerformed(const Tizen::Ui::Control& source, int actionId)
{
    switch(actionId)
    {
    case ID_BUTTON:
        __pLabel->SetText(L"Button is clicked!");
        AppLog("Button is pressed! \n");
        {
            static const int NELEM = 10000000;
            unique_ptr< vector< int > > pData(
                new vector< int >(NELEM)
                );
            pData->assign(NELEM, 3);
            __pStatisticsCalculator->CalculateAsync(
                std::move(pData2), *this
                );
        }
        break;
    }
    Invalidate(true);
}
```

If you execute the preceding code on the Emulator, you'll see something like the following log:

```
... : INFO / PTAP : OnActionPerformed(...)(147) > \
Button is pressed!
... : INFO / PTAP : CalculateAsync(...) > Entered
... : INFO / PTAP : OnRequestReceived(...) > Entered
... : INFO / PTAP : OnRequestReceived(...) > \
Returning sum = 30000000 & average = 3.000000
... : INFO / PTAP : OnResponseReceived(...) > \
sum = 30000000, average = 3.000000
... : INFO / PTAP : OnActionPerformed(...) > Button is pressed!
... : INFO / PTAP : CalculateAsync(...) > Entered
... : INFO / PTAP : OnRequestReceived(...) > Entered
... : ERROR / Tizen::Base::Runtime : AddListener(...) > [E_OBJ_ALREADY_EXIST] ...
... : INFO / PTAP : CalculateAsync(...) > error occurred
... : INFO / PTAP : OnRequestReceived(...) > \
Returning sum = 30000000 & average = 3.000000
... : INFO / PTAP : OnResponseReceived(...) > \
sum = 30000000, average = 3.000000
```

The preceding log will be generated when you press the button twice. You'll see that an error is shown for the second request. This happens because currently the StatisticsCalculator does not remove the listener when the response is received and any subsequent request to add the listener will result in an error.

To fix this problem, you may want to modify ResponseEvent::FireImpl() as follows:

```cpp
class ResponseEvent
    : public Tizen::Base::Runtime::Event
{
protected:
    virtual void FireImpl(
        Tizen::Base::Runtime::IEventListener& listener,
        const Tizen::Base::Runtime::IEventArg& arg
        )
    {
        IResponseListener* pListener =
            dynamic_cast< IResponseListener* >(&listener);
        const ResponseEventArg* pArg =
            dynamic_cast< const ResponseEventArg* >(&arg);
        pListener->OnResponseReceived(pArg->sum, pArg->avg);
        result r = RemoveListener(*pListener);
        TryLogTag("PTAP", r == E_SUCCESS, "error occurred");
    }
};
```

However, you will always get the following error for the RemoveListener() call:

```
[E_INVALID_OPERATION] The source collection is modified after \
the creation of this enumerator.
```

This happens because the Event class manages multiple listeners as a collection internally and it is not possible to modify the collection while firing an event. The Event class is designed to support a generic mechanism for events and callbacks, not just for inter-thread communication. This error can be avoided if you remove the listener after the event has been fired. Unfortunately, the Event class does not provide any callback which can be called after the event has been fired. Instead, you can delegate the task of removing the listener to StatisticsCalculator's thread.

EventDrivenThread provides user event APIs such as the following:

➤ SendUserEvent(reqId, pArgs) — Sends a user event to the current thread. The ownership of pArgs is transferred to the recipient thread.

➤ OnUserEventReceivedN(reqId, pArgs) — This is a callback which is called in the context of the recipient thread when a user event is received. pArgs should be freed by the user.

The EventDrivenThread::SendUserEvent() and EventDrivenThread::OnUserEventReceivedN() methods provide an easy-to-use event transfer mechanism between EventDrivenThreads which doesn't require you to create Events. SendUserEvent() can be called in any thread context but OnUserEventReceivedN() will be called in the context of the EventDrivenThread.

If you send an event "The response has been processed" to the StatisticsCalculator's thread using SendUserEvent() with an IResponseListener instance, StatisticsCalculator::OnUserEventReceivedN() will be called in the context of StatisticsCalculator's thread and the listener can be removed in this callback.

The remaining problem with this approach is where and how you should send the event. As far as the "where" is concerned, it is appropriate to send the event in ResponseEvent::FireImpl() after calling IResponseListener::OnResponseReceived().

You'll need to define a method for sending the "response has been processed" event, which we'll name ResponseProcessed(). It is also necessary for the ResponseEvent instance to store the StatisticsCalculator instance in order to call StatisticsCalculator::ResponseProcessed(). This can be achieved if you modify the StatisticsCalculator::Construct() method. Note that StatisticsCalculator::OnUserEventReceivedN() and StatisticsCalculator::ResponseProcessed() should not be public because they are purely implementation details to which users of your library do not need to be exposed.

The following code shows how to implement the preceding concept and how to use the EventDrivenThread::SendUserEvent() and EventDrivenThread::OnUserEventReceivedN() methods:

```
class StatisticsCalculator
    : private Tizen::Base::Runtime::EventDrivenThread
{
private:
    class ResponseEvent
        : public Tizen::Base::Runtime::Event
    {
    public:
        StatisticsCalculator* pCalc;

    protected:
        virtual void FireImpl(
            Tizen::Base::Runtime::IEventListener& listener,
            const Tizen::Base::Runtime::IEventArg& arg
            )
```

```
            {
                AppLogTag("PTAP", "Entered");
                IResponseListener* pListener =
                dynamic_cast< IResponseListener* >(&listener);
                const ResponseEventArg* pArg =
                    dynamic_cast< const ResponseEventArg* >(&arg);
                pListener->OnResponseReceived(pArg->sum, pArg->avg);
                pCalc->ResponseProcessed(*pListener);
            }
    };

    // These two member functions should be private
    virtual void OnUserEventReceivedN(
        RequestId reqId,
        Tizen::Base::Collection::IList* pArgs
        );
    void ResponseProcessed(IResponseListener& listener);
...
};

result
StatisticsCalculator::Construct()
{
    AppLogTag("PTAP", "Creating thread...");
    EventDrivenThread::Construct();
    Start();
    // to call ResponseProcessed() in ResponseEvent::FireImpl()
    __pResponseEvent->pCalc = this;
    AppLogTag("PTAP", "Thread successfully started");

    return r;
}

void
StatisticsCalculator::ResponseProcessed(
    IResponseListener& listener
    )
{
    AppLogTag("PTAP", "Entered");
    ArrayList* pList = new ArrayList();
    pList->Add(dynamic_cast< Object* >(&listener));
    AppLogTag("PTAP", "Request to remove the listener");
    SendUserEvent(0, pList);
}

void
StatisticsCalculator::OnUserEventReceivedN(
    RequestId reqId, IList* pArgs
    )
{
    std::unique_ptr< IList > pList(pArgs);
    IResponseListener* pListener =
        dynamic_cast< IResponseListener* >(pList->GetAt(0));
```

```
    result r = __pResponseEvent->RemoveListener(*pListener);
    TryLogTag("PTAP", r == E_SUCCESS, "error occurred");
    AppLogTag("PTAP", "Response listener removed");
}
```

Now everything is in place and you're ready to ship your library. The following code shows the library's final public interface:

```
class StatisticsCalculator
    : private Tizen::Base::Runtime::EventDrivenThread
{
public:
    struct IResponseListener
        : public Tizen::Base::Runtime::IEventListener
    {
        virtual void OnResponseReceived(
            int sum, double average
            ) = 0;
    };

    StatisticsCalculator();
    virtual ~StatisticsCalculator();
    result Construct();
    void CalculateAsync(
        std::unique_ptr< std::vector< int > > pData,
        IResponseListener& listener
        );
};
```

The only difference now is that IResponseListener inherits from IEventListener. You have successfully managed to expose only what users should really know, not the implementation details.

SUMMARY

In this chapter you gained a practical introduction to threads in Tizen native applications. You learned about worker threads and event-driven threads and how to use them. By working through the early code examples, you discovered that a worker thread performs its processing from beginning to the end, but an event-driven thread runs an event loop and responds to events until it is told to terminate.

Then things got a lot more complex with detailed code examples covering monitors and mutexes, which are essential if you're writing multithreaded code and want to control access to shared resources in a safe way. You also learned about event-driven threads and inter-thread communication, looking at coding techniques which will save you time when writing your own applications.

19

Inter-Application Communication and Hybrid Applications

WHAT'S IN THIS CHAPTER?

➤ The message port

➤ Sending and receiving messages

➤ Web and native applications, working together

➤ Building a hybrid application package

WROX.COM CODE DOWNLOADS FOR THIS CHAPTER

The wrox.com code downloads for this chapter are found at www.wrox.com/go/professionaltizen on the Download Code tab. The code is in the Chapter 19 download, and after decompressing the downloaded Zip file you will have a tizen-iac directory that contains the StatisticsServiceApp and StatisticsUI applications developed in this chapter.

In this chapter you'll build two applications, a web application that provides a UI and a native service application that runs in the background and is delegated to perform some tasks. You'll learn how to use Tizen's inter-application communications features to enable these applications to work together, combining them into one hybrid application package.

Many client applications for Internet services need to run continuously, even when there is no interaction with users, and these operations are often implemented as a background service. This lends itself to the creation of a multi-process application, with one process providing the UI and the other the background service.

The multi-process architecture for an application is also helpful for web applications because the web application sometimes needs to delegate some tasks to native applications, either to access features not available to the web API or to perform processor-intensive tasks. Inter-application communication is vital to enable these applications to work together. This chapter will help you understand how inter-application communication works in Tizen and how to build your own hybrid apps.

INTER-APPLICATION COMMUNICATION

The Tizen platform provides various inter-application communication methods, the most common of which is the message port. Message ports are used for peer-to-peer asynchronous communication between applications. You can use trusted or non-trusted message ports, the latter of which is used for communication between two applications that are signed with a certificate assigned to the developer.

Message Ports

The message port is a communication method which supports one-way asynchronous message passing, although two-way communication is also possible with a pair of message ports. This communication method is available in both the Tizen Web and native frameworks. Two interfaces (in a web application) or classes (in a native application) are used to implement message port functionality:

➤ `RemoteMessagePort` — Used to send messages to another application.

➤ `LocalMessagePort` — Used to receive messages from another application. You can send a message without using a `LocalMessagePort`, but you need to create a `LocalMessagePort` to receive a response from the other application.

Tizen currently supports inter-application communication between the following combination of UI and service applications:

➤ A web UI application and a native background service application

➤ A native UI application and a native background service application

Combining a web UI application with a native background service application gives you the best of both worlds: a front end built with standard web technologies and a back end able to access all the features of a native application. In the following sections, you'll build two applications which work together: a web application and a native service application. The web application will provide a user interface to some statistical functions, while the actual calculations will be carried out by the native service application running in the background, which takes the requests from the web application and returns the results.

You'll start by creating the native service application and then build the web front end, pausing along the way to define the message-passing protocol used to allow the two applications to communicate.

Creating a LocalMessagePort in a Native Application

The first thing you should do within native service application is to create a `LocalMessagePort` for receiving requests. You create a `LocalMessagePort` as shown in the following code. A separate class, `StatisticsMessagePort`, is used for the `LocalMessagePort` code.

STATISTICSMESSAGEPORT

```
// file: StatisticsMessagePort.h
#include <FBase.h>
// (1)
#include <FIo.h>

class StatisticsMessagePort
    : public Tizen::Io::IMessagePortListener  // (2)
{
public :
    StatisticsMessagePort();
    ~StatisticsMessagePort();
    result Construct();
    // (3)
    virtual void OnMessageReceivedN(
        Tizen::Io::RemoteMessagePort* pRemoteMessagePort,
        Tizen::Base::Collection::IMap* pMessage
        );

private:
    // (4)
    Tizen::Io::LocalMessagePort* __pLocalMessagePort;
};

// file: StatisticsMessagePort.cpp
#include "StatisticsMessagePort.h"

using namespace Tizen::Base;
using namespace Tizen::Base::Collection;
using namespace Tizen::Io;


StatisticsMessagePort::StatisticsMessagePort(void)
    : __pLocalMessagePort(null)
{
}

StatisticsMessagePort::~StatisticsMessagePort(void)
{
    // (5)
}

result
StatisticsMessagePort::Construct()
{
    // (6)
    __pLocalMessagePort =
```

```
        MessagePortManager::RequestLocalMessagePort(
            L"STATISTICS_PORT"
            );
    TryReturnTag(
        "PTAP", __pLocalMessagePort != null, E_FAILURE,
        "[%s] Failed to get LocalMessagePort instance.",
        GetErrorMessage(GetLastResult())
        );
    // (7)
    result r = __pLocalMessagePort->AddMessagePortListener(*this);
    TryReturnTag(
        "PTAP", r == E_SUCCESS, E_FAILURE,
        "[%s] Failed to add a listener", GetErrorMessage(r)
        );
    AppLogTag(
        "PTAP", "LocalMessagePort(\"%ls\") is ready !!!",
        __pLocalMessagePort->GetName().GetPointer()
        );

    return E_SUCCESS;
}
```

(1) Because the message port classes are part of the `Io` namespace, you need to include `<FIo.h>`.

(2) Implements the `IMessagePortListener` interface to receive messages from other applications.

(3) The `IMessagePortListener` defines two callbacks:

➤ `virtual void OnMessageReceivedN(RemoteMessagePort* pRemoteMessagePort, Tizen::Base::Collection::IMap* pMessage)`.

  ➤ Called when the other application sends a message with `RemoteMessagePort.sendMessage(data, localMessagePort)`.

  ➤ Used for bidirectional communication. The other application specifies a message port to be used for the response.

➤ `virtual void OnMessageReceivedN(Tizen::Base::Collection::IMap* pMessage)`

  ➤ Called when the other application sends a message with `RemoteMessagePort.sendMessage(data)`.

  ➤ This method is used for unidirectional communication, whereby the other application does not require a response.

`StatisticsServiceApp` needs to receive messages from the web application and send a response to the request, so it should implement the `OnMessageReceivedN(pRemoteMessagePort, pMessage)` callback.

(4) The `LocalMessagePort`'s fully scoped name is `Tizen::Io::LocalMessagePort`.

(5) You need not free the `LocalMessagePort` instance returned in step (6).

(6) Obtains a `LocalMessagePort` instance by calling `MessagePortManager::RequestLoca lMessagePort(portName)`. The returned `LocalMessagePort` instance will be managed by the platform and you should not release it. The `MessagePortManager` class contains a set of static methods for managing message ports.

(7) Registers a callback to receive `LocalMessagePort` events by calling `LocalMessagePort:: AddMessagePortListener()`. The `StatisticsMessagePort` instance will implement the `OnMessageReceivedN(pRemoteMessagePort, pMessage)` callback.

Sending a Message to Another Application

To send a message to another application, you need to request a remote message port to it. The following JavaScript code shows you how to send a message to another application from a web application, although the same approach is used to send a message from a native application:

```
// (1)
var gServiceAppId = "r9vrpxzuyp.StatisticsServiceApp";
// (2)
var gServicePortName = "STATISTICS_PORT";
// (3)
var remotePort =
    tizen.messageport.requestRemoteMessagePort(
        gServiceAppId, gServicePortName
        );
// (4)
remotePort.sendMessage([{ key: "data", value: "1,2,3" }]);
```

(1) You need to know the identifier of the remote application. The application ID is composed of an auto-generated alphanumeric package ID, a period ('.'), and the application name. For the example application here, assume that the application ID is `"r9vrpxzuyp. StatisticsServiceApp"`.

(2) You also need to know the port name because each application can create as many ports as necessary. For the example application, the port name is `"STATISTICS_PORT"`.

(3) The message port API is accessed from the `tizen.messageport` object.

You can get a `RemoteMessagePort` instance by calling `tizen.messageport.request-RemoteMessagePort()`, and passing the remote application ID and port name as parameters.

(4) You send a message by calling the `sendMessage()` function of the `RemoteMessagePort` object which was returned at step (3). The message is composed of an array of key-value pairs, and in this case there will only be one key element: the `"data"` key. The value of the `"data"` key is a comma-separated sequence of integral values. This data will be received in the Tizen native application as a `HashMap` instance, for which keys and values are of the type `Tizen::Base::String`. See Chapter 11, "Native Application Fundamentals," for more information on these fundamental types.

Receiving a Message Response

The example application needs to send and receive messages in a bidirectional way — that is, it needs to send a message from the web application to the service application and receive a response.

To receive reply messages from the `StatisticsServiceApp`, create a `LocalMessagePort` in the same way that you earlier created one for the native service application, `StatisticsServiceApp`.

The following code snippet shows how to create a `LocalMessagePort` in a web application:

```
var localPort =
    tizen.messageport.requestLocalMessagePort(
        "STATISTICS_UI_PORT"
        );
```

To receive a response for a message you sent to the native application, pass the `localPort` object as a parameter in the call to `remotePort.sendMessage()`:

```
remotePort.sendMessage(
    [{ key: "data", value: "1,2,3" }],
    localPort
    );
```

The reply will be sent back by the native application using the message port that you specified.

When the message is sent from the web application, the `IMessagePortListener::OnMes sageReceivedN(pRemoteMessagePort, pMessage)` method will be called in the native `StatisticsServiceApp` and this application will then send back a response.

In the web application, you need to register a callback function to receive these responses by calling `addMessagePortListener()` and passing a `MessagePortCallback` function which will be invoked when a message is received:

```
watchId = localPort.addMessagePortListener(
    function (data, remote) {
        for (var i in data) {
            if (data[i].key == "average") {
                writeToScreen("Average: " + data[i].value);
            }
            else if (data[i].key == "sum") {
                writeToScreen("Average: " + data[i].value);
            }
        }
    });
```

Here you can assume that the `StatisticsServiceApp` returns the result using key-value pairs whose keys are `"average"` and `"sum"`. The Tizen native application sends a reply message using a `HashMap` instance in which the keys and values are of the type `Tizen::Base::String`.

The `MessagePortCallback` callback function is defined as follows:

```
[Callback=FunctionOnly, NoInterfaceObject] interface
MessagePortCallback {
    void onreceived(
        MessagePortDataItem[] data,
        RemoteMessagePort? remoteMessagePort
    );
};

dictionary MessagePortDataItem {
```

```
        DOMString key;
        DOMString value;
    };
```

As you can see, the data argument is mandatory and the `remoteMessagePort` argument is optional. The message port contained in the `remoteMessagePort` argument would be used to send a reply.

Defining a Message Protocol

You need to define a protocol between the two applications to help them collaborate. In this example, the most important request is "calculate" which requests the result of a statistical operation. The exit request is also necessary to make the `StatisticsServiceApp` exit, because the application will continue running in the background until told to exit.

The message protocol is defined as follows:

- ➤ Calculate
  - ➤ Request data
    - ➤ key = `"request"`, value = `"calculate"`
    - ➤ key = `"data"`, value = comma separated integral values (e.g., "1,2,3,4,5")
  - ➤ Response data
    - ➤ key = `"response"`, value = `"result"`
    - ➤ key = `"average"`, value = `"average value"`
    - ➤ key = `"sum"`, value = `"sum value"`
- ➤ Exit
  - ➤ Request data
    - ➤ key = `"request"`, value = `"exit"`
  - ➤ Response data
    - ➤ key = `"response"`, value = `"exit"`
- ➤ Other responses
  - ➤ Unsupported request
    - ➤ key = `"response"`, value = `"unsupported"`
  - ➤ Missing data when the request is calculate but there is no `"data"` key element
    - ➤ key = `"response"`, value = `"missing data"`

As you can see, a request message always has the `"request"` key and a response message the `"response"` key. More keys and values may be present depending on the request or response type. For example, the calculate request has the `"data"` key and its value, and the calculate response has the `"average"` and `"sum"` keys and their values.

As explained in the "Creating a LocalMessagePort in a Native Application" section, you register a callback to receive messages. Whenever a remote application sends a message to the StatisticsServiceApp, the StatisticsMessagePort::OnMessageReceivedN() method is called. This callback needs to implement the messaging protocol:

HANDLING PROTOCOL IN STATISTICSSERVICEAPP

```
// (5)
std::vector<int>
StatisticsMessagePort::Parse(const String& str)
{
    Tizen::Base::Utility::StringTokenizer strTok(str, L",");
    String elem;
    int val;
    std::vector<int> rv;
    while (strTok.HasMoreTokens())
    {
        strTok.GetNextToken(elem);
        AppLogTag("PTAP", "Parsing %ls...", elem.GetPointer());
        Integer::Parse(elem, val);
        AppLogTag("PTAP", "Parsed value = %d", val);
        rv.push_back(val);
    }
    return rv;
}

void
StatisticsMessagePort::OnMessageReceivedN(
    RemoteMessagePort* pRemoteMessagePort, IMap* pMessage
    )
{
    AppLogTag("PTAP", "OnMessageReceivedN is invoked");
    std::unique_ptr<IMap> pReceivedMessage(pMessage);

    std::unique_ptr<HashMap> pMap(
        new HashMap(SingleObjectDeleter)
        );
    pMap->Construct();

    // (1)
    String* pRequest = static_cast<String *>(pMessage->GetValue(
        String(L"request"))
        );
    // (2)
    TryCatchTag(
        "PTAP", pRequest &&
            (*pRequest == L"exit" || *pRequest == "calculate"),
        pMap->Add(new String(L"response"),
            new String(L"unsupported")),
        "Invalid message"
        );
```

```
        AppLogTag("PTAP", "request = %ls", pRequest->GetPointer());

    // (3)
    if (*pRequest == L"exit")
    {
        pMap->Add(new String(L"response"), new String(L"exit"));
        App* pApp = App::GetInstance();
        pApp->SendUserEvent(APP_EXIT, null);
    }
    // (4)
    else if (*pRequest == L"calculate")
    {
        String* pData = static_cast<String *>(pMessage->GetValue(
            String(L"data")
            ));
        TryCatchTag(
            "PTAP", pData,
            pMap->Add(new String(L"response"),
                new String(L"missing data")),
            "Missing data"
            );
        AppLogTag("PTAP", "data = %ls", pData->GetPointer());


        // (5)
        std::vector<int> data = Parse(*pData);
        int sum = std::accumulate(data.begin(), data.end(), 0);
        double avg = sum / static_cast< double >(data.size());
        AppLogTag(
            "PTAP", "Sending result: sum = %d, avg = %f",
            sum, avg
            );

        // (6)
        pMap->Add(new String(L"response"), new String(L"result"));
        pMap->Add(
            new String(L"average"),
            new String(Double::ToString(avg))
            );
        pMap->Add(
            new String(L"sum"),
            new String(Integer::ToString(sum))
            );
    }

CATCH:
    // (7)
    pRemoteMessagePort->SendMessage(
        __pLocalMessagePort, pMap.get()
        );
}
```

(1) The callback checks which request has been received.

(2) Checks whether the request message is valid. According to the protocol, there should be a `"request"` key, and the value of the key should be either `"calculate"` or `"exit"`. Otherwise, an `"unsupported"` response message will be sent back to the web application.

(3) Handles an exit request. It sends an `APP_EXIST` user event which will be handled in the application's `OnUserEventReceivedN()` method, forcing the application to terminate:

HANDLING AN EXIT REQUEST

```
class StatisticsServiceApp
{
public:
    ...
    virtual void OnUserEventReceivedN(
        RequestId requestId,
        Tizen::Base::Collection::IList* pArgs
        );
};

void
StatisticsServiceApp::OnUserEventReceivedN(
    RequestId requestId, IList* pArgs
    )
{
    AppLogTag(
        "PTAP",
        "OnUserEventReceivedN is called. requestId is %d",
        requestId
        );

    if (requestId == APP_EXIT)
    {
        Terminate();
    }

    delete pArgs;
}
```

(4) Handles a calculate request. First, it checks whether the data is present, and if absent sends a `"missing data"` response message.

(5) `Parse()` will parse comma-separated integral values into `vector<int>` using `Tizen::Base::Utility::StringTokenizer`. The callback computes the sum and average based on the parsed values.

(6) Composes the response message for the calculation result. According to the protocol, the response message should contain `"response"`, `"average"`, and `"sum"` keys and their values.

(7) Sends the response message.

Sending Requests to a Native Application from a Web Application

Now that the functionality of the `StatisticsServiceApp` is in place, you are ready to build the client web application. The web application is named `StatisticsUI` and features the user interface shown in Figure 19-1.

The buttons at the bottom of the screen describe the following behaviour:

➤ **CALC** — When a user clicks the CALC button, the calculate request is sent to the `StatisticsServiceApp` and the result is displayed on the screen.

➤ **NODATA** — This button is similar to the CALC button but it intentionally violates the message protocol for demonstration purposes. When a user clicks the NODATA button, the calculate request, with no data, is sent and an error response is received.

FIGURE 19-1

➤ **STOP** — When a user clicks the STOP button, the exit request is sent to the `StatisticsServiceApp` and the connection to it is reset.

➤ **CLEAR** — When a user clicks the CLEAR button, the screen is cleared.

Figure 19-2 shows the result when a user clicks the CALC, NODATA, and STOP buttons sequentially.

The following code shows the UI design of the web application:

```html
<!DOCTYPE html>
<html>
  <head>
    ...
    <!-- (1) -->
    <script type="text/javascript" src="./js/main.js">
    </script>
  </head>
  <body>
    <div data-role="page" id="main">
      <!-- (2) -->
      <div data-role="header" data-position="fixed">
        <h1>Statistics UI</h1>
      </div>


      <!-- (3) -->
      <div data-role="content" id="history">
        <ul id="logs" data-role="listview"></ul>

        <div id="alert-popup" data-role="popup">
          <p id="message"></p>
          <div id="button">
            <a href="#" data-role="button"
```

FIGURE 19-2

```
                                   data-inline="true"
                                   data-rel="back">OK</a>
                     </div>
                 </div>
             </div>


             <!-- (4) -->
             <div data-role="footer" data-position="fixed">
                 <div data-role="tabbar" data-style="toolbar">
                     <ul>
                         <li><a id="btn-calc">CALC</a></li>
                         <li><a id="btn-no-data">NODATA</a></li>
                         <li><a id="btn-stop">STOP</a></li>
                         <li><a id="btn-clear">CLEAR</a></li>
                     </ul>
                 </div>
             </div>
         </div>
     </body>
</html>
```

As you can see, the UI is composed of three parts: header, content, and footer. The content is composed of logs and an alert pop-up. The header is used for displaying the application's title, the footer for buttons, and the content for message logs and the alert pop-up window.

When a user clicks the CALC or NODATA buttons, the StatisticsUI application tries to launch the StatisticsServiceApp if it's not running. The following code shows this logic where the important code is in bold:

```
var app = tizen.application.getCurrentApplication();
var gServiceAppId = "r9vrpxzuyp.StatisticsServiceApp";
var isStarting = false;
var isStarted = false;

function launchServiceApp() {
    function onSuccess() {
        console.log("Service App launched successfully!");
        console.log("Restart...");
        start();
    }

    function onError(err) {
        console.log("Service Applaunch failed");
        isStarting = false;
        showAlert("Failed to launch StatisticsServiceApp!");
    }

    try {
        console.log("Launching [" + gServiceAppId + "] ...");
        tizen.application.launch(
            gServiceAppId, onSuccess, onError
            );
    }
    catch (exc) {
```

```
            console.log(
                "Exception while launching StatisticsServiceApp: "
                + exc.message
                );
            showAlert(
                "Exception while launching StatisticsServiceApp:<br>"
                + exc.message
            );
    }
}

function start() {
    function onGetAppsContextSuccess(contexts) {
        for (var i = 0; i < contexts.length; i++) {
            var appInfo =
                tizen.application.getAppInfo(contexts[i].appId);
            if (appInfo.id == gServiceAppId) {
                console.log("Service App running");
                break;
            }
        }
        if (i >= contexts.length) {
            console.log(
                "Service App not running. Launching it");
            launchServiceApp();
        }
        else {
            startMessagePort();
        }
    }

    function onGetAppsContextError(err) {
        console.log("getAppsContext exc");
    }

    try {
        tizen.application.getAppsContext(
            onGetAppsContextSuccess, onGetAppsContextError
            );
    }
    catch (exc) {
        writeToScreen("Get AppContext Error");
    }
}

function makeSureServiceAppRunning()
{
    if (gLocalMessagePort) {
        writeToScreen("Cannot start: already running");
    }
    else if (isStarting) {
        writeToScreen("Cannot start: service is starting");
    }
    else {
        isStarting = true;
```

```
            start();
        }
    }
```

The `start()` function determines whether the service application is already running by calling `tizen.application.getAppsContext()`. The success callback for `getAppsContext()` checks if the application ID of the service application is among the IDs of running applications and if it's not, calls `launchServiceApp()`. If the service application is already running, `startMessagePort()` is called.

`launchServiceApp()` launches the service application by calling `tizen.application.launch()`. This function requires the `http://tizen.org/privilege/application.launch` privilege, which you should declare in `config.xml`, as explained in Chapter 2, "Tizen Application Packages."

The `startMessagePort()` function sets up the message port connection with the service application as follows:

```
var gServicePortName = "STATISTICS_PORT";
var gServiceAppId = "r9vrpxzuyp.StatisticsServiceApp";
var gLocalMessagePortName = "RESPONSE_PORT";
var gLocalMessagePort;
var gRemoteMessagePort;
var gWatchId;
var noData = false;

function startMessagePort() {
    try {
        // (1)
        gLocalMessagePort =
            tizen.messageport.requestLocalMessagePort(
                gLocalMessagePortName
                );
        gWatchId =
            gLocalMessagePort.addMessagePortListener(onReceive);
    }
    catch (e) {
        gLocalMessagePort = null;
        writeToScreen(e.name);
    }


    try {
        // (2)
        gRemoteMessagePort =
            tizen.messageport.requestRemoteMessagePort(
                gServiceAppId, gServicePortName
                );
    }
    catch (e) {
        gRemoteMessagePort = null;
        writeToScreen(e.name);
    }

    isStarting = false;
```

```
        isStarted = true;


        // (3)
        if (noData)
            calculateNoData();
        else
            calculate();
    }
```

(1) Gets a `LocalMessagePort` and registers the callback, `onReceive()`.

(2) Gets a `RemoteMessagePort` for the `"STATISTICS_PORT"` of the service application, which has the application ID `"r9vrpxzuyp.StatisticsServiceApp"`.

(3) `startMessagePort()` may be called when handling the click events of either the CALC or NODATA buttons. Each button's handlers will set the `noData` flag so that the appropriate request is sent to the service application. The following code snippet shows the button click handlers:

```
function makeSureServiceAppRunning()
{
    if (gLocalMessagePort) {
        writeToScreen("Cannot start: already running");
    }
    else if (isStarting) {
        writeToScreen("Cannot start: service is starting");
    }
    else {
        isStarting = true;
        start();
    }
}

$(document).delegate("#main", "pageinit", function() {
    $("#btn-calc").bind("click", function() {
        noData = false;
        if (!isStarted) {
            makeSureServiceAppRunning();
        }
        else {
            calculate();
        }
        return false;
    });
    $("#btn-no-data").bind("click", function() {
        noData = true;
        if (!isStarted) {
            makeSureServiceAppRunning();
        }
        else {
            calculateNoData();
        }
        return false;
    });
    $("#btn-stop").bind("click", function() {
```

```
            if(isStarting) {
                writeToScreen("Cannot stop: service is starting");
            }
            else if(gRemoteMessagePort) {
                sendRequest("exit");
            }
            else {
                writeToScreen("Cannot stop: not running");
            }
            return false;
        });
        $("#btn-clear").bind("click", function() {
            $("#logs").empty().listview("refresh");
            return false;
        });
        $(window).on('tizenhwkey', function (e) {
            if (e.originalEvent.keyName === "back") {
                if ($.mobile.activePage.attr('id') === 'main') {
                    tizen.application.getCurrentApplication().exit();
                }
                else {
                    history.back();
                }
            }
        });
    });
```

The CALC button handler first ensures that the service application is running; if it is, it calls the following `calculate()` function:

```
function sendData() {
    gRemoteMessagePort.sendMessage([
        { key: "request", value: "calculate" },
        { key: "data", value: "1,2,3,4,5,6,7,8,9,10" }
        ], gLocalMessagePort);
    writeToScreen("Sending a calculate request");
}

function calculate() {
    sendData();
}
```

As you can see, it sends pairs of keys and values to the service application. Note that each key and value are mapped to the `Tizen::Base::String` instance in the native application. Currently, no other data type is allowed.

Similarly, the NODATA button handler first ensures that the service application is running and then calls the following `calculateNoData()` function:

```
function calculateNoData() {
    gRemoteMessagePort.sendMessage([
        { key: "request", value: "calculate" }
        ], gLocalMessagePort);
    writeToScreen("Sending a calculate request");
}
```

Note there is no "`data`" key and related value. This message causes the service application to return the error response "`missing data`". Note that it provides the `gLocalMessagePort` to receive responses. When a response message is received, `onReceive()` is called.

The STOP button handler sends a `sendRequest("exit")` request, telling the service application to terminate:

```
function sendRequest(command) {
    gRemoteMessagePort.sendMessage([
        { key: "request", value: command }
        ], gLocalMessagePort);
    writeToScreen("Sending a " + command + " request");
}
```

According to the defined protocol, it will add a "`request=exit`" key-value pair and send the message to the service application.

The following code shows the `onReceive()` callback which is called when a response message is received from the service application:

```
function onReceive(data, remote) {
    var message;
    var average;
    var sum;

    for (var i in data) {
        if(data[i].key == "response")
            message = data[i].value;
        else if (data[i].key == "average")
            average = data[i].value;
        else if (data[i].key == "sum")
            sum = data[i].value;
    }

    if (message)
        writeToScreen("Received: " + message);
    else
        writeToScreen("Received: unknown");

    if (message == "result") {
        writeToScreen("  Average: " + average);
        writeToScreen("  Sum: " + sum);
    }
    else if (message == "exit") {
        if (gRemoteMessagePort)
            gRemoteMessagePort = null;
        if (gLocalMessagePort) {
            gLocalMessagePort.removeMessagePortListener(gWatchId);
            gLocalMessagePort = null;
        }
        isStarted = false;
    }
}
```

The callback first checks the response type. If the response is the calculation result, it prints out the average and sum to the screen; if the response is exit, it resets the connection with the service application.

Using a Trusted Message Port

In some cases, such as when dealing with sensitive data, you need a way to communicate securely between trusted applications. Tizen provides its own secure inter-application communication mechanism: the trusted message port.

The trusted message port enables applications signed with the same author certificate to communicate with each other. This policy assumes that the applications are well known to each other and thus can be trusted by each application.

A trusted message port is used in exactly the same way as a plain message port except that you can request a trusted `LocalMessagePort` or `RemoteMessagePort` from a web application by calling `tizen.messageport.requestTrustedLocalMessagePort()` or `tizen.messageport .requestTrustedRemoteMessagePort()`.

In a native application, call `Tizen::Io::MessagePortManager::RequestTrustedLocalMessage Port()` or `Tizen::Io::MessagePortManager::RequestTrustedRemoteMessagePort()`.

If you want the `StatisticsUI` and `StatisticsServiceApp` to communicate with each other in a secure way, the `StatisticsUI` code should be modified as follows:

```
function startMessagePort() {
    try {
        gLocalMessagePort =
            tizen.messageport.requestTrustedLocalMessagePort(
                gLocalMessagePortName
                );
        gWatchId =
            gLocalMessagePort.addMessagePortListener(
                onReceive
                );
    }
    catch (e) {
        gLocalMessagePort = null;
        writeToScreen(e.name);
    }

    try {
        gRemoteMessagePort =
            tizen.messageport.requestTrustedRemoteMessagePort(
                gServiceAppId, gServicePortName
                );
    }
    catch (e) {
        gRemoteMessagePort = null;
        writeToScreen(e.name);
    }

    isStarting = false;
```

```
            isStarted = true;

            if (noData)
                calculateNoData();
            else
                calculate();
    }
```

The `StatisticsServiceApp` should be modified as follows:

```
    result
    StatisticsMessagePort::Construct()
    {
        __pLocalMessagePort =
            MessagePortManager::RequestTrustedLocalMessagePort(
                L"STATISTICS_PORT"
                );
        TryReturnTag(
            "PTAP", __pLocalMessagePort != null, E_FAILURE,
            "[%s] Failed to get LocalMessagePort instance.",
            GetErrorMessage(GetLastResult())
            );
        result r = __pLocalMessagePort->AddMessagePortListener(*this);
        TryReturnTag(
            "PTAP", r == E_SUCCESS, E_FAILURE,
            "[%s] Failed to add a listener", GetErrorMessage(r)
            );
        AppLogTag(
            "PTAP", "LocalMessagePort(\"%ls\") is ready !!!",
            __pLocalMessagePort->GetName().GetPointer()
            );

        return E_SUCCESS;
    }
```

MAKING A HYBRID PACKAGE

Even though the `StatisticsUI` and `StatisticsServiceApp` are separate applications, they provide users with one well-defined feature: calculation of statistics. As such, it would be convenient for users to install them in one package. As explained in Chapter 2, Tizen supports hybrid application packages, which consist of one web application and multiple service apps. In this section, you'll combine the `StatisticsUI` and `StatisticsServiceApp` into one hybrid package.

In order to build the web application and service application in one package, the web application project needs to refer to the native service application project. In the IDE, right-click the web application in the Project Explorer, choose Properties ⇨ Project References, and set up a reference to the `StatisticsServiceApp` project as shown in Figure 19-3.

After setting the project references of the `StatisticsUI` application, the `StatisticsServiceApp` is marked with [with StatisticsUI] as shown at Figure 19-4. Now if you build the `StatisticsUI` application, the hybrid application package will be built.

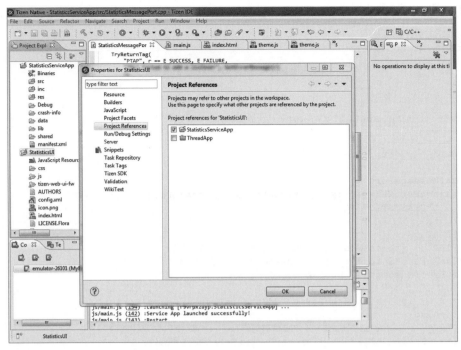

FIGURE 19-3

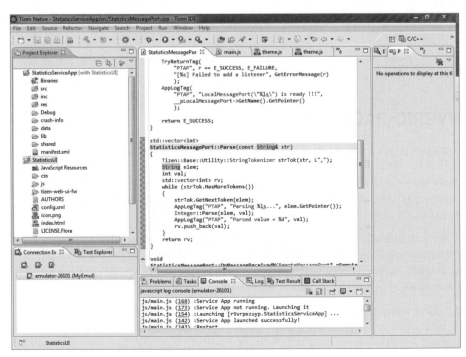

FIGURE 19-4

If you didn't install the `StatisticsServiceApp` and you build and install the hybrid application package for the first time, you will get the error shown in Figure 19-5.

This error occurs because the application ID of the `StatisticsServiceApp`'s was modified after it became a part of the hybrid application package. For example, if the `StatisticsServiceApp`'s package ID were `"r9vrpxzuyp"` and the `StatisticsUI` application package ID were `"pnyZLRCKmg"`, now the `StatisticsServiceApp`'s application ID would be `"pnyZLRCKmg.StatisticsServiceApp"`. Therefore, you should modify the `StatisticsUI` code as follows:

```
var gServiceAppId = "pnyZLRCKmg.StatisticsServiceApp";
```

FIGURE 19-5

SUMMARY

In this chapter you learned how to make applications work together using message ports for inter-application communication. Message ports are available in both web and native applications and they're a great way for the two to communicate. You can also use trusted message ports, which enable two applications to communicate securely.

Building the sample application in this chapter, you created a web UI application which works together with a native service application running in the background. You also implemented a message protocol so that the two apps could talk to each other, and combined the apps into one hybrid application package.

Two applications working together and combining the features of web and native development seems an ideal way to conclude our introduction to Tizen development. You now have everything you need to put your application ideas into action. It's time to start coding.

INDEX

J-K